LUCAS STAND™

D1361882

BOOM! STUDIOS

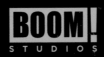

LUCAS STAND, May 2017. Published by BOOM! Studios, a division of Boom Entertainment, Inc. Lucas Stand is ™ & © 2017 Twentieth Century Fox Film Corporation. All Rights Reserved. Originally published in single magazine form as LUCAS STAND No. 1-6. ™ & © 2016 Twentieth Century Fox Film Corporation. All Rights Reserved. BOOM! Studios™ and the BOOM! Studios logo are trademarks of Boom Entertainment, Inc., registered in various countries and categories. All characters, events, and institutions depicted herein are fictional. Any similarity between any of the names, characters, persons, events, and/or institutions in this publication to actual names, characters, and persons, whether living or dead, events, and/or institutions is unintended and purely coincidental. BOOM! Studios does not read or accept unsolicited submissions of ideas, stories, or artwork.

A catalog record of this book is available from OCLC and from the BOOM! Studios website, www.boom-studios.com, on the Librarians Page.

BOOM! Studios, 5670 Wilshire Boulevard, Suite 450, Los Angeles, CA 90036-5679. Printed in China. First Printing.

ISBN: 978-1-60886-961-9, eISBN: 978-1-61398-632-5

LUCAS STAND ™

CREATED BY KURT SUTTER

WRITTEN BY
KURT SUTTER
& CAITLIN KITTREDGE

ILLUSTRATED BY
JESÚS HERVÁS

COLORS BY
ADAM METCALFE

LETTERS BY
JIM CAMPBELL

COVER BY
LEE BERMEJO

DESIGN
KELSEY DIETERICH

ASSOCIATE EDITOR
CHRIS ROSA

EDITORS
DAFNA PLEBAN
MATT GAGNON

CHAPTER
ONE

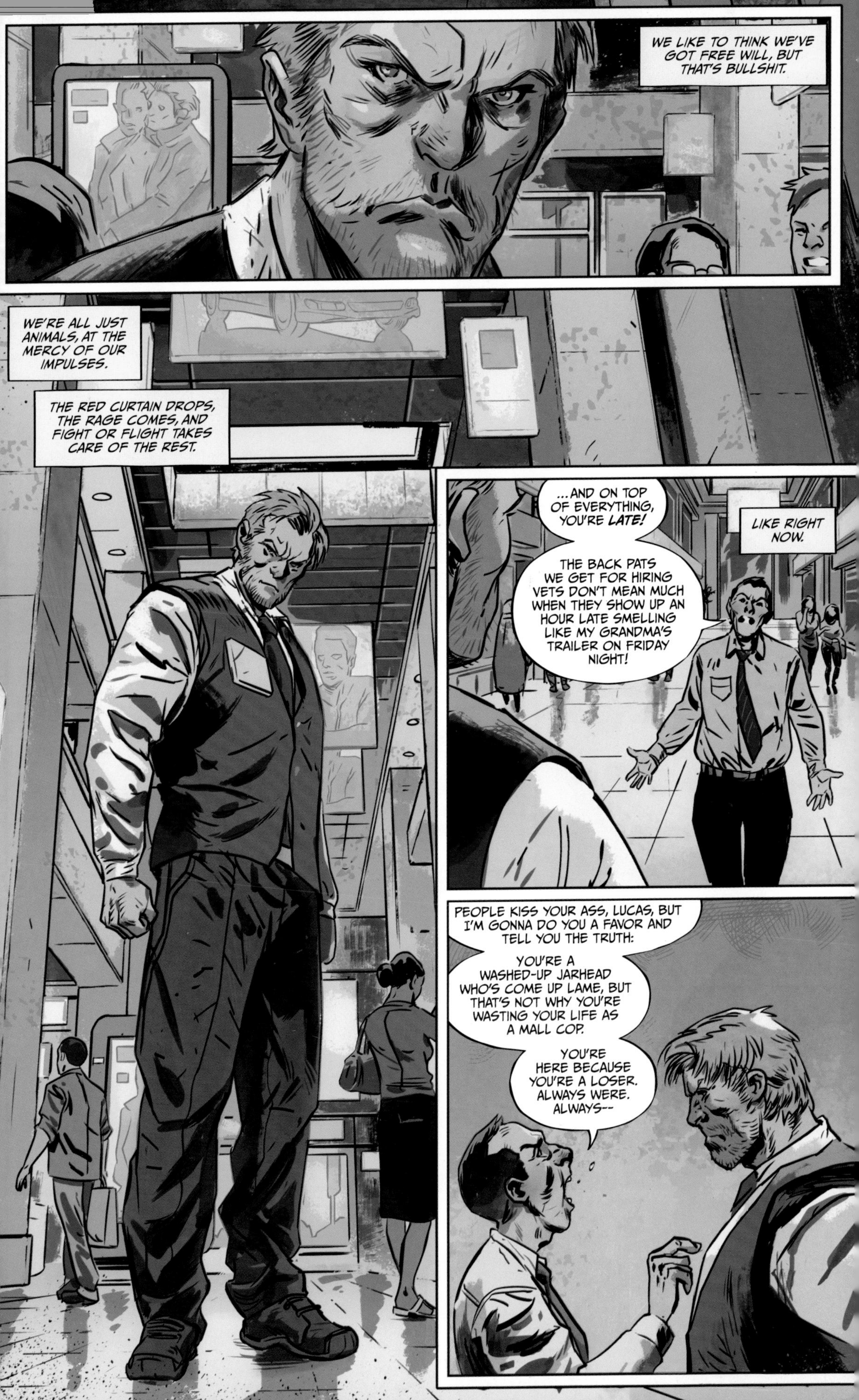
WE LIKE TO THINK WE'VE GOT FREE WILL, BUT THAT'S BULLSHIT.
WE'RE ALL JUST ANIMALS, AT THE MERCY OF OUR IMPULSES.
THE RED CURTAIN DROPS, THE RAGE COMES, AND FIGHT OR FLIGHT TAKES CARE OF THE REST.
...AND ON TOP OF EVERYTHING, YOU'RE LATE!
LIKE RIGHT NOW.
THE BACK PATS WE GET FOR HIRING VETS DON'T MEAN MUCH WHEN THEY SHOW UP AN HOUR LATE SMELLING LIKE MY GRANDMA'S TRAILER ON FRIDAY NIGHT!
PEOPLE KISS YOUR ASS, LUCAS, BUT I'M GONNA DO YOU A FAVOR AND TELL YOU THE TRUTH:
YOU'RE A WASHED-UP JARHEAD WHO'S COME UP LAME, BUT THAT'S NOT WHY YOU'RE WASTING YOUR LIFE AS A MALL COP.
YOU'RE HERE BECAUSE YOU'RE A LOSER. ALWAYS WERE. ALWAYS--

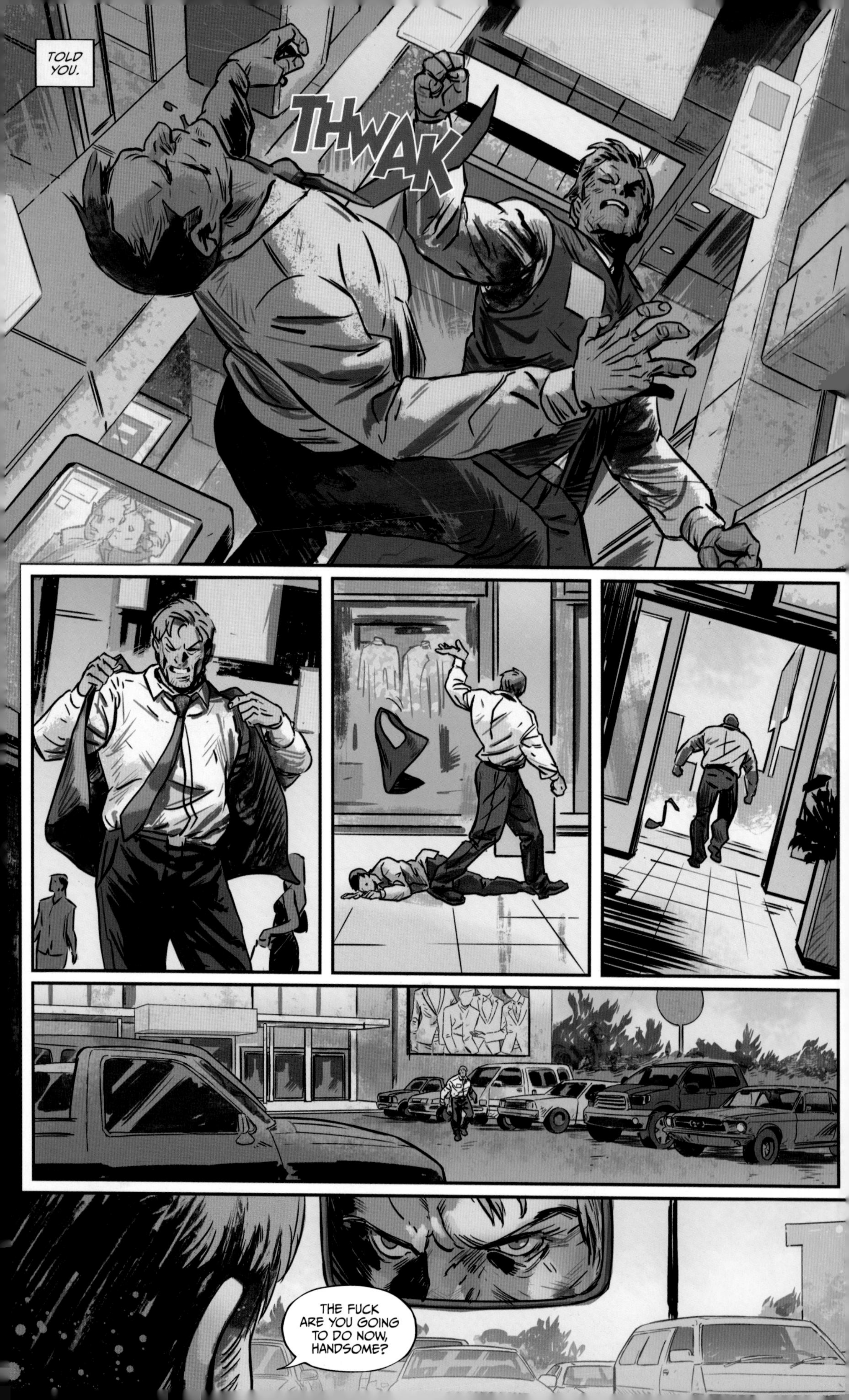
TOLD YOU.
THWAK
THE FUCK ARE YOU GOING TO DO NOW, HANDSOME?

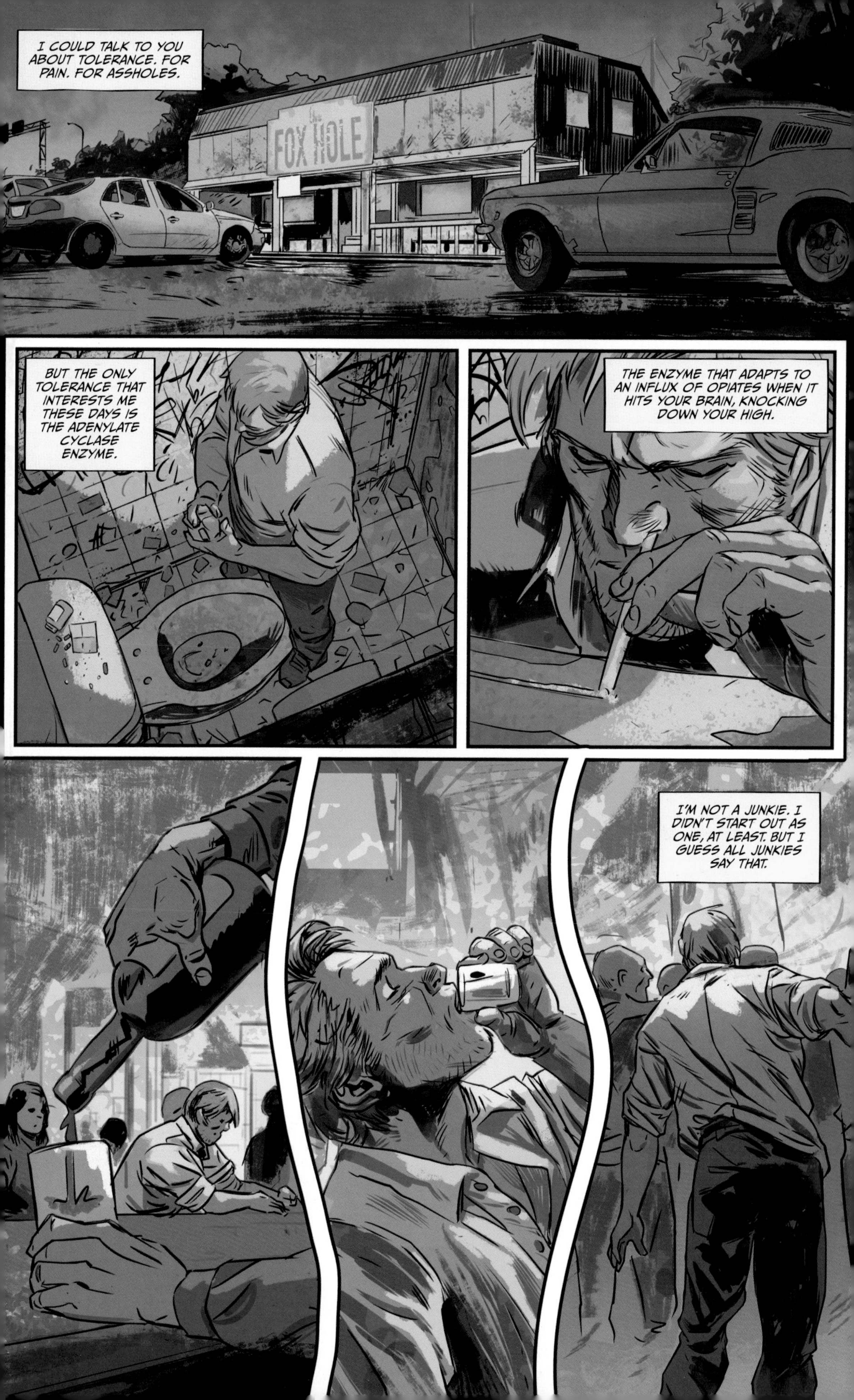
I COULD TALK TO YOU ABOUT TOLERANCE. FOR PAIN. FOR ASSHOLES.
FOX HOLE
BUT THE ONLY TOLERANCE THAT INTERESTS ME THESE DAYS IS THE ADENYLATE CYCLASE ENZYME.
THE ENZYME THAT ADAPTS TO AN INFLUX OF OPIATES WHEN IT HITS YOUR BRAIN, KNOCKING DOWN YOUR HIGH.
I'M NOT A JUNKIE. I DIDN'T START OUT AS ONE, AT LEAST. BUT I GUESS ALL JUNKIES SAY THAT.

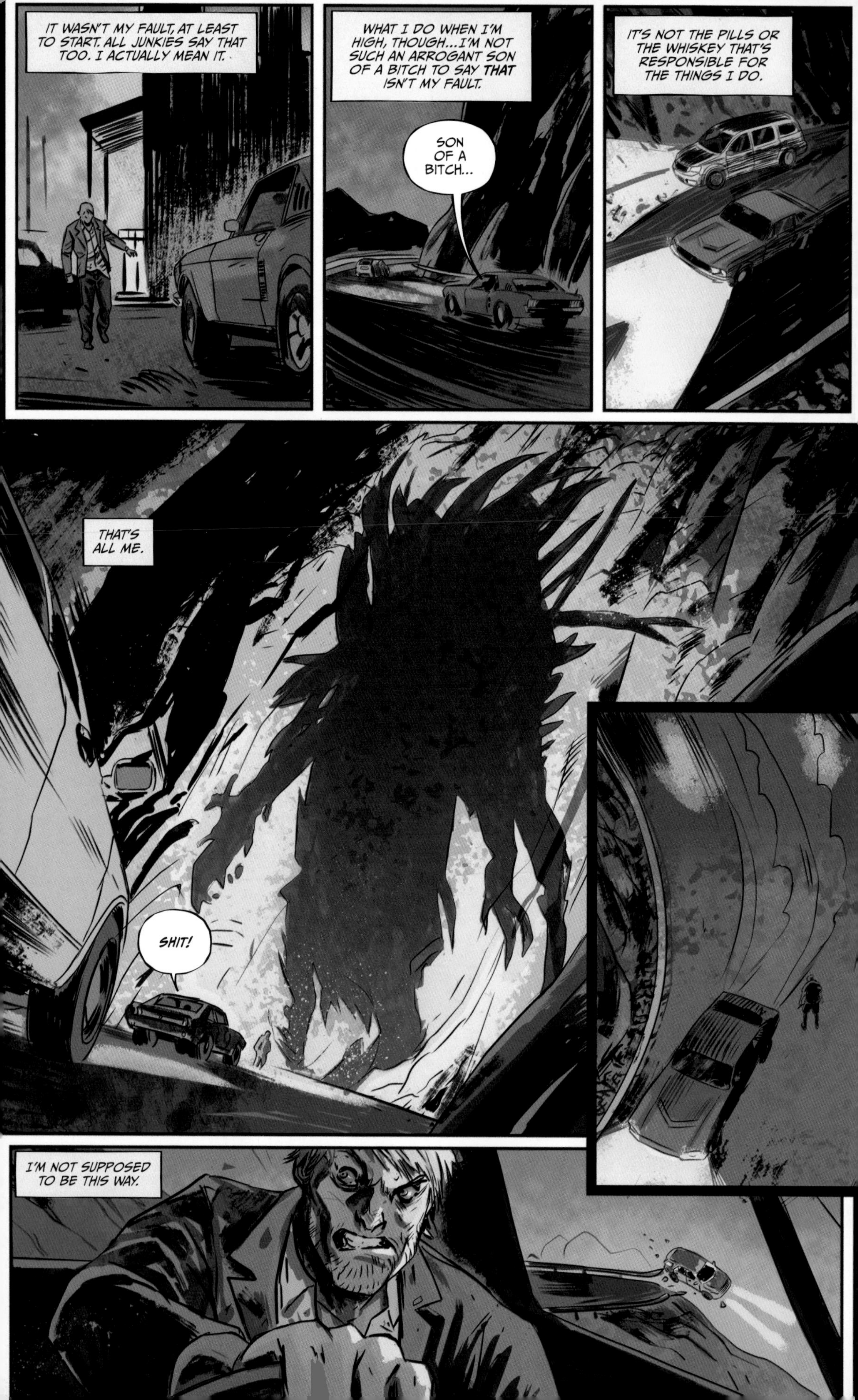
IT WASN'T MY FAULT, AT LEAST TO START. ALL JUNKIES SAY THAT TOO. I ACTUALLY MEAN IT.
WHAT I DO WHEN I'M HIGH, THOUGH...I'M NOT SUCH AN ARROGANT SON OF A BITCH TO SAY THAT ISN'T MY FAULT.
SON OF A BITCH...
IT'S NOT THE PILLS OR THE WHISKEY THAT'S RESPONSIBLE FOR THE THINGS I DO.
THAT'S ALL ME.
SHIT!
I'M NOT SUPPOSED TO BE THIS WAY.

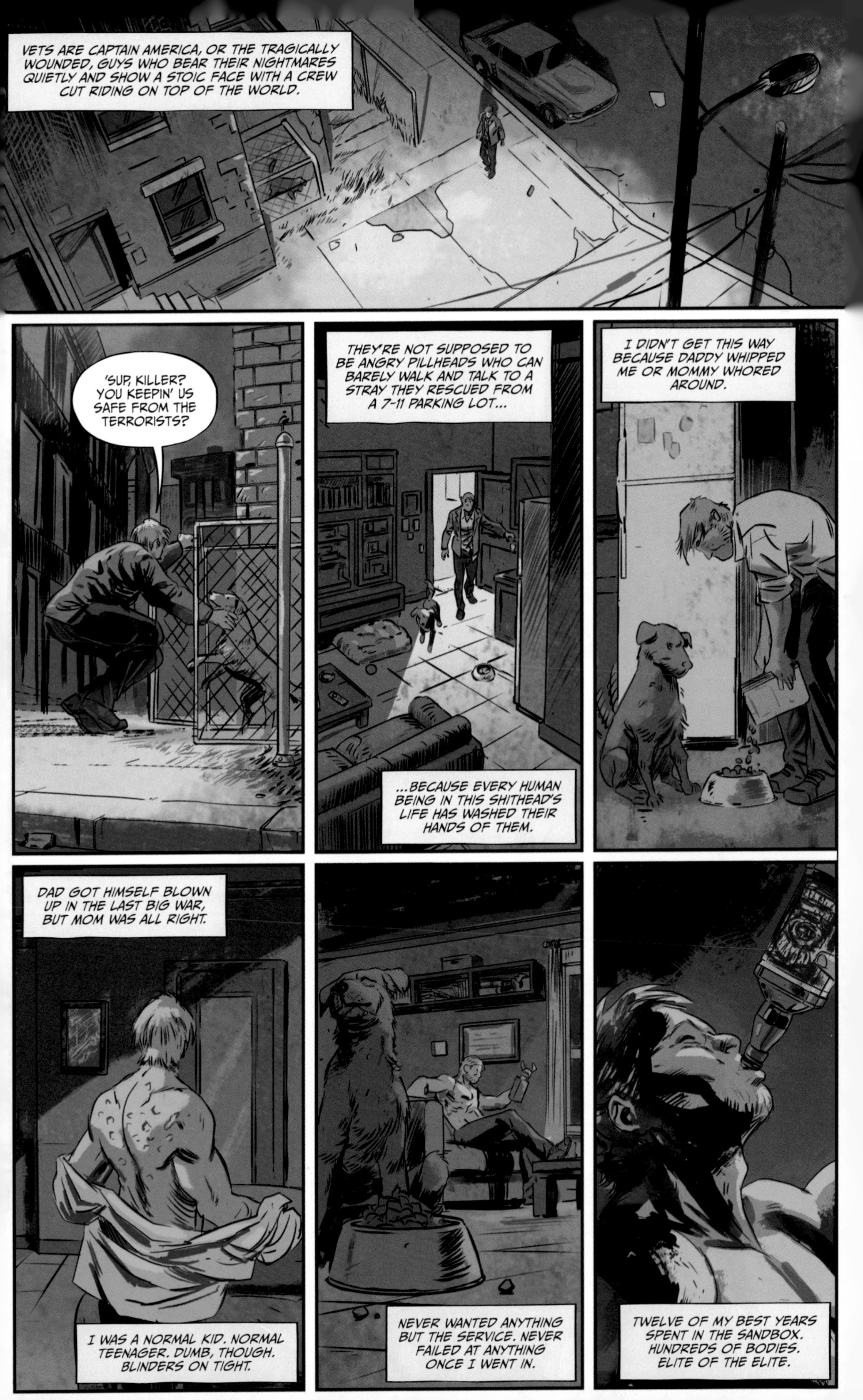
VETS ARE CAPTAIN AMERICA, OR THE TRAGICALLY WOUNDED, GUYS WHO BEAR THEIR NIGHTMARES QUIETLY AND SHOW A STOIC FACE WITH A CREW CUT RIDING ON TOP OF THE WORLD.
'SUP, KILLER? YOU KEEPIN' US SAFE FROM THE TERRORISTS?
THEY'RE NOT SUPPOSED TO BE ANGRY PILLHEADS WHO CAN BARELY WALK AND TALK TO A STRAY THEY RESCUED FROM A 7-11 PARKING LOT...
...BECAUSE EVERY HUMAN BEING IN THIS SHITHEAD'S LIFE HAS WASHED THEIR HANDS OF THEM.
I DIDN'T GET THIS WAY BECAUSE DADDY WHIPPED ME OR MOMMY WHORED AROUND.
DAD GOT HIMSELF BLOWN UP IN THE LAST BIG WAR, BUT MOM WAS ALL RIGHT.
I WAS A NORMAL KID. NORMAL TEENAGER. DUMB, THOUGH. BLINDERS ON TIGHT.
NEVER WANTED ANYTHING BUT THE SERVICE. NEVER FAILED AT ANYTHING ONCE I WENT IN.
TWELVE OF MY BEST YEARS SPENT IN THE SANDBOX. HUNDREDS OF BODIES. ELITE OF THE ELITE.

ALL OVER IN THE TEN SECONDS IT TOOK A TALIBAN FIGHTER TO PUMP SIX AK ROUNDS INTO MY SPINE.

OUR TOP STORY THIS MORNING...

FROM "YOU'LL NEVER WALK AGAIN" TO "YOU'LL WALK AND EVERY STEP FEELS LIKE AN ARROW OF PURE FIRE IN YOUR BACK."

FUUUUUUCK.

KISS A JOB IN LAW ENFORCEMENT OR PRIVATE SECURITY GOODBYE, ALONG WITH YOUR MOBILITY AND YOUR DIGNITY.

OF GODDAMN COURSE.

PAIN MANAGEMENT TURNS TO PAIN OBLITERATION, WHICH YOU HELP OUT WITH THE CHEAPEST LIQUOR YOU CAN FIND. THEN SPEED TO CUT THROUGH THE OPIATES SO YOU CAN FUNCTION.

YOU KNOW THE REST. EVERY PATHETIC DOWNWARD SPIRAL IS BASICALLY THE SAME.

WE TAKE YOU LIVE TO ROUTE 27, WHERE A DEADLY SINGLE-CAR ACCIDENT CLAIMED THE LIVES OF KEITH DONLAN, 45, HIS WIFE MARIE AND THEIR TWO CHILDREN.

STATE POLICE ARE STILL INVESTIGATING THE INCIDENT BUT ACCORDING TO A SPOKESPERSON, THERE APPEARS TO BE NO EVIDENCE OF FOUL PLAY.

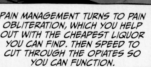

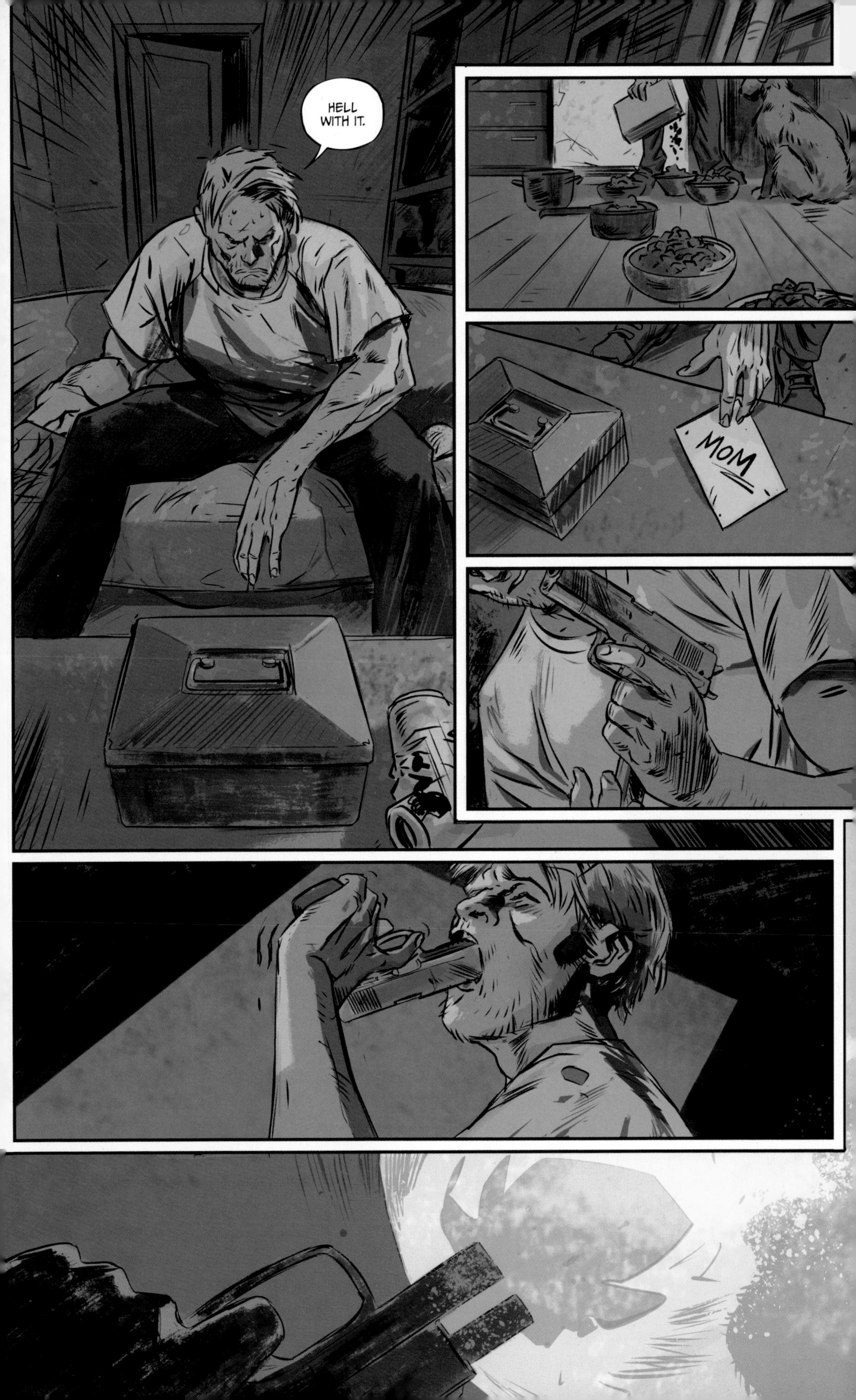
HELL WITH IT.
MOM

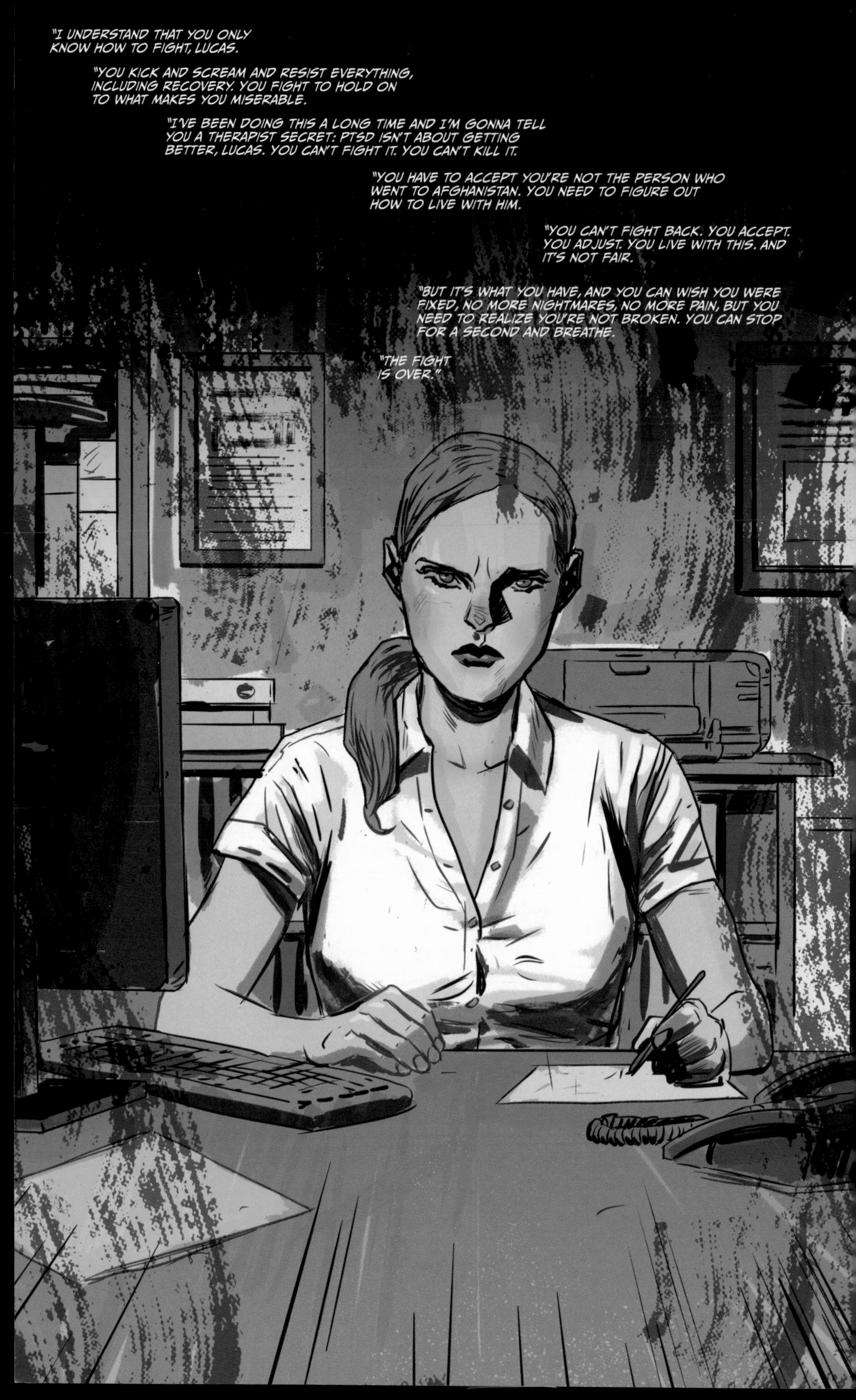
"I UNDERSTAND THAT YOU ONLY KNOW HOW TO FIGHT, LUCAS.
"YOU KICK AND SCREAM AND RESIST EVERYTHING, INCLUDING RECOVERY. YOU FIGHT TO HOLD ON TO WHAT MAKES YOU MISERABLE.
"I'VE BEEN DOING THIS A LONG TIME AND I'M GONNA TELL YOU A THERAPIST SECRET: PTSD ISN'T ABOUT GETTING BETTER, LUCAS. YOU CAN'T FIGHT IT. YOU CAN'T KILL IT.
"YOU HAVE TO ACCEPT YOU'RE NOT THE PERSON WHO WENT TO AFGHANISTAN. YOU NEED TO FIGURE OUT HOW TO LIVE WITH HIM.
"YOU CAN'T FIGHT BACK. YOU ACCEPT. YOU ADJUST. YOU LIVE WITH THIS. AND IT'S NOT FAIR.
"BUT IT'S WHAT YOU HAVE, AND YOU CAN WISH YOU WERE FIXED, NO MORE NIGHTMARES, NO MORE PAIN, BUT YOU NEED TO REALIZE YOU'RE NOT BROKEN. YOU CAN STOP FOR A SECOND AND BREATHE.
"THE FIGHT IS OVER."

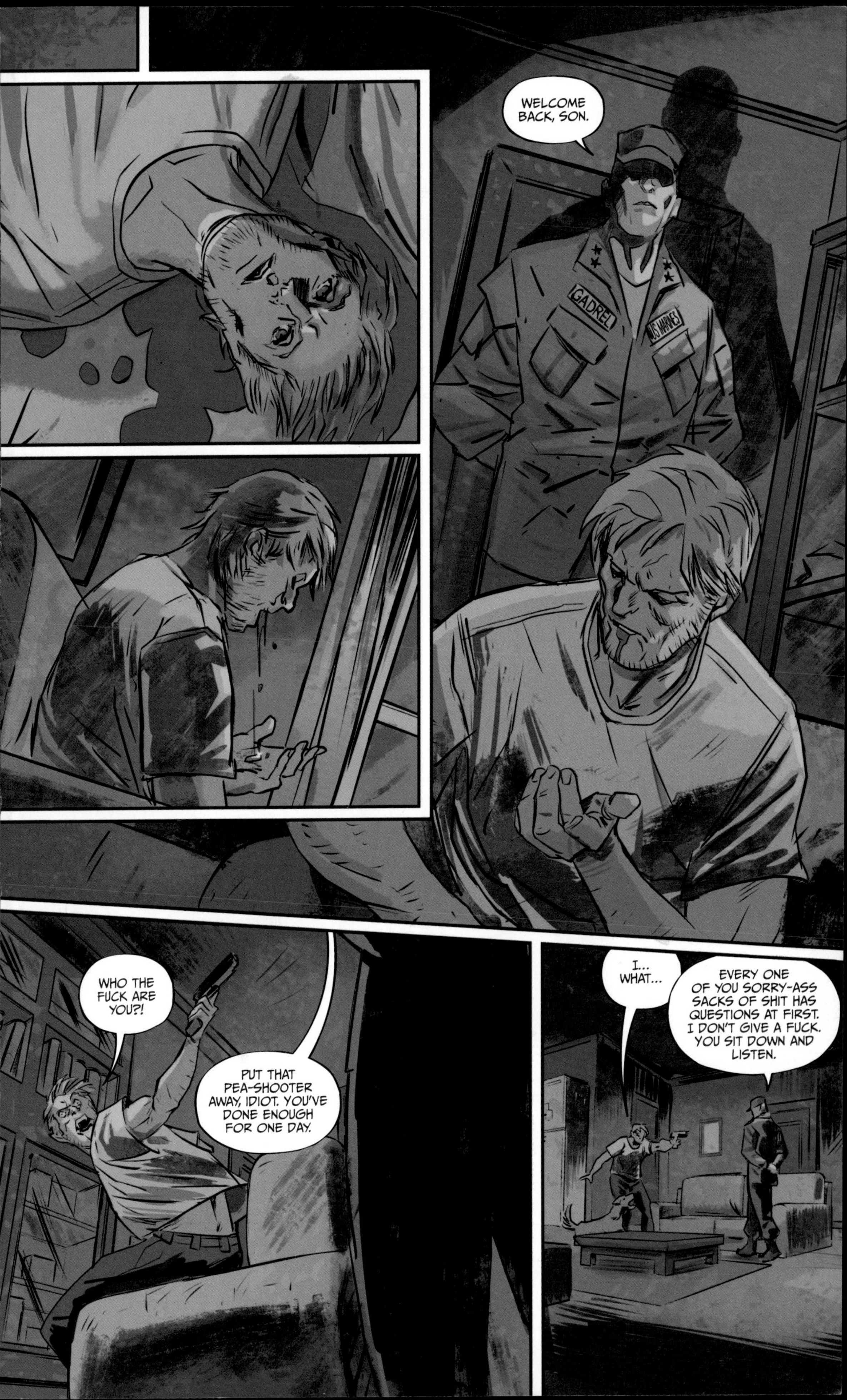
WELCOME BACK, SON.
GADREL
U.S. MARINES
WHO THE FUCK ARE YOU?!
PUT THAT PEA-SHOOTER AWAY, IDIOT. YOU'VE DONE ENOUGH FOR ONE DAY.
I... WHAT...
EVERY ONE OF YOU SORRY-ASS SACKS OF SHIT HAS QUESTIONS AT FIRST. I DON'T GIVE A FUCK. YOU SIT DOWN AND LISTEN.

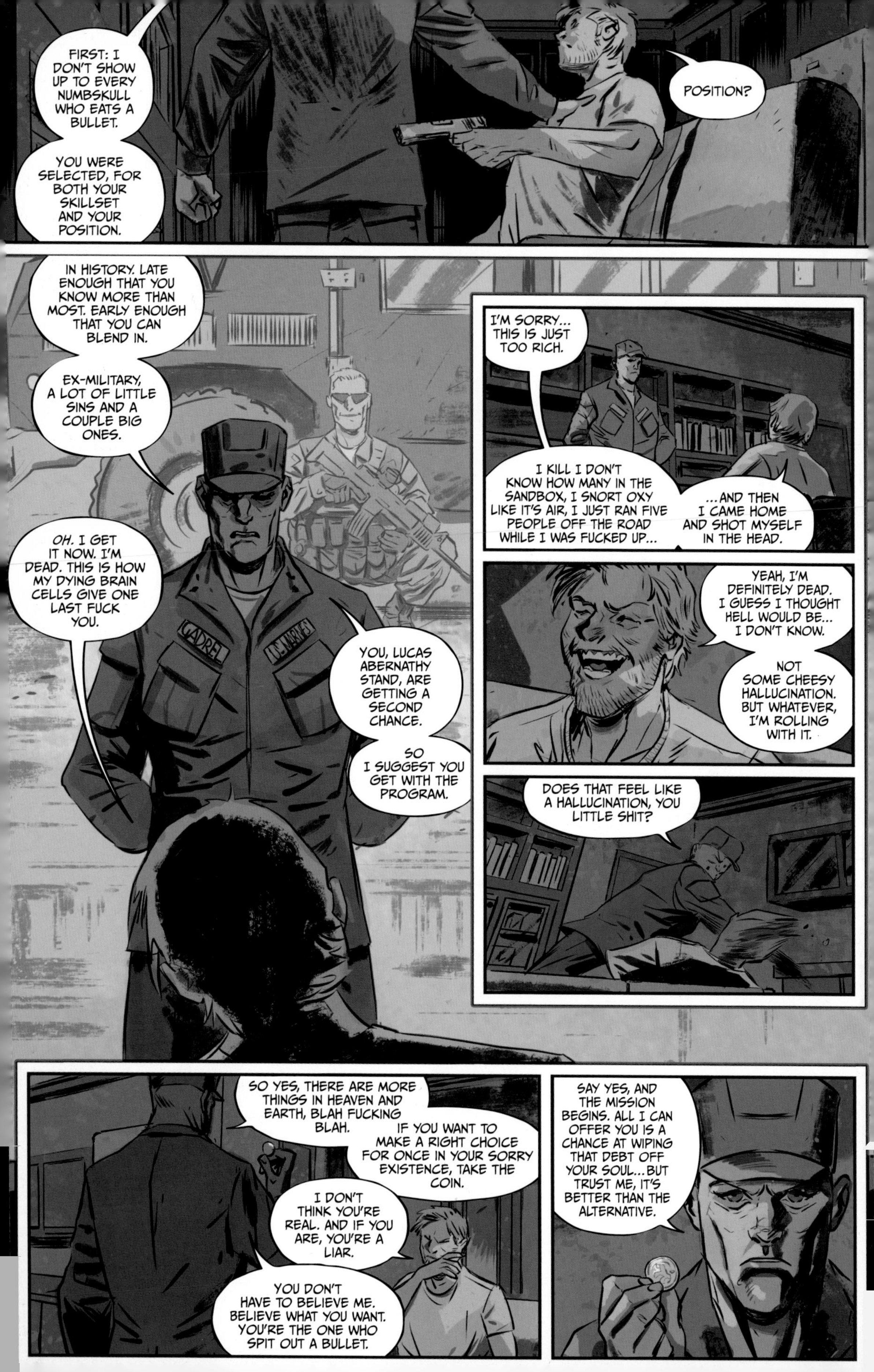
FIRST: I DON'T SHOW UP TO EVERY NUMBSKULL WHO EATS A BULLET.
YOU WERE SELECTED, FOR BOTH YOUR SKILLSET AND YOUR POSITION.
POSITION?
IN HISTORY. LATE ENOUGH THAT YOU KNOW MORE THAN MOST. EARLY ENOUGH THAT YOU CAN BLEND IN.
EX-MILITARY, A LOT OF LITTLE SINS AND A COUPLE BIG ONES.
GADREL
U.S. MARINES
OH. I GET IT NOW. I'M DEAD. THIS IS HOW MY DYING BRAIN CELLS GIVE ONE LAST FUCK YOU.
YOU, LUCAS ABERNATHY STAND, ARE GETTING A SECOND CHANCE.
SO I SUGGEST YOU GET WITH THE PROGRAM.
I'M SORRY... THIS IS JUST TOO RICH.
I KILL I DON'T KNOW HOW MANY IN THE SANDBOX, I SNORT OXY LIKE IT'S AIR, I JUST RAN FIVE PEOPLE OFF THE ROAD WHILE I WAS FUCKED UP...
...AND THEN I CAME HOME AND SHOT MYSELF IN THE HEAD.
YEAH, I'M DEFINITELY DEAD. I GUESS I THOUGHT HELL WOULD BE... I DON'T KNOW.
NOT SOME CHEESY HALLUCINATION. BUT WHATEVER, I'M ROLLING WITH IT.
DOES THAT FEEL LIKE A HALLUCINATION, YOU LITTLE SHIT?
SO YES, THERE ARE MORE THINGS IN HEAVEN AND EARTH, BLAH FUCKING BLAH.
IF YOU WANT TO MAKE A RIGHT CHOICE FOR ONCE IN YOUR SORRY EXISTENCE, TAKE THE COIN.
I DON'T THINK YOU'RE REAL. AND IF YOU ARE, YOU'RE A LIAR.
YOU DON'T HAVE TO BELIEVE ME. BELIEVE WHAT YOU WANT. YOU'RE THE ONE WHO SPIT OUT A BULLET.
SAY YES, AND THE MISSION BEGINS. ALL I CAN OFFER YOU IS A CHANCE AT WIPING THAT DEBT OFF YOUR SOUL... BUT TRUST ME, IT'S BETTER THAN THE ALTERNATIVE.

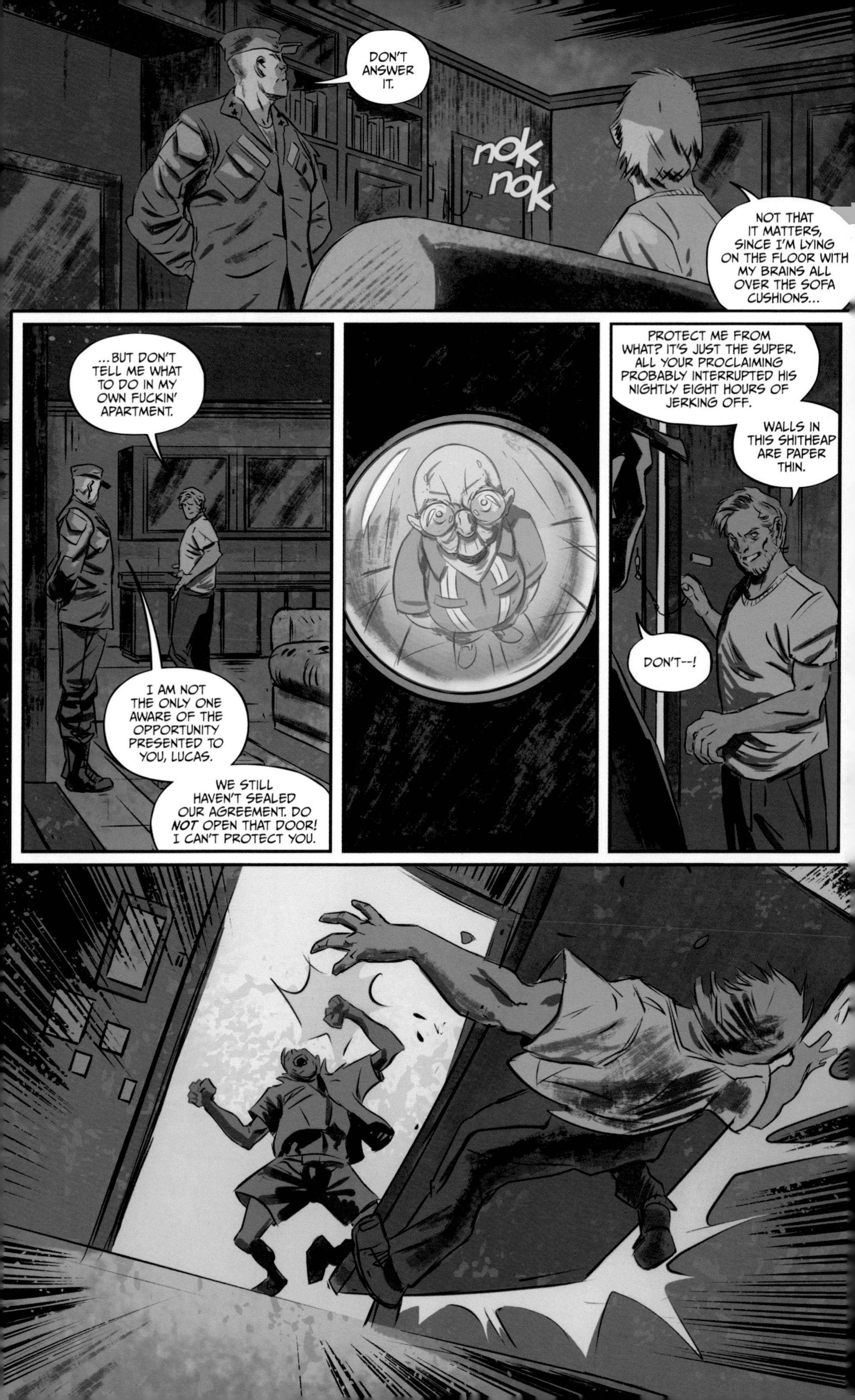
DON'T ANSWER IT.
nok nok
NOT THAT IT MATTERS, SINCE I'M LYING ON THE FLOOR WITH MY BRAINS ALL OVER THE SOFA CUSHIONS...
...BUT DON'T TELL ME WHAT TO DO IN MY OWN FUCKIN' APARTMENT.
I AM NOT THE ONLY ONE AWARE OF THE OPPORTUNITY PRESENTED TO YOU, LUCAS.
WE STILL HAVEN'T SEALED OUR AGREEMENT. DO NOT OPEN THAT DOOR! I CAN'T PROTECT YOU.
PROTECT ME FROM WHAT? IT'S JUST THE SUPER. ALL YOUR PROCLAIMING PROBABLY INTERRUPTED HIS NIGHTLY EIGHT HOURS OF JERKING OFF.
WALLS IN THIS SHITHEAP ARE PAPER THIN.
DON'T--!

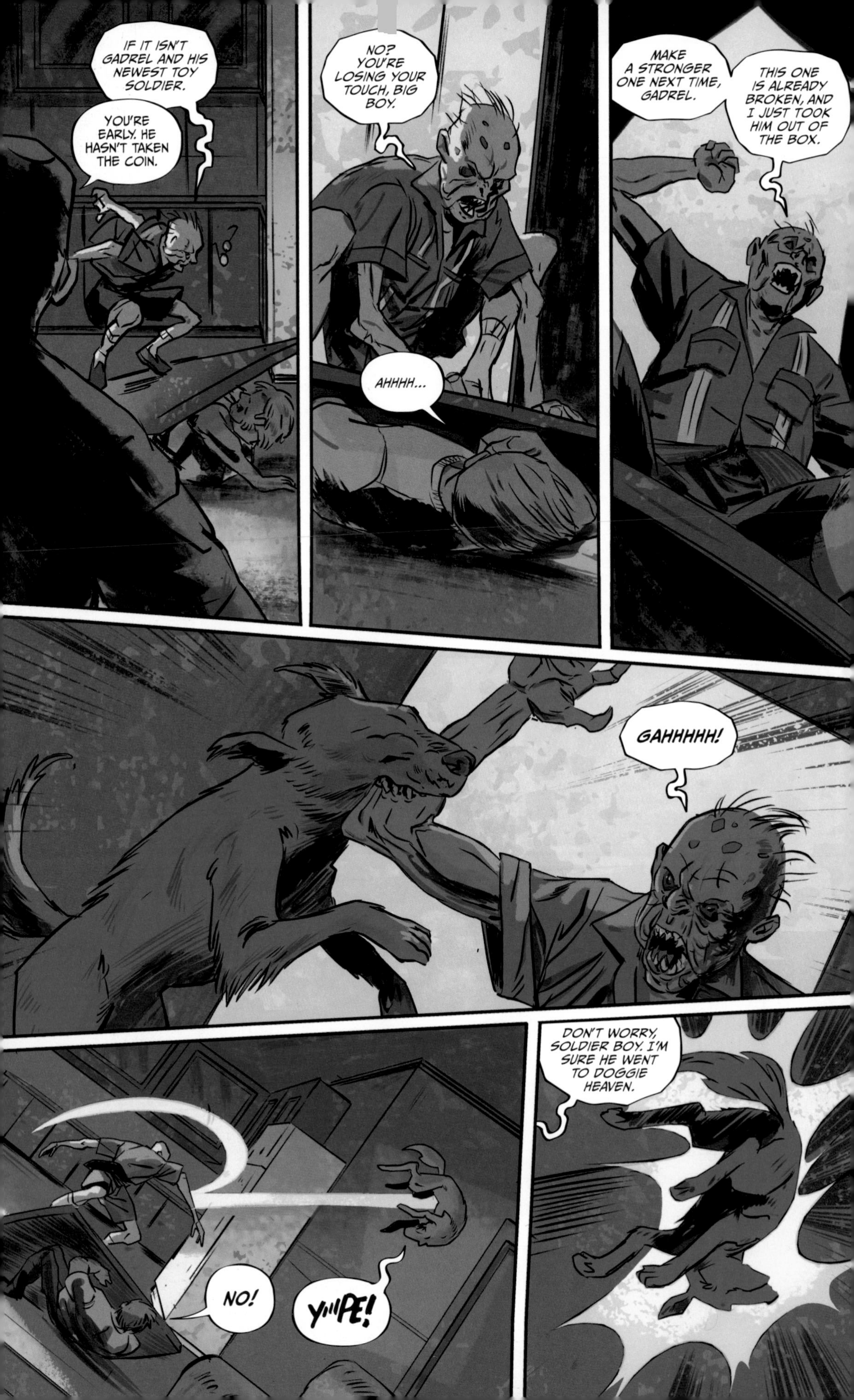
IF IT ISN'T GADREL AND HIS NEWEST TOY SOLDIER.
YOU'RE EARLY. HE HASN'T TAKEN THE COIN.
NO? YOU'RE LOSING YOUR TOUCH, BIG BOY.
AHHHH...
MAKE A STRONGER ONE NEXT TIME, GADREL.
THIS ONE IS ALREADY BROKEN, AND I JUST TOOK HIM OUT OF THE BOX.
GAHHHHH!
NO!
Y''IPE!
DON'T WORRY, SOLDIER BOY. I'M SURE HE WENT TO DOGGIE HEAVEN.

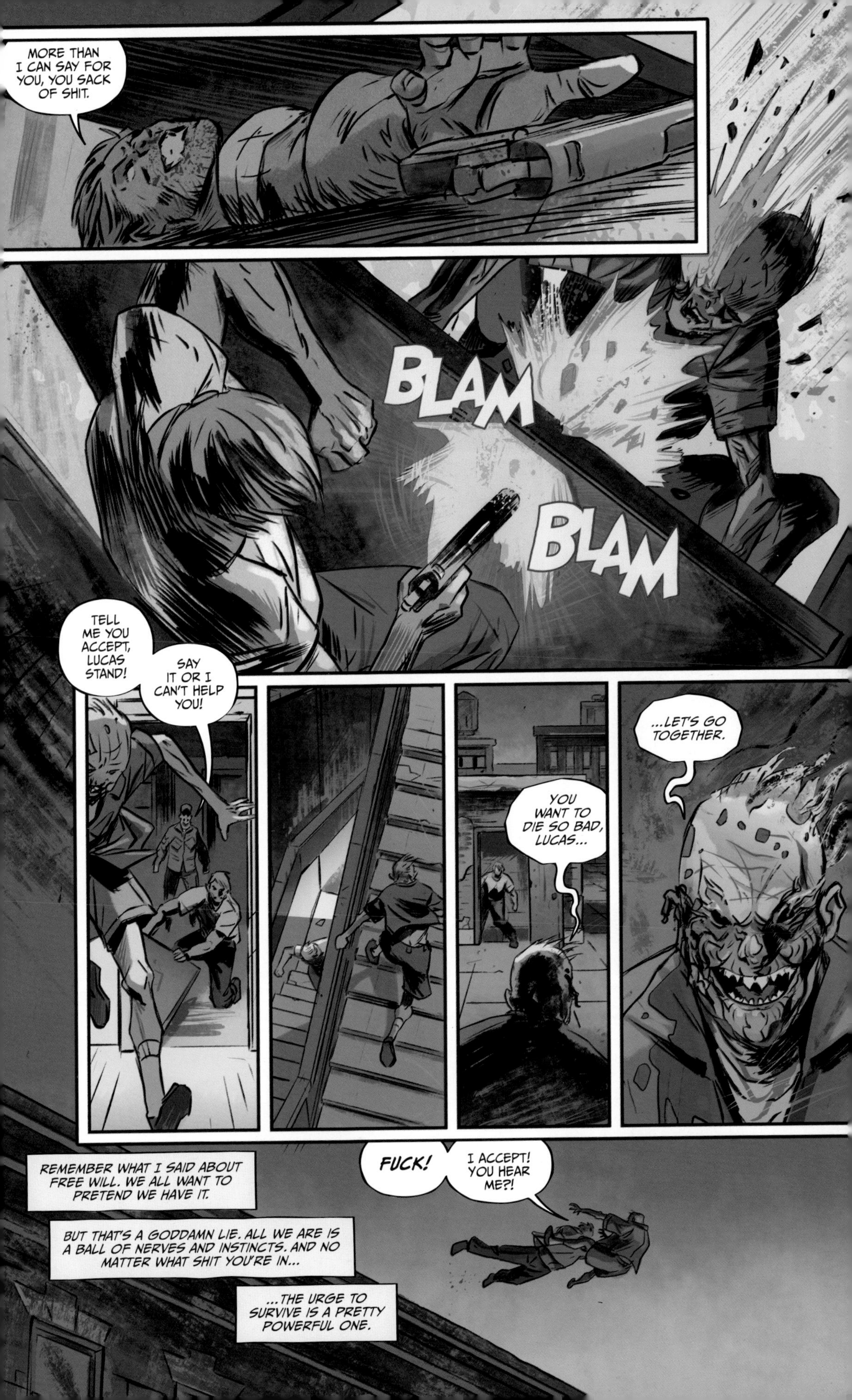

MORE THAN I CAN SAY FOR YOU, YOU SACK OF SHIT.
BLAM
BLAM
TELL ME YOU ACCEPT, LUCAS STAND!
SAY IT OR I CAN'T HELP YOU!
YOU WANT TO DIE SO BAD, LUCAS...
...LET'S GO TOGETHER.
REMEMBER WHAT I SAID ABOUT FREE WILL. WE ALL WANT TO PRETEND WE HAVE IT.
FUCK!
I ACCEPT! YOU HEAR ME?!
BUT THAT'S A GODDAMN LIE. ALL WE ARE IS A BALL OF NERVES AND INSTINCTS. AND NO MATTER WHAT SHIT YOU'RE IN...
...THE URGE TO SURVIVE IS A PRETTY POWERFUL ONE.

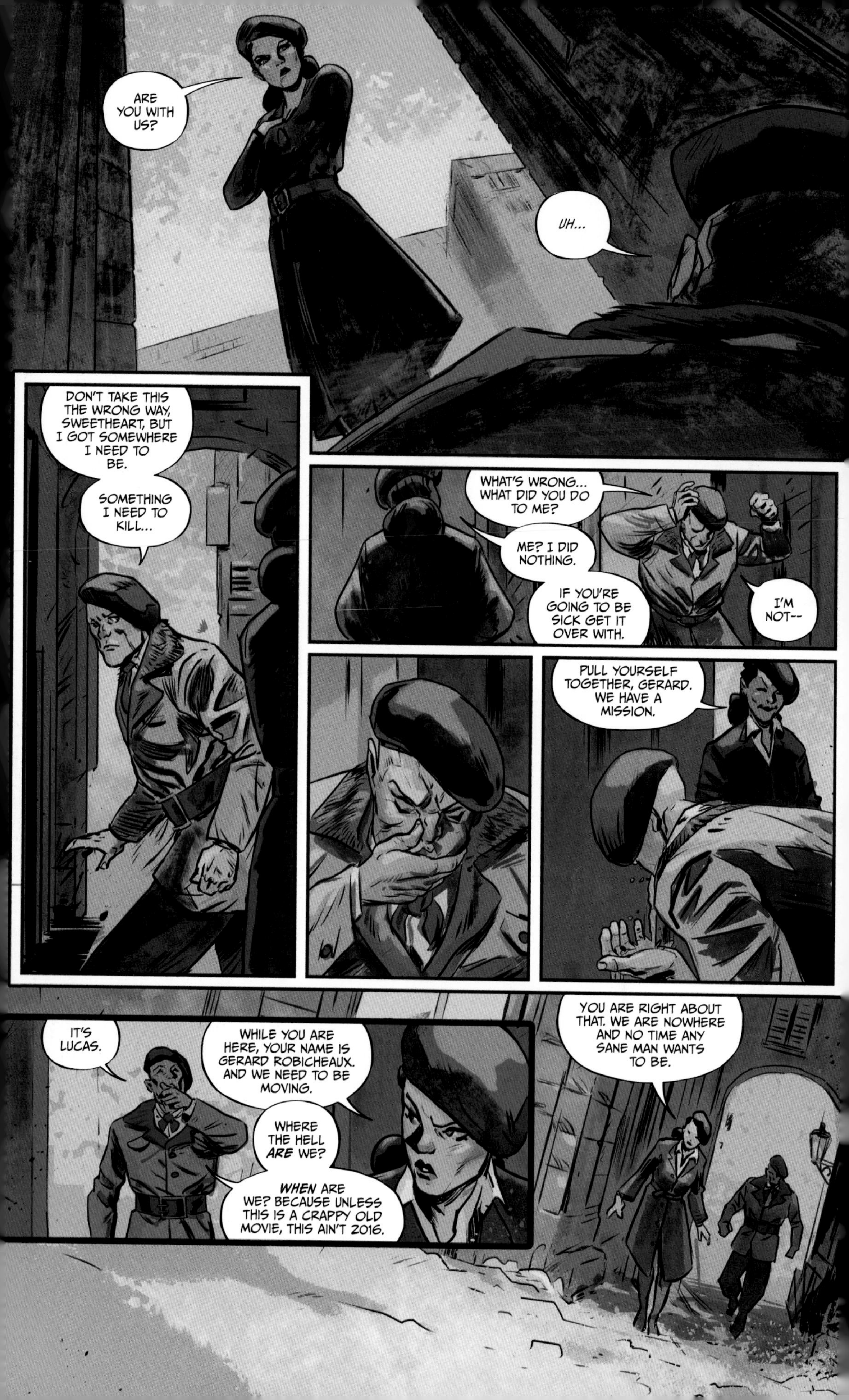
ARE YOU WITH US?
UH...
DON'T TAKE THIS THE WRONG WAY, SWEETHEART, BUT I GOT SOMEWHERE I NEED TO BE.
SOMETHING I NEED TO KILL...
WHAT'S WRONG... WHAT DID YOU DO TO ME?
ME? I DID NOTHING.
IF YOU'RE GOING TO BE SICK GET IT OVER WITH.
I'M NOT--
PULL YOURSELF TOGETHER, GERARD. WE HAVE A MISSION.
IT'S LUCAS.
WHILE YOU ARE HERE, YOUR NAME IS GERARD ROBICHEAUX. AND WE NEED TO BE MOVING.
WHERE THE HELL *ARE* WE?
WHEN ARE WE? BECAUSE UNLESS THIS IS A CRAPPY OLD MOVIE, THIS AIN'T 2016.
YOU ARE RIGHT ABOUT THAT. WE ARE NOWHERE AND NO TIME ANY SANE MAN WANTS TO BE.

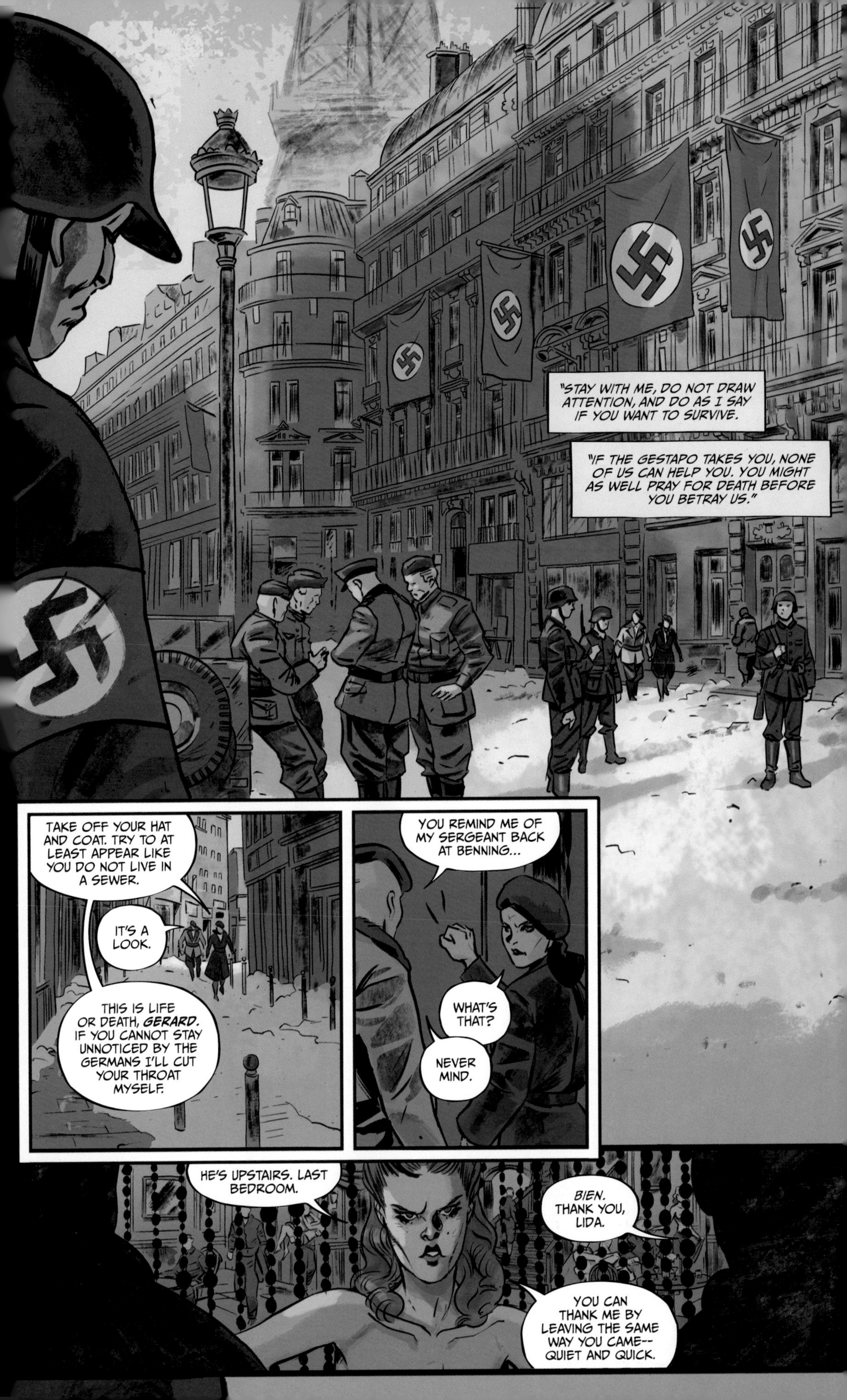

"STAY WITH ME, DO NOT DRAW ATTENTION, AND DO AS I SAY IF YOU WANT TO SURVIVE.
"IF THE GESTAPO TAKES YOU, NONE OF US CAN HELP YOU. YOU MIGHT AS WELL PRAY FOR DEATH BEFORE YOU BETRAY US."
TAKE OFF YOUR HAT AND COAT. TRY TO AT LEAST APPEAR LIKE YOU DO NOT LIVE IN A SEWER.
IT'S A LOOK.
THIS IS LIFE OR DEATH, *GERARD*. IF YOU CANNOT STAY UNNOTICED BY THE GERMANS I'LL CUT YOUR THROAT MYSELF.
YOU REMIND ME OF MY SERGEANT BACK AT BENNING...
WHAT'S THAT?
NEVER MIND.
HE'S UPSTAIRS. LAST BEDROOM.
BIEN. THANK YOU, LIDA.
YOU CAN THANK ME BY LEAVING THE SAME WAY YOU CAME-- QUIET AND QUICK.

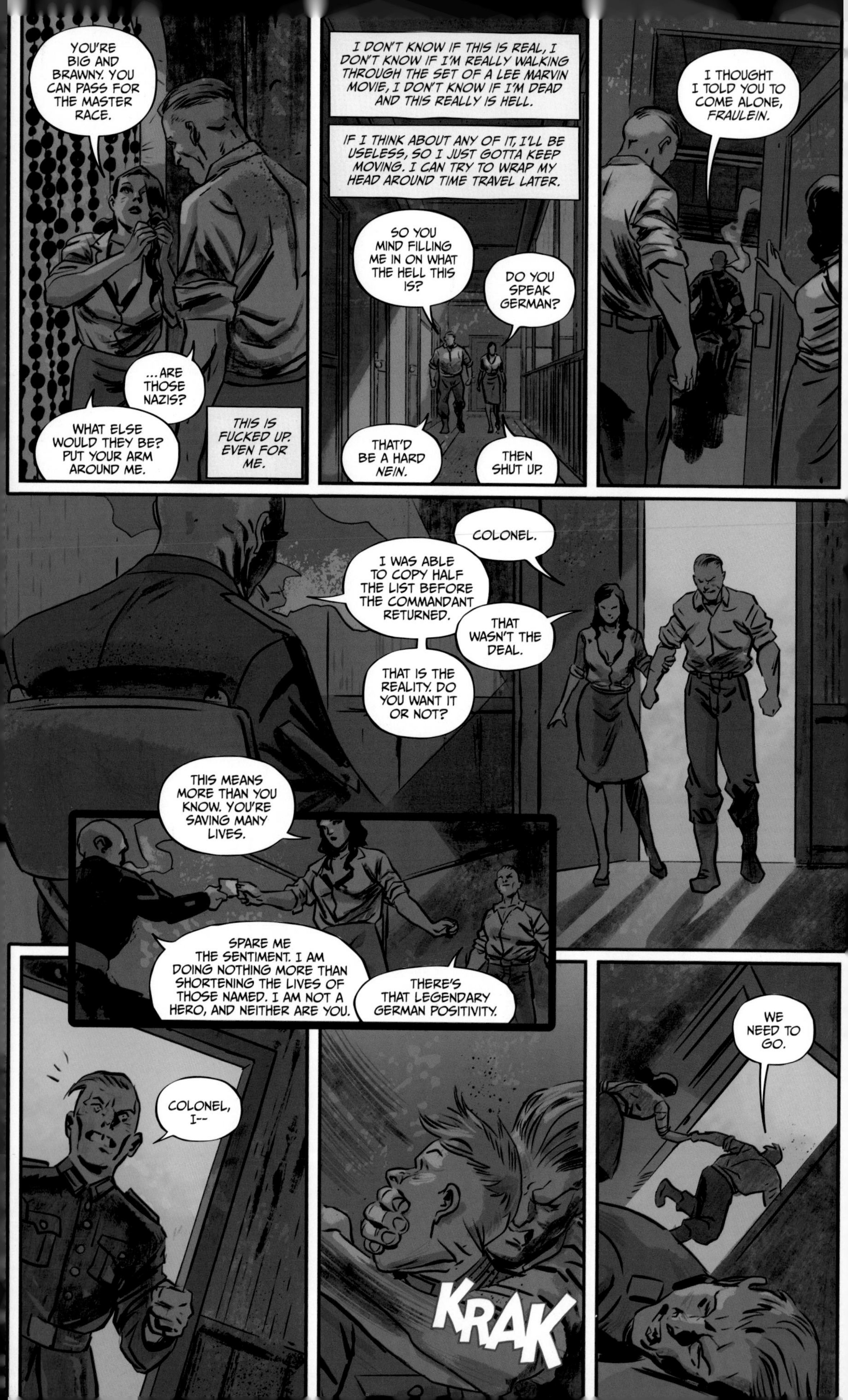
YOU'RE BIG AND BRAWNY. YOU CAN PASS FOR THE MASTER RACE.
...ARE THOSE NAZIS?
WHAT ELSE WOULD THEY BE? PUT YOUR ARM AROUND ME.
THIS IS FUCKED UP. EVEN FOR ME.
I DON'T KNOW IF THIS IS REAL, I DON'T KNOW IF I'M REALLY WALKING THROUGH THE SET OF A LEE MARVIN MOVIE, I DON'T KNOW IF I'M DEAD AND THIS REALLY IS HELL.
IF I THINK ABOUT ANY OF IT, I'LL BE USELESS, SO I JUST GOTTA KEEP MOVING. I CAN TRY TO WRAP MY HEAD AROUND TIME TRAVEL LATER.
SO YOU MIND FILLING ME IN ON WHAT THE HELL THIS IS?
DO YOU SPEAK GERMAN?
THAT'D BE A HARD NEIN.
THEN SHUT UP.
I THOUGHT I TOLD YOU TO COME ALONE, FRAULEIN.
COLONEL.
I WAS ABLE TO COPY HALF THE LIST BEFORE THE COMMANDANT RETURNED.
THAT WASN'T THE DEAL.
THAT IS THE REALITY. DO YOU WANT IT OR NOT?
THIS MEANS MORE THAN YOU KNOW. YOU'RE SAVING MANY LIVES.
SPARE ME THE SENTIMENT. I AM DOING NOTHING MORE THAN SHORTENING THE LIVES OF THOSE NAMED. I AM NOT A HERO, AND NEITHER ARE YOU.
THERE'S THAT LEGENDARY GERMAN POSITIVITY.
COLONEL, I--
KRAK
WE NEED TO GO.

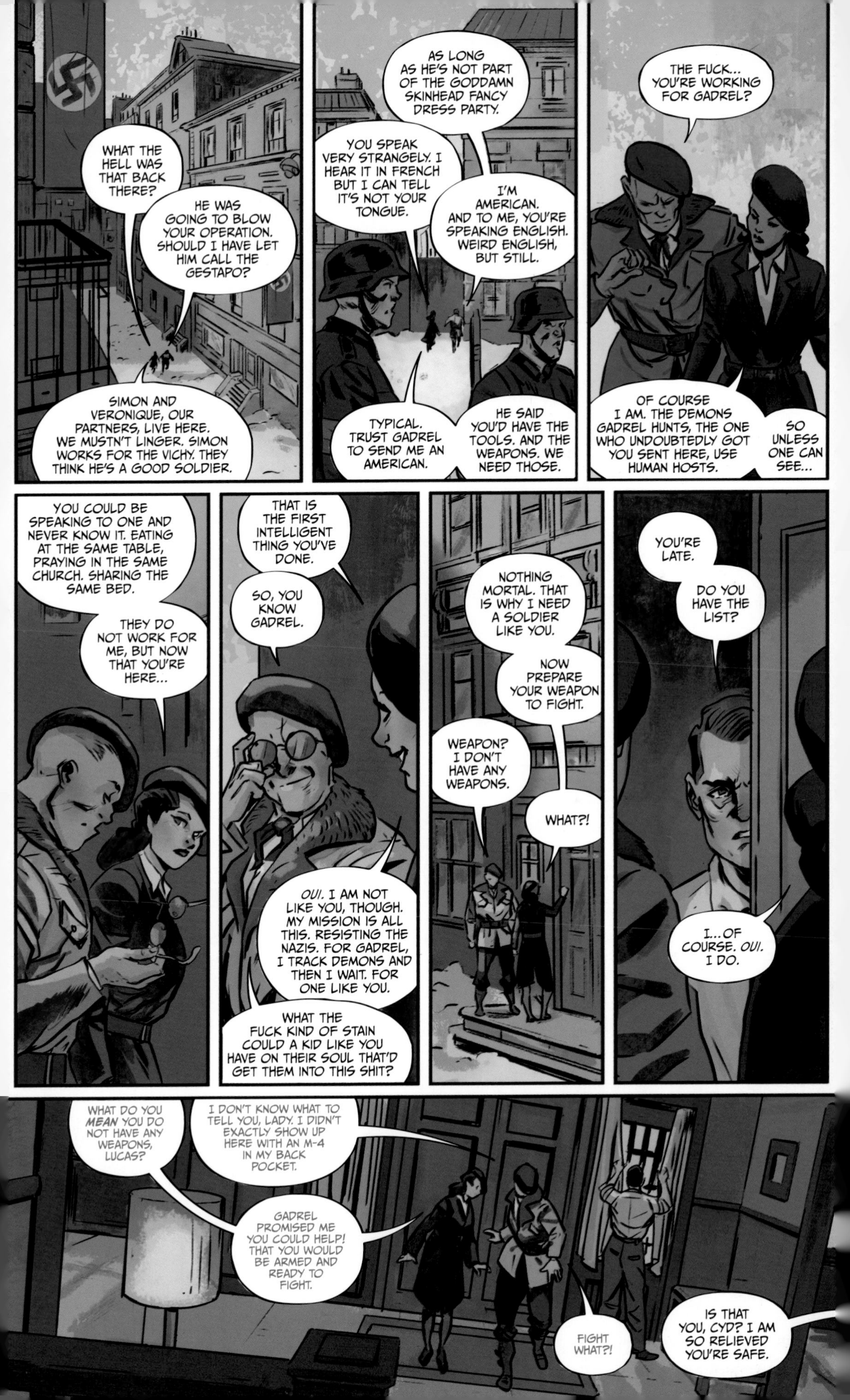
WHAT THE HELL WAS THAT BACK THERE?
HE WAS GOING TO BLOW YOUR OPERATION. SHOULD I HAVE LET HIM CALL THE GESTAPO?
SIMON AND VERONIQUE, OUR PARTNERS, LIVE HERE. WE MUSTN'T LINGER. SIMON WORKS FOR THE VICHY. THEY THINK HE'S A GOOD SOLDIER.
AS LONG AS HE'S NOT PART OF THE GODDAMN SKINHEAD FANCY DRESS PARTY.
YOU SPEAK VERY STRANGELY. I HEAR IT IN FRENCH BUT I CAN TELL IT'S NOT YOUR TONGUE.
I'M AMERICAN. AND TO ME, YOU'RE SPEAKING ENGLISH. WEIRD ENGLISH, BUT STILL.
TYPICAL. TRUST GADREL TO SEND ME AN AMERICAN.
HE SAID YOU'D HAVE THE TOOLS. AND THE WEAPONS. WE NEED THOSE.
THE FUCK... YOU'RE WORKING FOR GADREL?
OF COURSE I AM. THE DEMONS GADREL HUNTS, THE ONE WHO UNDOUBTEDLY GOT YOU SENT HERE, USE HUMAN HOSTS.
SO UNLESS ONE CAN SEE...
YOU COULD BE SPEAKING TO ONE AND NEVER KNOW IT. EATING AT THE SAME TABLE, PRAYING IN THE SAME CHURCH. SHARING THE SAME BED.
THEY DO NOT WORK FOR ME, BUT NOW THAT YOU'RE HERE...
THAT IS THE FIRST INTELLIGENT THING YOU'VE DONE.
SO, YOU KNOW GADREL.
OUI. I AM NOT LIKE YOU, THOUGH. MY MISSION IS ALL THIS. RESISTING THE NAZIS. FOR GADREL, I TRACK DEMONS AND THEN I WAIT. FOR ONE LIKE YOU.
WHAT THE FUCK KIND OF STAIN COULD A KID LIKE YOU HAVE ON THEIR SOUL THAT'D GET THEM INTO THIS SHIT?
NOTHING MORTAL. THAT IS WHY I NEED A SOLDIER LIKE YOU.
NOW PREPARE YOUR WEAPON TO FIGHT.
WEAPON? I DON'T HAVE ANY WEAPONS.
WHAT?!
YOU'RE LATE.
DO YOU HAVE THE LIST?
I...OF COURSE. *OUI*. I DO.
WHAT DO YOU *MEAN* YOU DO NOT HAVE ANY WEAPONS, LUCAS?
I DON'T KNOW WHAT TO TELL YOU, LADY. I DIDN'T EXACTLY SHOW UP HERE WITH AN M-4 IN MY BACK POCKET.
GADREL PROMISED ME YOU COULD HELP! THAT YOU WOULD BE ARMED AND READY TO FIGHT.
FIGHT WHAT?!
IS THAT YOU, CYD? I AM SO RELIEVED YOU'RE SAFE.

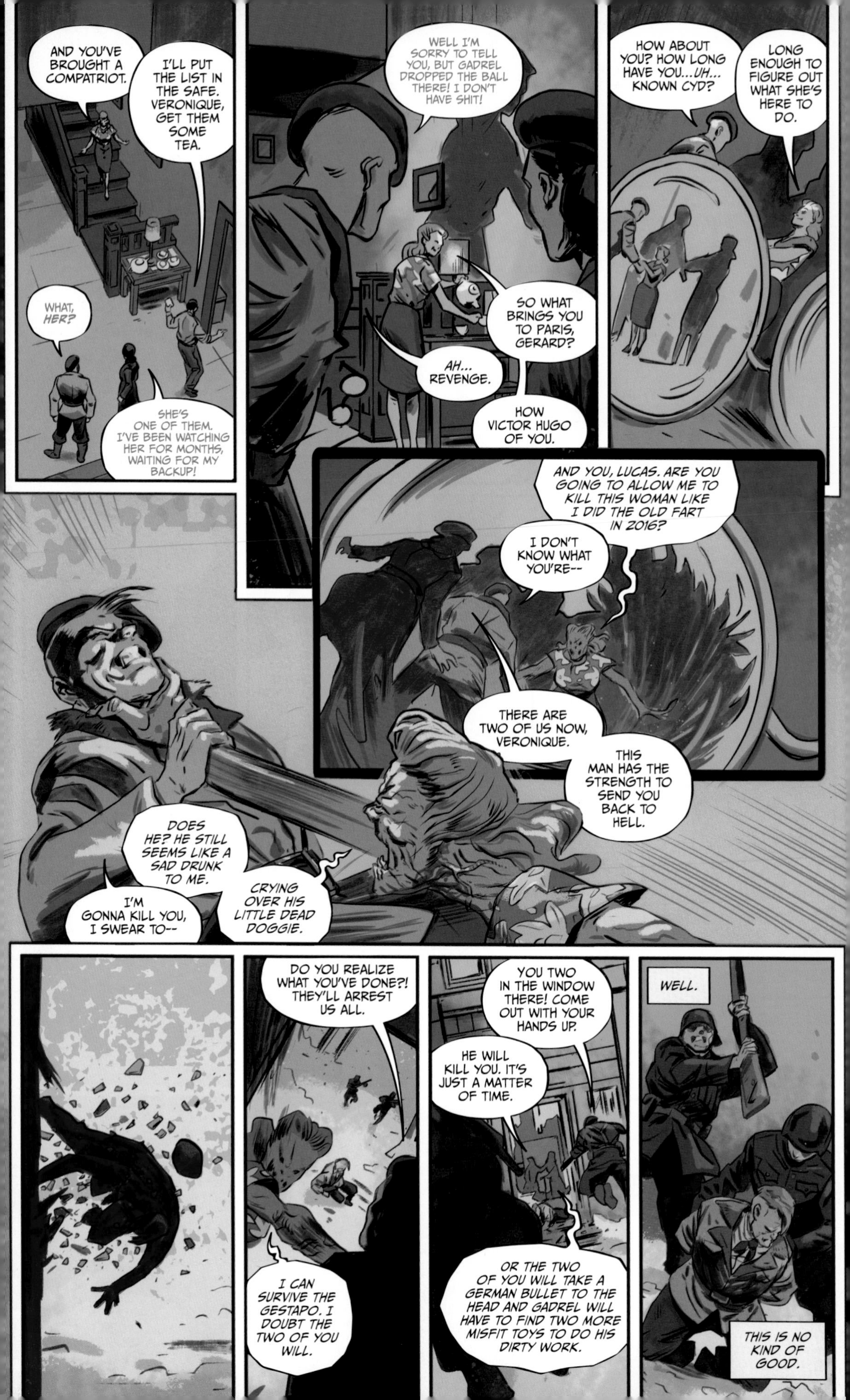
AND YOU'VE BROUGHT A COMPATRIOT.
I'LL PUT THE LIST IN THE SAFE. VERONIQUE, GET THEM SOME TEA.
WHAT, HER?
SHE'S ONE OF THEM. I'VE BEEN WATCHING HER FOR MONTHS, WAITING FOR MY BACKUP!
WELL I'M SORRY TO TELL YOU, BUT GADREL DROPPED THE BALL THERE! I DON'T HAVE SHIT!
SO WHAT BRINGS YOU TO PARIS, GERARD?
AH... REVENGE.
HOW VICTOR HUGO OF YOU.
HOW ABOUT YOU? HOW LONG HAVE YOU...UH... KNOWN CYD?
LONG ENOUGH TO FIGURE OUT WHAT SHE'S HERE TO DO.
AND YOU, LUCAS. ARE YOU GOING TO ALLOW ME TO KILL THIS WOMAN LIKE I DID THE OLD FART IN 2016?
I DON'T KNOW WHAT YOU'RE--
THERE ARE TWO OF US NOW, VERONIQUE.
THIS MAN HAS THE STRENGTH TO SEND YOU BACK TO HELL.
DOES HE? HE STILL SEEMS LIKE A SAD DRUNK TO ME.
CRYING OVER HIS LITTLE DEAD DOGGIE.
I'M GONNA KILL YOU, I SWEAR TO--
DO YOU REALIZE WHAT YOU'VE DONE?! THEY'LL ARREST US ALL.
I CAN SURVIVE THE GESTAPO. I DOUBT THE TWO OF YOU WILL.
YOU TWO IN THE WINDOW THERE! COME OUT WITH YOUR HANDS UP.
HE WILL KILL YOU. IT'S JUST A MATTER OF TIME.
OR THE TWO OF YOU WILL TAKE A GERMAN BULLET TO THE HEAD AND GADREL WILL HAVE TO FIND TWO MORE MISFIT TOYS TO DO HIS DIRTY WORK.
WELL.
THIS IS NO KIND OF GOOD.

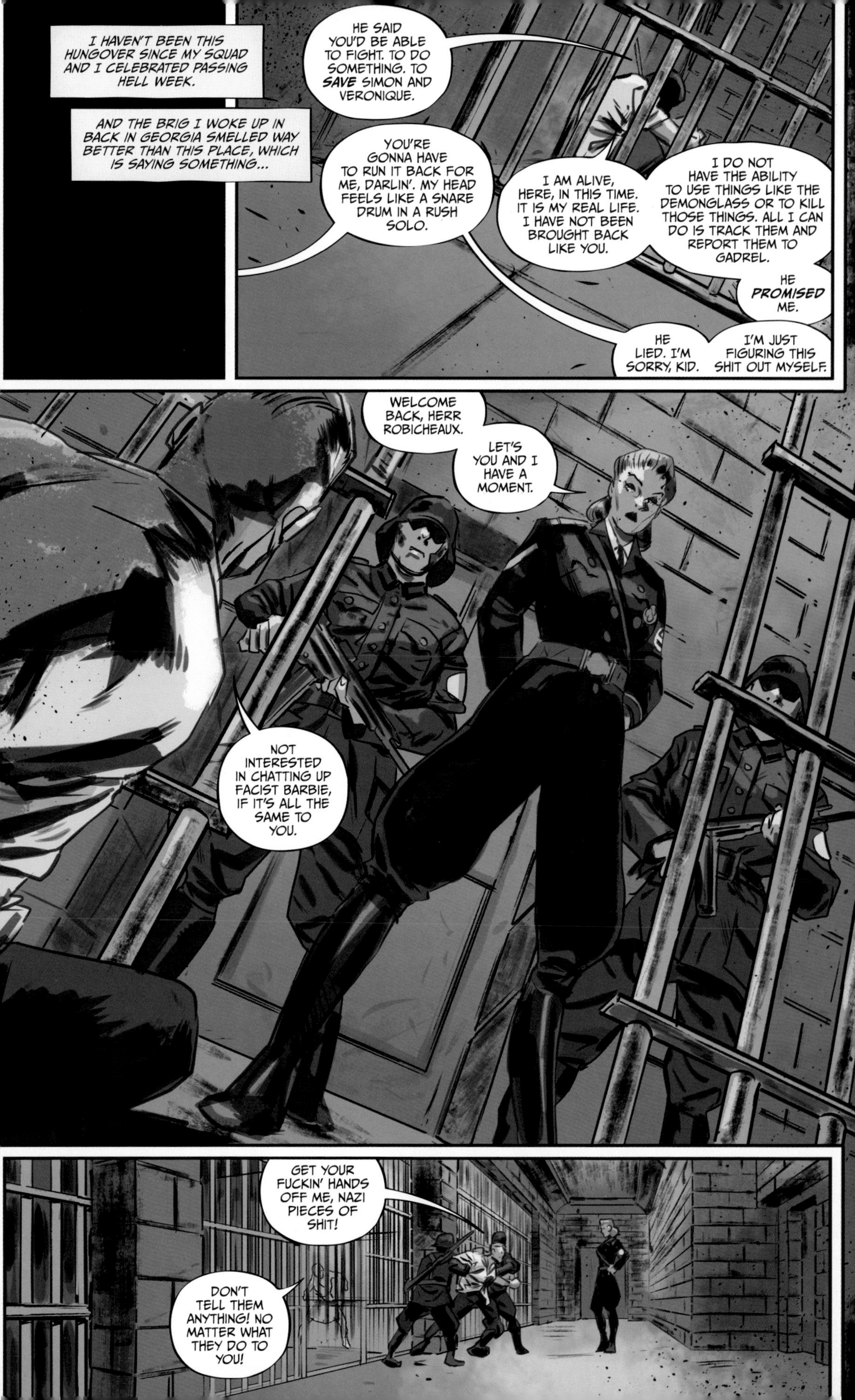
I HAVEN'T BEEN THIS HUNGOVER SINCE MY SQUAD AND I CELEBRATED PASSING HELL WEEK.
AND THE BRIG I WOKE UP IN BACK IN GEORGIA SMELLED WAY BETTER THAN THIS PLACE, WHICH IS SAYING SOMETHING...
HE SAID YOU'D BE ABLE TO FIGHT. TO DO SOMETHING. TO SAVE SIMON AND VERONIQUE.
YOU'RE GONNA HAVE TO RUN IT BACK FOR ME, DARLIN'. MY HEAD FEELS LIKE A SNARE DRUM IN A RUSH SOLO.
I AM ALIVE, HERE, IN THIS TIME. IT IS MY REAL LIFE. I HAVE NOT BEEN BROUGHT BACK LIKE YOU.
I DO NOT HAVE THE ABILITY TO USE THINGS LIKE THE DEMONGLASS OR TO KILL THOSE THINGS. ALL I CAN DO IS TRACK THEM AND REPORT THEM TO GADREL.
HE PROMISED ME.
HE LIED. I'M SORRY, KID.
I'M JUST FIGURING THIS SHIT OUT MYSELF.
WELCOME BACK, HERR ROBICHEAUX.
LET'S YOU AND I HAVE A MOMENT.
NOT INTERESTED IN CHATTING UP FACIST BARBIE, IF IT'S ALL THE SAME TO YOU.
GET YOUR FUCKIN' HANDS OFF ME, NAZI PIECES OF SHIT!
DON'T TELL THEM ANYTHING! NO MATTER WHAT THEY DO TO YOU!

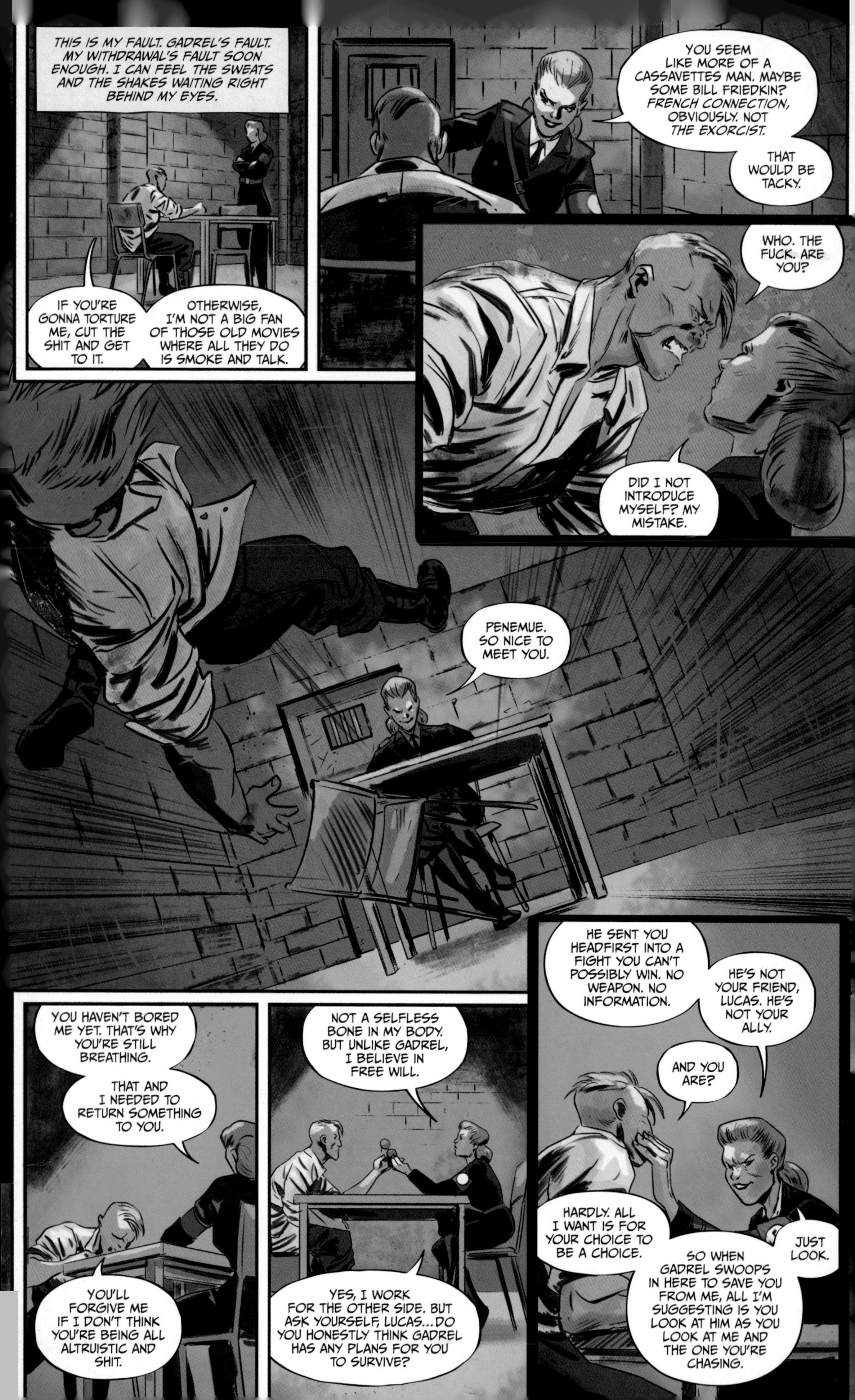
THIS IS MY FAULT. GADREL'S FAULT. MY WITHDRAWAL'S FAULT SOON ENOUGH. I CAN FEEL THE SWEATS AND THE SHAKES WAITING RIGHT BEHIND MY EYES.
IF YOU'RE GONNA TORTURE ME, CUT THE SHIT AND GET TO IT.
OTHERWISE, I'M NOT A BIG FAN OF THOSE OLD MOVIES WHERE ALL THEY DO IS SMOKE AND TALK.
YOU SEEM LIKE MORE OF A CASSAVETTES MAN. MAYBE SOME BILL FRIEDKIN? *FRENCH CONNECTION*, OBVIOUSLY. NOT *THE EXORCIST*.
THAT WOULD BE TACKY.
WHO. THE FUCK. ARE YOU?
DID I NOT INTRODUCE MYSELF? MY MISTAKE.
PENEMUE. SO NICE TO MEET YOU.
YOU HAVEN'T BORED ME YET. THAT'S WHY YOU'RE STILL BREATHING.
THAT AND I NEEDED TO RETURN SOMETHING TO YOU.
YOU'LL FORGIVE ME IF I DON'T THINK YOU'RE BEING ALL ALTRUISTIC AND SHIT.
NOT A SELFLESS BONE IN MY BODY. BUT UNLIKE GADREL, I BELIEVE IN FREE WILL.
YES, I WORK FOR THE OTHER SIDE. BUT ASK YOURSELF, LUCAS...DO YOU HONESTLY THINK GADREL HAS ANY PLANS FOR YOU TO SURVIVE?
HE SENT YOU HEADFIRST INTO A FIGHT YOU CAN'T POSSIBLY WIN. NO WEAPON. NO INFORMATION.
HE'S NOT YOUR FRIEND, LUCAS. HE'S NOT YOUR ALLY.
AND YOU ARE?
HARDLY. ALL I WANT IS FOR YOUR CHOICE TO BE A CHOICE.
JUST LOOK.
SO WHEN GADREL SWOOPS IN HERE TO SAVE YOU FROM ME, ALL I'M SUGGESTING IS YOU LOOK AT HIM AS YOU LOOK AT ME AND THE ONE YOU'RE CHASING.

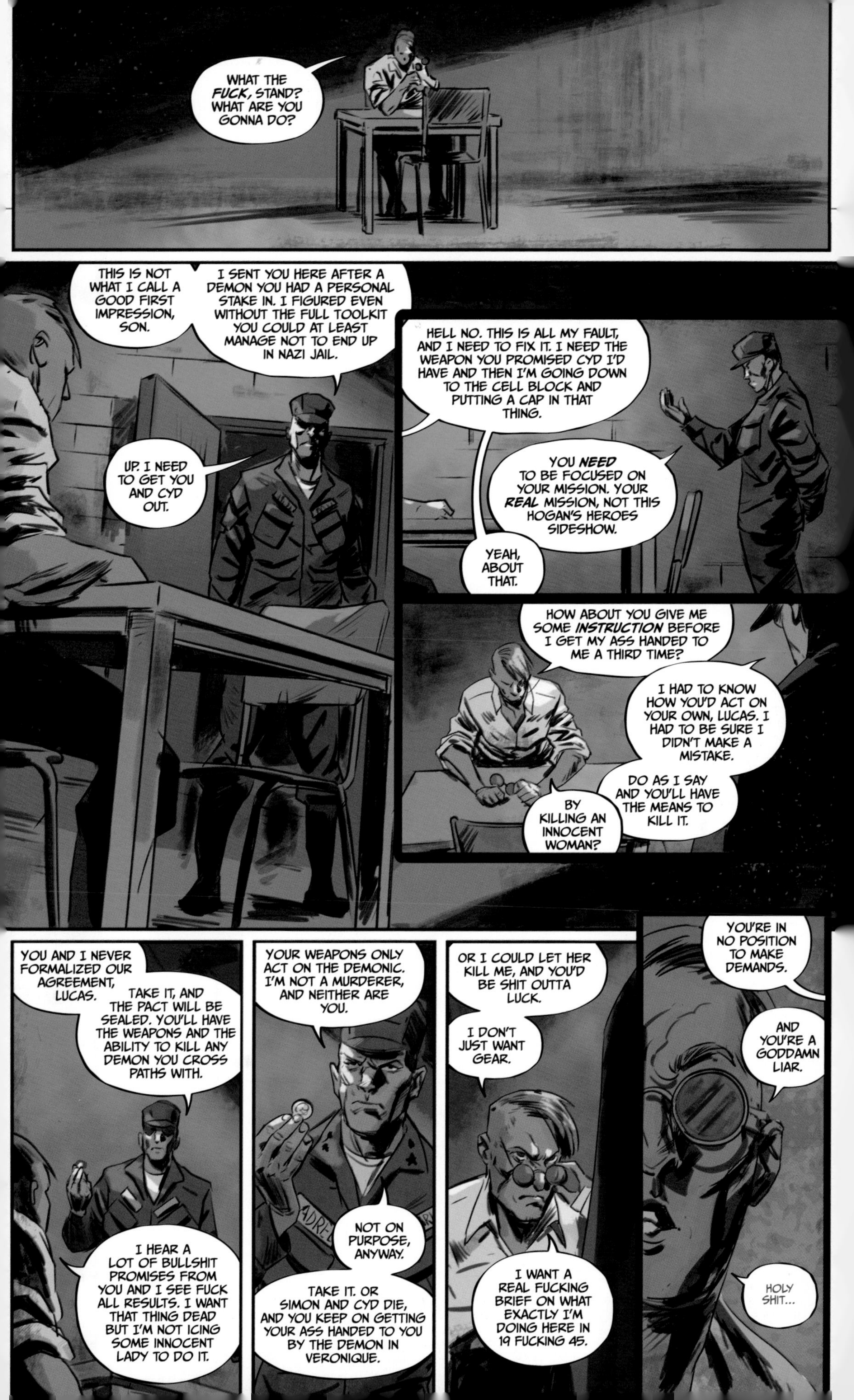
WHAT THE FUCK, STAND? WHAT ARE YOU GONNA DO?
THIS IS NOT WHAT I CALL A GOOD FIRST IMPRESSION, SON.
I SENT YOU HERE AFTER A DEMON YOU HAD A PERSONAL STAKE IN. I FIGURED EVEN WITHOUT THE FULL TOOLKIT YOU COULD AT LEAST MANAGE NOT TO END UP IN NAZI JAIL.
UP. I NEED TO GET YOU AND CYD OUT.
HELL NO. THIS IS ALL MY FAULT, AND I NEED TO FIX IT. I NEED THE WEAPON YOU PROMISED CYD I'D HAVE AND THEN I'M GOING DOWN TO THE CELL BLOCK AND PUTTING A CAP IN THAT THING.
YOU NEED TO BE FOCUSED ON YOUR MISSION. YOUR REAL MISSION, NOT THIS HOGAN'S HEROES SIDESHOW.
YEAH, ABOUT THAT.
HOW ABOUT YOU GIVE ME SOME INSTRUCTION BEFORE I GET MY ASS HANDED TO ME A THIRD TIME?
I HAD TO KNOW HOW YOU'D ACT ON YOUR OWN, LUCAS. I HAD TO BE SURE I DIDN'T MAKE A MISTAKE.
DO AS I SAY AND YOU'LL HAVE THE MEANS TO KILL IT.
BY KILLING AN INNOCENT WOMAN?
YOU AND I NEVER FORMALIZED OUR AGREEMENT, LUCAS.
TAKE IT, AND THE PACT WILL BE SEALED. YOU'LL HAVE THE WEAPONS AND THE ABILITY TO KILL ANY DEMON YOU CROSS PATHS WITH.
I HEAR A LOT OF BULLSHIT PROMISES FROM YOU AND I SEE FUCK ALL RESULTS. I WANT THAT THING DEAD BUT I'M NOT ICING SOME INNOCENT LADY TO DO IT.
YOUR WEAPONS ONLY ACT ON THE DEMONIC. I'M NOT A MURDERER, AND NEITHER ARE YOU.
NOT ON PURPOSE, ANYWAY.
TAKE IT. OR SIMON AND CYD DIE, AND YOU KEEP ON GETTING YOUR ASS HANDED TO YOU BY THE DEMON IN VERONIQUE.
OR I COULD LET HER KILL ME, AND YOU'D BE SHIT OUTTA LUCK.
I DON'T JUST WANT GEAR.
I WANT A REAL FUCKING BRIEF ON WHAT EXACTLY I'M DOING HERE IN 19 FUCKING 45.
YOU'RE IN NO POSITION TO MAKE DEMANDS.
AND YOU'RE A GODDAMN LIAR.
HOLY SHIT...

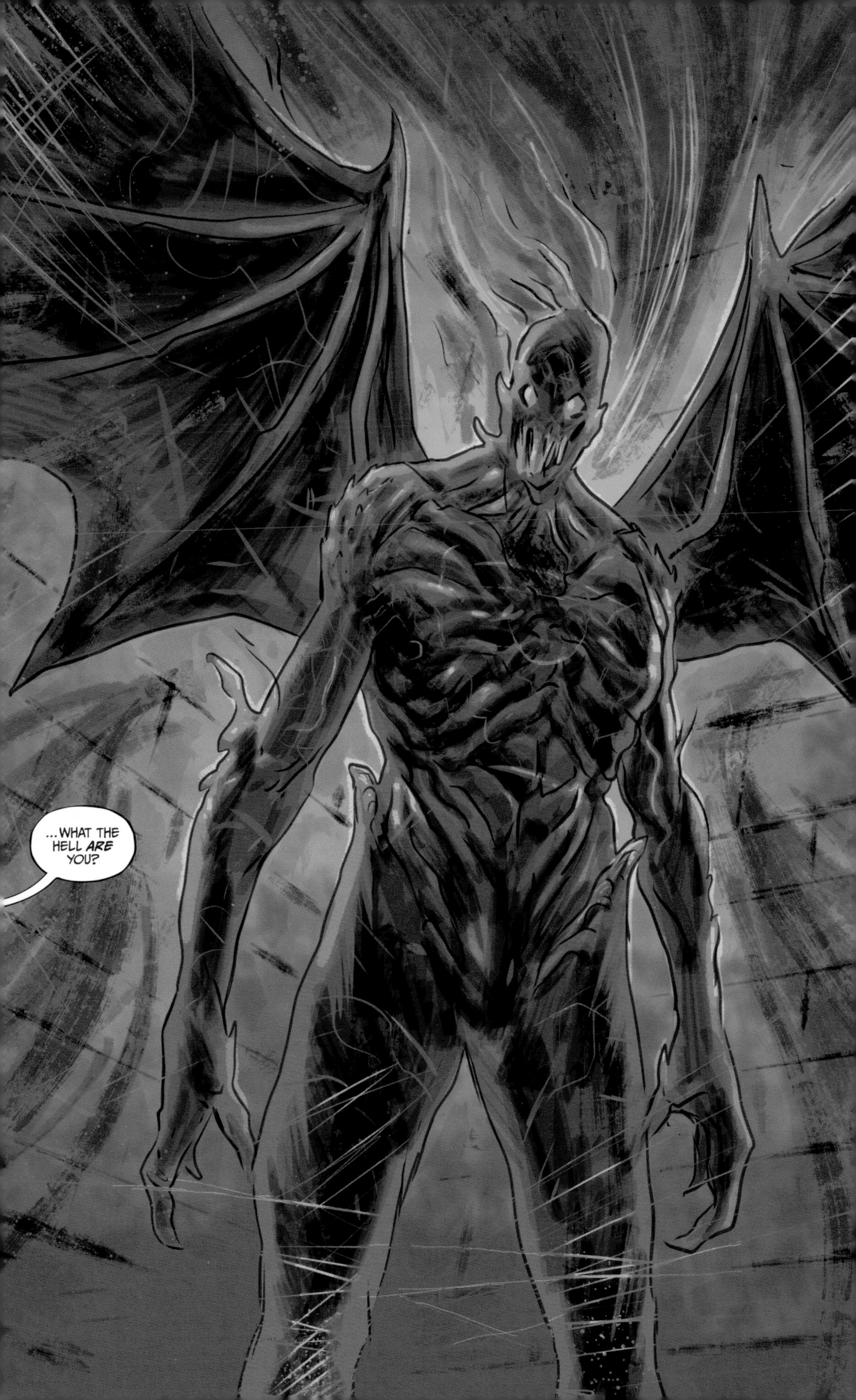
...WHAT THE HELL ARE YOU?

UNITED STATES MARINE CORPS

SEMPER FIDELIS

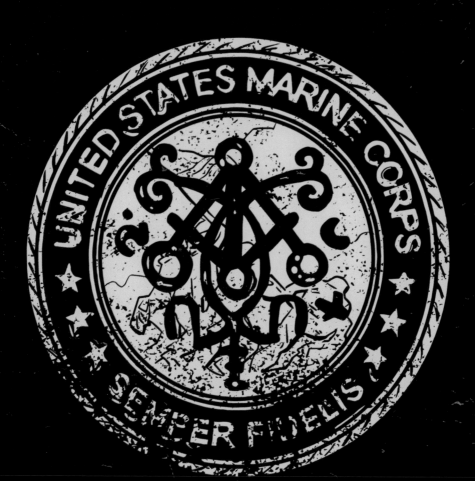

CHAPTER
TWO

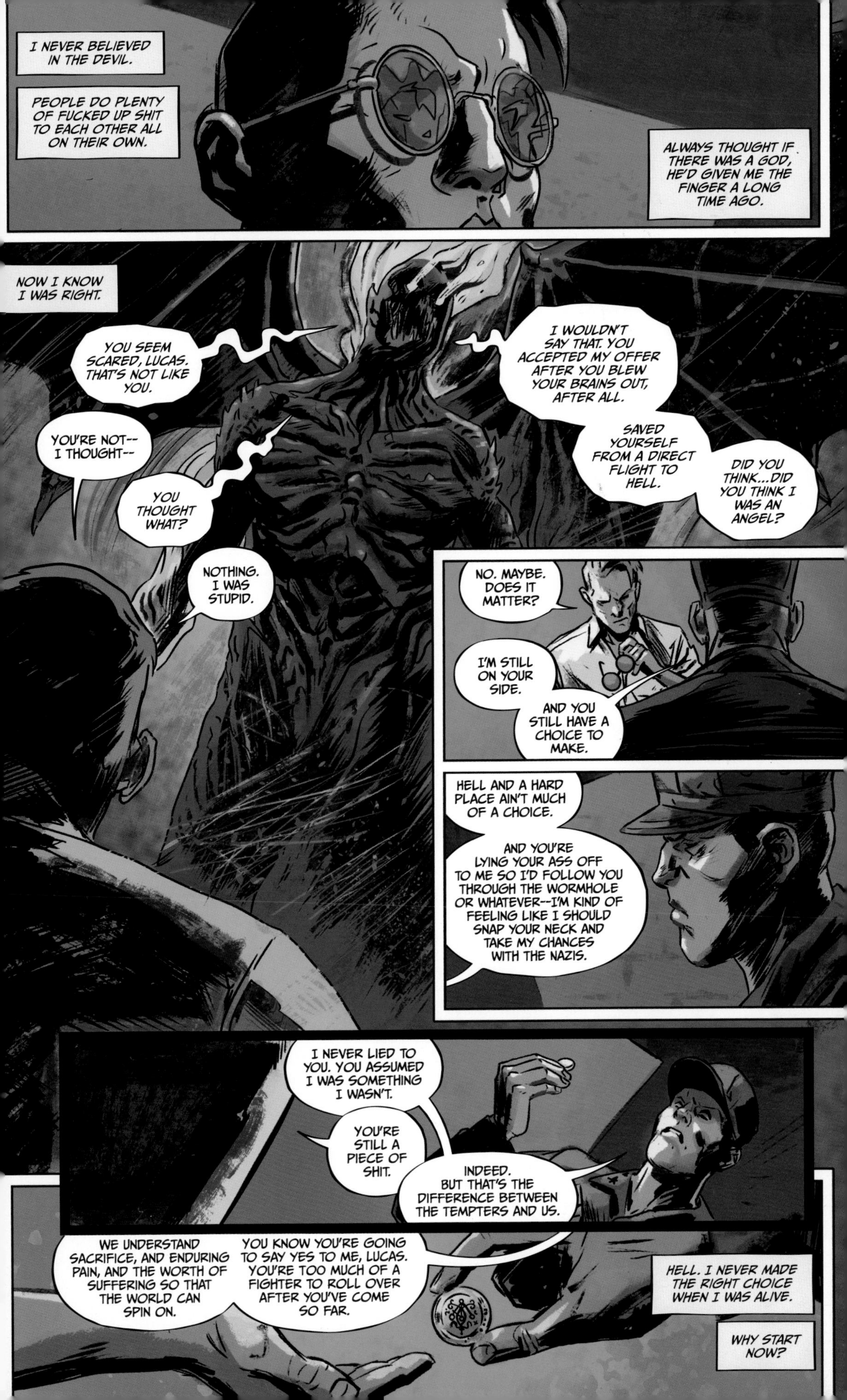

I NEVER BELIEVED IN THE DEVIL.
PEOPLE DO PLENTY OF FUCKED UP SHIT TO EACH OTHER ALL ON THEIR OWN.
ALWAYS THOUGHT IF THERE WAS A GOD, HE'D GIVEN ME THE FINGER A LONG TIME AGO.
NOW I KNOW I WAS RIGHT.
YOU SEEM SCARED, LUCAS. THAT'S NOT LIKE YOU.
YOU'RE NOT-- I THOUGHT--
YOU THOUGHT WHAT?
NOTHING. I WAS STUPID.
I WOULDN'T SAY THAT. YOU ACCEPTED MY OFFER AFTER YOU BLEW YOUR BRAINS OUT, AFTER ALL.
SAVED YOURSELF FROM A DIRECT FLIGHT TO HELL.
DID YOU THINK...DID YOU THINK I WAS AN ANGEL?
NO. MAYBE. DOES IT MATTER?
I'M STILL ON YOUR SIDE.
AND YOU STILL HAVE A CHOICE TO MAKE.
HELL AND A HARD PLACE AIN'T MUCH OF A CHOICE.
AND YOU'RE LYING YOUR ASS OFF TO ME SO I'D FOLLOW YOU THROUGH THE WORMHOLE OR WHATEVER--I'M KIND OF FEELING LIKE I SHOULD SNAP YOUR NECK AND TAKE MY CHANCES WITH THE NAZIS.
I NEVER LIED TO YOU. YOU ASSUMED I WAS SOMETHING I WASN'T.
YOU'RE STILL A PIECE OF SHIT.
INDEED. BUT THAT'S THE DIFFERENCE BETWEEN THE TEMPTERS AND US.
WE UNDERSTAND SACRIFICE, AND ENDURING PAIN, AND THE WORTH OF SUFFERING SO THAT THE WORLD CAN SPIN ON.
YOU KNOW YOU'RE GOING TO SAY YES TO ME, LUCAS. YOU'RE TOO MUCH OF A FIGHTER TO ROLL OVER AFTER YOU'VE COME SO FAR.
HELL. I NEVER MADE THE RIGHT CHOICE WHEN I WAS ALIVE.
WHY START NOW?

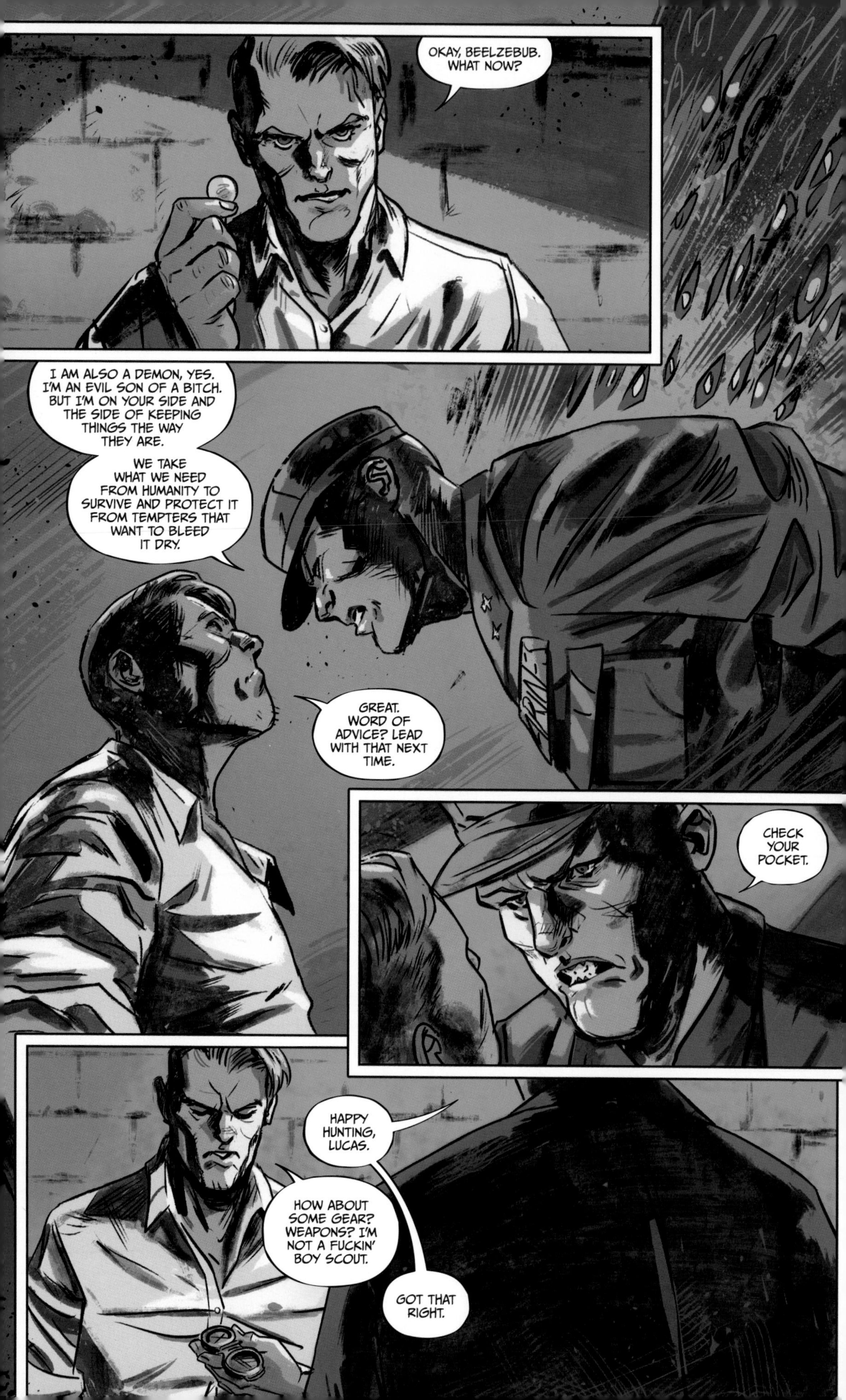
OKAY, BEELZEBUB. WHAT NOW?
I AM ALSO A DEMON, YES. I'M AN EVIL SON OF A BITCH. BUT I'M ON YOUR SIDE AND THE SIDE OF KEEPING THINGS THE WAY THEY ARE.
WE TAKE WHAT WE NEED FROM HUMANITY TO SURVIVE AND PROTECT IT FROM TEMPTERS THAT WANT TO BLEED IT DRY.
GREAT. WORD OF ADVICE? LEAD WITH THAT NEXT TIME.
CHECK YOUR POCKET.
HAPPY HUNTING, LUCAS.
HOW ABOUT SOME GEAR? WEAPONS? I'M NOT A FUCKIN' BOY SCOUT.
GOT THAT RIGHT.

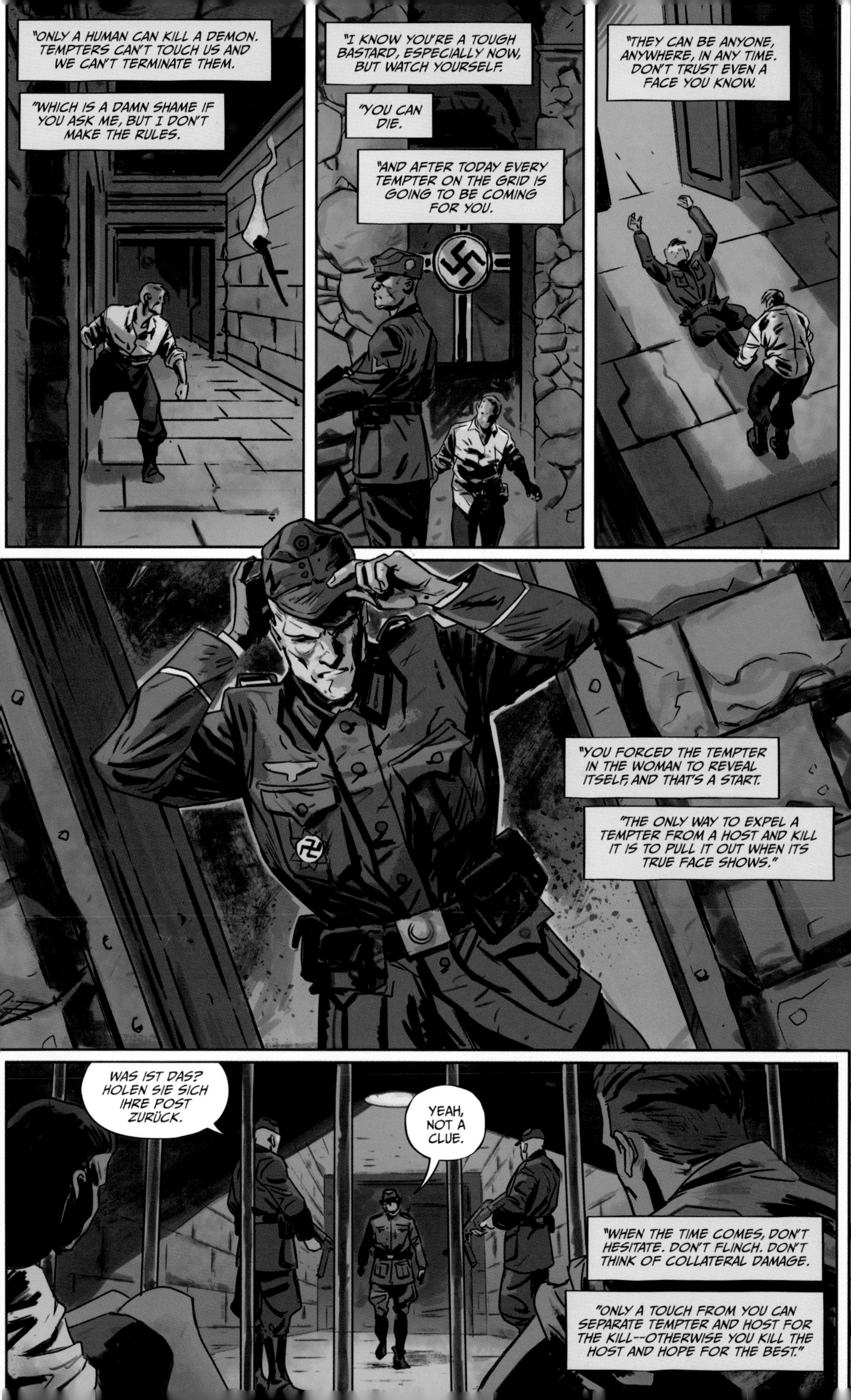
"ONLY A HUMAN CAN KILL A DEMON. TEMPTERS CAN'T TOUCH US AND WE CAN'T TERMINATE THEM.
"WHICH IS A DAMN SHAME IF YOU ASK ME, BUT I DON'T MAKE THE RULES.
"I KNOW YOU'RE A TOUGH BASTARD, ESPECIALLY NOW, BUT WATCH YOURSELF.
"YOU CAN DIE.
"AND AFTER TODAY EVERY TEMPTER ON THE GRID IS GOING TO BE COMING FOR YOU.
"THEY CAN BE ANYONE, ANYWHERE, IN ANY TIME. DON'T TRUST EVEN A FACE YOU KNOW.
"YOU FORCED THE TEMPTER IN THE WOMAN TO REVEAL ITSELF, AND THAT'S A START.
"THE ONLY WAY TO EXPEL A TEMPTER FROM A HOST AND KILL IT IS TO PULL IT OUT WHEN ITS TRUE FACE SHOWS."
WAS IST DAS? HOLEN SIE SICH IHRE POST ZURÜCK.
YEAH, NOT A CLUE.
"WHEN THE TIME COMES, DON'T HESITATE. DON'T FLINCH. DON'T THINK OF COLLATERAL DAMAGE.
"ONLY A TOUCH FROM YOU CAN SEPARATE TEMPTER AND HOST FOR THE KILL--OTHERWISE YOU KILL THE HOST AND HOPE FOR THE BEST."

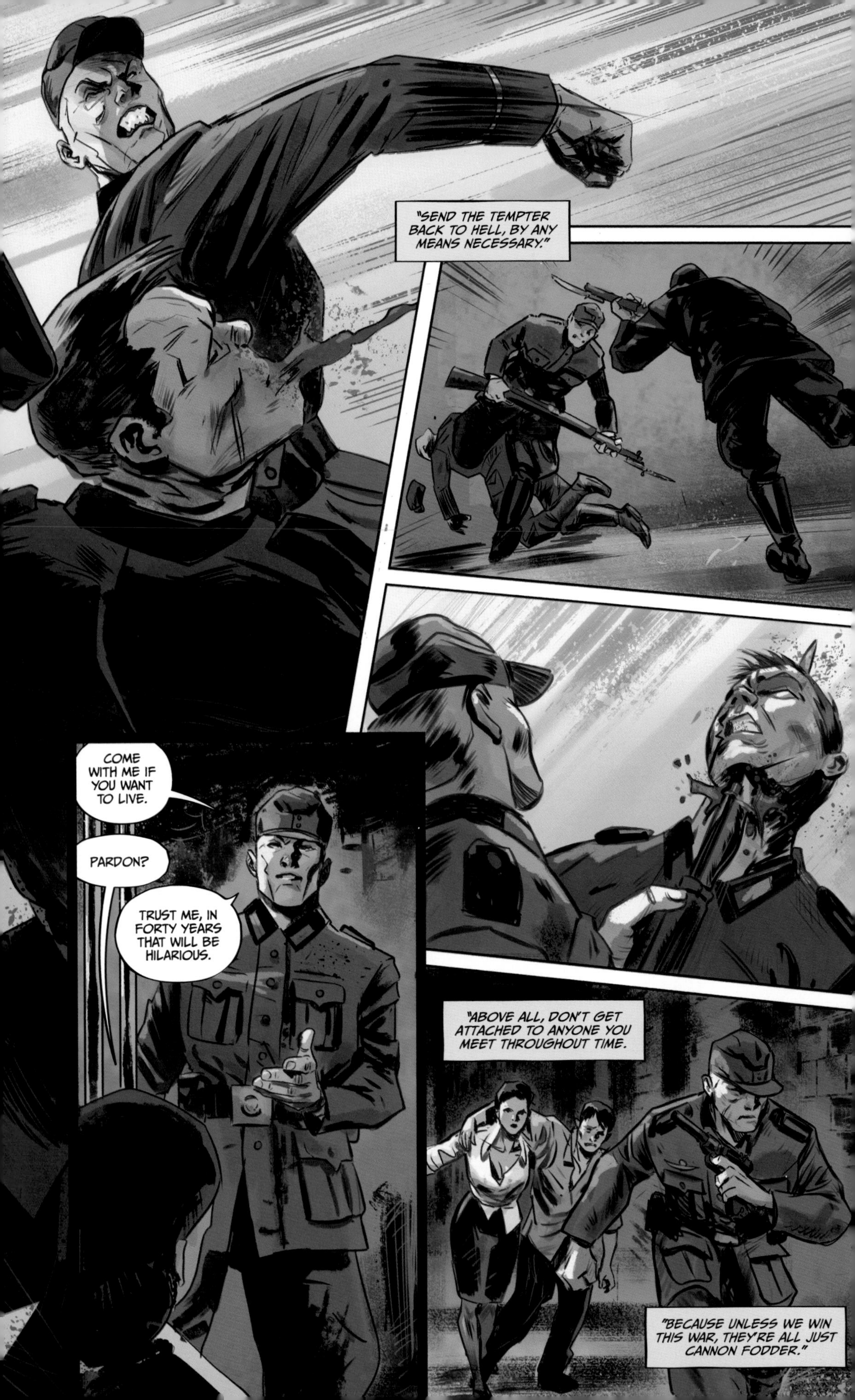
"SEND THE TEMPTER BACK TO HELL, BY ANY MEANS NECESSARY."
COME WITH ME IF YOU WANT TO LIVE.
PARDON?
TRUST ME, IN FORTY YEARS THAT WILL BE HILARIOUS.
"ABOVE ALL, DON'T GET ATTACHED TO ANYONE YOU MEET THROUGHOUT TIME.
"BECAUSE UNLESS WE WIN THIS WAR, THEY'RE ALL JUST CANNON FODDER."

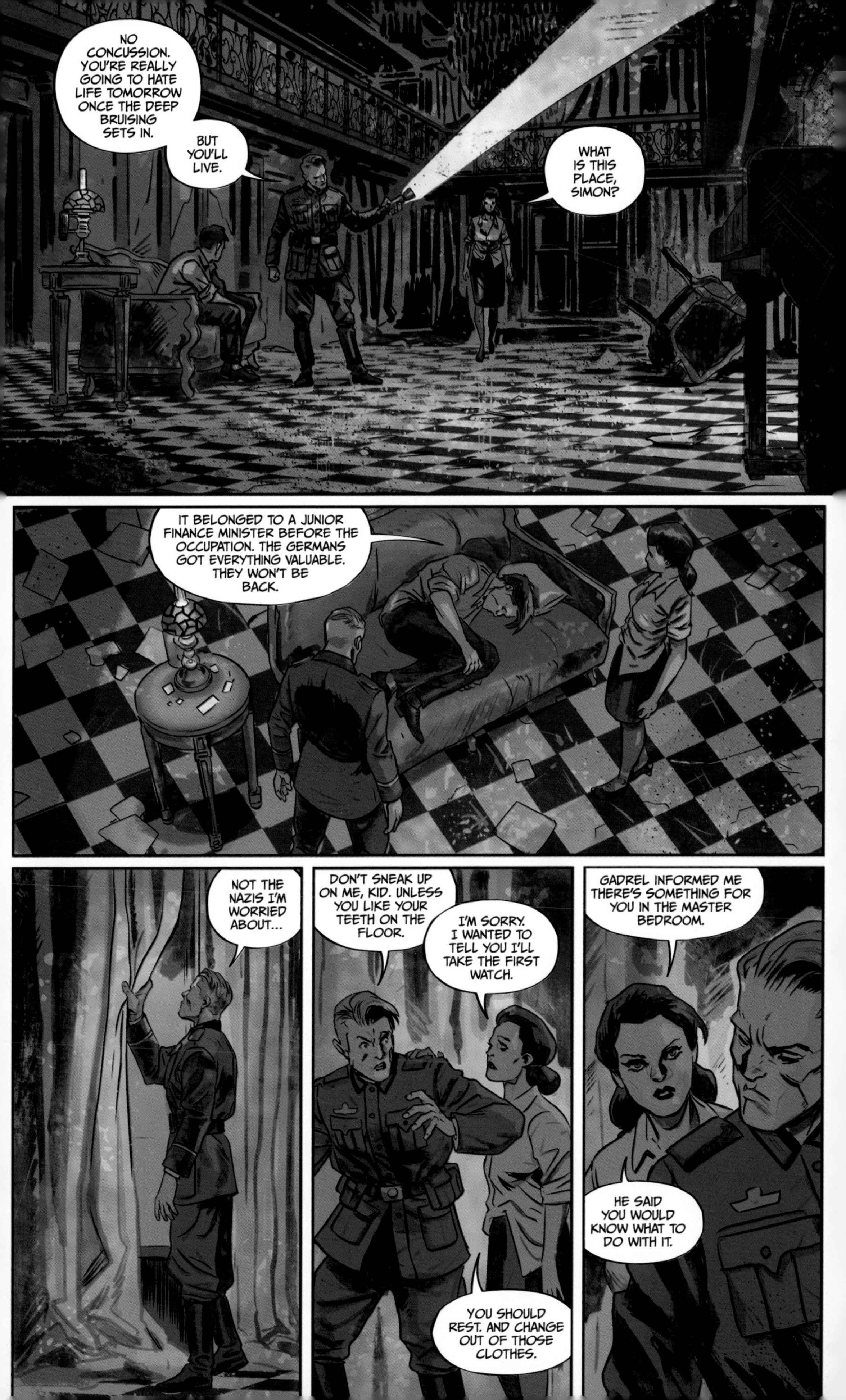
NO CONCUSSION. YOU'RE REALLY GOING TO HATE LIFE TOMORROW ONCE THE DEEP BRUISING SETS IN.
BUT YOU'LL LIVE.
WHAT IS THIS PLACE, SIMON?
IT BELONGED TO A JUNIOR FINANCE MINISTER BEFORE THE OCCUPATION. THE GERMANS GOT EVERYTHING VALUABLE. THEY WON'T BE BACK.
NOT THE NAZIS I'M WORRIED ABOUT...
DON'T SNEAK UP ON ME, KID. UNLESS YOU LIKE YOUR TEETH ON THE FLOOR.
I'M SORRY. I WANTED TO TELL YOU I'LL TAKE THE FIRST WATCH.
YOU SHOULD REST. AND CHANGE OUT OF THOSE CLOTHES.
GADREL INFORMED ME THERE'S SOMETHING FOR YOU IN THE MASTER BEDROOM.
HE SAID YOU WOULD KNOW WHAT TO DO WITH IT.

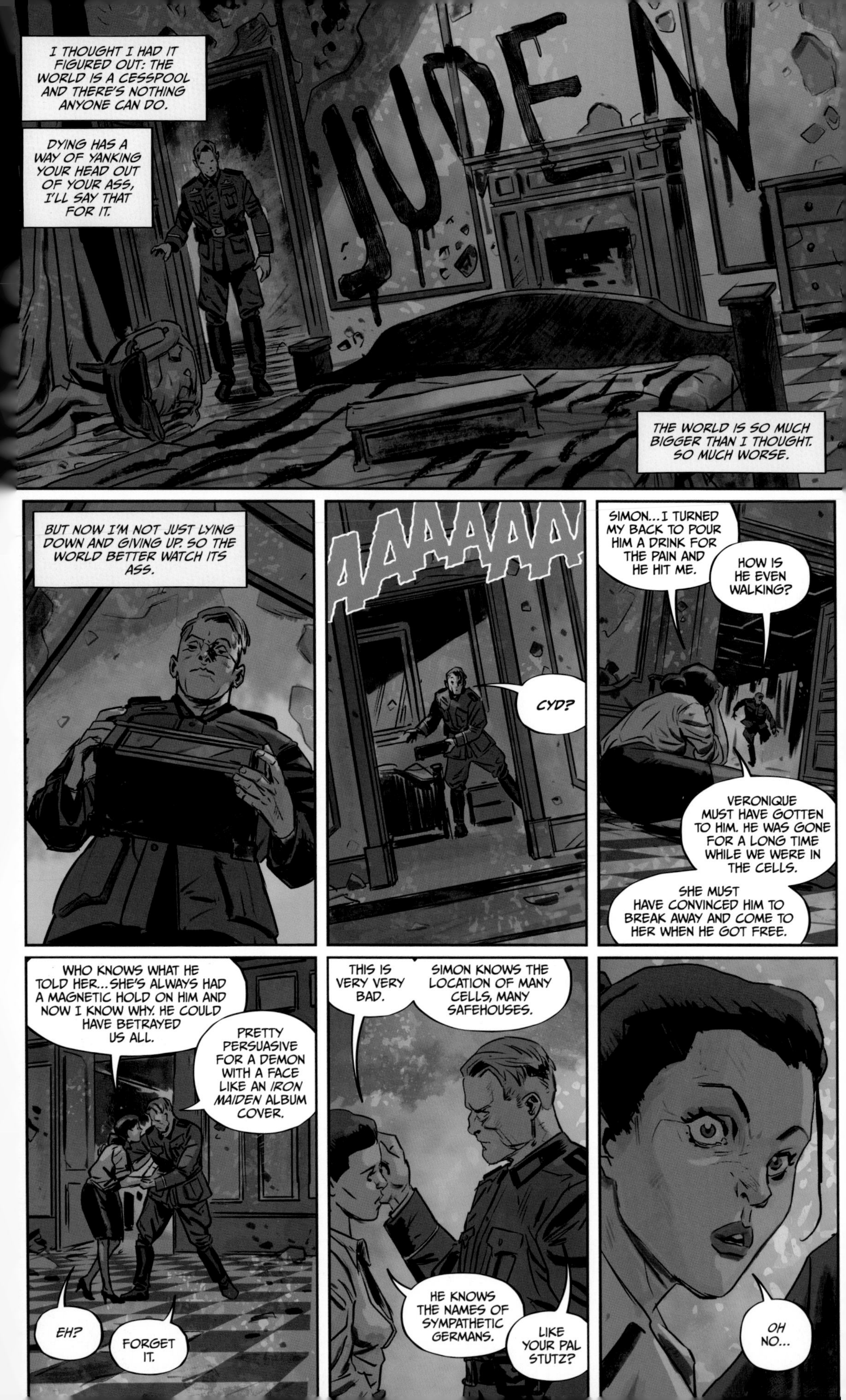
I THOUGHT I HAD IT FIGURED OUT: THE WORLD IS A CESSPOOL AND THERE'S NOTHING ANYONE CAN DO.
DYING HAS A WAY OF YANKING YOUR HEAD OUT OF YOUR ASS, I'LL SAY THAT FOR IT.
JUDEN
THE WORLD IS SO MUCH BIGGER THAN I THOUGHT. SO MUCH WORSE.
BUT NOW I'M NOT JUST LYING DOWN AND GIVING UP. SO THE WORLD BETTER WATCH ITS ASS.
AAAAAAA
CYD?
SIMON...I TURNED MY BACK TO POUR HIM A DRINK FOR THE PAIN AND HE HIT ME.
HOW IS HE EVEN WALKING?
VERONIQUE MUST HAVE GOTTEN TO HIM. HE WAS GONE FOR A LONG TIME WHILE WE WERE IN THE CELLS.
SHE MUST HAVE CONVINCED HIM TO BREAK AWAY AND COME TO HER WHEN HE GOT FREE.
WHO KNOWS WHAT HE TOLD HER...SHE'S ALWAYS HAD A MAGNETIC HOLD ON HIM AND NOW I KNOW WHY. HE COULD HAVE BETRAYED US ALL.
PRETTY PERSUASIVE FOR A DEMON WITH A FACE LIKE AN IRON MAIDEN ALBUM COVER.
EH?
FORGET IT.
THIS IS VERY VERY BAD.
SIMON KNOWS THE LOCATION OF MANY CELLS, MANY SAFEHOUSES.
HE KNOWS THE NAMES OF SYMPATHETIC GERMANS.
LIKE YOUR PAL STUTZ?
OH NO...

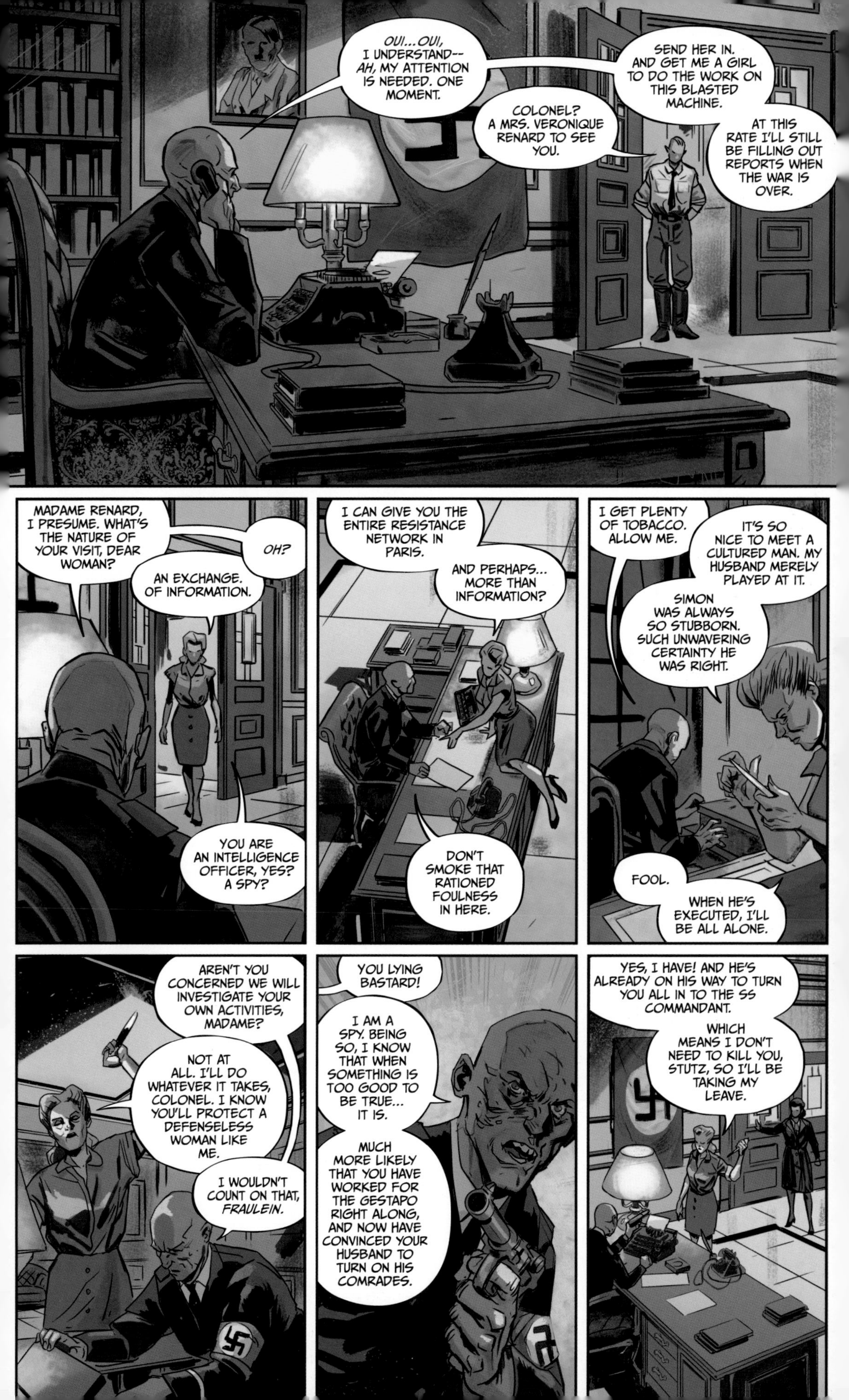
OUI...OUI, I UNDERSTAND-- AH, MY ATTENTION IS NEEDED. ONE MOMENT.
COLONEL? A MRS. VERONIQUE RENARD TO SEE YOU.
SEND HER IN. AND GET ME A GIRL TO DO THE WORK ON THIS BLASTED MACHINE.
AT THIS RATE I'LL STILL BE FILLING OUT REPORTS WHEN THE WAR IS OVER.
MADAME RENARD, I PRESUME. WHAT'S THE NATURE OF YOUR VISIT, DEAR WOMAN?
AN EXCHANGE. OF INFORMATION.
OH?
YOU ARE AN INTELLIGENCE OFFICER, YES? A SPY?
I CAN GIVE YOU THE ENTIRE RESISTANCE NETWORK IN PARIS.
AND PERHAPS... MORE THAN INFORMATION?
DON'T SMOKE THAT RATIONED FOULNESS IN HERE.
I GET PLENTY OF TOBACCO. ALLOW ME.
IT'S SO NICE TO MEET A CULTURED MAN. MY HUSBAND MERELY PLAYED AT IT.
SIMON WAS ALWAYS SO STUBBORN. SUCH UNWAVERING CERTAINTY HE WAS RIGHT.
FOOL.
WHEN HE'S EXECUTED, I'LL BE ALL ALONE.
AREN'T YOU CONCERNED WE WILL INVESTIGATE YOUR OWN ACTIVITIES, MADAME?
NOT AT ALL. I'LL DO WHATEVER IT TAKES, COLONEL. I KNOW YOU'LL PROTECT A DEFENSELESS WOMAN LIKE ME.
I WOULDN'T COUNT ON THAT, FRAULEIN.
YOU LYING BASTARD!
I AM A SPY. BEING SO, I KNOW THAT WHEN SOMETHING IS TOO GOOD TO BE TRUE... IT IS.
MUCH MORE LIKELY THAT YOU HAVE WORKED FOR THE GESTAPO RIGHT ALONG, AND NOW HAVE CONVINCED YOUR HUSBAND TO TURN ON HIS COMRADES.
YES, I HAVE! AND HE'S ALREADY ON HIS WAY TO TURN YOU ALL IN TO THE SS COMMANDANT.
WHICH MEANS I DON'T NEED TO KILL YOU, STUTZ, SO I'LL BE TAKING MY LEAVE.

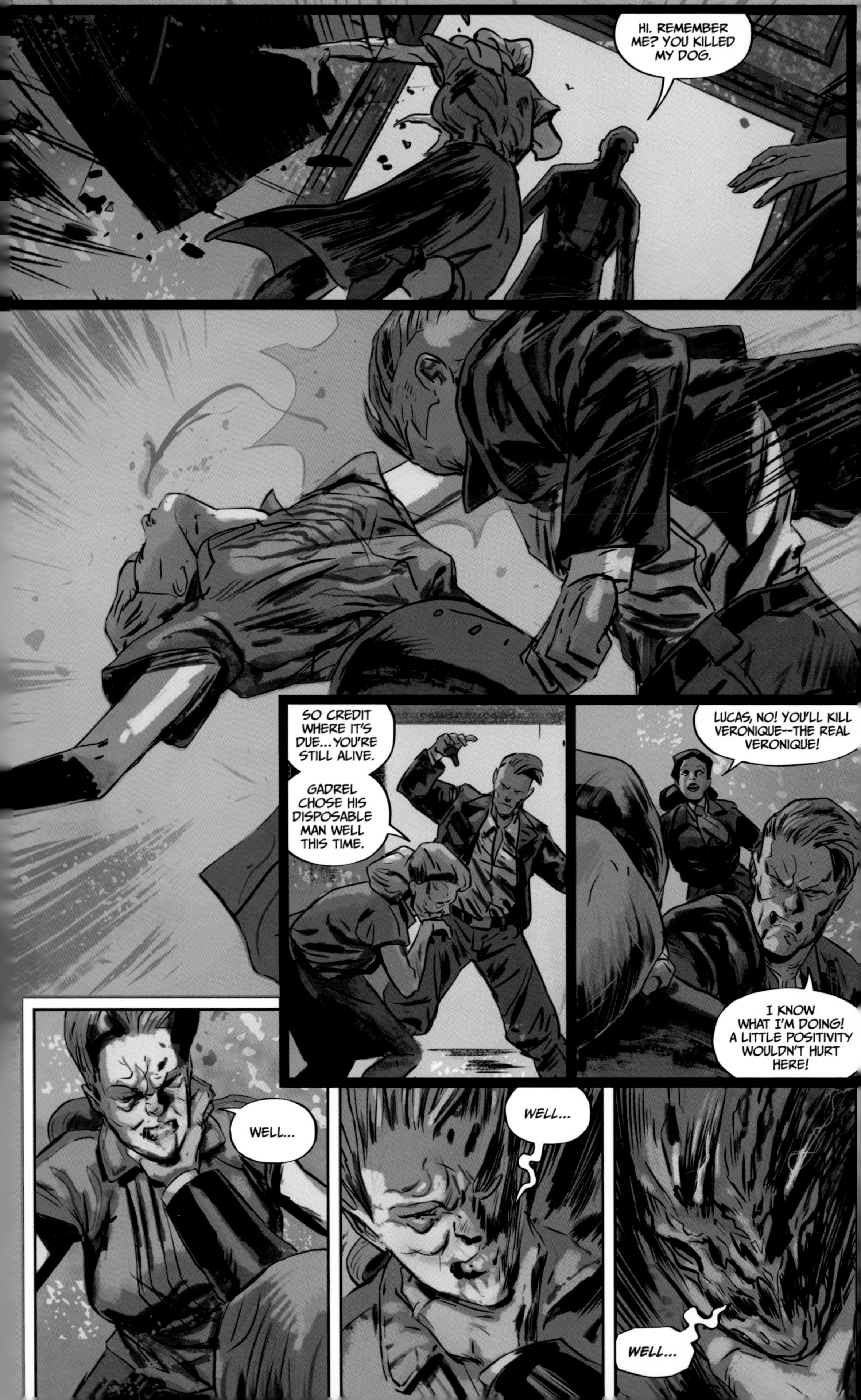
HI. REMEMBER ME? YOU KILLED MY DOG.
SO CREDIT WHERE IT'S DUE... YOU'RE STILL ALIVE.
GADREL CHOSE HIS DISPOSABLE MAN WELL THIS TIME.
LUCAS, NO! YOU'LL KILL VERONIQUE--THE REAL VERONIQUE!
I KNOW WHAT I'M DOING! A LITTLE POSITIVITY WOULDN'T HURT HERE!
WELL...
WELL...
WELL...

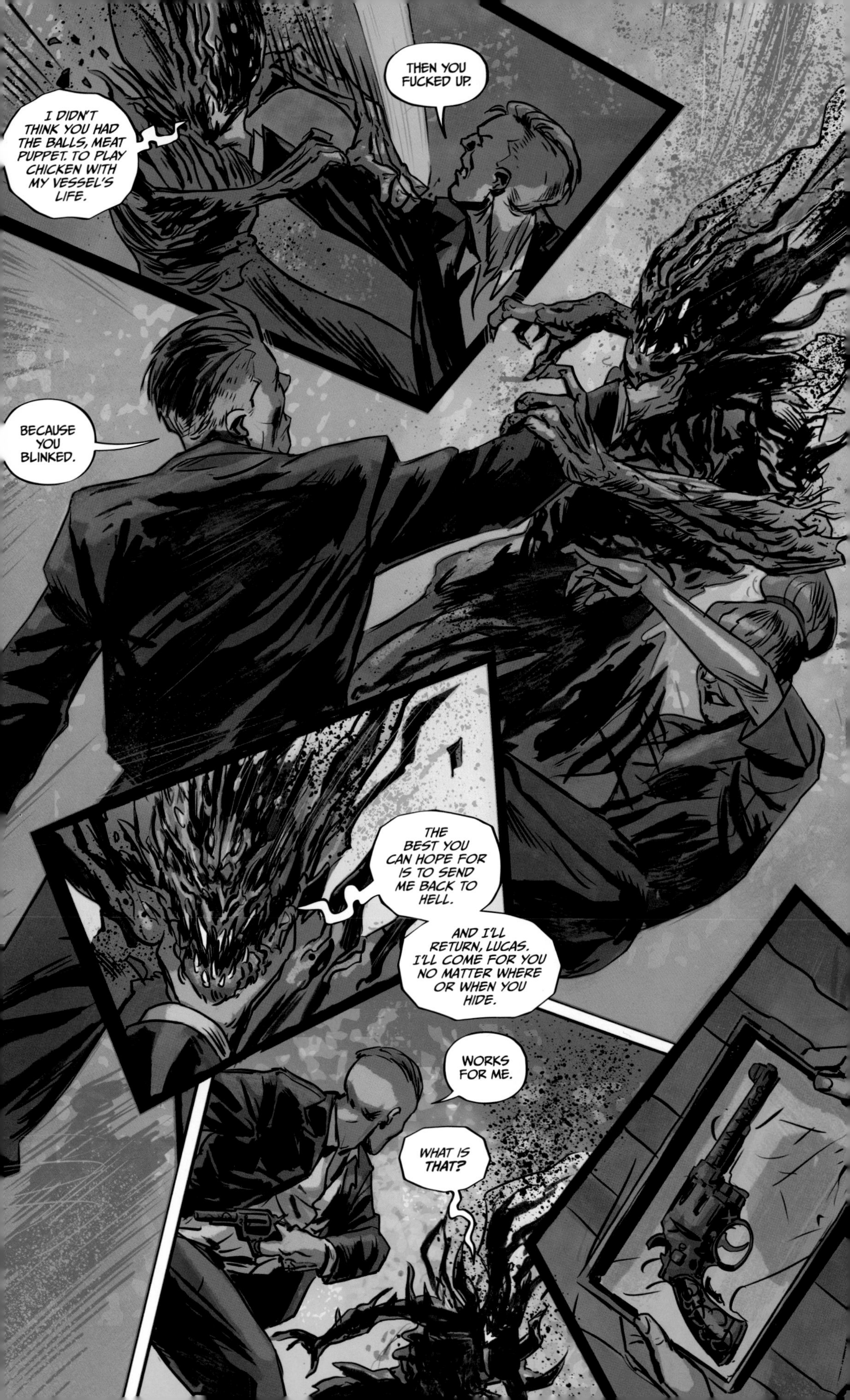
I DIDN'T THINK YOU HAD THE BALLS, MEAT PUPPET. TO PLAY CHICKEN WITH MY VESSEL'S LIFE.
THEN YOU FUCKED UP.
BECAUSE YOU BLINKED.
THE BEST YOU CAN HOPE FOR IS TO SEND ME BACK TO HELL.
AND I'LL RETURN, LUCAS. I'LL COME FOR YOU NO MATTER WHERE OR WHEN YOU HIDE.
WORKS FOR ME.
WHAT IS THAT?

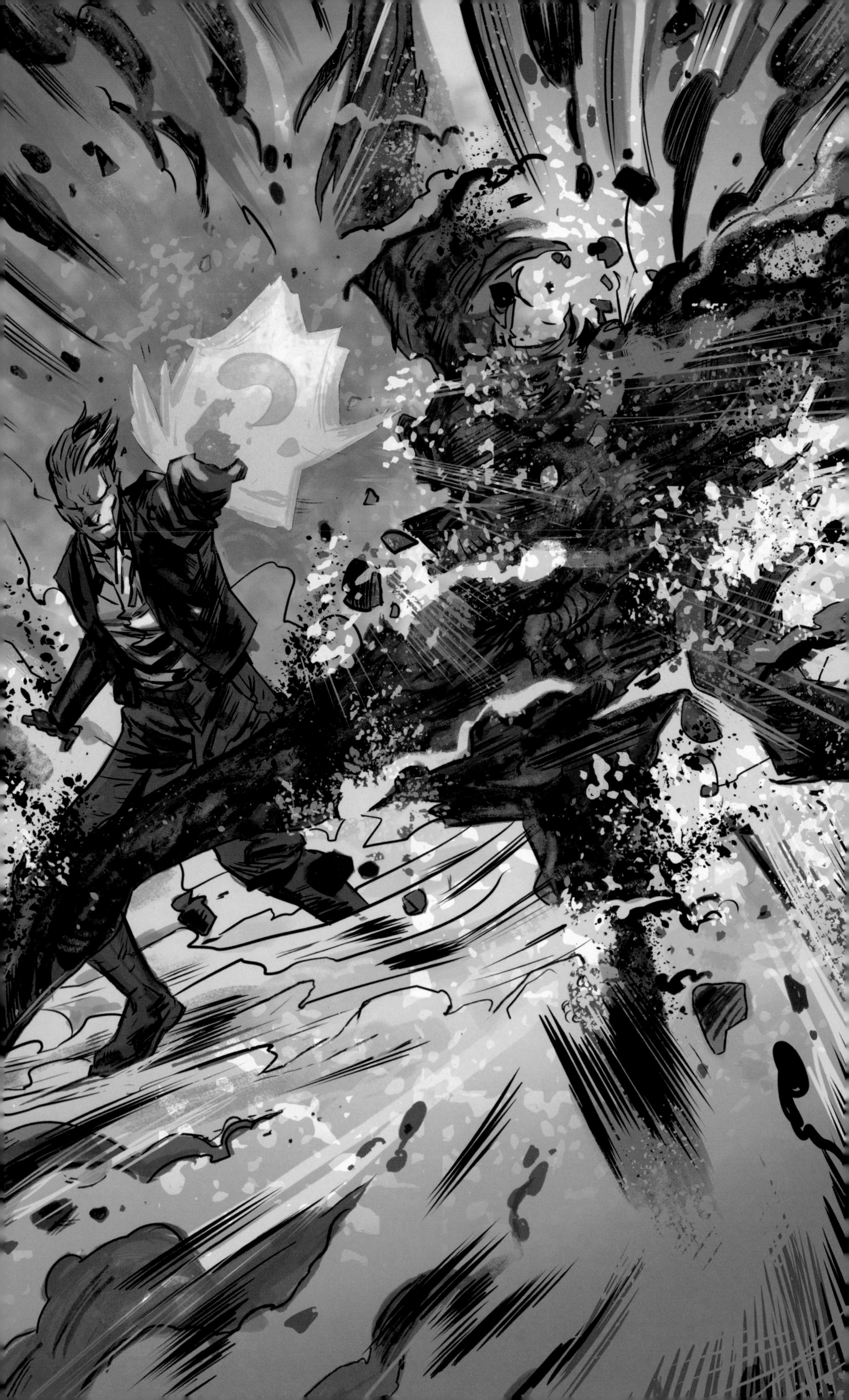

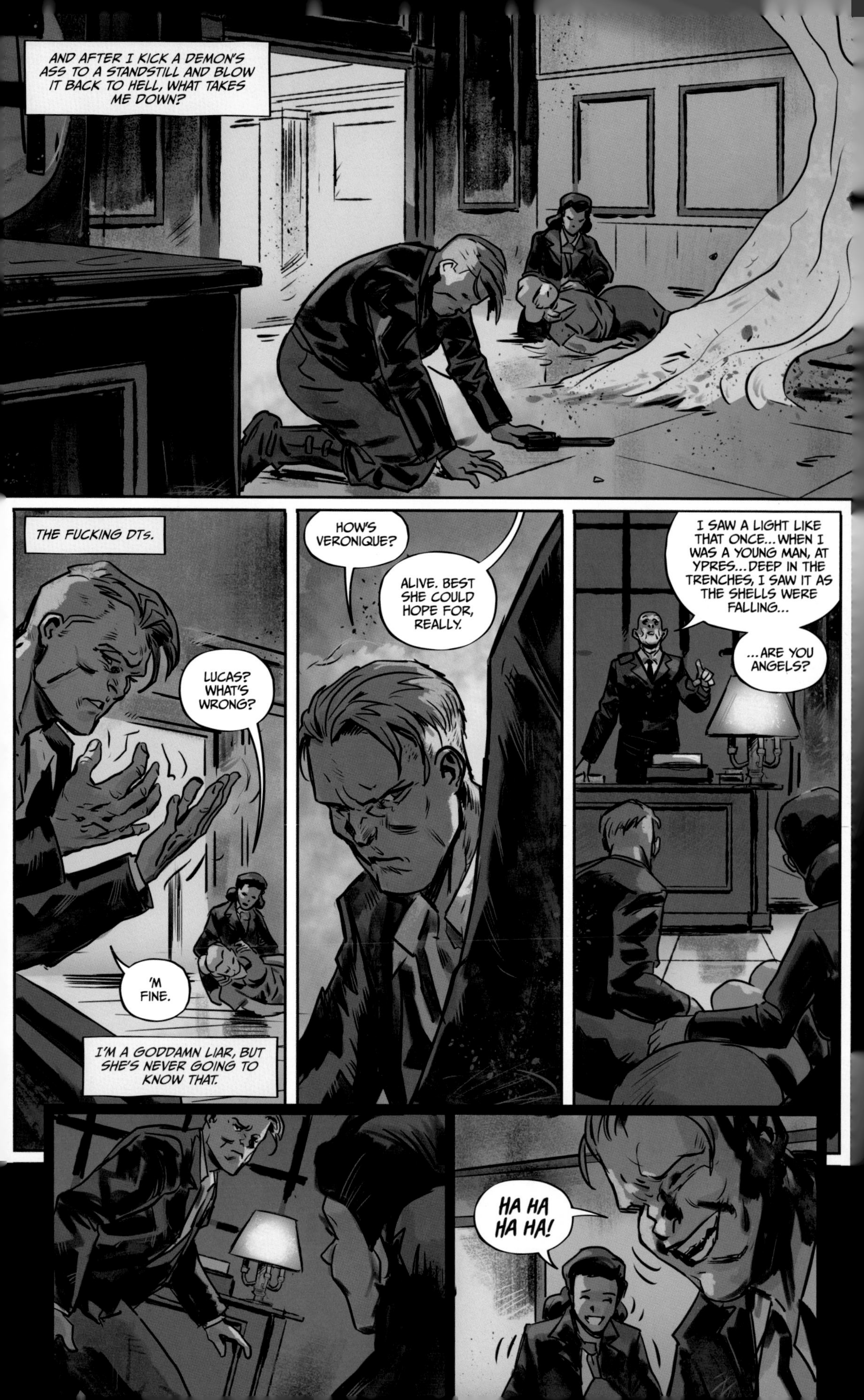
AND AFTER I KICK A DEMON'S ASS TO A STANDSTILL AND BLOW IT BACK TO HELL, WHAT TAKES ME DOWN?
THE FUCKING DTs.
LUCAS? WHAT'S WRONG?
'M FINE.
I'M A GODDAMN LIAR, BUT SHE'S NEVER GOING TO KNOW THAT.
HOW'S VERONIQUE?
ALIVE. BEST SHE COULD HOPE FOR, REALLY.
I SAW A LIGHT LIKE THAT ONCE...WHEN I WAS A YOUNG MAN, AT YPRES...DEEP IN THE TRENCHES, I SAW IT AS THE SHELLS WERE FALLING...
...ARE YOU ANGELS?
HA HA HA HA!

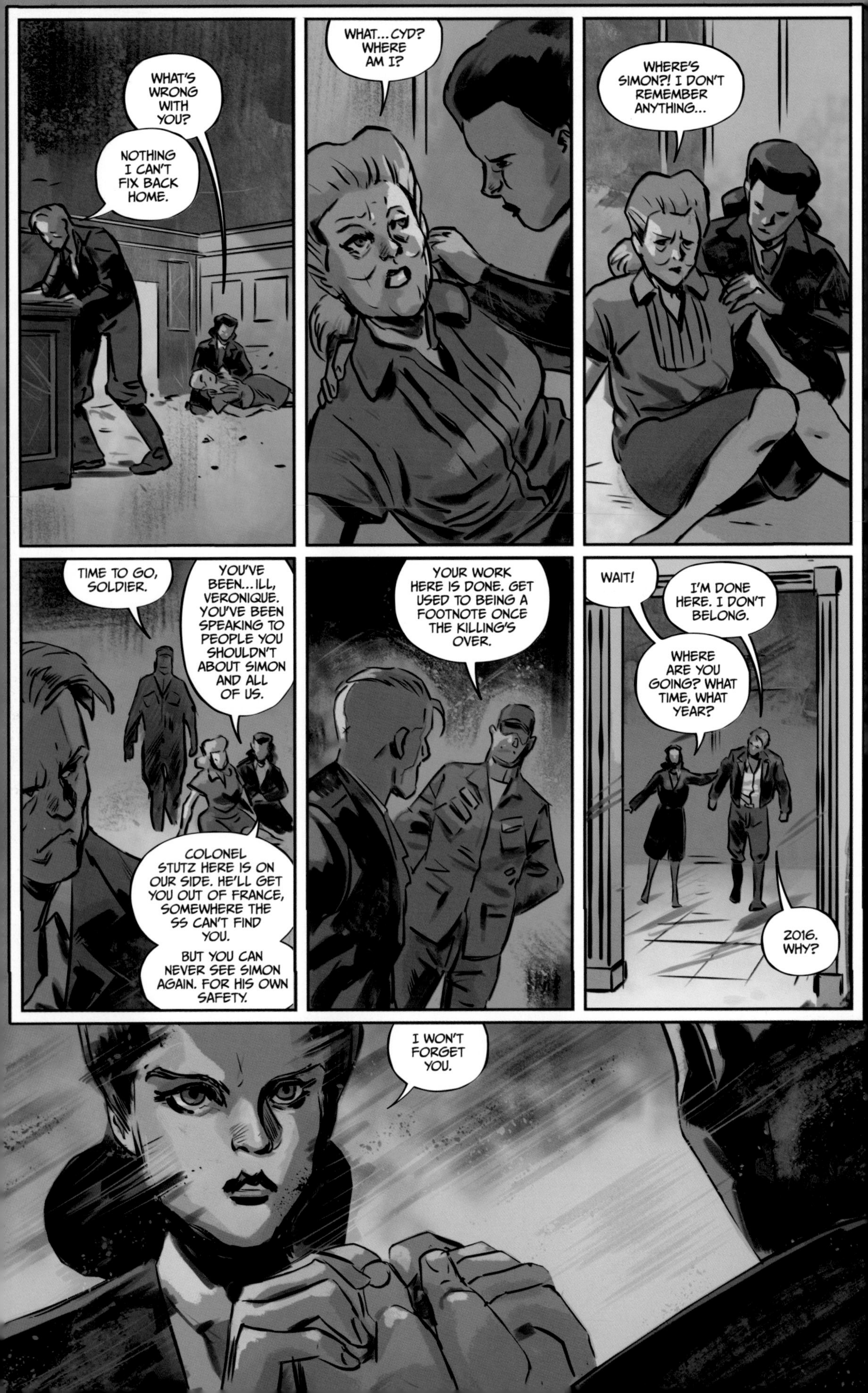
WHAT'S WRONG WITH YOU?
NOTHING I CAN'T FIX BACK HOME.
WHAT... CYD? WHERE AM I?
WHERE'S SIMON?! I DON'T REMEMBER ANYTHING...
TIME TO GO, SOLDIER.
YOU'VE BEEN... ILL, VERONIQUE. YOU'VE BEEN SPEAKING TO PEOPLE YOU SHOULDN'T ABOUT SIMON AND ALL OF US.
COLONEL STUTZ HERE IS ON OUR SIDE. HE'LL GET YOU OUT OF FRANCE, SOMEWHERE THE SS CAN'T FIND YOU.
BUT YOU CAN NEVER SEE SIMON AGAIN. FOR HIS OWN SAFETY.
YOUR WORK HERE IS DONE. GET USED TO BEING A FOOTNOTE ONCE THE KILLING'S OVER.
WAIT!
I'M DONE HERE. I DON'T BELONG.
WHERE ARE YOU GOING? WHAT TIME, WHAT YEAR?
2016. WHY?
I WON'T FORGET YOU.

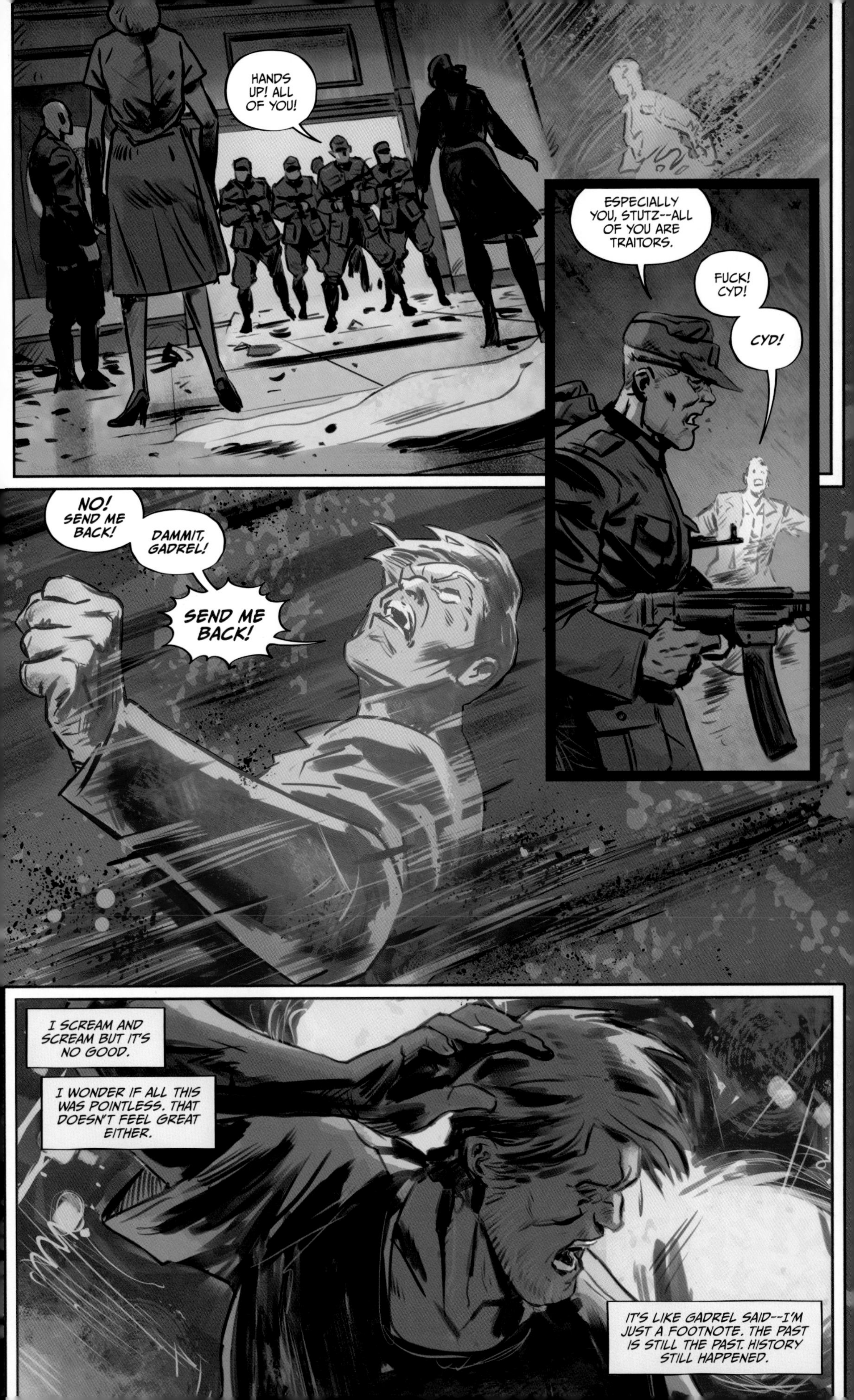
HANDS UP! ALL OF YOU!
ESPECIALLY YOU, STUTZ--ALL OF YOU ARE TRAITORS.
FUCK! CYD!
CYD!
NO! SEND ME BACK!
DAMMIT, GADREL!
SEND ME BACK!
I SCREAM AND SCREAM BUT IT'S NO GOOD.
I WONDER IF ALL THIS WAS POINTLESS. THAT DOESN'T FEEL GREAT EITHER.
IT'S LIKE GADREL SAID--I'M JUST A FOOTNOTE. THE PAST IS STILL THE PAST. HISTORY STILL HAPPENED.

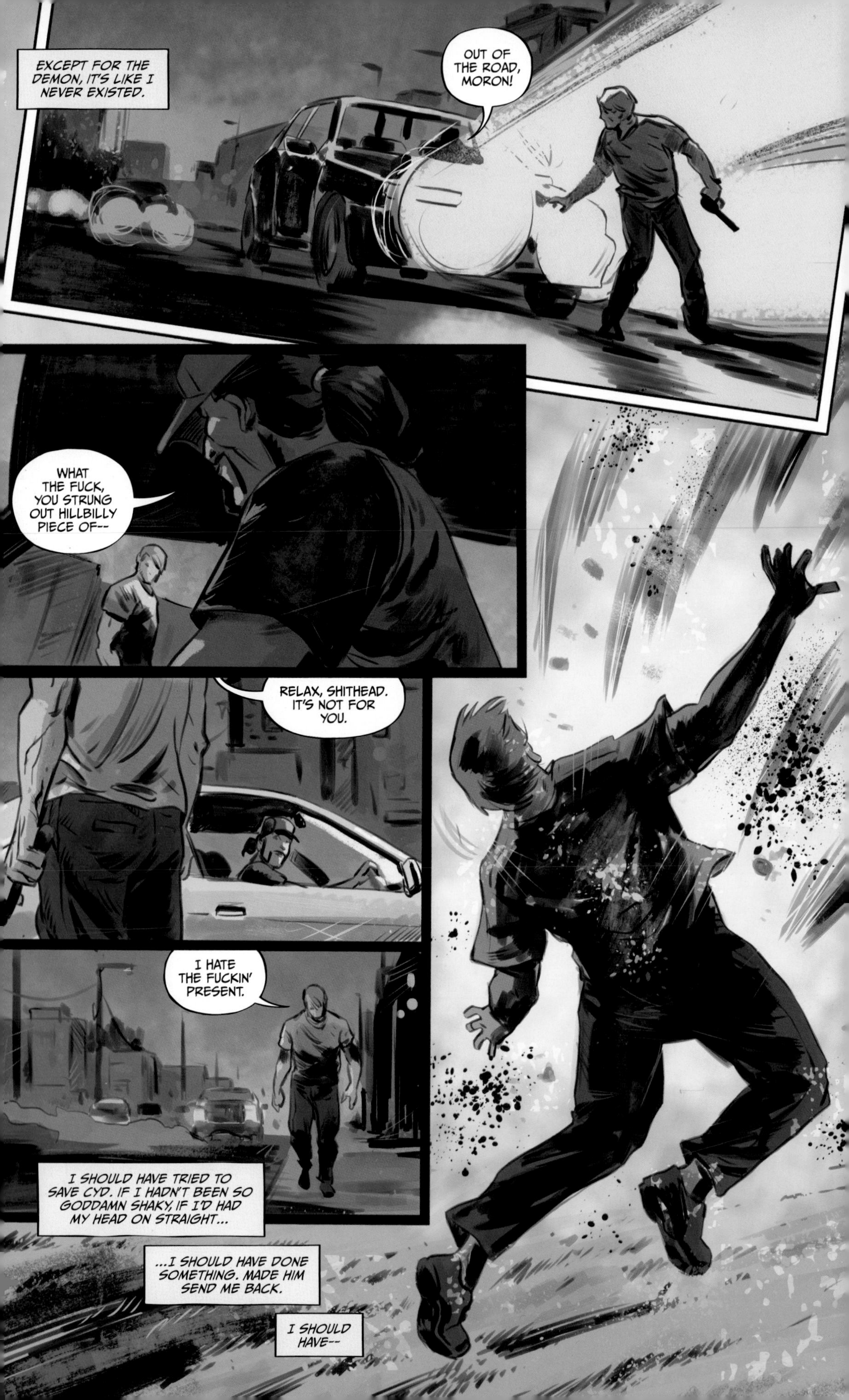
EXCEPT FOR THE DEMON, IT'S LIKE I NEVER EXISTED.
OUT OF THE ROAD, MORON!
WHAT THE FUCK, YOU STRUNG OUT HILLBILLY PIECE OF--
RELAX, SHITHEAD. IT'S NOT FOR YOU.
I HATE THE FUCKIN' PRESENT.
I SHOULD HAVE TRIED TO SAVE CYD. IF I HADN'T BEEN SO GODDAMN SHAKY, IF I'D HAD MY HEAD ON STRAIGHT...
...I SHOULD HAVE DONE SOMETHING. MADE HIM SEND ME BACK.
I SHOULD HAVE--

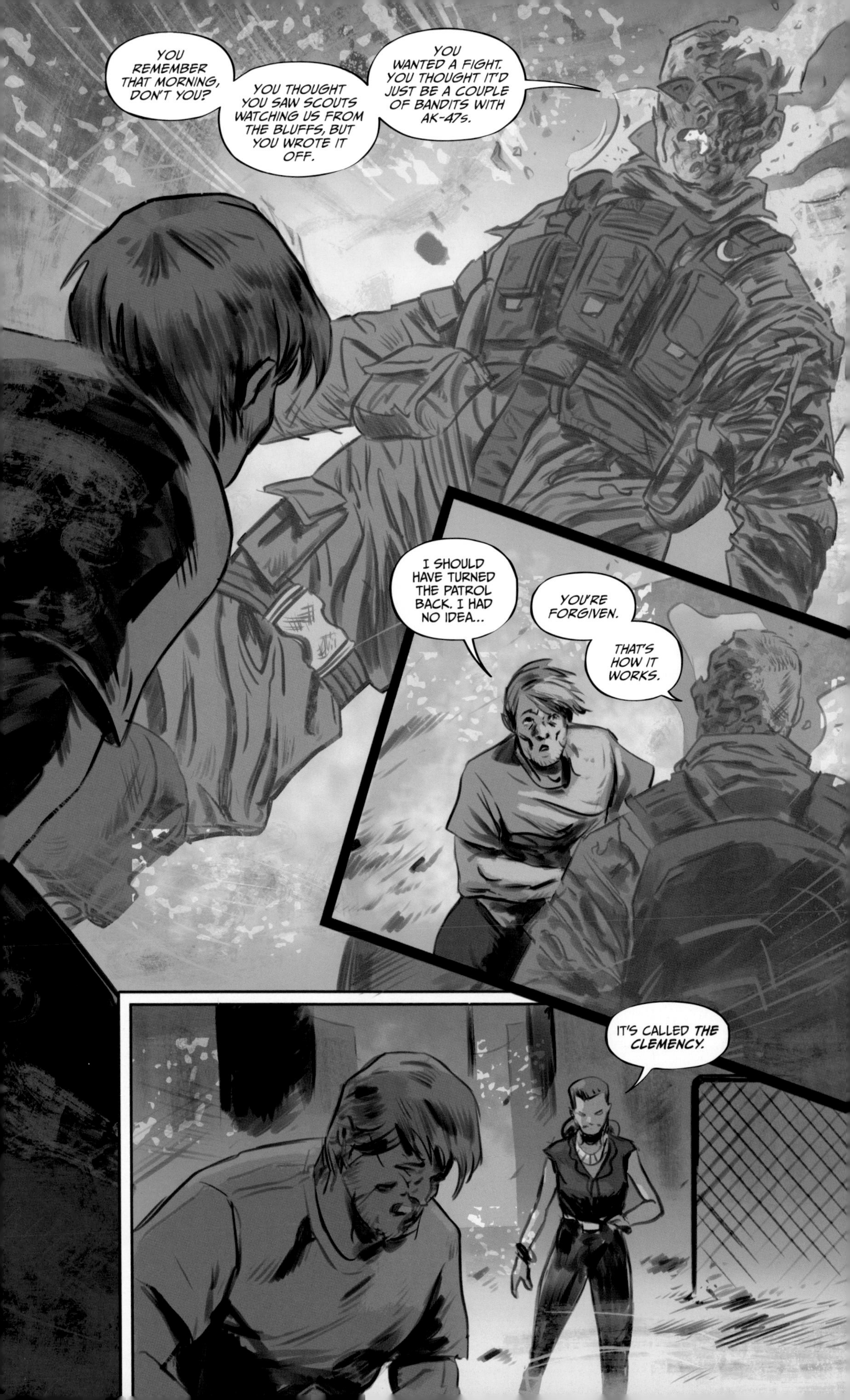
YOU REMEMBER THAT MORNING, DON'T YOU?
YOU THOUGHT YOU SAW SCOUTS WATCHING US FROM THE BLUFFS, BUT YOU WROTE IT OFF.
YOU WANTED A FIGHT. YOU THOUGHT IT'D JUST BE A COUPLE OF BANDITS WITH AK-47s.
I SHOULD HAVE TURNED THE PATROL BACK. I HAD NO IDEA...
YOU'RE FORGIVEN.
THAT'S HOW IT WORKS.
IT'S CALLED THE CLEMENCY.

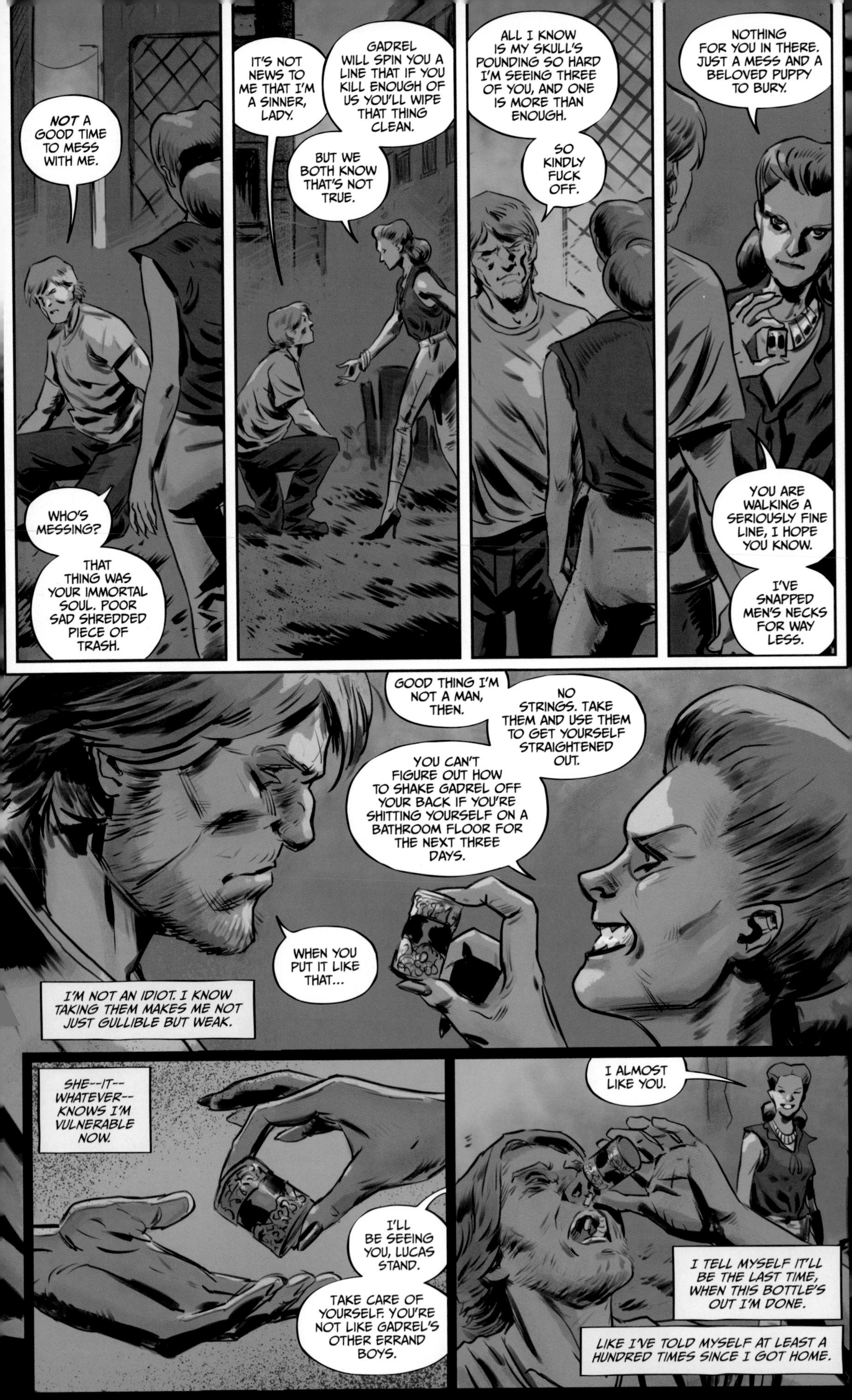
NOT A GOOD TIME TO MESS WITH ME.
WHO'S MESSING?
THAT THING WAS YOUR IMMORTAL SOUL. POOR SAD SHREDDED PIECE OF TRASH.
IT'S NOT NEWS TO ME THAT I'M A SINNER, LADY.
GADREL WILL SPIN YOU A LINE THAT IF YOU KILL ENOUGH OF US YOU'LL WIPE THAT THING CLEAN.
BUT WE BOTH KNOW THAT'S NOT TRUE.
ALL I KNOW IS MY SKULL'S POUNDING SO HARD I'M SEEING THREE OF YOU, AND ONE IS MORE THAN ENOUGH.
SO KINDLY FUCK OFF.
NOTHING FOR YOU IN THERE. JUST A MESS AND A BELOVED PUPPY TO BURY.
YOU ARE WALKING A SERIOUSLY FINE LINE, I HOPE YOU KNOW.
I'VE SNAPPED MEN'S NECKS FOR WAY LESS.
GOOD THING I'M NOT A MAN, THEN.
NO STRINGS. TAKE THEM AND USE THEM TO GET YOURSELF STRAIGHTENED OUT.
YOU CAN'T FIGURE OUT HOW TO SHAKE GADREL OFF YOUR BACK IF YOU'RE SHITTING YOURSELF ON A BATHROOM FLOOR FOR THE NEXT THREE DAYS.
WHEN YOU PUT IT LIKE THAT...
I'M NOT AN IDIOT. I KNOW TAKING THEM MAKES ME NOT JUST GULLIBLE BUT WEAK.
SHE--IT--WHATEVER--KNOWS I'M VULNERABLE NOW.
I'LL BE SEEING YOU, LUCAS STAND.
TAKE CARE OF YOURSELF. YOU'RE NOT LIKE GADREL'S OTHER ERRAND BOYS.
I ALMOST LIKE YOU.
I TELL MYSELF IT'LL BE THE LAST TIME, WHEN THIS BOTTLE'S OUT I'M DONE.
LIKE I'VE TOLD MYSELF AT LEAST A HUNDRED TIMES SINCE I GOT HOME.

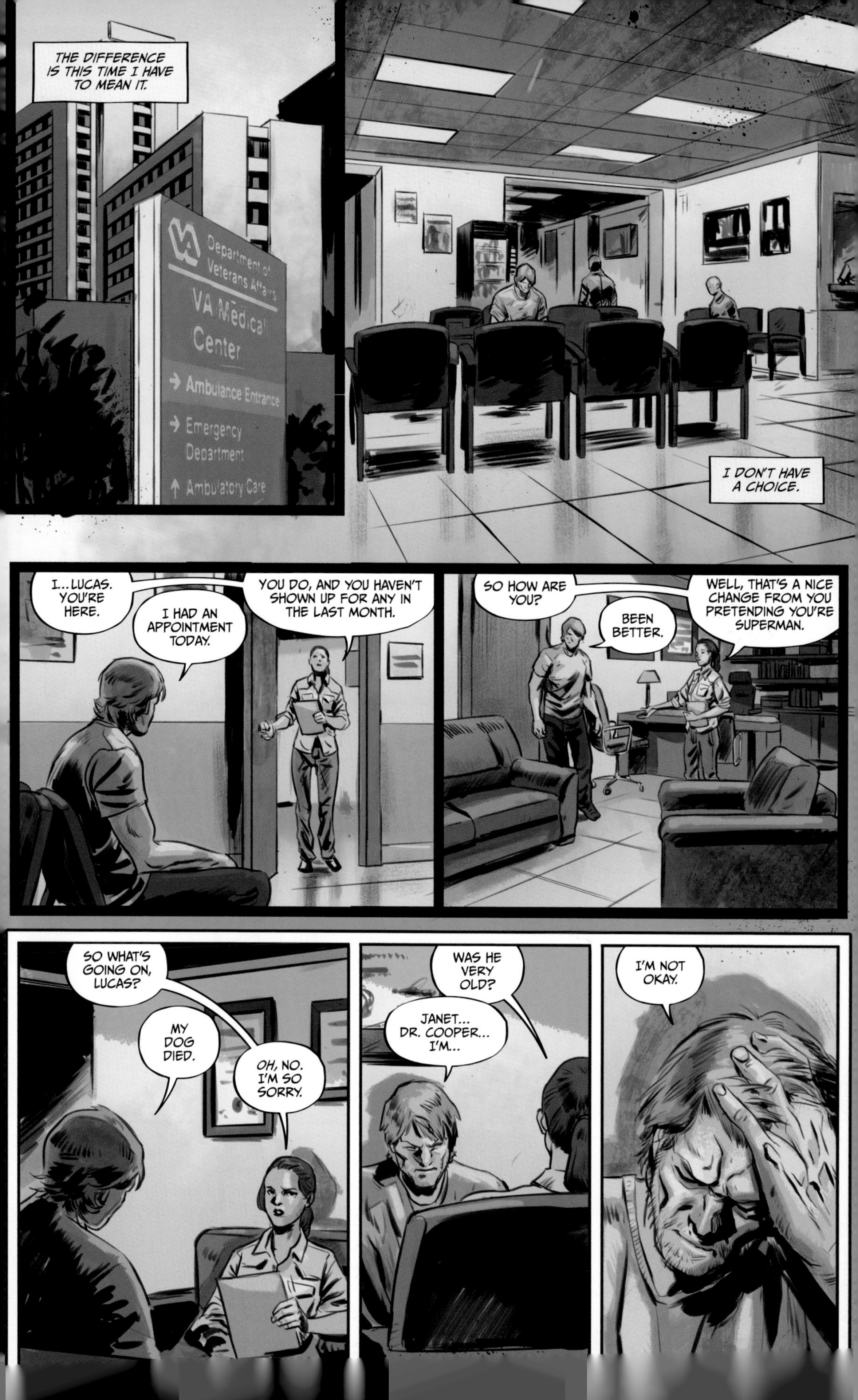
THE DIFFERENCE IS THIS TIME I HAVE TO MEAN IT.
Department of Veterans Affairs
VA Medical Center
Ambulance Entrance
Emergency Department
Ambulatory Care
I DON'T HAVE A CHOICE.
I...LUCAS. YOU'RE HERE.
I HAD AN APPOINTMENT TODAY.
YOU DO, AND YOU HAVEN'T SHOWN UP FOR ANY IN THE LAST MONTH.
SO HOW ARE YOU?
BEEN BETTER.
WELL, THAT'S A NICE CHANGE FROM YOU PRETENDING YOU'RE SUPERMAN.
SO WHAT'S GOING ON, LUCAS?
MY DOG DIED.
OH, NO. I'M SO SORRY.
WAS HE VERY OLD?
JANET... DR. COOPER... I'M...
I'M NOT OKAY.

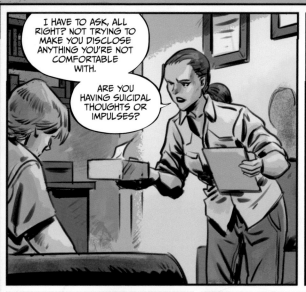

I HAVE TO ASK, ALL RIGHT? NOT TRYING TO MAKE YOU DISCLOSE ANYTHING YOU'RE NOT COMFORTABLE WITH.

ARE YOU HAVING SUICIDAL THOUGHTS OR IMPULSES?

DO YOU FEEL THAT YOU'RE AT RISK TO ACT ON THESE THOUGHTS?

UH... NOT AT THE MOMENT. NO.

I KNOW YOU DON'T LIKE THE IDEA OF PSYCH MEDS...

THAT'S FUNNY, RIGHT? I KNOW YOU'RE LAUGHING ON THE INSIDE.

I WOULD NEVER LAUGH AT YOU, LUCAS. I WILL NEVER PITY YOU OR JUDGE YOU OR HOLD YOU IN ANYTHING BUT UNCONDITIONAL POSITIVE REGARD.

I'M STILL USING. BEFORE, WHEN I GOT THIRTY DAYS FOR POSSESSION?

HAD TO COME TO THAT STUPID NA GROUP HERE EVERY DAY?

NEVER STOPPED. NOT FOR AN HOUR.

I KNOW. I'M NOT A TOTAL IDIOT.

I REALLY DO THINK AN ANTIDEPRESSANT...

NO. I KNOW WHAT I GOTTA DO.

LUCAS, THIS IS A LOT AND I'D REALLY LIKE YOU TO STAY AND PROCESS THIS WITH ME.

I CAN'T. I CAN'T.

I'M SORRY, DR. COOPER. JANET. YOU'RE THE ONLY PERSON WHO DIDN'T TELL ME TO GO TO HELL.

I'M JUST REALLY SORRY I'M SUCH A FUCK-UP.

I DON'T NEED YOU TO APOLOGIZE, LUCAS. I DON'T NEED ANYTHING FROM YOU. I JUST WANT TO HELP YOU.

THAT WAS YOUR FIRST MISTAKE, DOC.

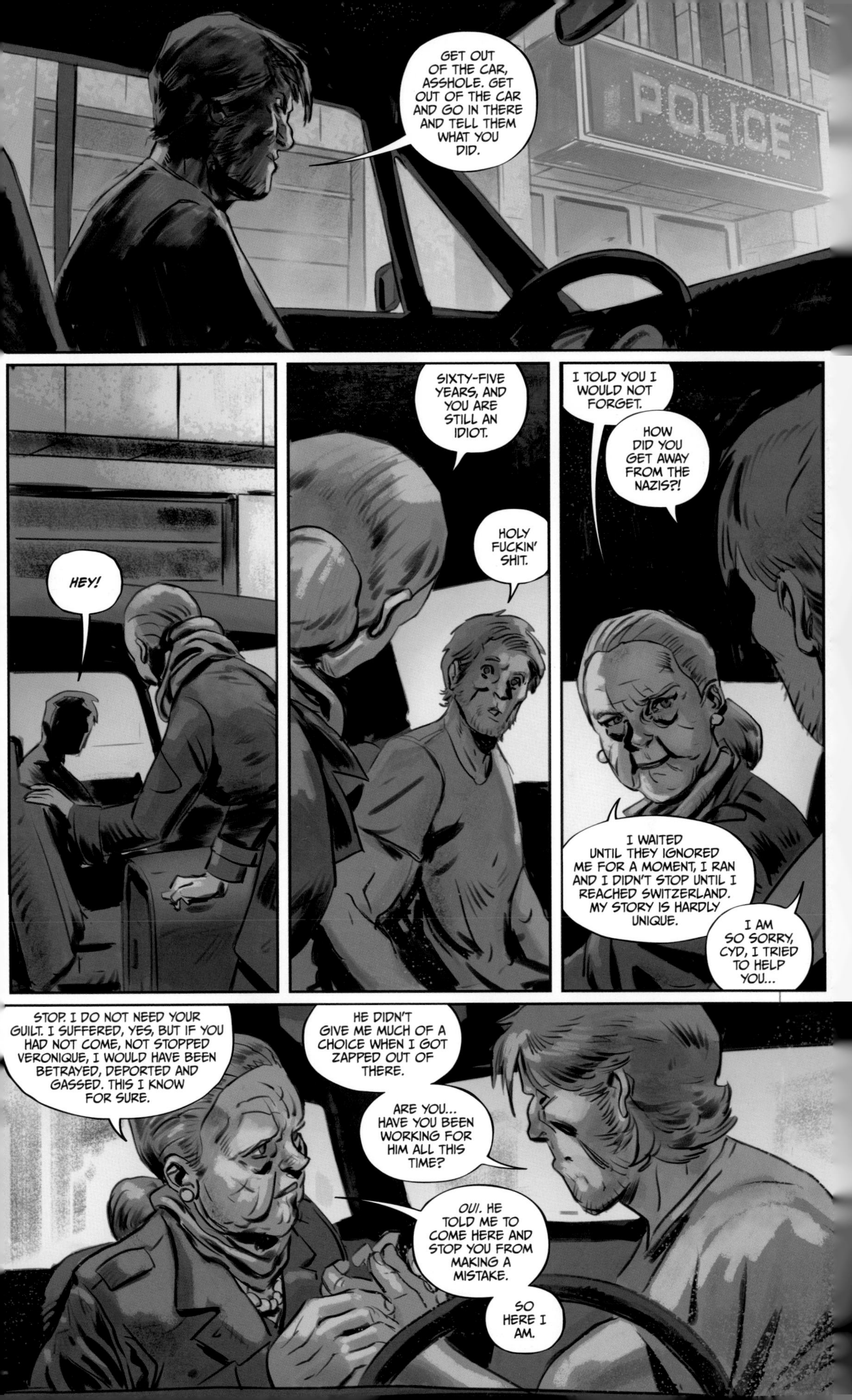
GET OUT OF THE CAR, ASSHOLE. GET OUT OF THE CAR AND GO IN THERE AND TELL THEM WHAT YOU DID.
POLICE
HEY!
SIXTY-FIVE YEARS, AND YOU ARE STILL AN IDIOT.
HOLY FUCKIN' SHIT.
I TOLD YOU I WOULD NOT FORGET.
HOW DID YOU GET AWAY FROM THE NAZIS?!
I WAITED UNTIL THEY IGNORED ME FOR A MOMENT, I RAN AND I DIDN'T STOP UNTIL I REACHED SWITZERLAND. MY STORY IS HARDLY UNIQUE.
I AM SO SORRY, CYD, I TRIED TO HELP YOU...
STOP. I DO NOT NEED YOUR GUILT. I SUFFERED, YES, BUT IF YOU HAD NOT COME, NOT STOPPED VERONIQUE, I WOULD HAVE BEEN BETRAYED, DEPORTED AND GASSED. THIS I KNOW FOR SURE.
HE DIDN'T GIVE ME MUCH OF A CHOICE WHEN I GOT ZAPPED OUT OF THERE.
ARE YOU... HAVE YOU BEEN WORKING FOR HIM ALL THIS TIME?
OUI. HE TOLD ME TO COME HERE AND STOP YOU FROM MAKING A MISTAKE.
SO HERE I AM.

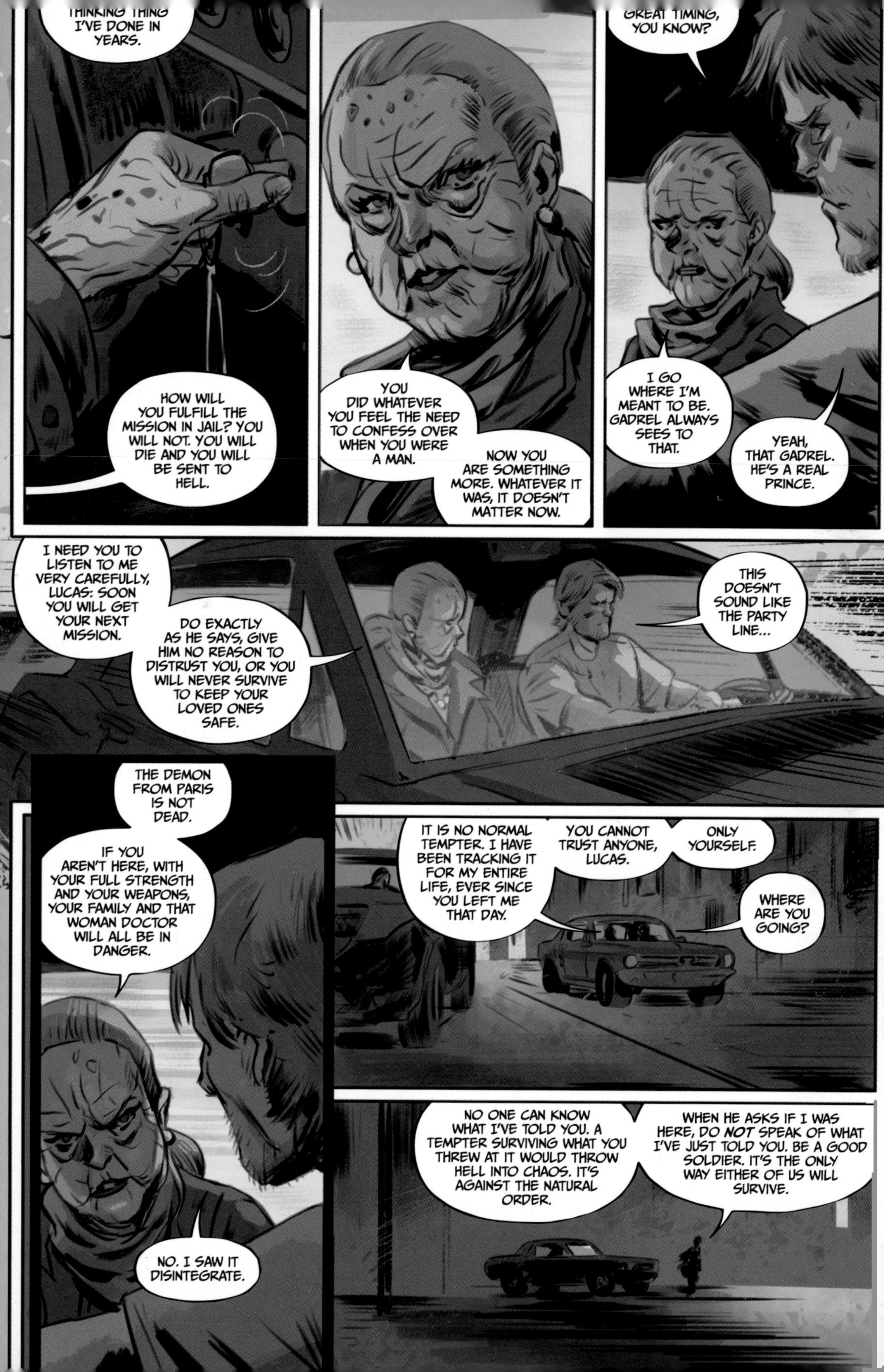
THINKING THING I'VE DONE IN YEARS.
HOW WILL YOU FULFILL THE MISSION IN JAIL? YOU WILL NOT. YOU WILL DIE AND YOU WILL BE SENT TO HELL.
YOU DID WHATEVER YOU FEEL THE NEED TO CONFESS OVER WHEN YOU WERE A MAN.
NOW YOU ARE SOMETHING MORE. WHATEVER IT WAS, IT DOESN'T MATTER NOW.
GREAT TIMING, YOU KNOW?
I GO WHERE I'M MEANT TO BE. GADREL ALWAYS SEES TO THAT.
YEAH, THAT GADREL. HE'S A REAL PRINCE.
I NEED YOU TO LISTEN TO ME VERY CAREFULLY, LUCAS: SOON YOU WILL GET YOUR NEXT MISSION.
DO EXACTLY AS HE SAYS, GIVE HIM NO REASON TO DISTRUST YOU, OR YOU WILL NEVER SURVIVE TO KEEP YOUR LOVED ONES SAFE.
THIS DOESN'T SOUND LIKE THE PARTY LINE...
THE DEMON FROM PARIS IS NOT DEAD.
IF YOU AREN'T HERE, WITH YOUR FULL STRENGTH AND YOUR WEAPONS, YOUR FAMILY AND THAT WOMAN DOCTOR WILL ALL BE IN DANGER.
NO. I SAW IT DISINTEGRATE.
IT IS NO NORMAL TEMPTER. I HAVE BEEN TRACKING IT FOR MY ENTIRE LIFE, EVER SINCE YOU LEFT ME THAT DAY.
YOU CANNOT TRUST ANYONE, LUCAS.
ONLY YOURSELF.
WHERE ARE YOU GOING?
NO ONE CAN KNOW WHAT I'VE TOLD YOU. A TEMPTER SURVIVING WHAT YOU THREW AT IT WOULD THROW HELL INTO CHAOS. IT'S AGAINST THE NATURAL ORDER.
WHEN HE ASKS IF I WAS HERE, DO NOT SPEAK OF WHAT I'VE JUST TOLD YOU. BE A GOOD SOLDIER. IT'S THE ONLY WAY EITHER OF US WILL SURVIVE.

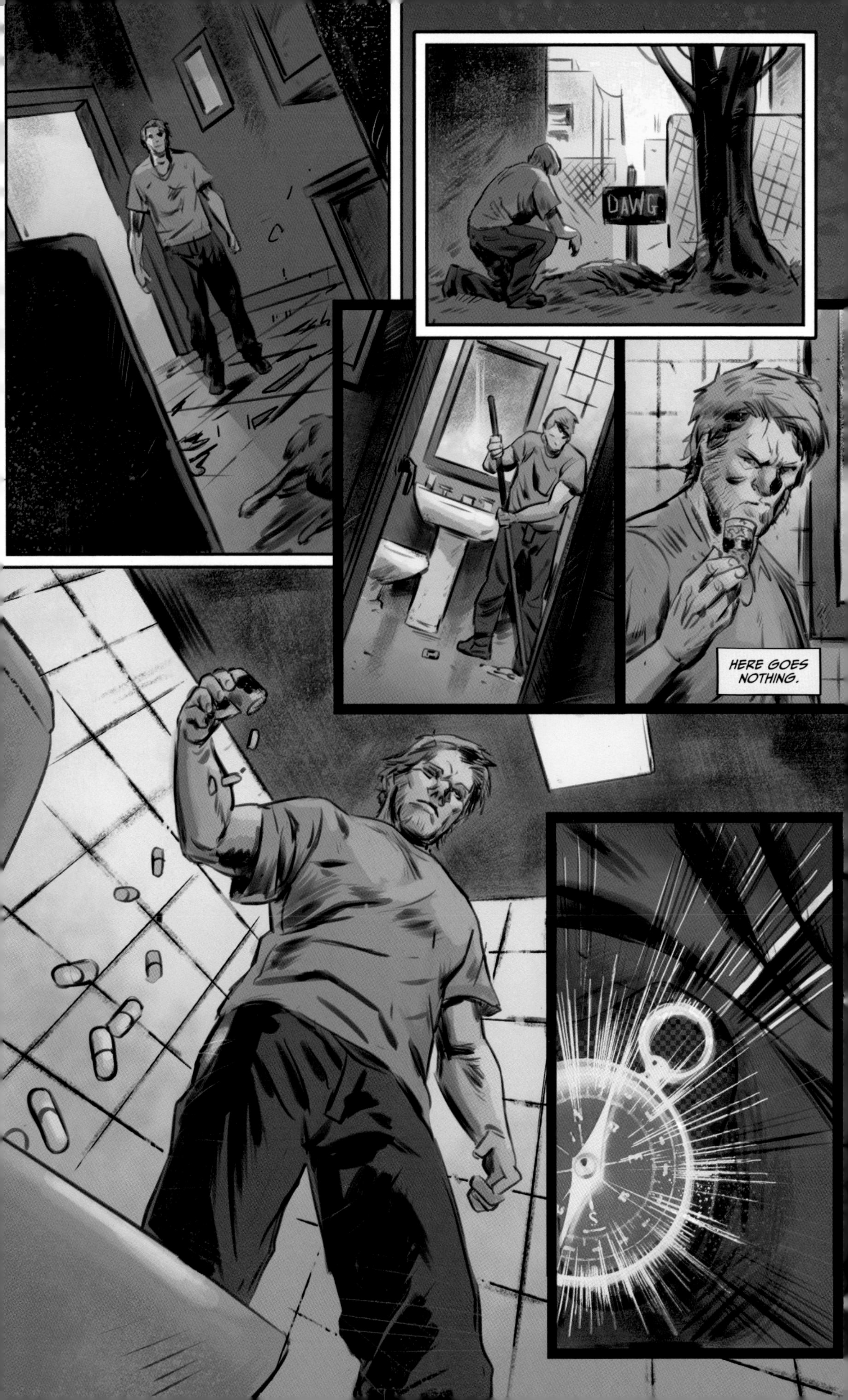
DAWG
HERE GOES NOTHING.

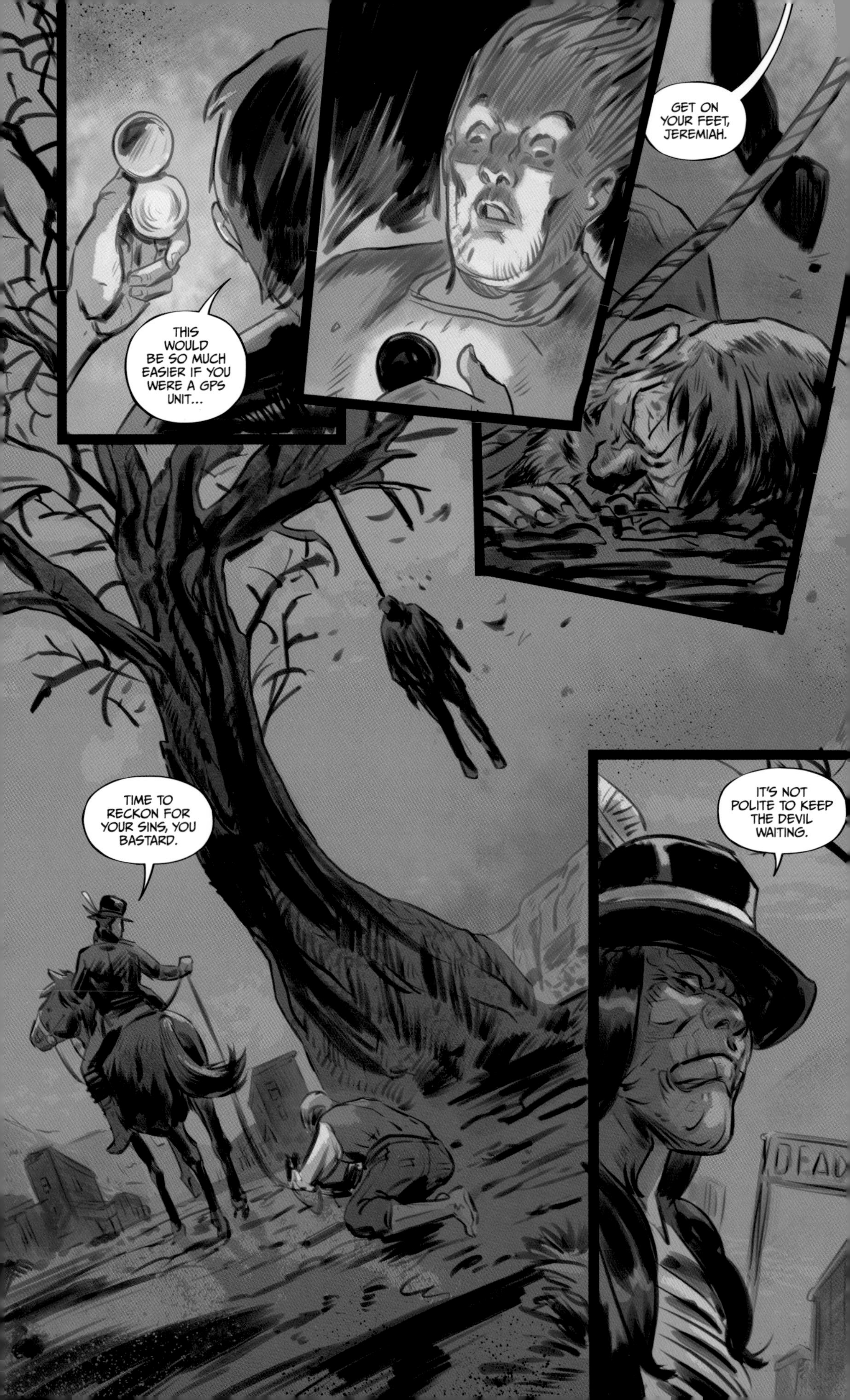
THIS WOULD BE SO MUCH EASIER IF YOU WERE A GPS UNIT...
GET ON YOUR FEET, JEREMIAH.
TIME TO RECKON FOR YOUR SINS, YOU BASTARD.
IT'S NOT POLITE TO KEEP THE DEVIL WAITING.
DEAD

UNITED STATES MARINE CORPS

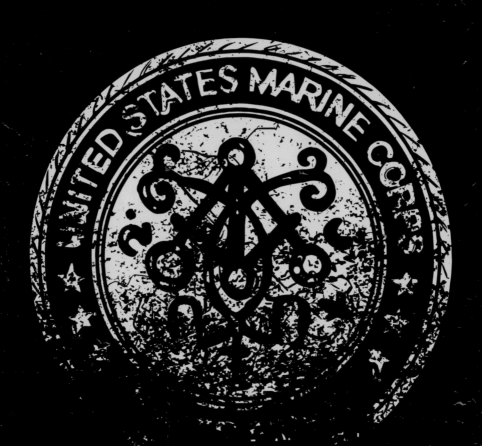

CHAPTER
THREE

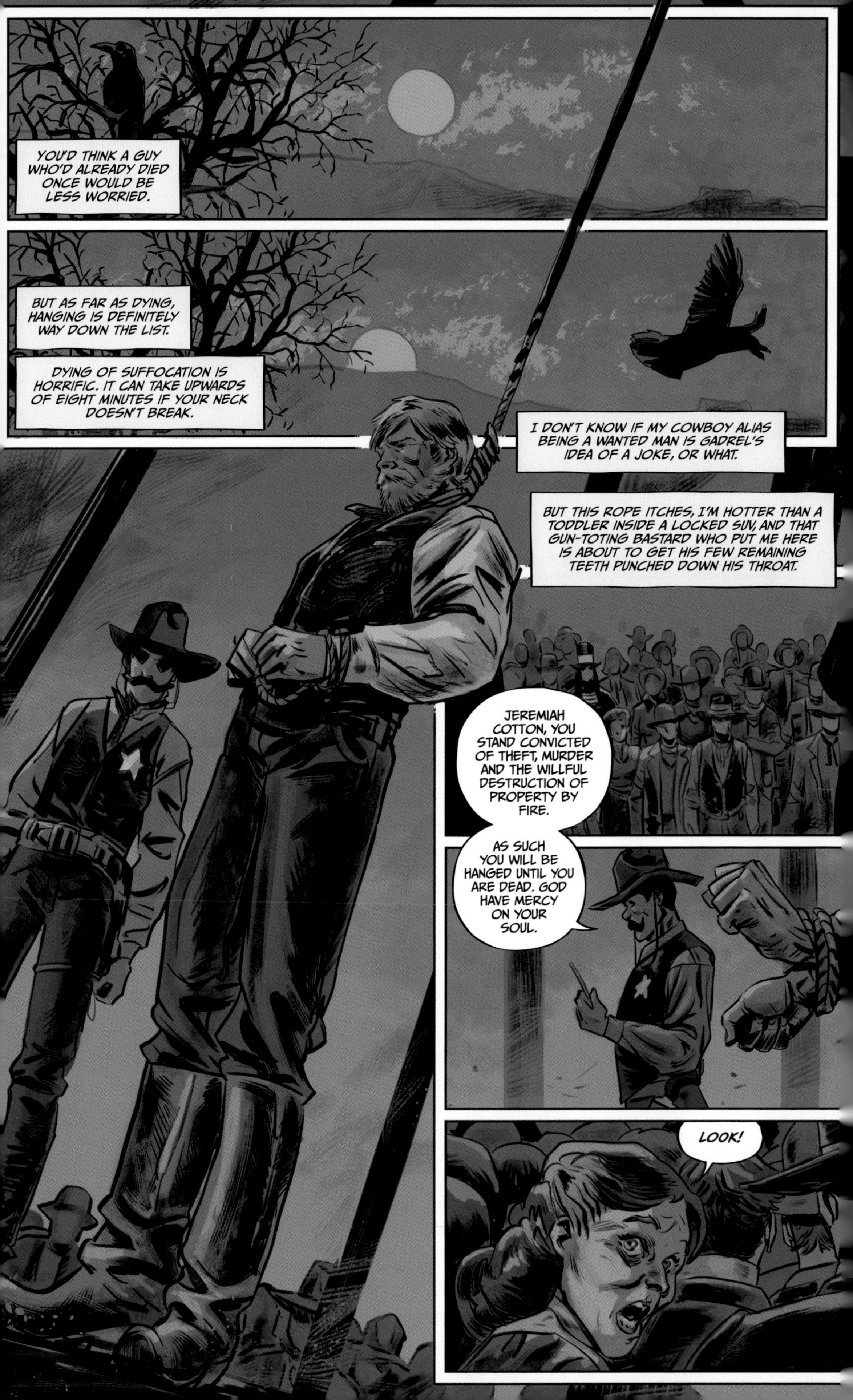
YOU'D THINK A GUY WHO'D ALREADY DIED ONCE WOULD BE LESS WORRIED.
BUT AS FAR AS DYING, HANGING IS DEFINITELY WAY DOWN THE LIST.
DYING OF SUFFOCATION IS HORRIFIC. IT CAN TAKE UPWARDS OF EIGHT MINUTES IF YOUR NECK DOESN'T BREAK.
I DON'T KNOW IF MY COWBOY ALIAS BEING A WANTED MAN IS GADREL'S IDEA OF A JOKE, OR WHAT.
BUT THIS ROPE ITCHES, I'M HOTTER THAN A TODDLER INSIDE A LOCKED SUV, AND THAT GUN-TOTING BASTARD WHO PUT ME HERE IS ABOUT TO GET HIS FEW REMAINING TEETH PUNCHED DOWN HIS THROAT.
JEREMIAH COTTON, YOU STAND CONVICTED OF THEFT, MURDER AND THE WILLFUL DESTRUCTION OF PROPERTY BY FIRE.
AS SUCH YOU WILL BE HANGED UNTIL YOU ARE DEAD. GOD HAVE MERCY ON YOUR SOUL.
LOOK!

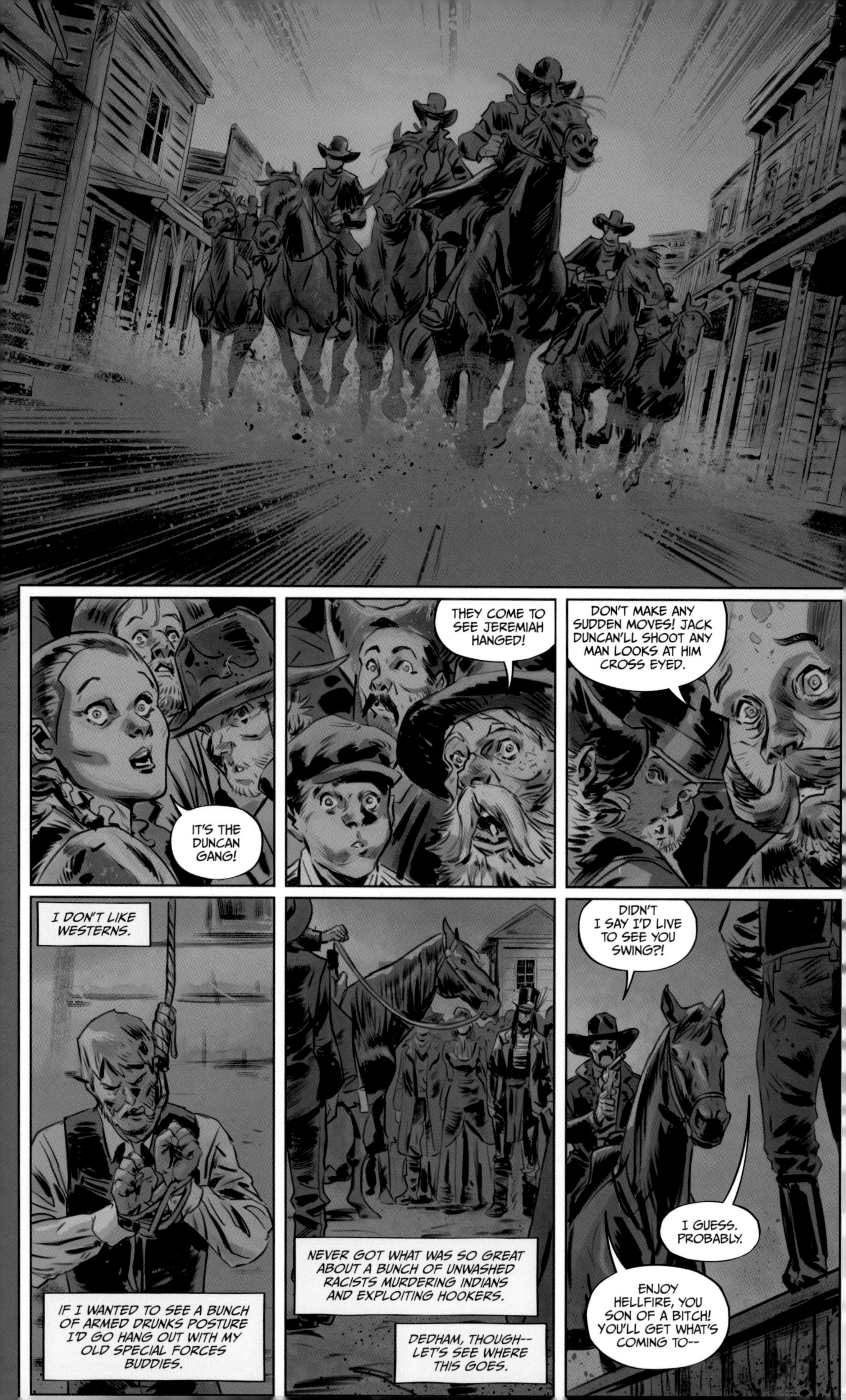
IT'S THE DUNCAN GANG!
THEY COME TO SEE JEREMIAH HANGED!
DON'T MAKE ANY SUDDEN MOVES! JACK DUNCAN'LL SHOOT ANY MAN LOOKS AT HIM CROSS EYED.
I DON'T LIKE WESTERNS.
IF I WANTED TO SEE A BUNCH OF ARMED DRUNKS POSTURE I'D GO HANG OUT WITH MY OLD SPECIAL FORCES BUDDIES.
NEVER GOT WHAT WAS SO GREAT ABOUT A BUNCH OF UNWASHED RACISTS MURDERING INDIANS AND EXPLOITING HOOKERS.
DEDHAM, THOUGH-- LET'S SEE WHERE THIS GOES.
DIDN'T I SAY I'D LIVE TO SEE YOU SWING?!
I GUESS. PROBABLY.
ENJOY HELLFIRE, YOU SON OF A BITCH! YOU'LL GET WHAT'S COMING TO--

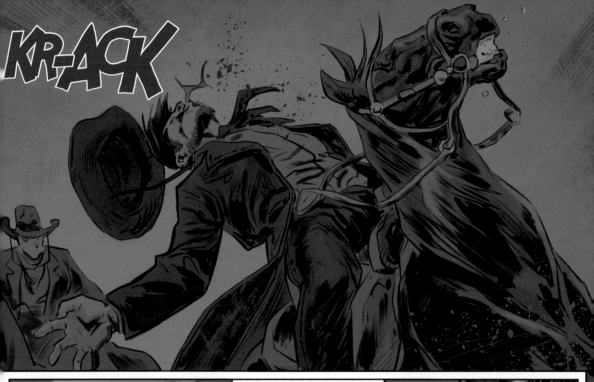

KR-ACK

JACK DUNCAN, YOU ARE WANTED IN OKLAHOMA TERRITORY FOR MURDER. DEAD OR ALIVE.

WELL, I CAN HONESTLY SAY I DIDN'T SEE THAT COMING.

GUESS DUNCAN DIDN'T EITHER.

WHATEVER YOU DO WON'T CHANGE THE FACT YOUR MAN WAS A KILLER AND A FIEND.

AND IF YOU MAKE A MOVE, I'LL BE TAKING AT LEAST SIX OF YOU TO HELL WITH ME.

EVEN THOUGH HE TRIED TO HANG ME, I KIND OF DIG THIS GUY. HE'S GOT WHAT MY DAD WOULD HAVE CALLED PANACHE, AND MY MOM WOULD CALL A SET OF BRASS ONES.

HEY!

YOU LIKE YOUR JAW WHERE IT IS, SHUT IT.

NEED SOME HELP?

I HAVE IT UNDER CONTROL.

I DON'T DOUBT IT. GUY ON THE FAR RIGHT LOOKS A LITTLE SQUIRRELLY, THOUGH.

HE HAS A SPENCER REPEATING RIFLE. NOW, I'M NOT A BIG HISTORY BUFF, BUT I BELIEVE THOSE THINGS HAD TWENTY SHOTS. YOU HAVE SIX.

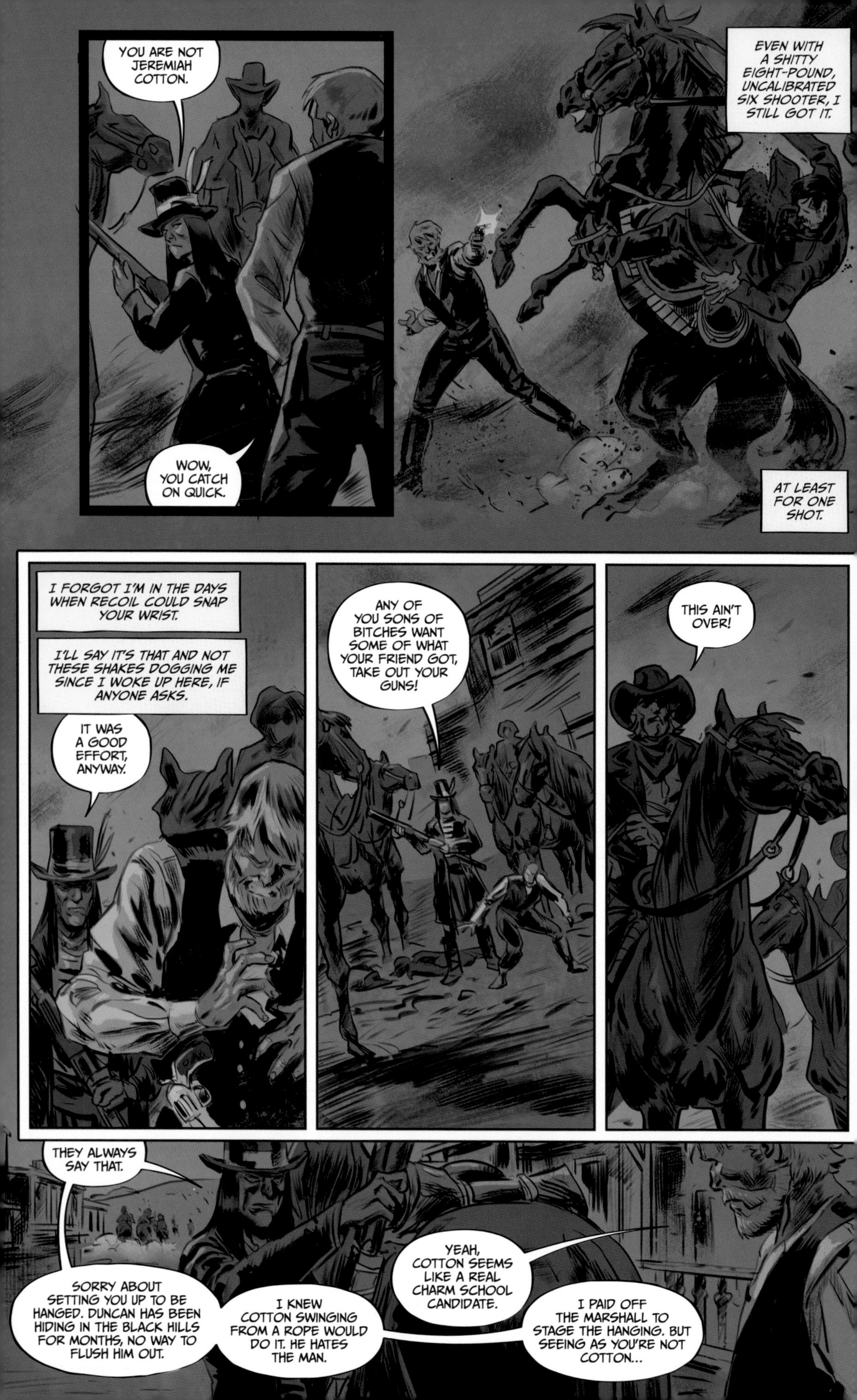
YOU ARE NOT JEREMIAH COTTON.
WOW, YOU CATCH ON QUICK.
EVEN WITH A SHITTY EIGHT-POUND, UNCALIBRATED SIX SHOOTER, I STILL GOT IT.
AT LEAST FOR ONE SHOT.
I FORGOT I'M IN THE DAYS WHEN RECOIL COULD SNAP YOUR WRIST.
I'LL SAY IT'S THAT AND NOT THESE SHAKES DOGGING ME SINCE I WOKE UP HERE, IF ANYONE ASKS.
IT WAS A GOOD EFFORT, ANYWAY.
ANY OF YOU SONS OF BITCHES WANT SOME OF WHAT YOUR FRIEND GOT, TAKE OUT YOUR GUNS!
THIS AIN'T OVER!
THEY ALWAYS SAY THAT.
SORRY ABOUT SETTING YOU UP TO BE HANGED. DUNCAN HAS BEEN HIDING IN THE BLACK HILLS FOR MONTHS, NO WAY TO FLUSH HIM OUT.
I KNEW COTTON SWINGING FROM A ROPE WOULD DO IT. HE HATES THE MAN.
YEAH, COTTON SEEMS LIKE A REAL CHARM SCHOOL CANDIDATE.
I PAID OFF THE MARSHALL TO STAGE THE HANGING. BUT SEEING AS YOU'RE NOT COTTON...

...IF YOU'RE NOT COTTON, YOU SHOULD RETURN TO WHEREVER YOU CAME FROM.

THIS IS NO PLACE FOR DECENT MEN.

SO WHO ARE YOU? A GHOST? A FRAGMENT OF COTTON'S OWN MIND?

WHOEVER TOLD YOU I WAS DECENT WAS A GODDAMN LIAR.

NEITHER. HOW ARE YOU SO OKAY WITH THIS?

I'M COMANCHE, BUT I LIVE AMONG THE WHITES. I SEE BOTH SIDES--SUPERNATURAL AND SCIENTIFIC. THERE'S ROOM FOR BOTH IN MY UNDERSTANDING.

ONE TINY BIT OF LUCK, FINALLY. A GUY WHO CAN MAKE A HEADSHOT WITH A WINCHESTER FROM TWO HUNDRED FEET NOT ONLY BELIEVES ME, BUT ISN'T SO TERRIFIED OF ME HE'S PEEING HIMSELF.

NAME'S LUCAS. WHY I'M HERE IS A LONG FUCKIN' STORY.

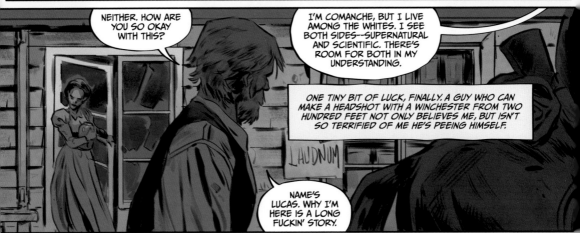

WHOA! YOU OKAY?

LEAVE HER. SHE'S AFFLICTED BY THE LOCAL SICKNESS.

I CAN'T JUST--

GET AWAY FROM ME!

YOU CAN FIND A PLACE TO CLEAN UP THERE.

I'LL BE IN THE STABLE.

YOU'RE NOT COMING IN?

I'M AN INDIAN.

IT TAKES A FULL SECOND TO CLICK. THEN I FEEL LIKE AN ASSHOLE.

LITERALLY ANY FLAT SURFACE SOUNDS GOOD RIGHT NOW. THE ADRENALINE'S WORN OFF, AND I CAN FEEL THE FEVER SWEATS DRENCHING EVERY INCH OF ME.

STABLE SOUNDS GOOD. LET'S GO.

GOOD THING MY CLOTHES ARE ALREADY FILTHY.

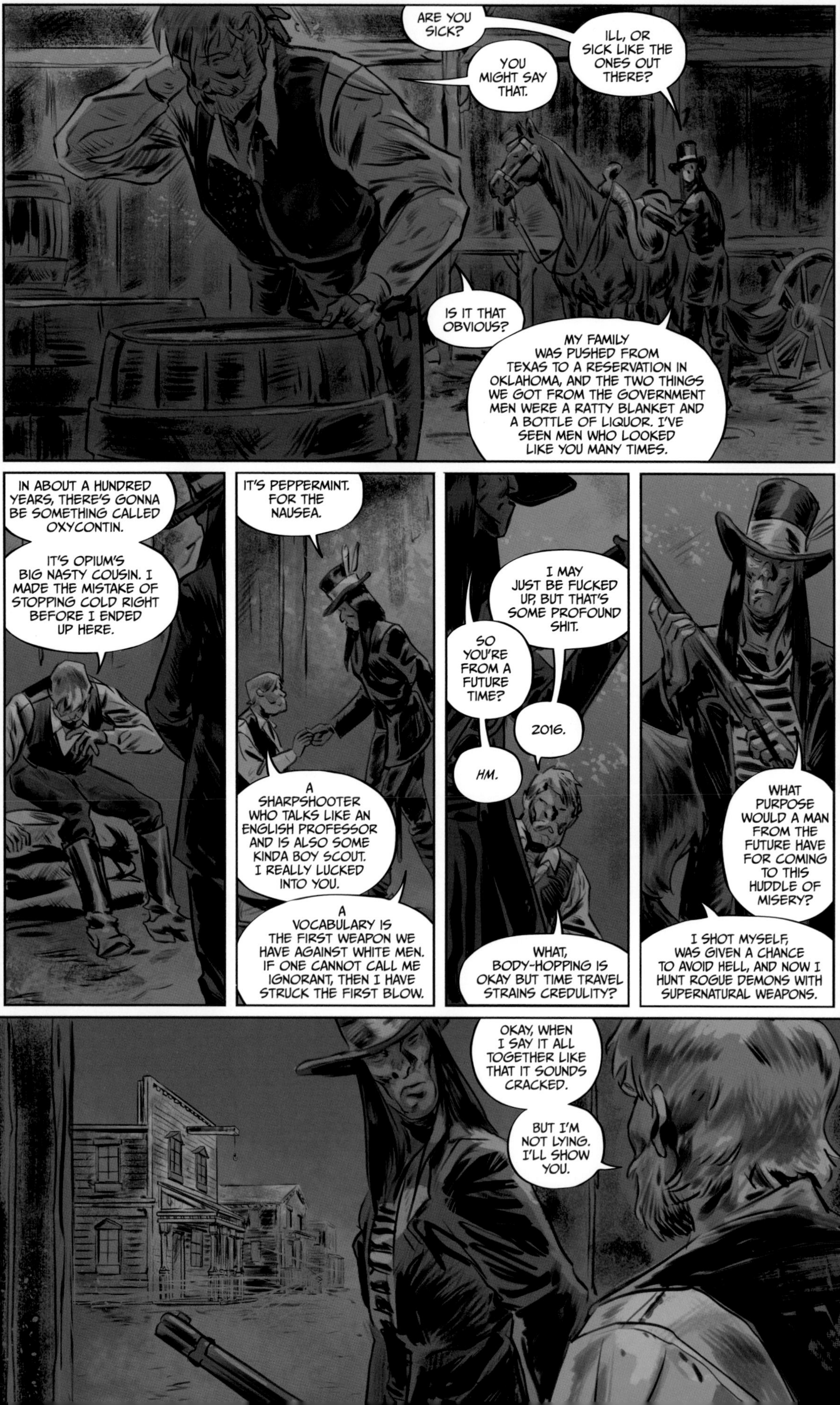
ARE YOU SICK?
YOU MIGHT SAY THAT.
ILL, OR SICK LIKE THE ONES OUT THERE?
IS IT THAT OBVIOUS?
MY FAMILY WAS PUSHED FROM TEXAS TO A RESERVATION IN OKLAHOMA, AND THE TWO THINGS WE GOT FROM THE GOVERNMENT MEN WERE A RATTY BLANKET AND A BOTTLE OF LIQUOR. I'VE SEEN MEN WHO LOOKED LIKE YOU MANY TIMES.
IN ABOUT A HUNDRED YEARS, THERE'S GONNA BE SOMETHING CALLED OXYCONTIN.
IT'S OPIUM'S BIG NASTY COUSIN. I MADE THE MISTAKE OF STOPPING COLD RIGHT BEFORE I ENDED UP HERE.
IT'S PEPPERMINT. FOR THE NAUSEA.
A SHARPSHOOTER WHO TALKS LIKE AN ENGLISH PROFESSOR AND IS ALSO SOME KINDA BOY SCOUT. I REALLY LUCKED INTO YOU.
A VOCABULARY IS THE FIRST WEAPON WE HAVE AGAINST WHITE MEN. IF ONE CANNOT CALL ME IGNORANT, THEN I HAVE STRUCK THE FIRST BLOW.
SO YOU'RE FROM A FUTURE TIME?
2016.
HM.
I MAY JUST BE FUCKED UP, BUT THAT'S SOME PROFOUND SHIT.
WHAT, BODY-HOPPING IS OKAY BUT TIME TRAVEL STRAINS CREDULITY?
WHAT PURPOSE WOULD A MAN FROM THE FUTURE HAVE FOR COMING TO THIS HUDDLE OF MISERY?
I SHOT MYSELF, WAS GIVEN A CHANCE TO AVOID HELL, AND NOW I HUNT ROGUE DEMONS WITH SUPERNATURAL WEAPONS.
OKAY, WHEN I SAY IT ALL TOGETHER LIKE THAT IT SOUNDS CRACKED.
BUT I'M NOT LYING. I'LL SHOW YOU.

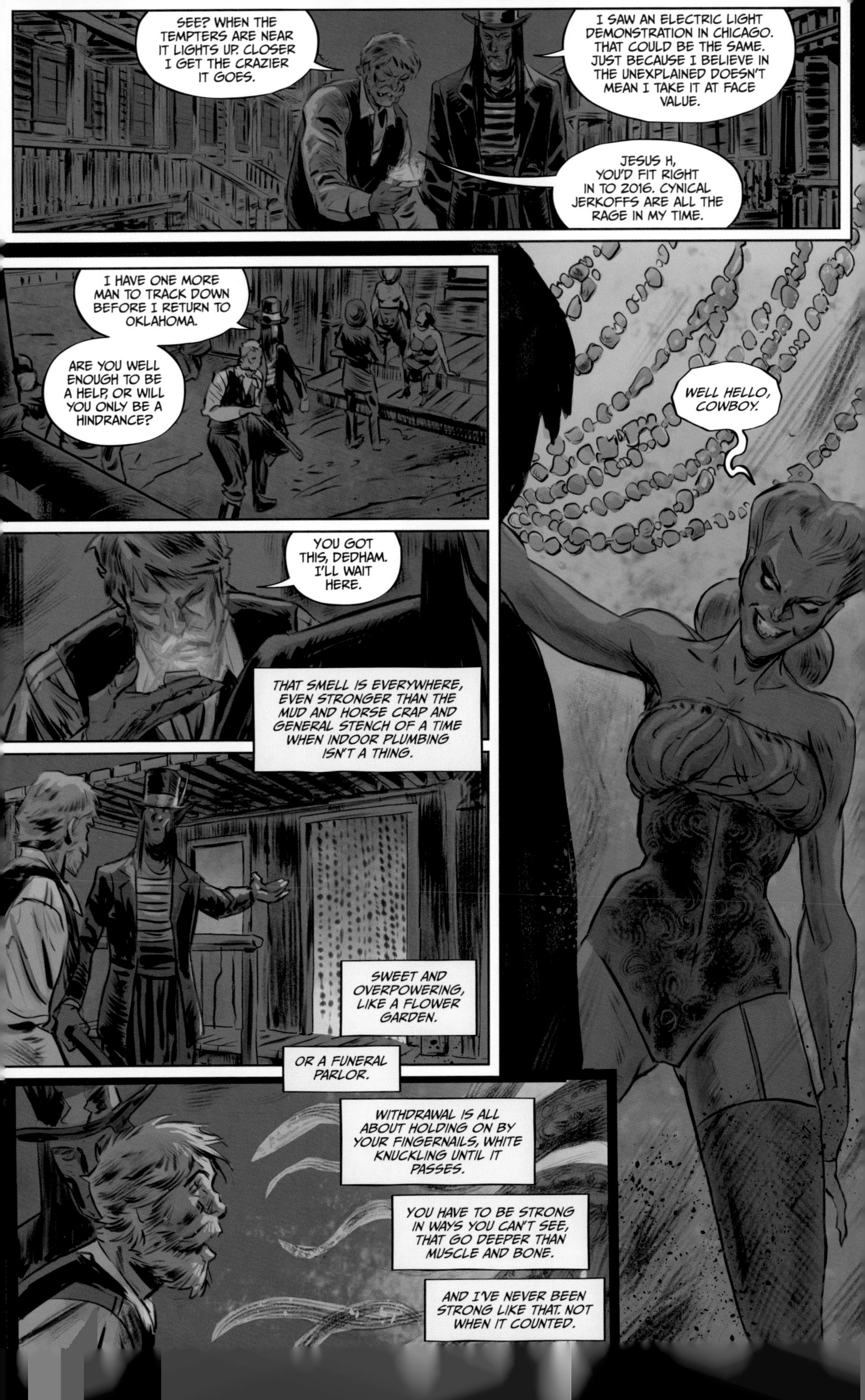
SEE? WHEN THE TEMPTERS ARE NEAR IT LIGHTS UP. CLOSER I GET THE CRAZIER IT GOES.
I SAW AN ELECTRIC LIGHT DEMONSTRATION IN CHICAGO. THAT COULD BE THE SAME. JUST BECAUSE I BELIEVE IN THE UNEXPLAINED DOESN'T MEAN I TAKE IT AT FACE VALUE.
JESUS H, YOU'D FIT RIGHT IN TO 2016. CYNICAL JERKOFFS ARE ALL THE RAGE IN MY TIME.
I HAVE ONE MORE MAN TO TRACK DOWN BEFORE I RETURN TO OKLAHOMA.
ARE YOU WELL ENOUGH TO BE A HELP, OR WILL YOU ONLY BE A HINDRANCE?
YOU GOT THIS, DEDHAM. I'LL WAIT HERE.
THAT SMELL IS EVERYWHERE, EVEN STRONGER THAN THE MUD AND HORSE CRAP AND GENERAL STENCH OF A TIME WHEN INDOOR PLUMBING ISN'T A THING.
SWEET AND OVERPOWERING, LIKE A FLOWER GARDEN.
OR A FUNERAL PARLOR.
WITHDRAWAL IS ALL ABOUT HOLDING ON BY YOUR FINGERNAILS, WHITE KNUCKLING UNTIL IT PASSES.
YOU HAVE TO BE STRONG IN WAYS YOU CAN'T SEE, THAT GO DEEPER THAN MUSCLE AND BONE.
AND I'VE NEVER BEEN STRONG LIKE THAT. NOT WHEN IT COUNTED.
WELL HELLO, COWBOY.

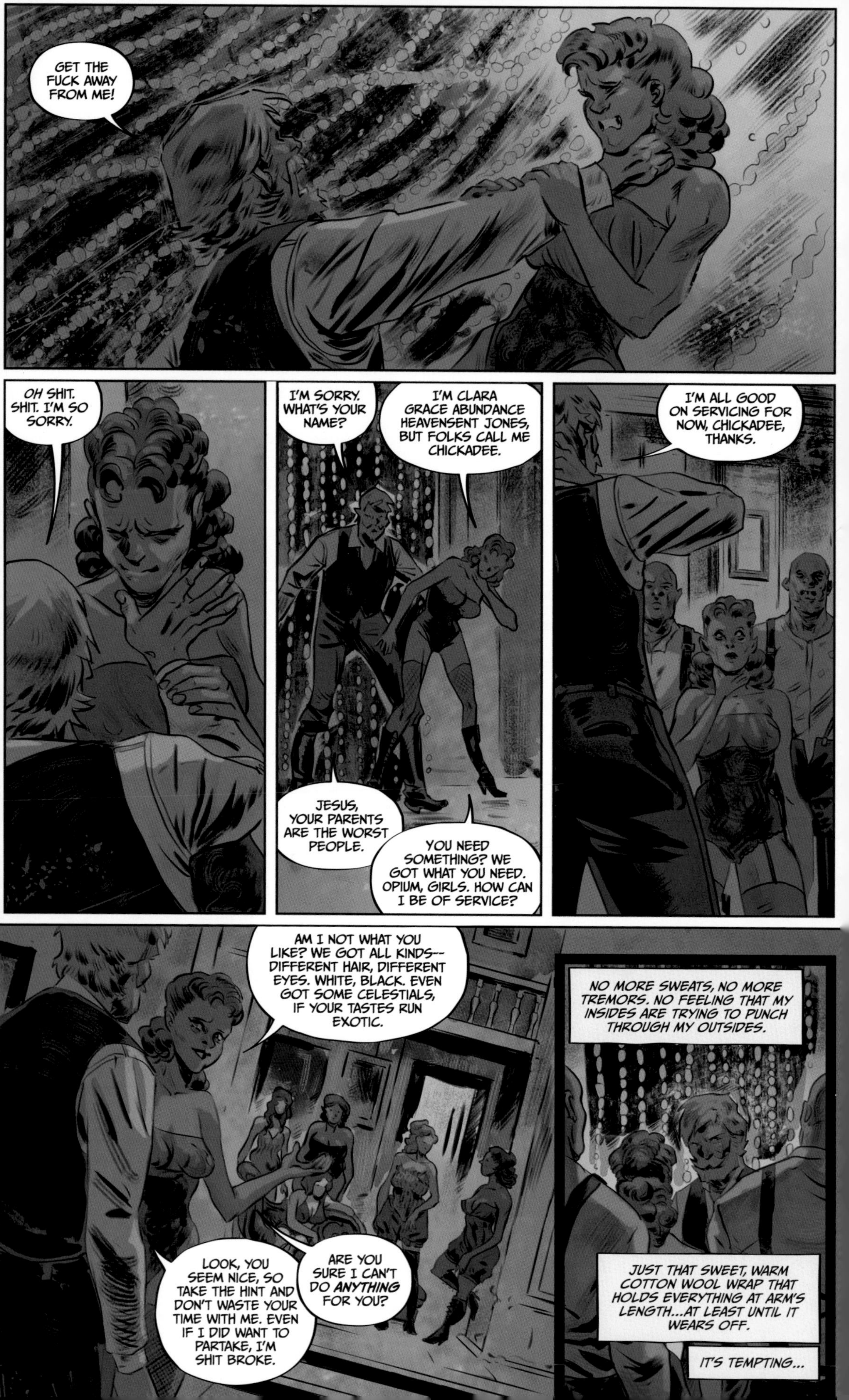
GET THE FUCK AWAY FROM ME!
OH SHIT. SHIT. I'M SO SORRY.
I'M SORRY. WHAT'S YOUR NAME?
I'M CLARA GRACE ABUNDANCE HEAVENSENT JONES, BUT FOLKS CALL ME CHICKADEE.
JESUS, YOUR PARENTS ARE THE WORST PEOPLE.
YOU NEED SOMETHING? WE GOT WHAT YOU NEED. OPIUM, GIRLS. HOW CAN I BE OF SERVICE?
I'M ALL GOOD ON SERVICING FOR NOW, CHICKADEE, THANKS.
AM I NOT WHAT YOU LIKE? WE GOT ALL KINDS-- DIFFERENT HAIR, DIFFERENT EYES. WHITE, BLACK. EVEN GOT SOME CELESTIALS, IF YOUR TASTES RUN EXOTIC.
LOOK, YOU SEEM NICE, SO TAKE THE HINT AND DON'T WASTE YOUR TIME WITH ME. EVEN IF I DID WANT TO PARTAKE, I'M SHIT BROKE.
ARE YOU SURE I CAN'T DO *ANYTHING* FOR YOU?
NO MORE SWEATS, NO MORE TREMORS. NO FEELING THAT MY INSIDES ARE TRYING TO PUNCH THROUGH MY OUTSIDES.
JUST THAT SWEET, WARM COTTON WOOL WRAP THAT HOLDS EVERYTHING AT ARM'S LENGTH...AT LEAST UNTIL IT WEARS OFF.
IT'S TEMPTING...

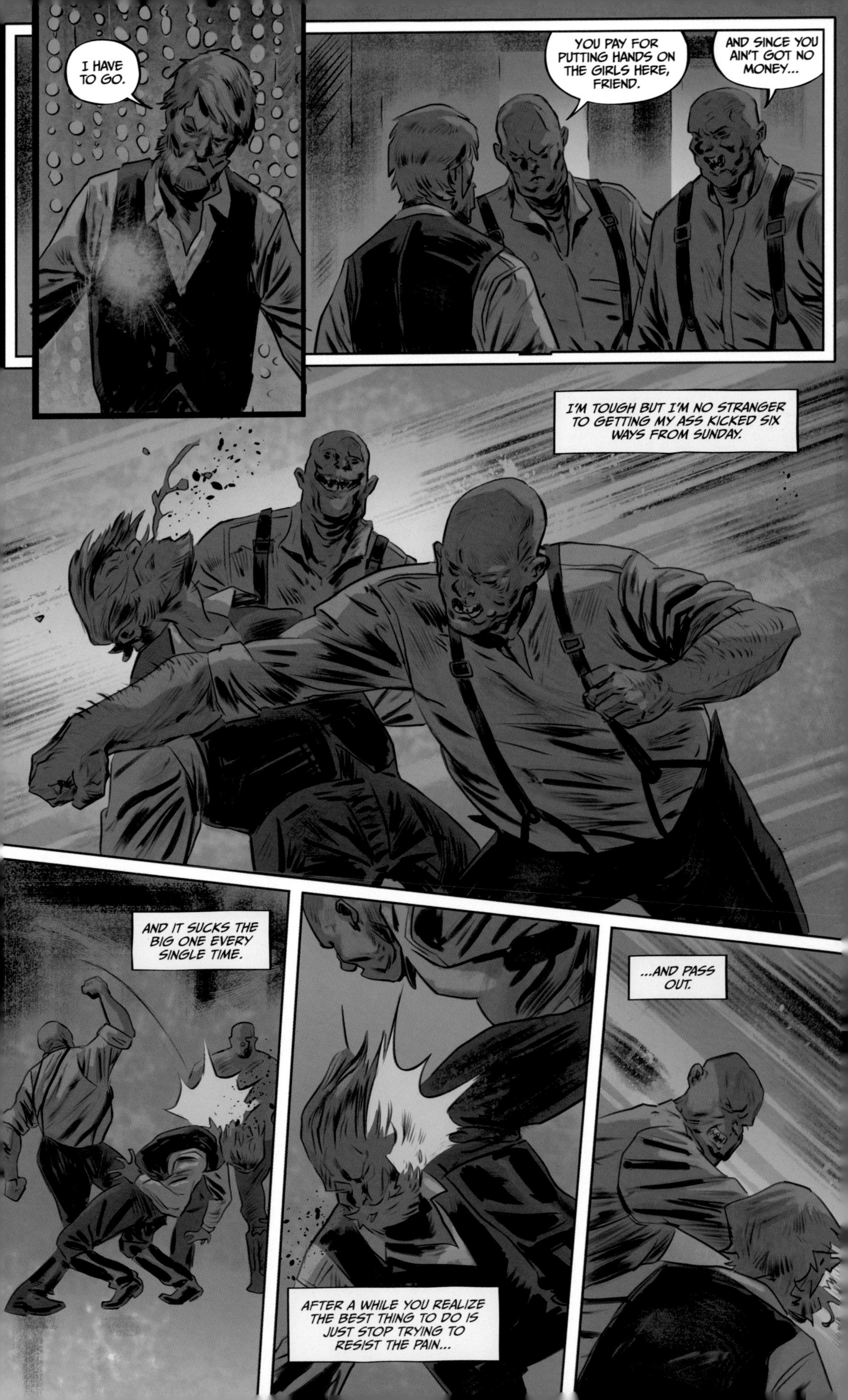
I HAVE TO GO.
YOU PAY FOR PUTTING HANDS ON THE GIRLS HERE, FRIEND.
AND SINCE YOU AIN'T GOT NO MONEY...
I'M TOUGH BUT I'M NO STRANGER TO GETTING MY ASS KICKED SIX WAYS FROM SUNDAY.
AND IT SUCKS THE BIG ONE EVERY SINGLE TIME.
AFTER A WHILE YOU REALIZE THE BEST THING TO DO IS JUST STOP TRYING TO RESIST THE PAIN...
...AND PASS OUT.

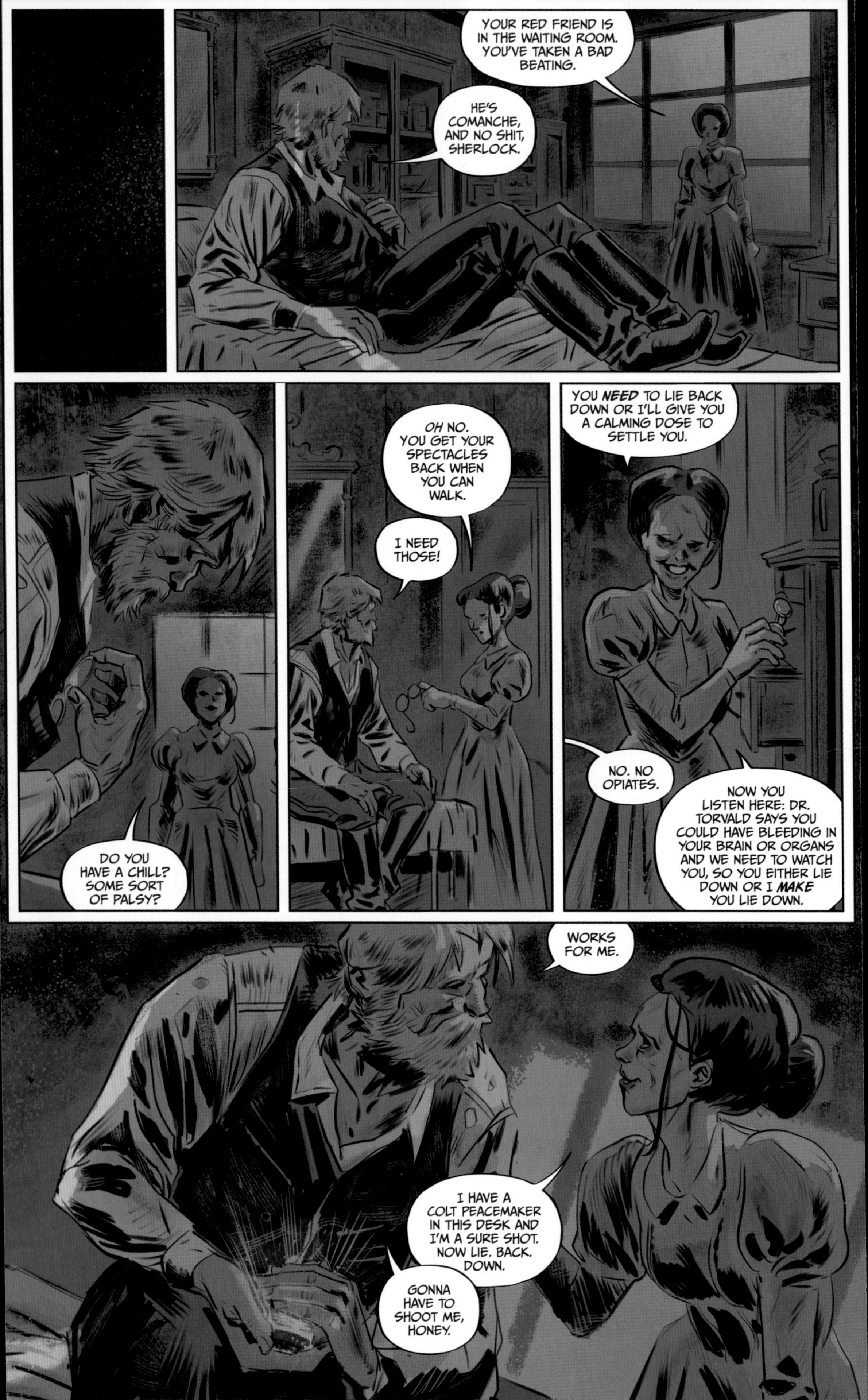
YOUR RED FRIEND IS IN THE WAITING ROOM. YOU'VE TAKEN A BAD BEATING.
HE'S COMANCHE, AND NO SHIT, SHERLOCK.
DO YOU HAVE A CHILL? SOME SORT OF PALSY?
OH NO. YOU GET YOUR SPECTACLES BACK WHEN YOU CAN WALK.
I NEED THOSE!
YOU NEED TO LIE BACK DOWN OR I'LL GIVE YOU A CALMING DOSE TO SETTLE YOU.
NO. NO OPIATES.
NOW YOU LISTEN HERE: DR. TORVALD SAYS YOU COULD HAVE BLEEDING IN YOUR BRAIN OR ORGANS AND WE NEED TO WATCH YOU, SO YOU EITHER LIE DOWN OR I MAKE YOU LIE DOWN.
WORKS FOR ME.
I HAVE A COLT PEACEMAKER IN THIS DESK AND I'M A SURE SHOT. NOW LIE. BACK. DOWN.
GONNA HAVE TO SHOOT ME, HONEY.

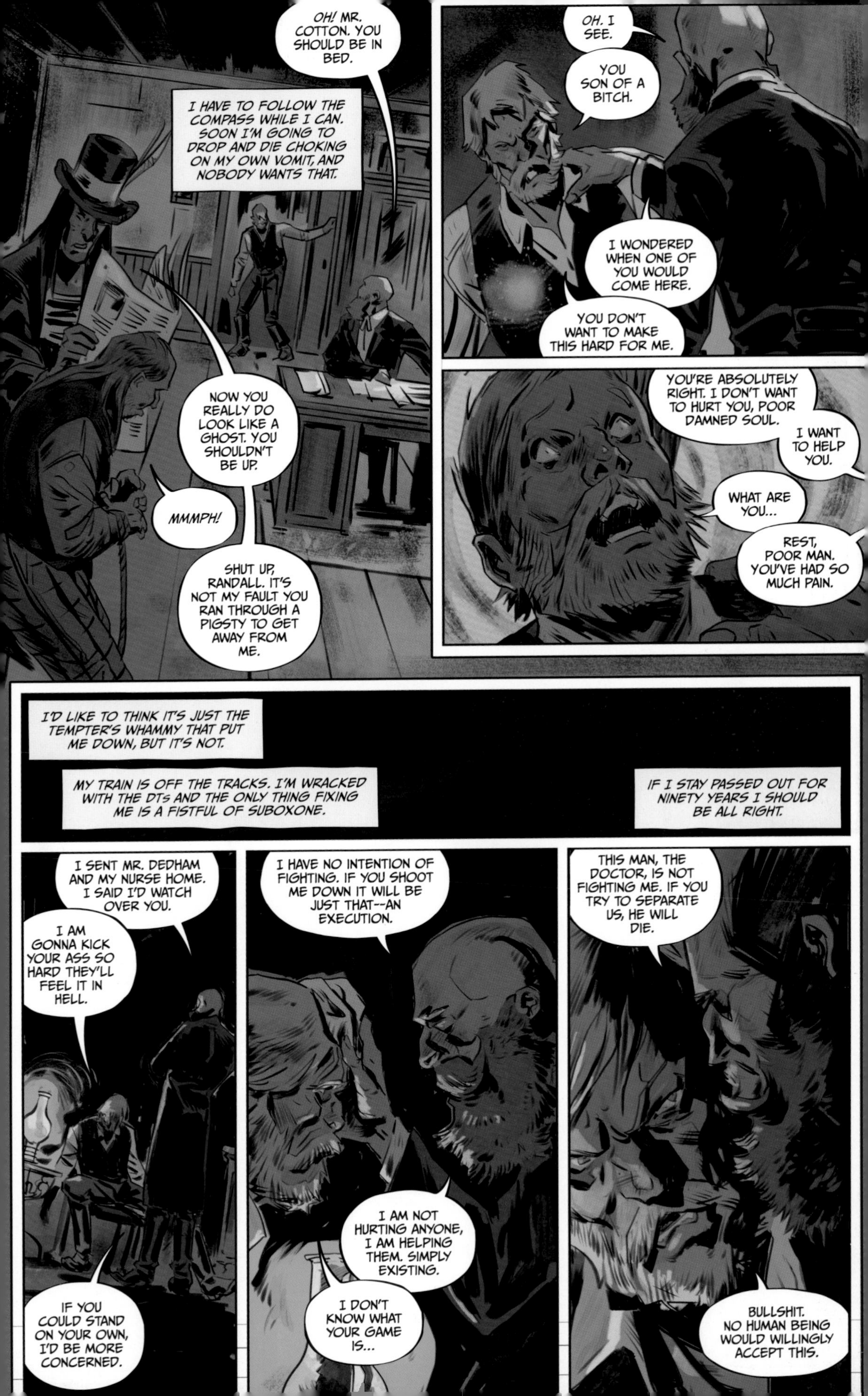
OH! MR. COTTON. YOU SHOULD BE IN BED.
I HAVE TO FOLLOW THE COMPASS WHILE I CAN. SOON I'M GOING TO DROP AND DIE CHOKING ON MY OWN VOMIT, AND NOBODY WANTS THAT.
NOW YOU REALLY DO LOOK LIKE A GHOST. YOU SHOULDN'T BE UP.
MMMPH!
SHUT UP, RANDALL. IT'S NOT MY FAULT YOU RAN THROUGH A PIGSTY TO GET AWAY FROM ME.
OH. I SEE.
YOU SON OF A BITCH.
I WONDERED WHEN ONE OF YOU WOULD COME HERE.
YOU DON'T WANT TO MAKE THIS HARD FOR ME.
YOU'RE ABSOLUTELY RIGHT. I DON'T WANT TO HURT YOU, POOR DAMNED SOUL.
I WANT TO HELP YOU.
WHAT ARE YOU...
REST, POOR MAN. YOU'VE HAD SO MUCH PAIN.
I'D LIKE TO THINK IT'S JUST THE TEMPTER'S WHAMMY THAT PUT ME DOWN, BUT IT'S NOT.
MY TRAIN IS OFF THE TRACKS. I'M WRACKED WITH THE DTs AND THE ONLY THING FIXING ME IS A FISTFUL OF SUBOXONE.
IF I STAY PASSED OUT FOR NINETY YEARS I SHOULD BE ALL RIGHT.
I SENT MR. DEDHAM AND MY NURSE HOME. I SAID I'D WATCH OVER YOU.
I AM GONNA KICK YOUR ASS SO HARD THEY'LL FEEL IT IN HELL.
IF YOU COULD STAND ON YOUR OWN, I'D BE MORE CONCERNED.
I HAVE NO INTENTION OF FIGHTING. IF YOU SHOOT ME DOWN IT WILL BE JUST THAT--AN EXECUTION.
I AM NOT HURTING ANYONE, I AM HELPING THEM. SIMPLY EXISTING.
I DON'T KNOW WHAT YOUR GAME IS...
THIS MAN, THE DOCTOR, IS NOT FIGHTING ME. IF YOU TRY TO SEPARATE US, HE WILL DIE.
BULLSHIT. NO HUMAN BEING WOULD WILLINGLY ACCEPT THIS.

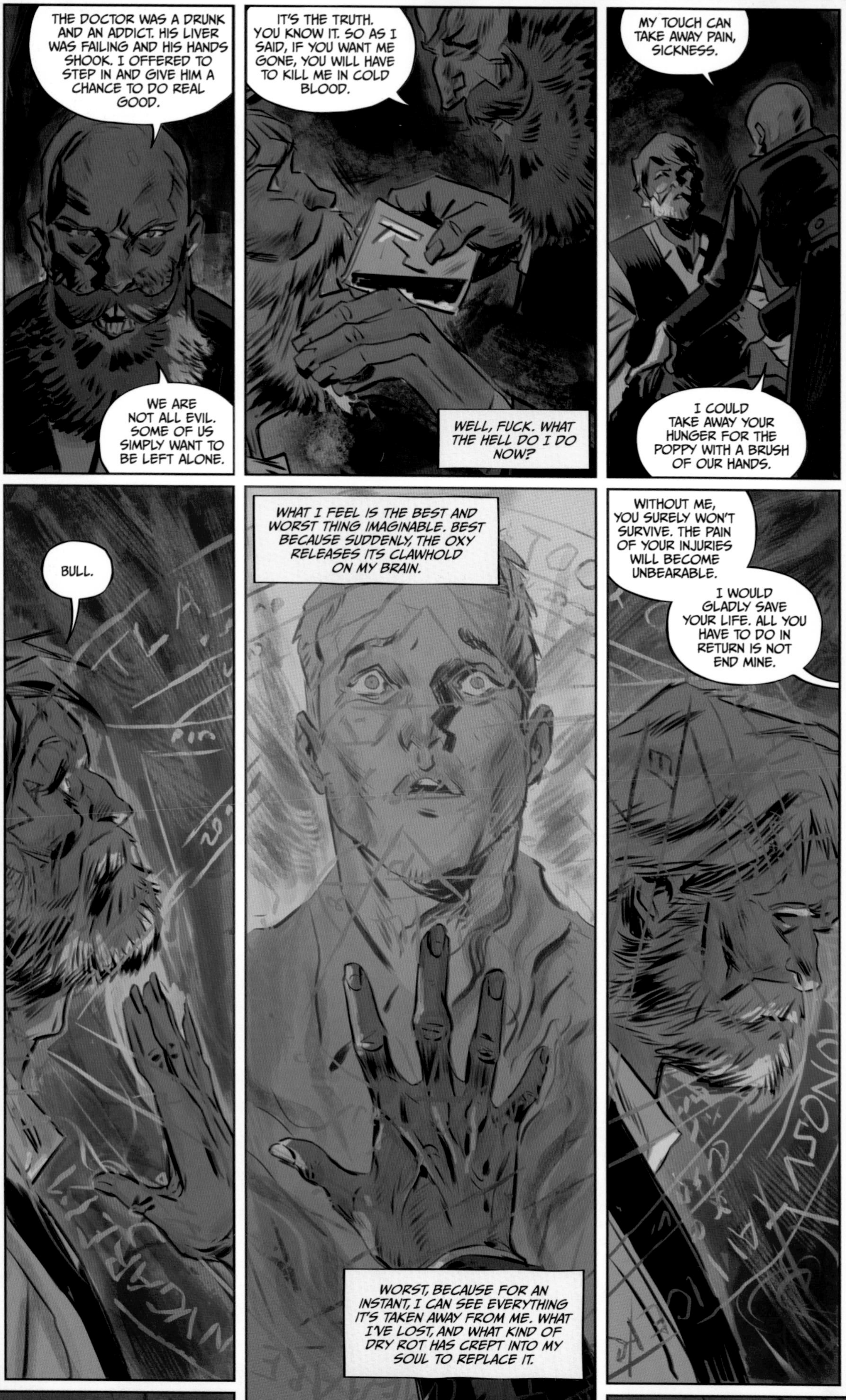
THE DOCTOR WAS A DRUNK AND AN ADDICT. HIS LIVER WAS FAILING AND HIS HANDS SHOOK. I OFFERED TO STEP IN AND GIVE HIM A CHANCE TO DO REAL GOOD.
WE ARE NOT ALL EVIL. SOME OF US SIMPLY WANT TO BE LEFT ALONE.
IT'S THE TRUTH. YOU KNOW IT. SO AS I SAID, IF YOU WANT ME GONE, YOU WILL HAVE TO KILL ME IN COLD BLOOD.
WELL, FUCK. WHAT THE HELL DO I DO NOW?
MY TOUCH CAN TAKE AWAY PAIN, SICKNESS.
I COULD TAKE AWAY YOUR HUNGER FOR THE POPPY WITH A BRUSH OF OUR HANDS.
BULL.
WHAT I FEEL IS THE BEST AND WORST THING IMAGINABLE. BEST BECAUSE SUDDENLY, THE OXY RELEASES ITS CLAWHOLD ON MY BRAIN.
WORST, BECAUSE FOR AN INSTANT, I CAN SEE EVERYTHING IT'S TAKEN AWAY FROM ME. WHAT I'VE LOST, AND WHAT KIND OF DRY ROT HAS CREPT INTO MY SOUL TO REPLACE IT.
WITHOUT ME, YOU SURELY WON'T SURVIVE. THE PAIN OF YOUR INJURIES WILL BECOME UNBEARABLE.
I WOULD GLADLY SAVE YOUR LIFE. ALL YOU HAVE TO DO IN RETURN IS NOT END MINE.

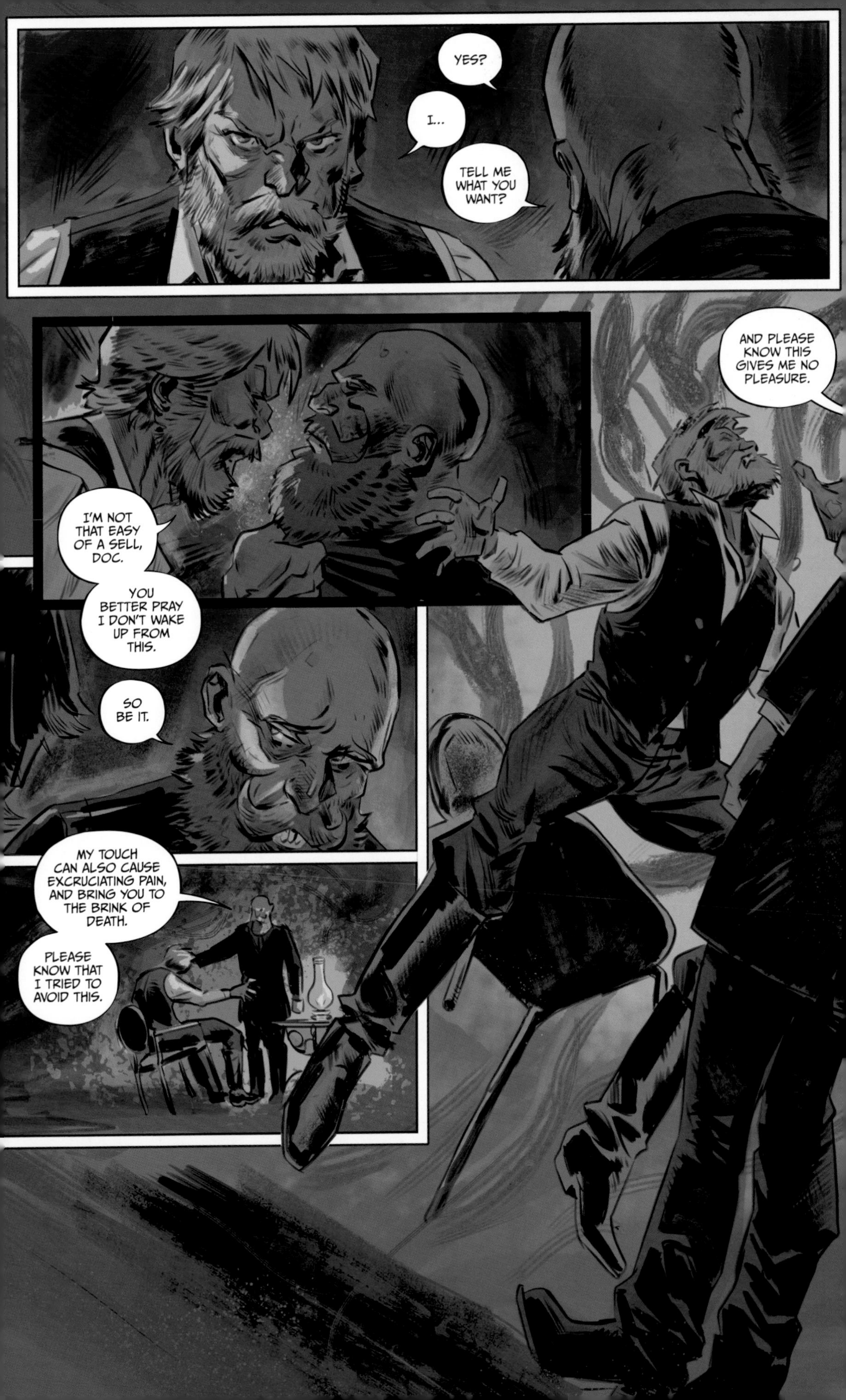
YES?
I...
TELL ME WHAT YOU WANT?
I'M NOT THAT EASY OF A SELL, DOC.
YOU BETTER PRAY I DON'T WAKE UP FROM THIS.
SO BE IT.
MY TOUCH CAN ALSO CAUSE EXCRUCIATING PAIN, AND BRING YOU TO THE BRINK OF DEATH.
PLEASE KNOW THAT I TRIED TO AVOID THIS.
AND PLEASE KNOW THIS GIVES ME NO PLEASURE.

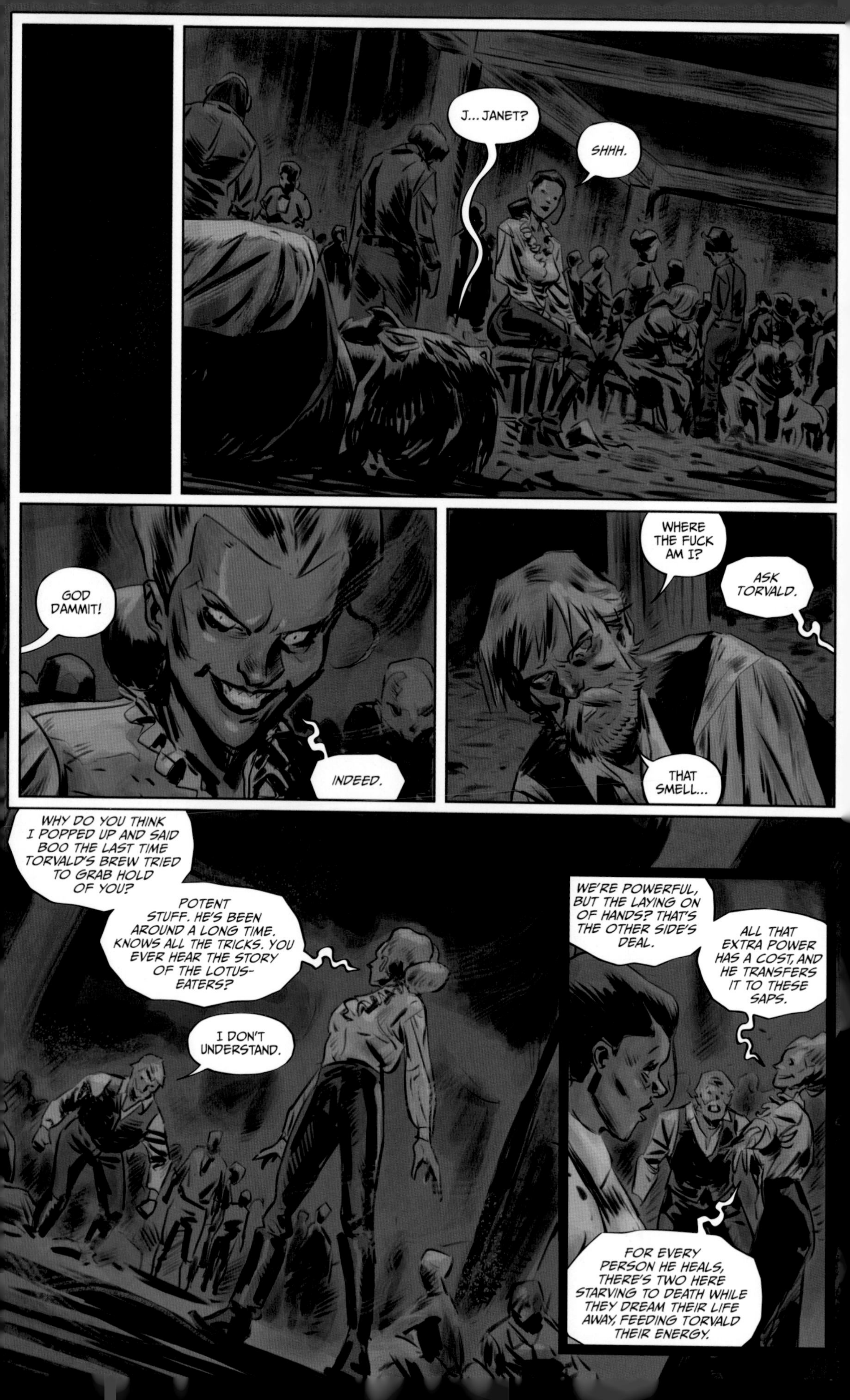
J... JANET?
SHHH.
GOD DAMMIT!
INDEED.
WHERE THE FUCK AM I?
ASK TORVALD.
THAT SMELL...
WHY DO YOU THINK I POPPED UP AND SAID BOO THE LAST TIME TORVALD'S BREW TRIED TO GRAB HOLD OF YOU?
POTENT STUFF. HE'S BEEN AROUND A LONG TIME. KNOWS ALL THE TRICKS. YOU EVER HEAR THE STORY OF THE LOTUS-EATERS?
I DON'T UNDERSTAND.
WE'RE POWERFUL, BUT THE LAYING ON OF HANDS? THAT'S THE OTHER SIDE'S DEAL.
ALL THAT EXTRA POWER HAS A COST, AND HE TRANSFERS IT TO THESE SAPS.
FOR EVERY PERSON HE HEALS, THERE'S TWO HERE STARVING TO DEATH WHILE THEY DREAM THEIR LIFE AWAY, FEEDING TORVALD THEIR ENERGY.

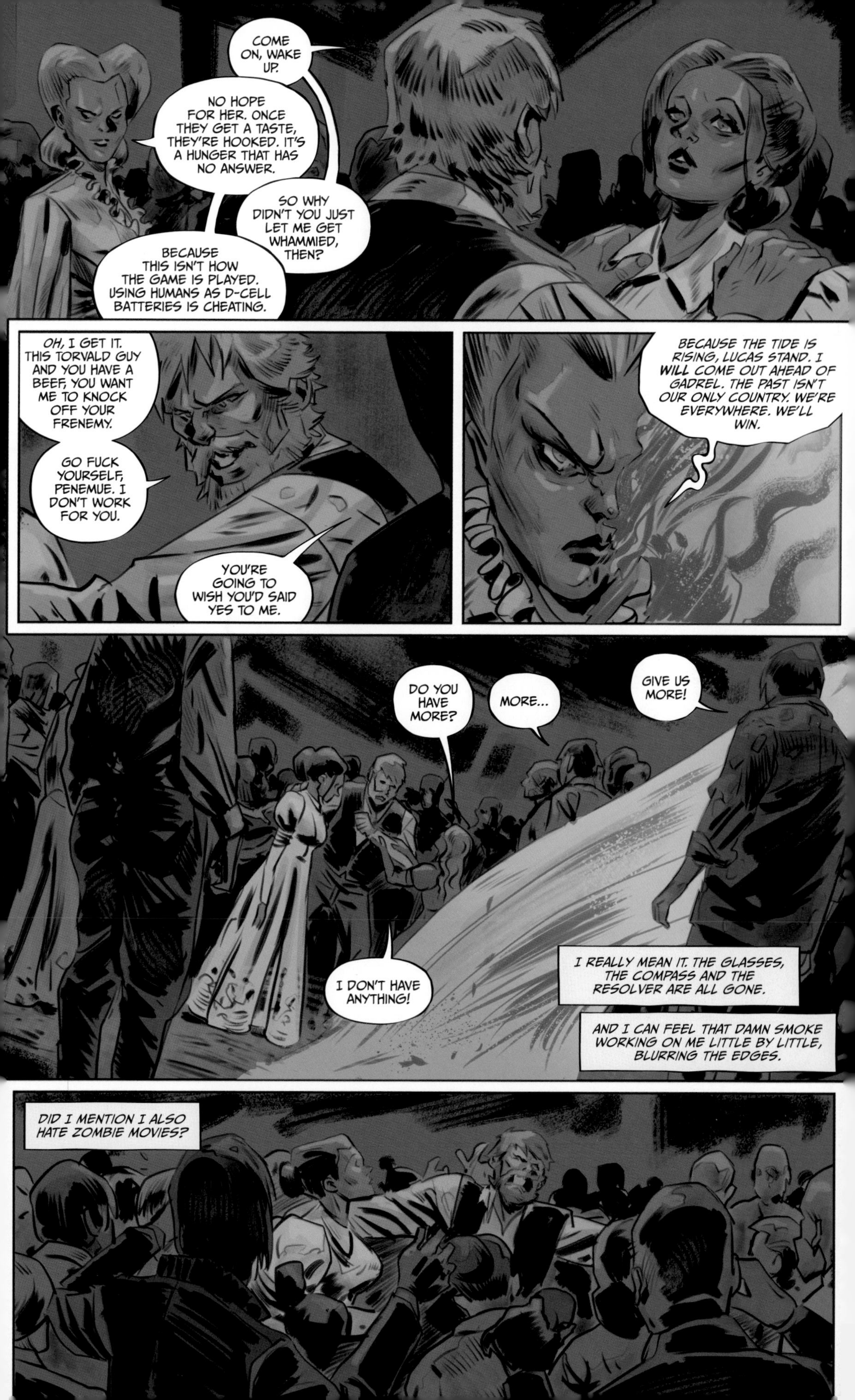
COME ON, WAKE UP.
NO HOPE FOR HER. ONCE THEY GET A TASTE, THEY'RE HOOKED. IT'S A HUNGER THAT HAS NO ANSWER.
SO WHY DIDN'T YOU JUST LET ME GET WHAMMIED, THEN?
BECAUSE THIS ISN'T HOW THE GAME IS PLAYED. USING HUMANS AS D-CELL BATTERIES IS CHEATING.
OH, I GET IT. THIS TORVALD GUY AND YOU HAVE A BEEF, YOU WANT ME TO KNOCK OFF YOUR FRENEMY.
GO FUCK YOURSELF, PENEMUE. I DON'T WORK FOR YOU.
YOU'RE GOING TO WISH YOU'D SAID YES TO ME.
BECAUSE THE TIDE IS RISING, LUCAS STAND. I WILL COME OUT AHEAD OF GADREL. THE PAST ISN'T OUR ONLY COUNTRY. WE'RE EVERYWHERE. WE'LL WIN.
DO YOU HAVE MORE?
MORE...
GIVE US MORE!
I DON'T HAVE ANYTHING!
I REALLY MEAN IT. THE GLASSES, THE COMPASS AND THE RESOLVER ARE ALL GONE.
AND I CAN FEEL THAT DAMN SMOKE WORKING ON ME LITTLE BY LITTLE, BLURRING THE EDGES.
DID I MENTION I ALSO HATE ZOMBIE MOVIES?

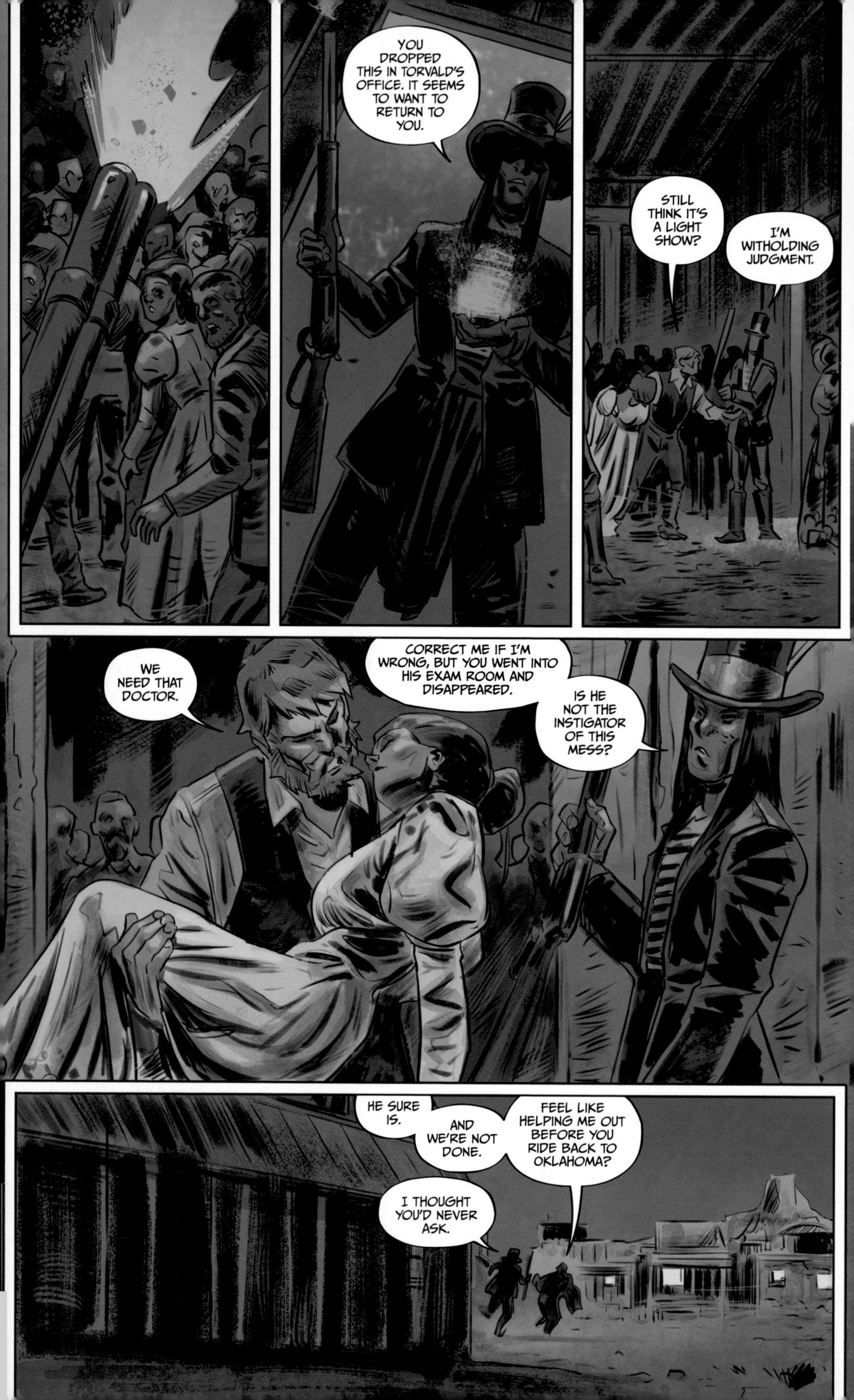
YOU DROPPED THIS IN TORVALD'S OFFICE. IT SEEMS TO WANT TO RETURN TO YOU.
STILL THINK IT'S A LIGHT SHOW?
I'M WITHOLDING JUDGMENT.
WE NEED THAT DOCTOR.
CORRECT ME IF I'M WRONG, BUT YOU WENT INTO HIS EXAM ROOM AND DISAPPEARED.
IS HE NOT THE INSTIGATOR OF THIS MESS?
HE SURE IS.
AND WE'RE NOT DONE.
FEEL LIKE HELPING ME OUT BEFORE YOU RIDE BACK TO OKLAHOMA?
I THOUGHT YOU'D NEVER ASK.

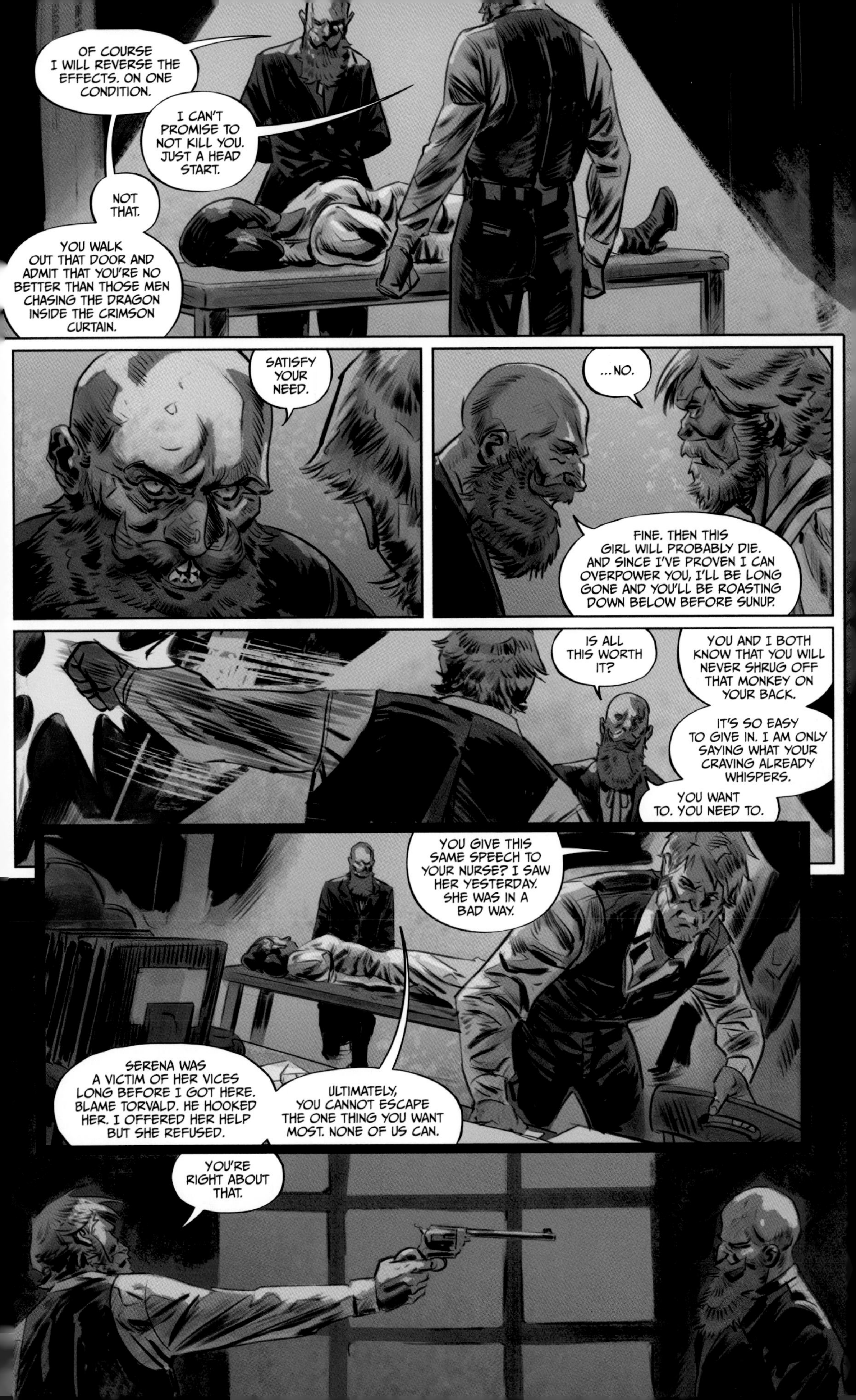
OF COURSE I WILL REVERSE THE EFFECTS. ON ONE CONDITION.
I CAN'T PROMISE TO NOT KILL YOU. JUST A HEAD START.
NOT THAT.
YOU WALK OUT THAT DOOR AND ADMIT THAT YOU'RE NO BETTER THAN THOSE MEN CHASING THE DRAGON INSIDE THE CRIMSON CURTAIN.
SATISFY YOUR NEED.
...NO.
FINE. THEN THIS GIRL WILL PROBABLY DIE. AND SINCE I'VE PROVEN I CAN OVERPOWER YOU, I'LL BE LONG GONE AND YOU'LL BE ROASTING DOWN BELOW BEFORE SUNUP.
IS ALL THIS WORTH IT?
YOU AND I BOTH KNOW THAT YOU WILL NEVER SHRUG OFF THAT MONKEY ON YOUR BACK.
IT'S SO EASY TO GIVE IN. I AM ONLY SAYING WHAT YOUR CRAVING ALREADY WHISPERS.
YOU WANT TO. YOU NEED TO.
YOU GIVE THIS SAME SPEECH TO YOUR NURSE? I SAW HER YESTERDAY. SHE WAS IN A BAD WAY.
SERENA WAS A VICTIM OF HER VICES LONG BEFORE I GOT HERE. BLAME TORVALD. HE HOOKED HER. I OFFERED HER HELP BUT SHE REFUSED.
ULTIMATELY, YOU CANNOT ESCAPE THE ONE THING YOU WANT MOST. NONE OF US CAN.
YOU'RE RIGHT ABOUT THAT.

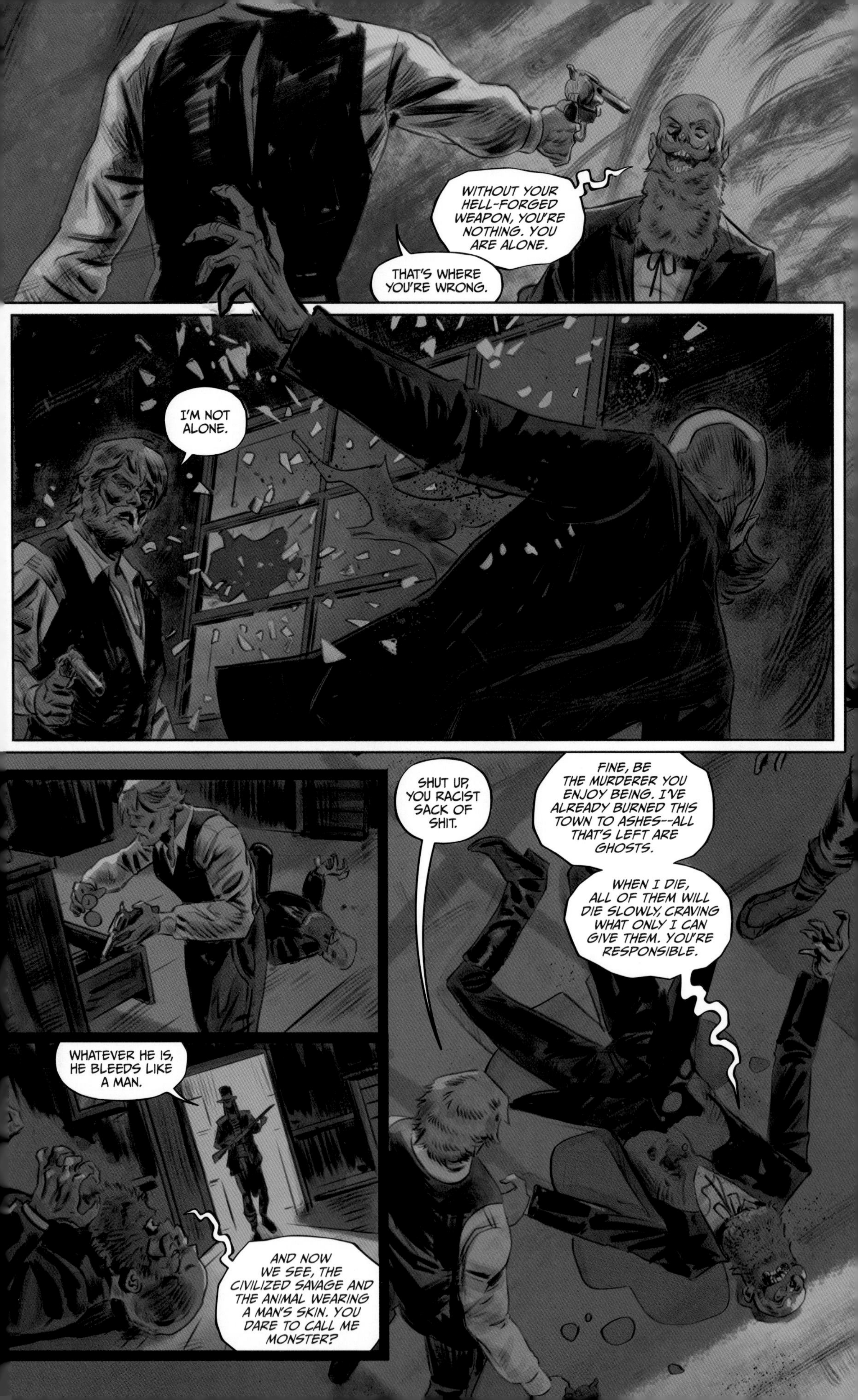
WITHOUT YOUR HELL-FORGED WEAPON, YOU'RE NOTHING. YOU ARE ALONE.
THAT'S WHERE YOU'RE WRONG.
I'M NOT ALONE.
WHATEVER HE IS, HE BLEEDS LIKE A MAN.
AND NOW WE SEE, THE CIVILIZED SAVAGE AND THE ANIMAL WEARING A MAN'S SKIN. YOU DARE TO CALL ME MONSTER?
SHUT UP, YOU RACIST SACK OF SHIT.
FINE, BE THE MURDERER YOU ENJOY BEING. I'VE ALREADY BURNED THIS TOWN TO ASHES--ALL THAT'S LEFT ARE GHOSTS.
WHEN I DIE, ALL OF THEM WILL DIE SLOWLY, CRAVING WHAT ONLY I CAN GIVE THEM. YOU'RE RESPONSIBLE.

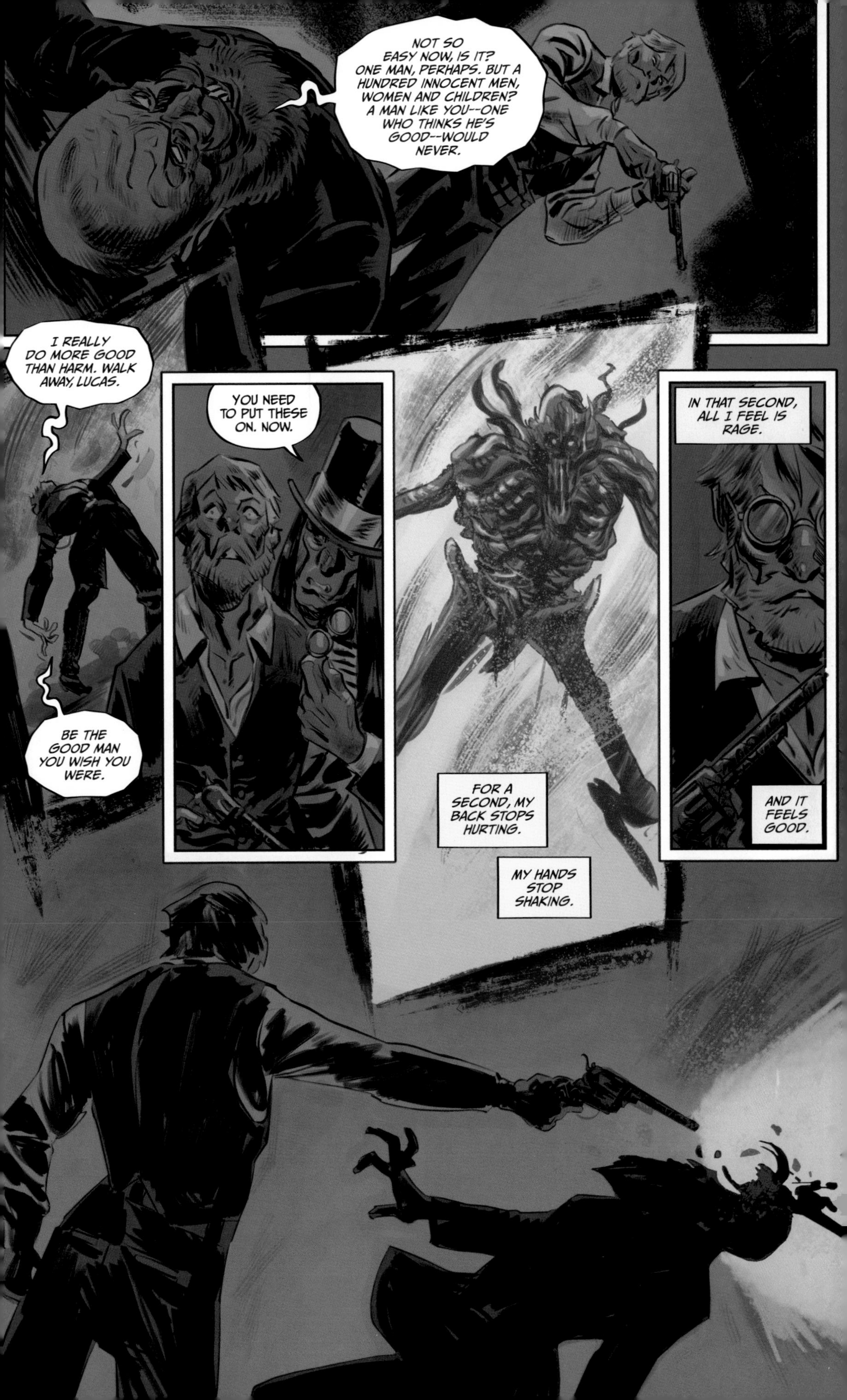
NOT SO EASY NOW, IS IT? ONE MAN, PERHAPS. BUT A HUNDRED INNOCENT MEN, WOMEN AND CHILDREN? A MAN LIKE YOU--ONE WHO THINKS HE'S GOOD--WOULD NEVER.
I REALLY DO MORE GOOD THAN HARM. WALK AWAY, LUCAS.
BE THE GOOD MAN YOU WISH YOU WERE.
YOU NEED TO PUT THESE ON. NOW.
FOR A SECOND, MY BACK STOPS HURTING.
MY HANDS STOP SHAKING.
IN THAT SECOND, ALL I FEEL IS RAGE.
AND IT FEELS GOOD.

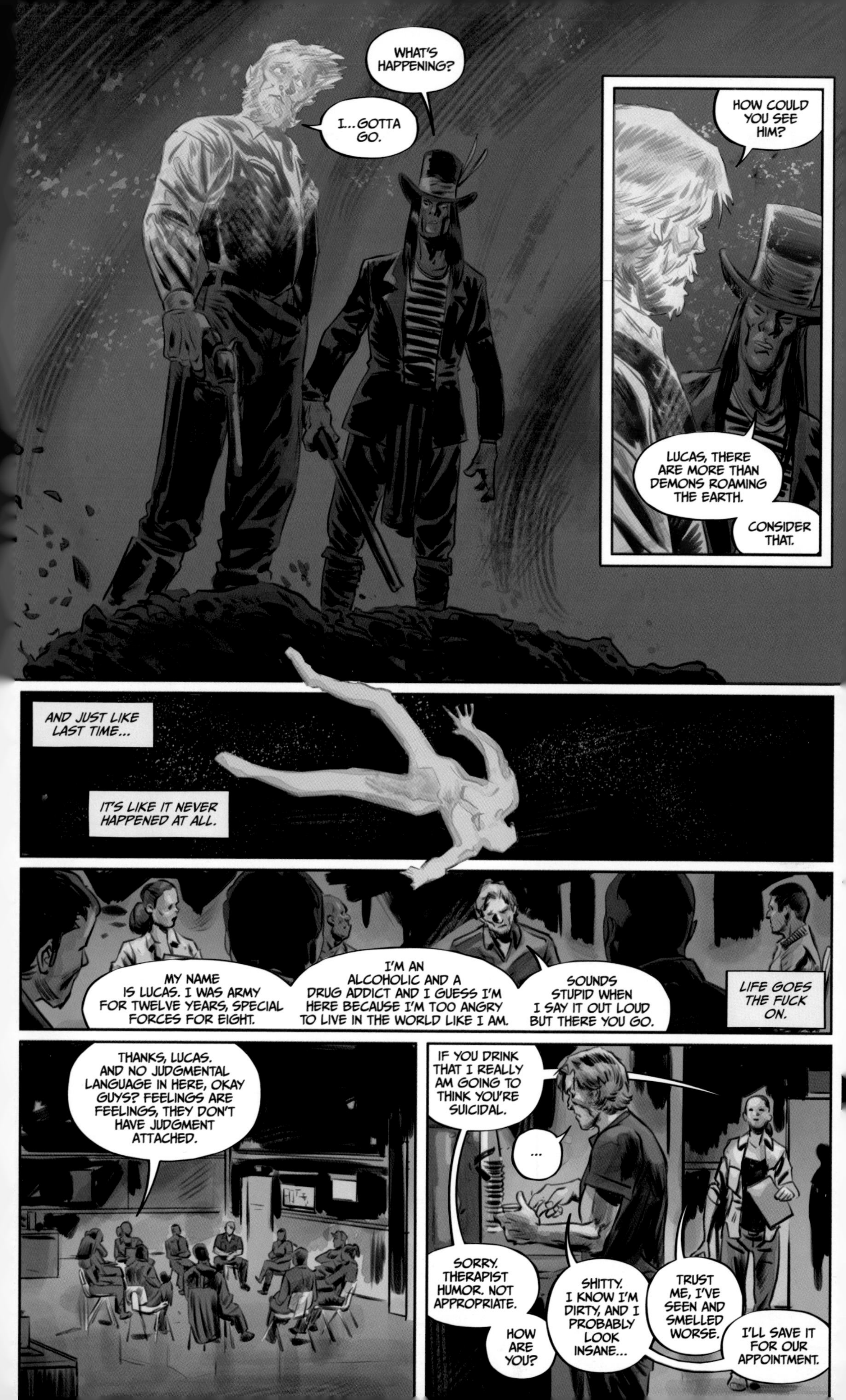
WHAT'S HAPPENING?
I...GOTTA GO.
HOW COULD YOU SEE HIM?
LUCAS, THERE ARE MORE THAN DEMONS ROAMING THE EARTH.
CONSIDER THAT.
AND JUST LIKE LAST TIME...
IT'S LIKE IT NEVER HAPPENED AT ALL.
MY NAME IS LUCAS. I WAS ARMY FOR TWELVE YEARS, SPECIAL FORCES FOR EIGHT.
I'M AN ALCOHOLIC AND A DRUG ADDICT AND I GUESS I'M HERE BECAUSE I'M TOO ANGRY TO LIVE IN THE WORLD LIKE I AM.
SOUNDS STUPID WHEN I SAY IT OUT LOUD BUT THERE YOU GO.
LIFE GOES THE FUCK ON.
THANKS, LUCAS. AND NO JUDGMENTAL LANGUAGE IN HERE, OKAY GUYS? FEELINGS ARE FEELINGS, THEY DON'T HAVE JUDGMENT ATTACHED.
IF YOU DRINK THAT I REALLY AM GOING TO THINK YOU'RE SUICIDAL.
...
SORRY. THERAPIST HUMOR. NOT APPROPRIATE.
HOW ARE YOU?
SHITTY. I KNOW I'M DIRTY, AND I PROBABLY LOOK INSANE...
TRUST ME, I'VE SEEN AND SMELLED WORSE.
I'LL SAVE IT FOR OUR APPOINTMENT.

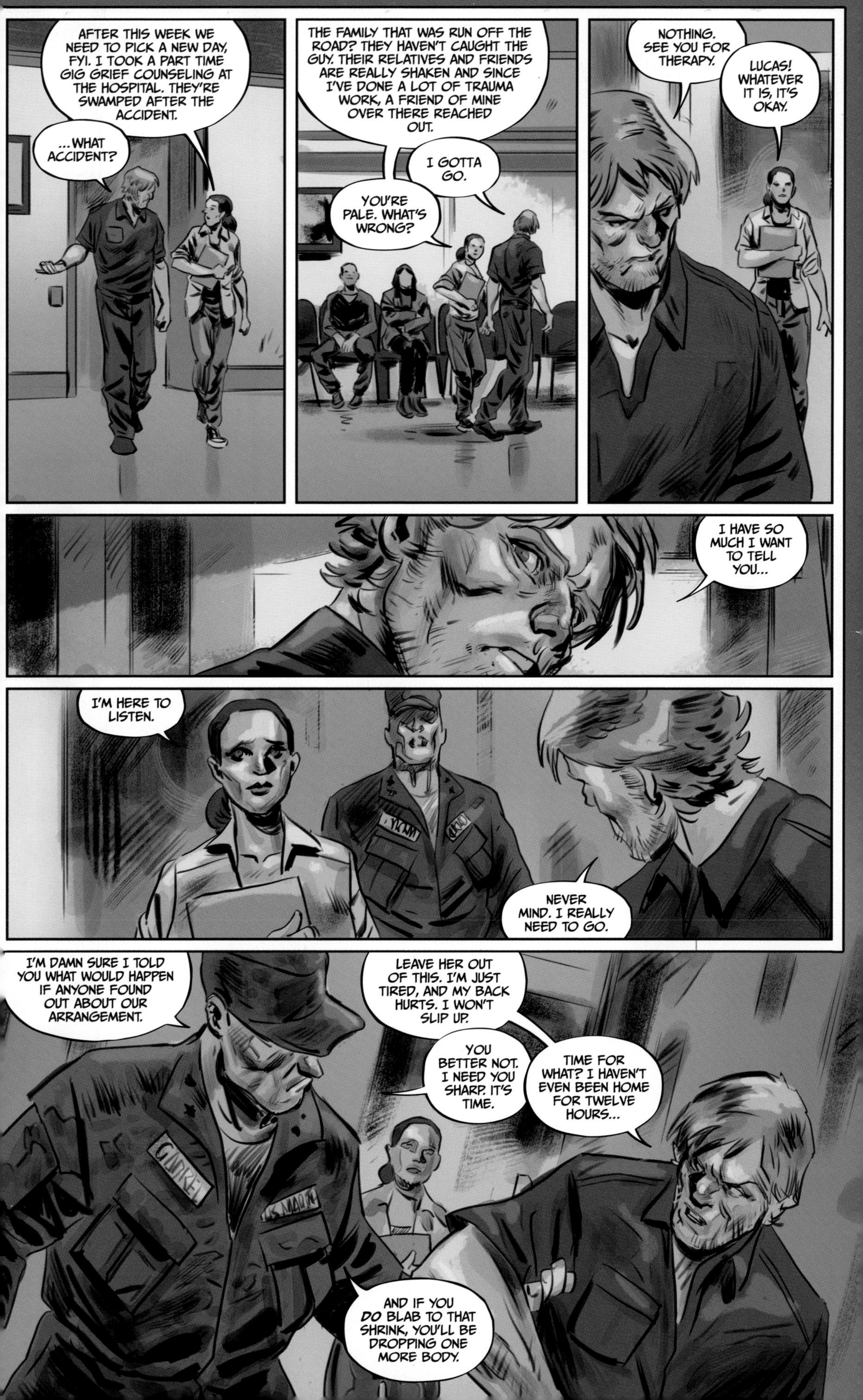
AFTER THIS WEEK WE NEED TO PICK A NEW DAY, FYI. I TOOK A PART TIME GIG GRIEF COUNSELING AT THE HOSPITAL. THEY'RE SWAMPED AFTER THE ACCIDENT.
...WHAT ACCIDENT?
THE FAMILY THAT WAS RUN OFF THE ROAD? THEY HAVEN'T CAUGHT THE GUY. THEIR RELATIVES AND FRIENDS ARE REALLY SHAKEN AND SINCE I'VE DONE A LOT OF TRAUMA WORK, A FRIEND OF MINE OVER THERE REACHED OUT.
I GOTTA GO.
YOU'RE PALE. WHAT'S WRONG?
NOTHING. SEE YOU FOR THERAPY.
LUCAS! WHATEVER IT IS, IT'S OKAY.
I HAVE SO MUCH I WANT TO TELL YOU...
I'M HERE TO LISTEN.
NEVER MIND. I REALLY NEED TO GO.
I'M DAMN SURE I TOLD YOU WHAT WOULD HAPPEN IF ANYONE FOUND OUT ABOUT OUR ARRANGEMENT.
LEAVE HER OUT OF THIS. I'M JUST TIRED, AND MY BACK HURTS. I WON'T SLIP UP.
YOU BETTER NOT. I NEED YOU SHARP. IT'S TIME.
TIME FOR WHAT? I HAVEN'T EVEN BEEN HOME FOR TWELVE HOURS...
AND IF YOU DO BLAB TO THAT SHRINK, YOU'LL BE DROPPING ONE MORE BODY.

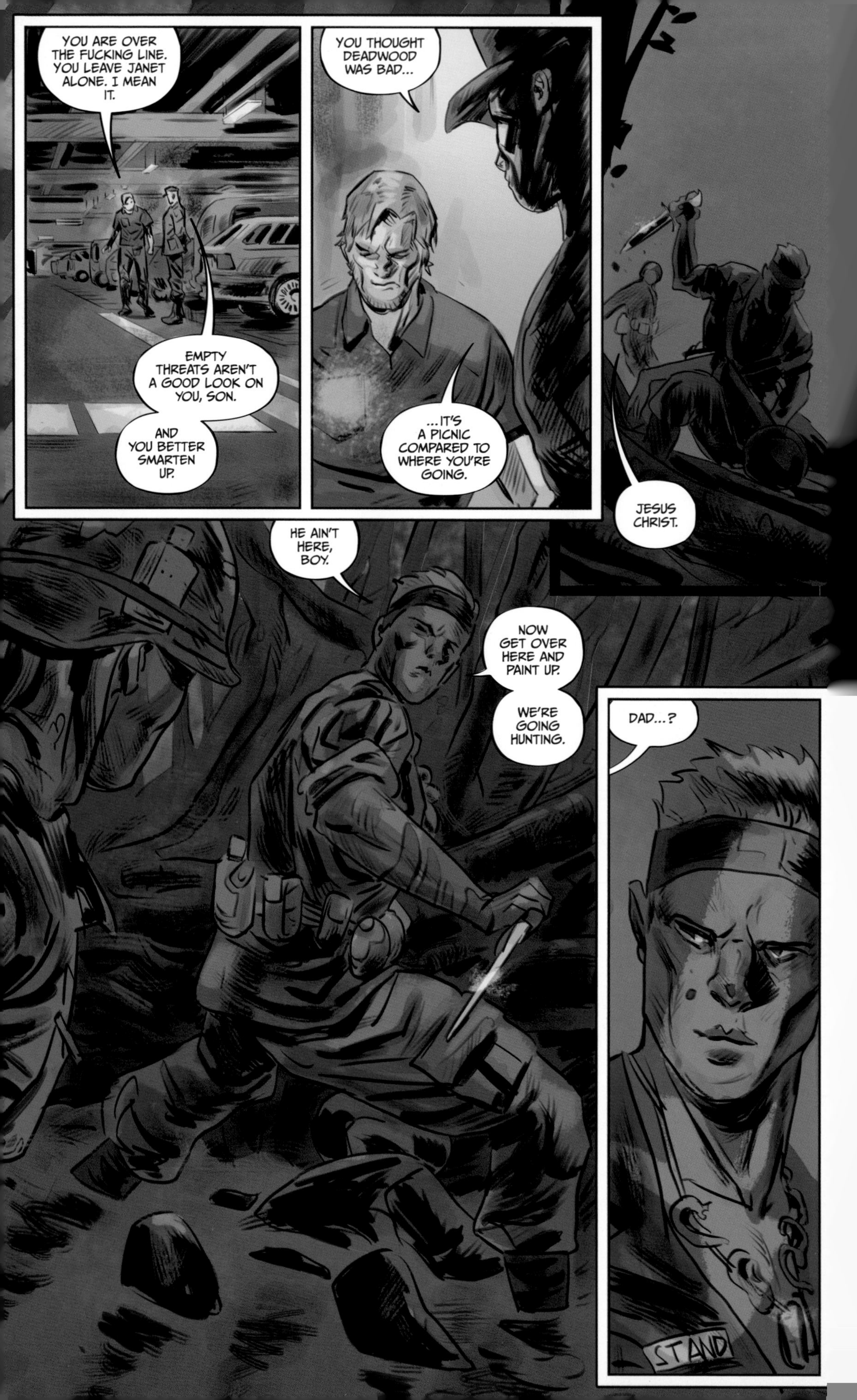
YOU ARE OVER THE FUCKING LINE. YOU LEAVE JANET ALONE. I MEAN IT.
EMPTY THREATS AREN'T A GOOD LOOK ON YOU, SON.
AND YOU BETTER SMARTEN UP.
YOU THOUGHT DEADWOOD WAS BAD...
...IT'S A PICNIC COMPARED TO WHERE YOU'RE GOING.
JESUS CHRIST.
HE AIN'T HERE, BOY.
NOW GET OVER HERE AND PAINT UP.
WE'RE GOING HUNTING.
DAD...?
STAND

UNITED STATES MARINE CORPS

CHAPTER
FOUR

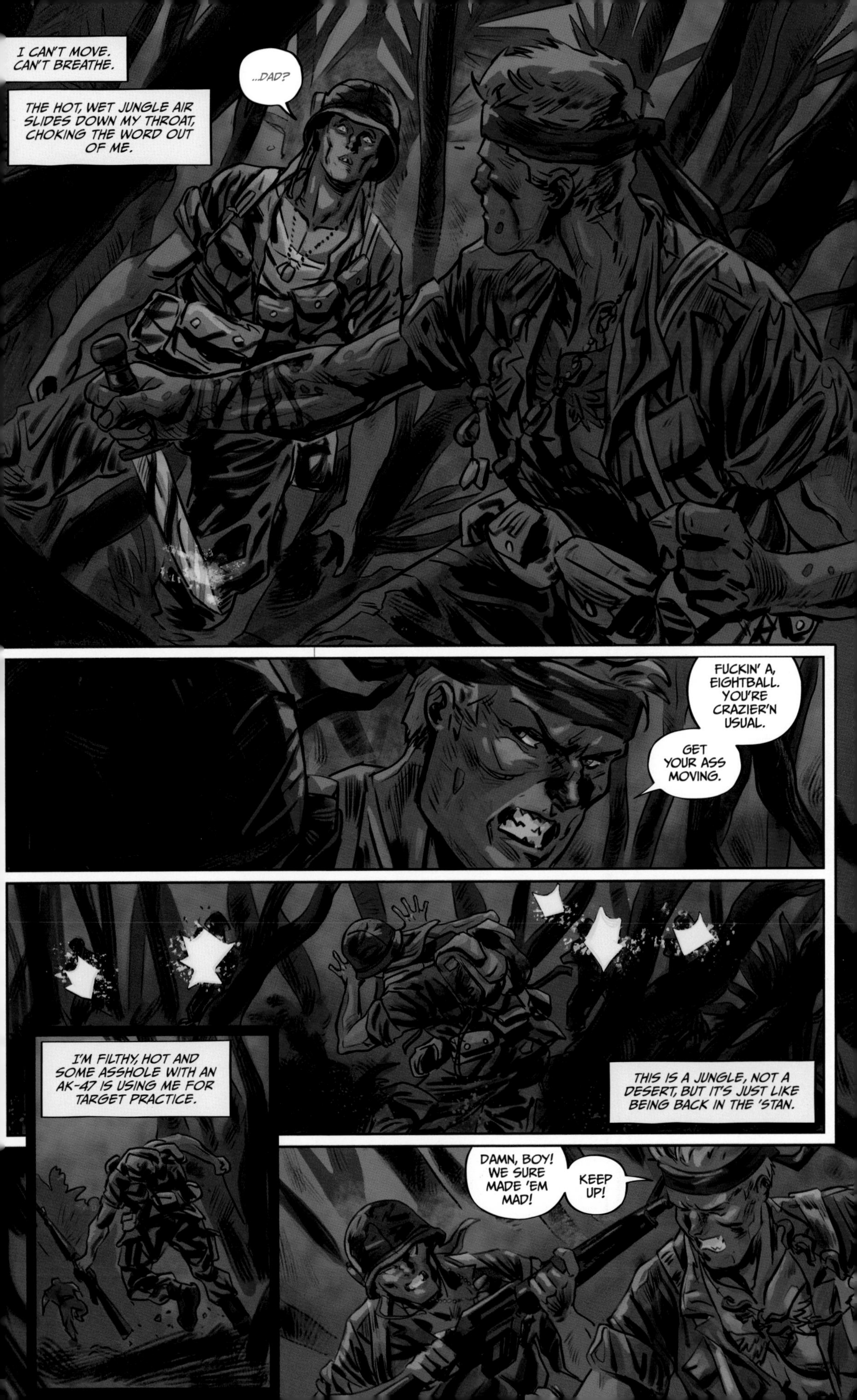
I CAN'T MOVE. CAN'T BREATHE.
...DAD?
THE HOT, WET JUNGLE AIR SLIDES DOWN MY THROAT, CHOKING THE WORD OUT OF ME.
FUCKIN' A, EIGHTBALL. YOU'RE CRAZIER'N USUAL.
GET YOUR ASS MOVING.
THIS IS A JUNGLE, NOT A DESERT, BUT IT'S JUST LIKE BEING BACK IN THE 'STAN.
I'M FILTHY, HOT AND SOME ASSHOLE WITH AN AK-47 IS USING ME FOR TARGET PRACTICE.
DAMN, BOY! WE SURE MADE 'EM MAD!
KEEP UP!

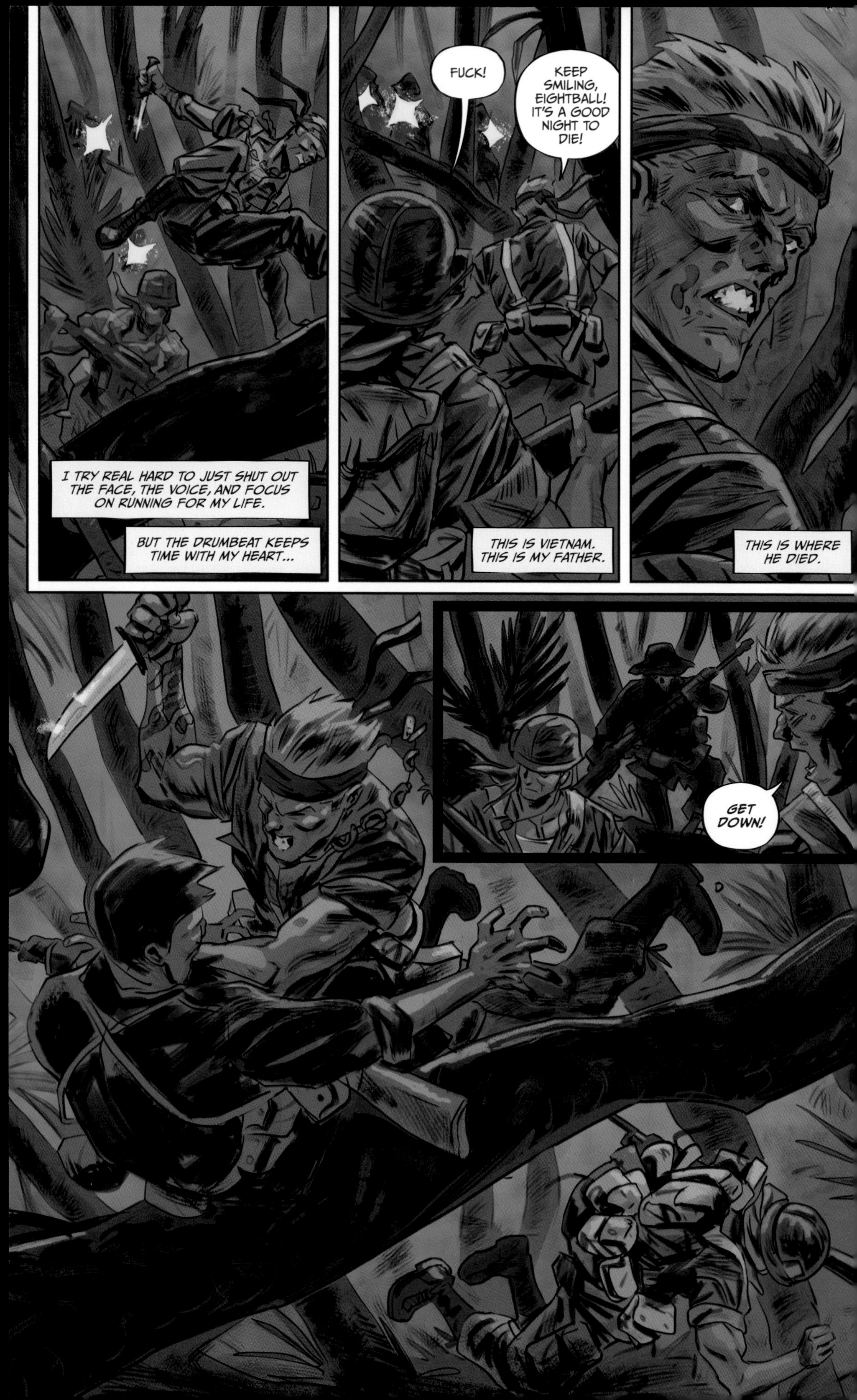
I TRY REAL HARD TO JUST SHUT OUT THE FACE, THE VOICE, AND FOCUS ON RUNNING FOR MY LIFE.
BUT THE DRUMBEAT KEEPS TIME WITH MY HEART...
FUCK!
KEEP SMILING, EIGHTBALL! IT'S A GOOD NIGHT TO DIE!
THIS IS VIETNAM. THIS IS MY FATHER.
THIS IS WHERE HE DIED.
GET DOWN!

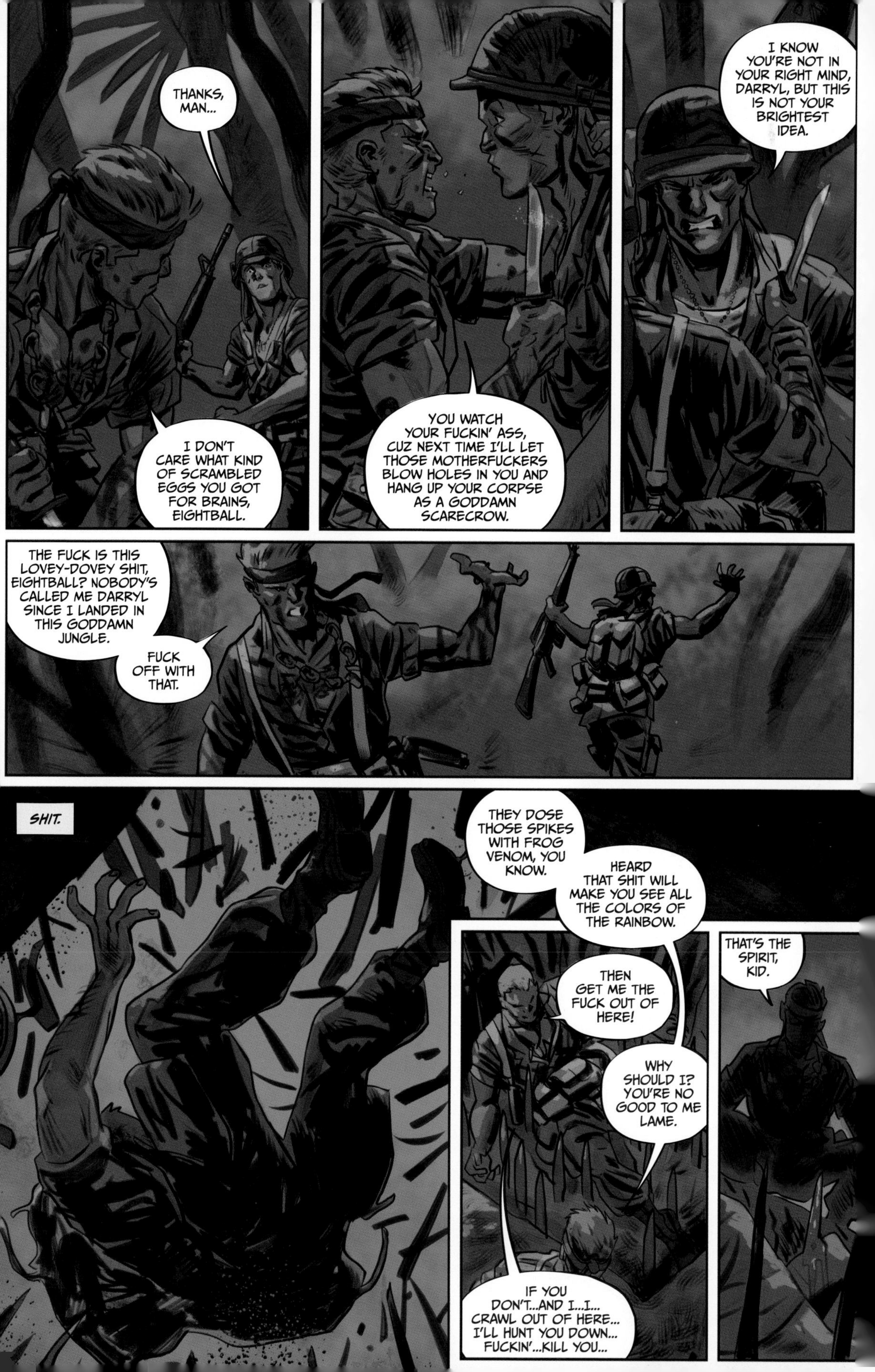
THANKS, MAN...
I DON'T CARE WHAT KIND OF SCRAMBLED EGGS YOU GOT FOR BRAINS, EIGHTBALL.
YOU WATCH YOUR FUCKIN' ASS, CUZ NEXT TIME I'LL LET THOSE MOTHERFUCKERS BLOW HOLES IN YOU AND HANG UP YOUR CORPSE AS A GODDAMN SCARECROW.
I KNOW YOU'RE NOT IN YOUR RIGHT MIND, DARRYL, BUT THIS IS NOT YOUR BRIGHTEST IDEA.
THE FUCK IS THIS LOVEY-DOVEY SHIT, EIGHTBALL? NOBODY'S CALLED ME DARRYL SINCE I LANDED IN THIS GODDAMN JUNGLE.
FUCK OFF WITH THAT.
SHIT.
THEY DOSE THOSE SPIKES WITH FROG VENOM, YOU KNOW.
HEARD THAT SHIT WILL MAKE YOU SEE ALL THE COLORS OF THE RAINBOW.
THEN GET ME THE FUCK OUT OF HERE!
WHY SHOULD I? YOU'RE NO GOOD TO ME LAME.
IF YOU DON'T...AND I...I... CRAWL OUT OF HERE... I'LL HUNT YOU DOWN... FUCKIN'...KILL YOU...
THAT'S THE SPIRIT, KID.

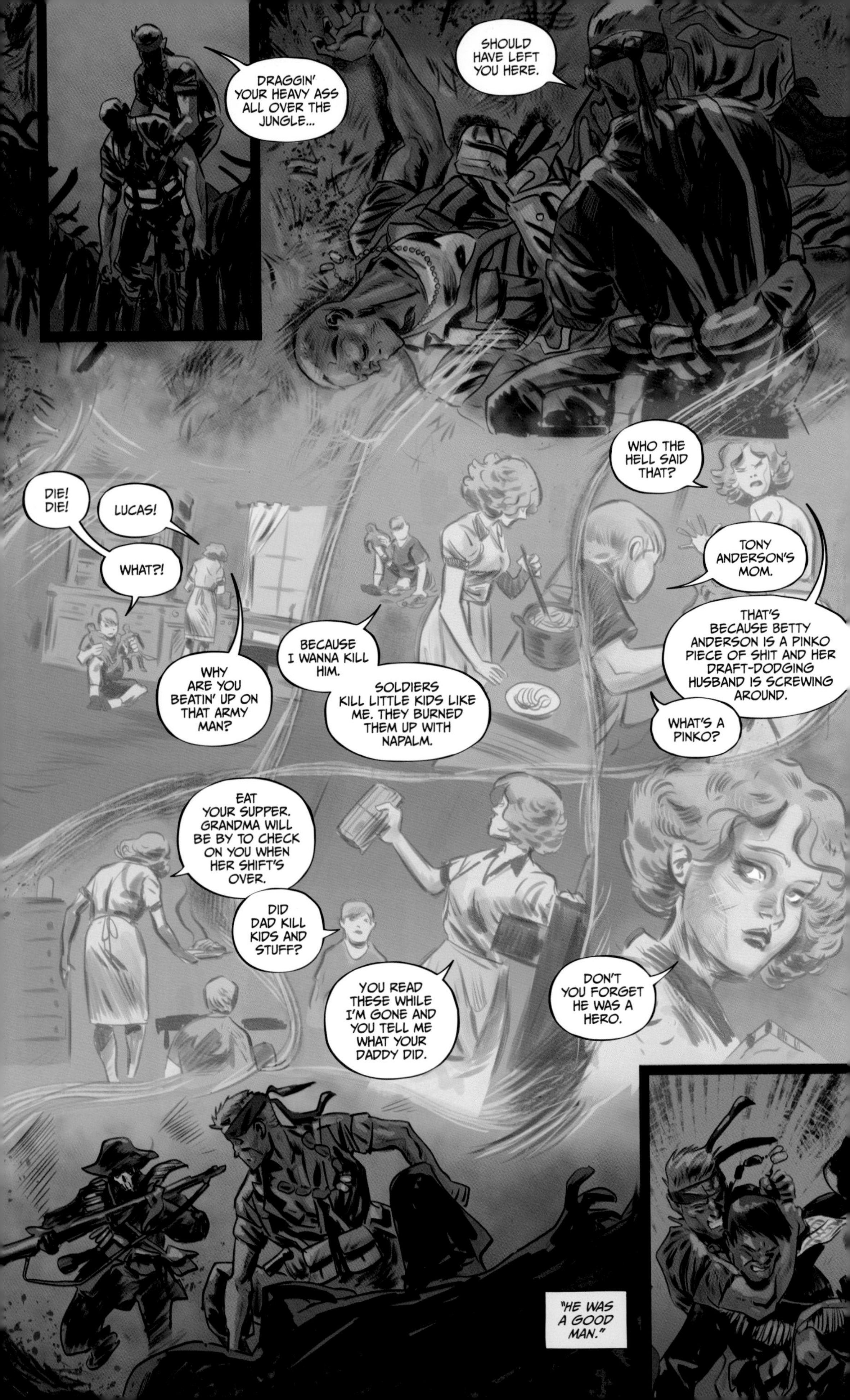
DRAGGIN' YOUR HEAVY ASS ALL OVER THE JUNGLE...
SHOULD HAVE LEFT YOU HERE.
DIE! DIE!
LUCAS!
WHAT?!
WHY ARE YOU BEATIN' UP ON THAT ARMY MAN?
BECAUSE I WANNA KILL HIM.
SOLDIERS KILL LITTLE KIDS LIKE ME. THEY BURNED THEM UP WITH NAPALM.
WHO THE HELL SAID THAT?
TONY ANDERSON'S MOM.
THAT'S BECAUSE BETTY ANDERSON IS A PINKO PIECE OF SHIT AND HER DRAFT-DODGING HUSBAND IS SCREWING AROUND.
WHAT'S A PINKO?
EAT YOUR SUPPER. GRANDMA WILL BE BY TO CHECK ON YOU WHEN HER SHIFT'S OVER.
DID DAD KILL KIDS AND STUFF?
YOU READ THESE WHILE I'M GONE AND YOU TELL ME WHAT YOUR DADDY DID.
DON'T YOU FORGET HE WAS A HERO.
"HE WAS A GOOD MAN."

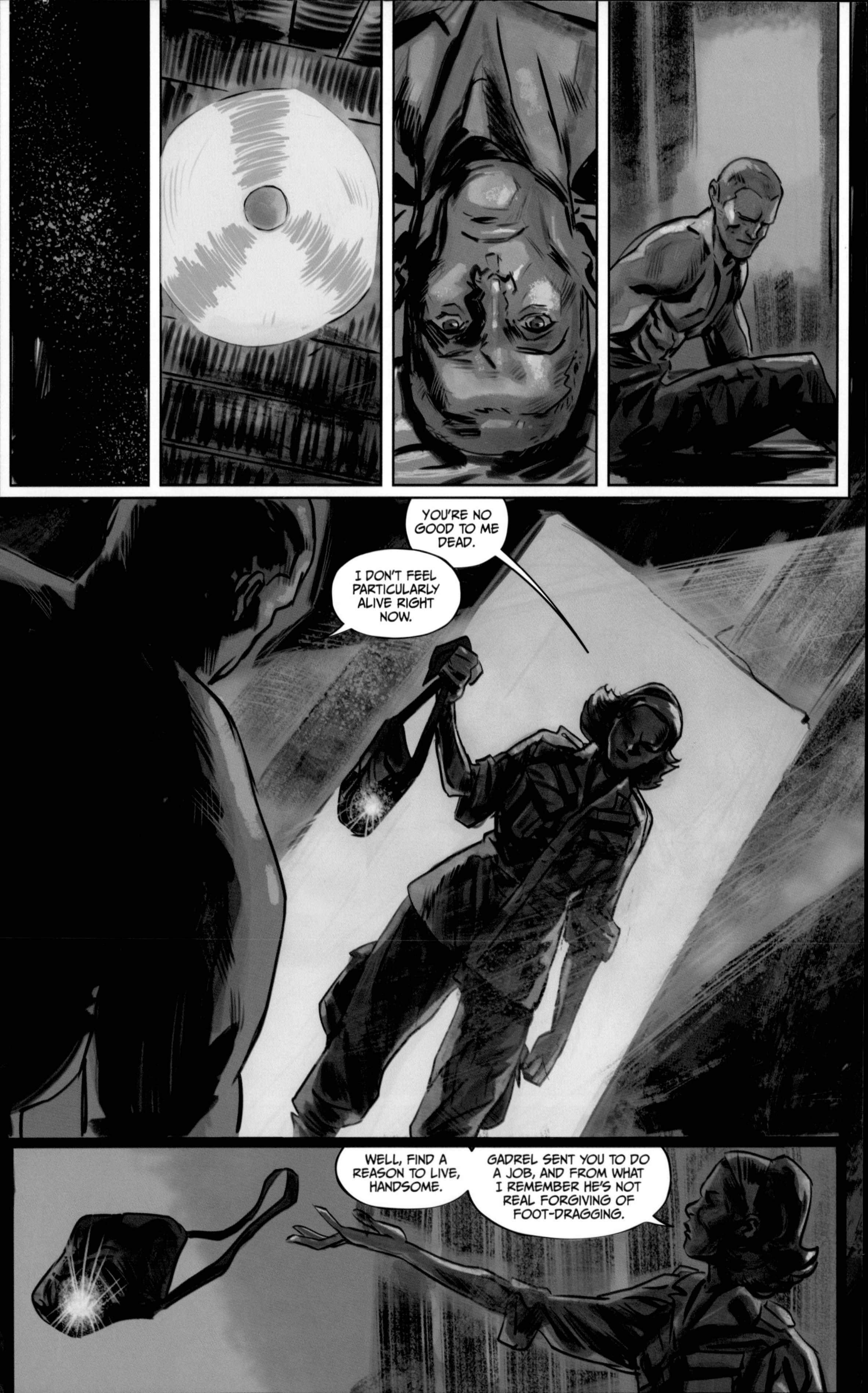
YOU'RE NO GOOD TO ME DEAD.
I DON'T FEEL PARTICULARLY ALIVE RIGHT NOW.
WELL, FIND A REASON TO LIVE, HANDSOME.
GADREL SENT YOU TO DO A JOB, AND FROM WHAT I REMEMBER HE'S NOT REAL FORGIVING OF FOOT-DRAGGING.

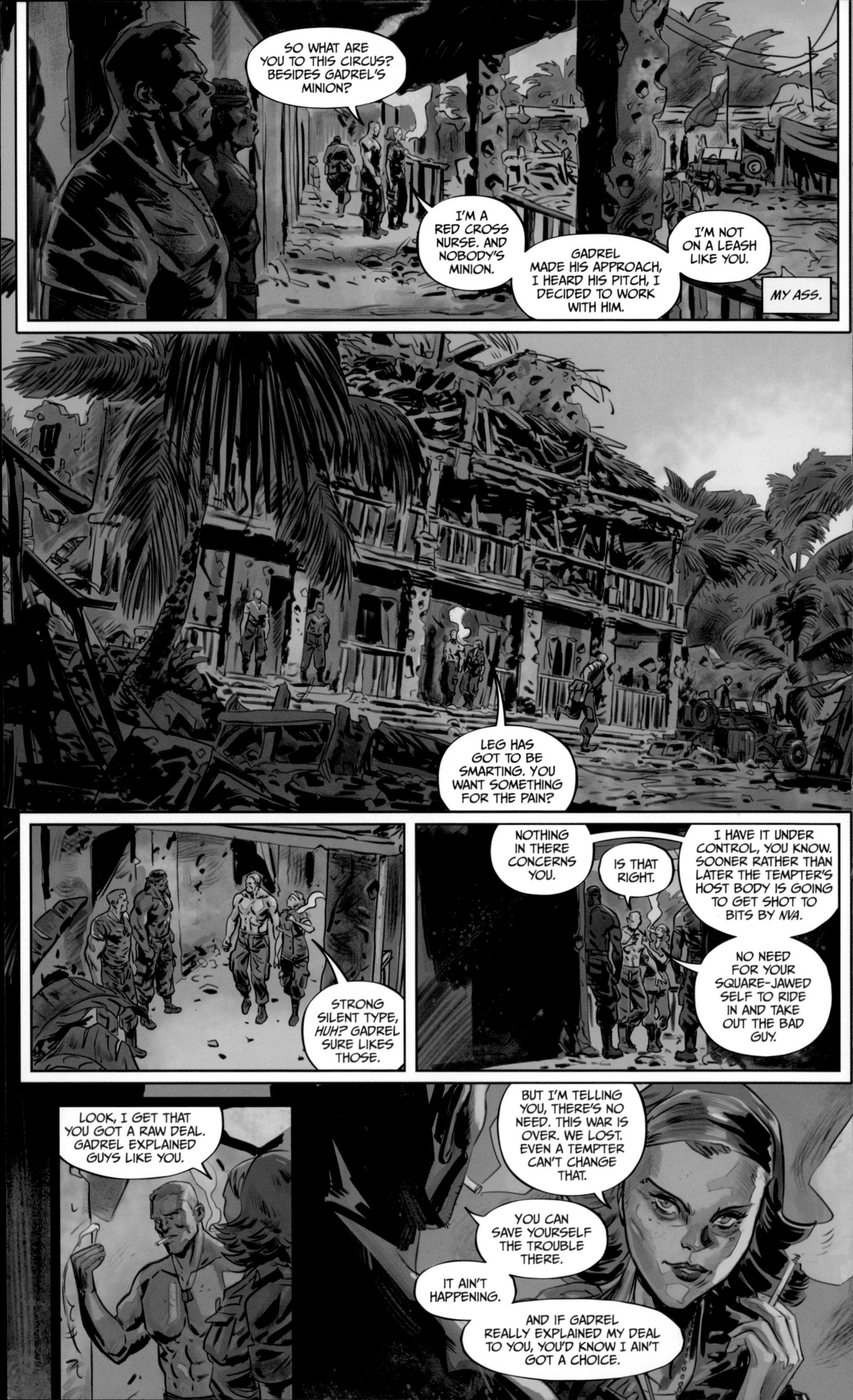
SO WHAT ARE YOU TO THIS CIRCUS? BESIDES GADREL'S MINION?
I'M A RED CROSS NURSE. AND NOBODY'S MINION.
GADREL MADE HIS APPROACH, I HEARD HIS PITCH, I DECIDED TO WORK WITH HIM.
I'M NOT ON A LEASH LIKE YOU.
MY ASS.
LEG HAS GOT TO BE SMARTING. YOU WANT SOMETHING FOR THE PAIN?
STRONG SILENT TYPE, HUH? GADREL SURE LIKES THOSE.
NOTHING IN THERE CONCERNS YOU.
IS THAT RIGHT.
I HAVE IT UNDER CONTROL, YOU KNOW. SOONER RATHER THAN LATER THE TEMPTER'S HOST BODY IS GOING TO GET SHOT TO BITS BY NVA.
NO NEED FOR YOUR SQUARE-JAWED SELF TO RIDE IN AND TAKE OUT THE BAD GUY.
LOOK, I GET THAT YOU GOT A RAW DEAL. GADREL EXPLAINED GUYS LIKE YOU.
BUT I'M TELLING YOU, THERE'S NO NEED. THIS WAR IS OVER. WE LOST. EVEN A TEMPTER CAN'T CHANGE THAT.
YOU CAN SAVE YOURSELF THE TROUBLE THERE.
IT AIN'T HAPPENING.
AND IF GADREL REALLY EXPLAINED MY DEAL TO YOU, YOU'D KNOW I AIN'T GOT A CHOICE.

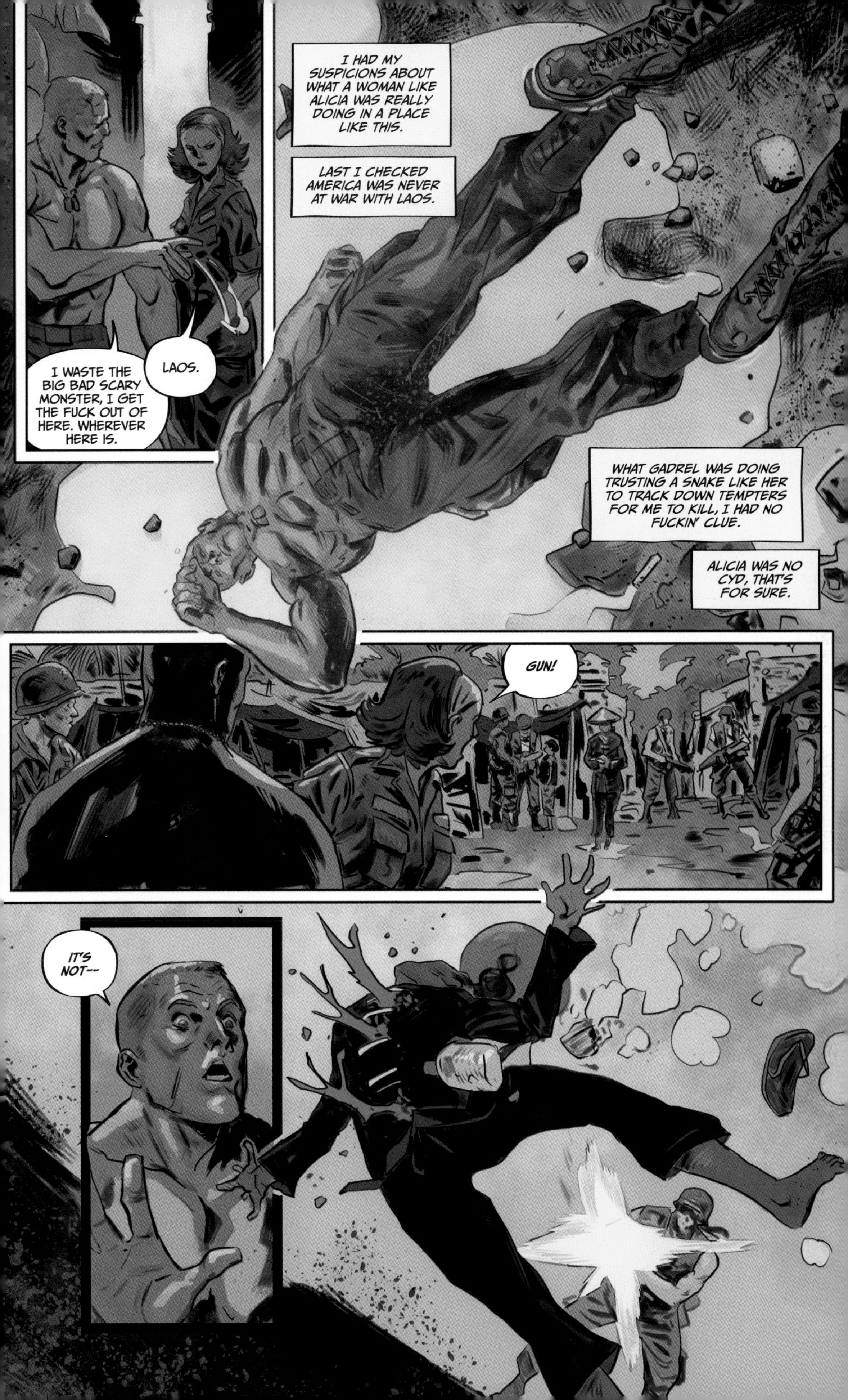
I HAD MY SUSPICIONS ABOUT WHAT A WOMAN LIKE ALICIA WAS REALLY DOING IN A PLACE LIKE THIS.
LAST I CHECKED AMERICA WAS NEVER AT WAR WITH LAOS.
I WASTE THE BIG BAD SCARY MONSTER, I GET THE FUCK OUT OF HERE. WHEREVER HERE IS.
LAOS.
WHAT GADREL WAS DOING TRUSTING A SNAKE LIKE HER TO TRACK DOWN TEMPTERS FOR ME TO KILL, I HAD NO FUCKIN' CLUE.
ALICIA WAS NO CYD, THAT'S FOR SURE.
GUN!
IT'S NOT--

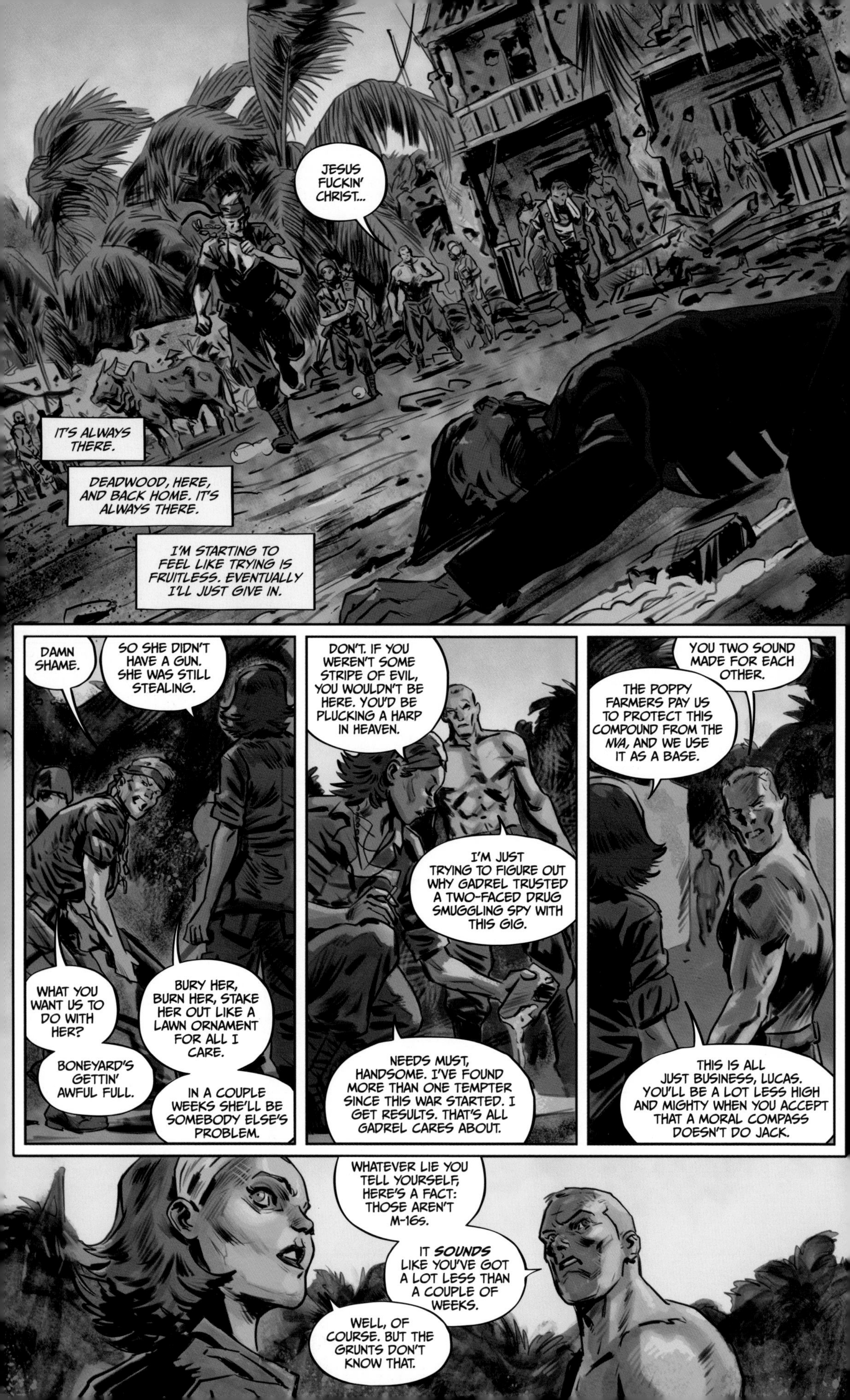
JESUS FUCKIN' CHRIST...
IT'S ALWAYS THERE.
DEADWOOD, HERE, AND BACK HOME. IT'S ALWAYS THERE.
I'M STARTING TO FEEL LIKE TRYING IS FRUITLESS. EVENTUALLY I'LL JUST GIVE IN.
DAMN SHAME.
SO SHE DIDN'T HAVE A GUN. SHE WAS STILL STEALING.
WHAT YOU WANT US TO DO WITH HER?
BONEYARD'S GETTIN' AWFUL FULL.
BURY HER, BURN HER, STAKE HER OUT LIKE A LAWN ORNAMENT FOR ALL I CARE.
IN A COUPLE WEEKS SHE'LL BE SOMEBODY ELSE'S PROBLEM.
DON'T. IF YOU WEREN'T SOME STRIPE OF EVIL, YOU WOULDN'T BE HERE. YOU'D BE PLUCKING A HARP IN HEAVEN.
I'M JUST TRYING TO FIGURE OUT WHY GADREL TRUSTED A TWO-FACED DRUG SMUGGLING SPY WITH THIS GIG.
NEEDS MUST, HANDSOME. I'VE FOUND MORE THAN ONE TEMPTER SINCE THIS WAR STARTED. I GET RESULTS. THAT'S ALL GADREL CARES ABOUT.
YOU TWO SOUND MADE FOR EACH OTHER.
THE POPPY FARMERS PAY US TO PROTECT THIS COMPOUND FROM THE NVA, AND WE USE IT AS A BASE.
THIS IS ALL JUST BUSINESS, LUCAS. YOU'LL BE A LOT LESS HIGH AND MIGHTY WHEN YOU ACCEPT THAT A MORAL COMPASS DOESN'T DO JACK.
WHATEVER LIE YOU TELL YOURSELF, HERE'S A FACT: THOSE AREN'T M-16S.
IT SOUNDS LIKE YOU'VE GOT A LOT LESS THAN A COUPLE OF WEEKS.
WELL, OF COURSE. BUT THE GRUNTS DON'T KNOW THAT.

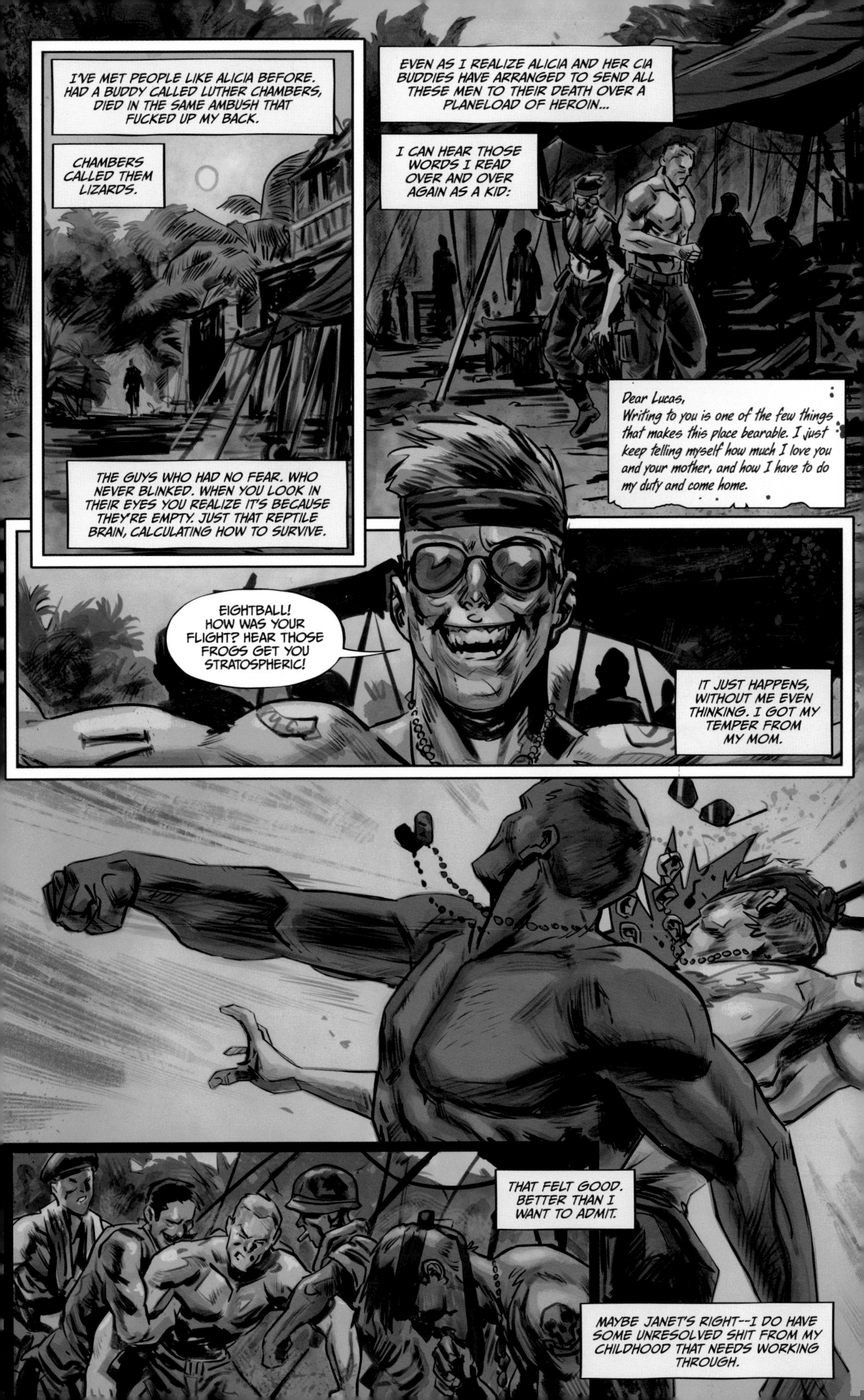
I'VE MET PEOPLE LIKE ALICIA BEFORE. HAD A BUDDY CALLED LUTHER CHAMBERS, DIED IN THE SAME AMBUSH THAT FUCKED UP MY BACK.
CHAMBERS CALLED THEM LIZARDS.
THE GUYS WHO HAD NO FEAR. WHO NEVER BLINKED. WHEN YOU LOOK IN THEIR EYES YOU REALIZE IT'S BECAUSE THEY'RE EMPTY. JUST THAT REPTILE BRAIN, CALCULATING HOW TO SURVIVE.
EVEN AS I REALIZE ALICIA AND HER CIA BUDDIES HAVE ARRANGED TO SEND ALL THESE MEN TO THEIR DEATH OVER A PLANELOAD OF HEROIN...
I CAN HEAR THOSE WORDS I READ OVER AND OVER AGAIN AS A KID:
Dear Lucas, Writing to you is one of the few things that makes this place bearable. I just keep telling myself how much I love you and your mother, and how I have to do my duty and come home.
EIGHTBALL! HOW WAS YOUR FLIGHT? HEAR THOSE FROGS GET YOU STRATOSPHERIC!
IT JUST HAPPENS, WITHOUT ME EVEN THINKING. I GOT MY TEMPER FROM MY MOM.
THAT FELT GOOD. BETTER THAN I WANT TO ADMIT.
MAYBE JANET'S RIGHT--I DO HAVE SOME UNRESOLVED SHIT FROM MY CHILDHOOD THAT NEEDS WORKING THROUGH.

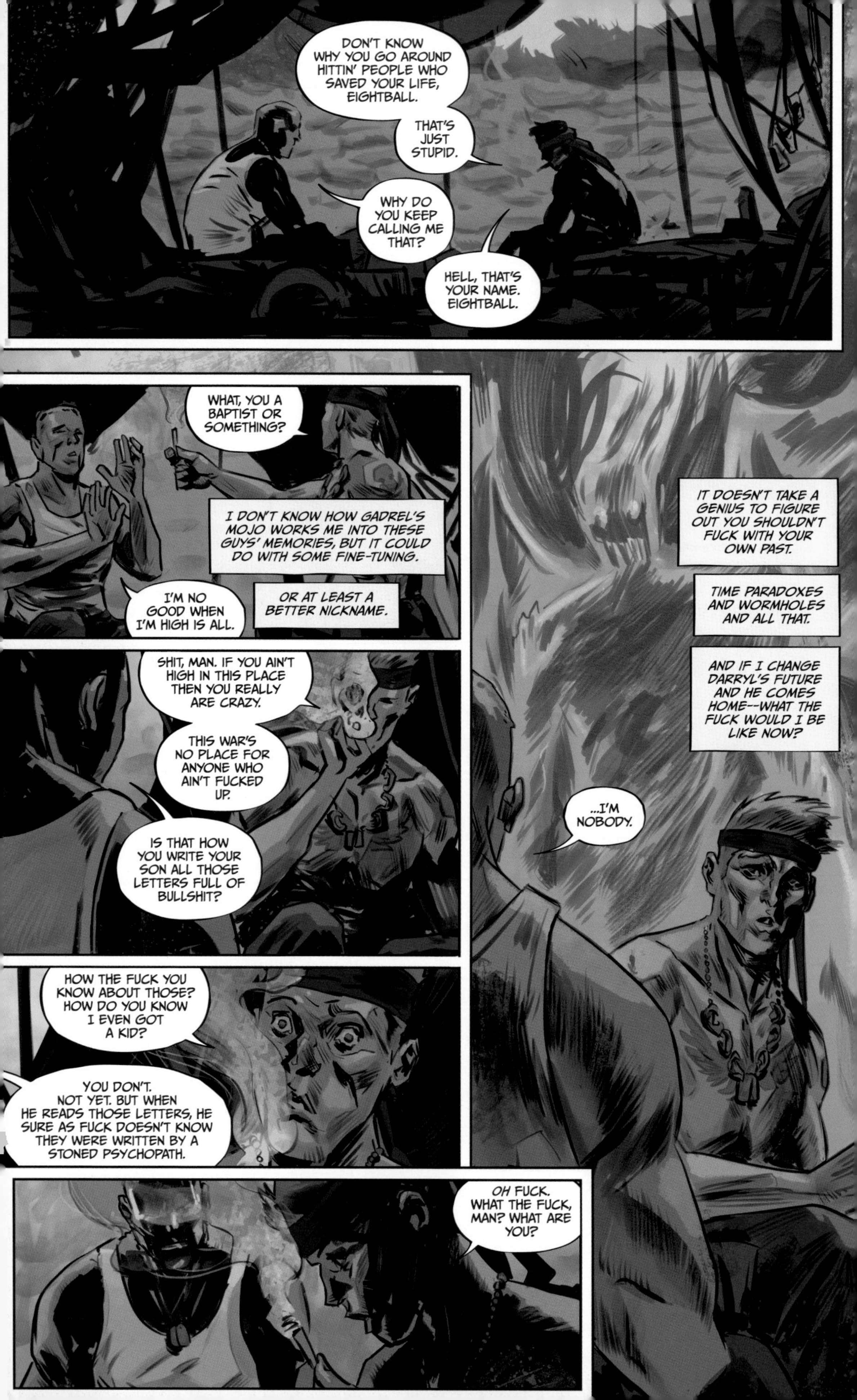
DON'T KNOW WHY YOU GO AROUND HITTIN' PEOPLE WHO SAVED YOUR LIFE, EIGHTBALL.
THAT'S JUST STUPID.
WHY DO YOU KEEP CALLING ME THAT?
HELL, THAT'S YOUR NAME. EIGHTBALL.
WHAT, YOU A BAPTIST OR SOMETHING?
I DON'T KNOW HOW GADREL'S MOJO WORKS ME INTO THESE GUYS' MEMORIES, BUT IT COULD DO WITH SOME FINE-TUNING.
I'M NO GOOD WHEN I'M HIGH IS ALL.
OR AT LEAST A BETTER NICKNAME.
SHIT, MAN. IF YOU AIN'T HIGH IN THIS PLACE THEN YOU REALLY ARE CRAZY.
THIS WAR'S NO PLACE FOR ANYONE WHO AIN'T FUCKED UP.
IS THAT HOW YOU WRITE YOUR SON ALL THOSE LETTERS FULL OF BULLSHIT?
HOW THE FUCK YOU KNOW ABOUT THOSE? HOW DO YOU KNOW I EVEN GOT A KID?
YOU DON'T. NOT YET. BUT WHEN HE READS THOSE LETTERS, HE SURE AS FUCK DOESN'T KNOW THEY WERE WRITTEN BY A STONED PSYCHOPATH.
IT DOESN'T TAKE A GENIUS TO FIGURE OUT YOU SHOULDN'T FUCK WITH YOUR OWN PAST.
TIME PARADOXES AND WORMHOLES AND ALL THAT.
AND IF I CHANGE DARRYL'S FUTURE AND HE COMES HOME--WHAT THE FUCK WOULD I BE LIKE NOW?
...I'M NOBODY.
OH FUCK. WHAT THE FUCK, MAN? WHAT ARE YOU?

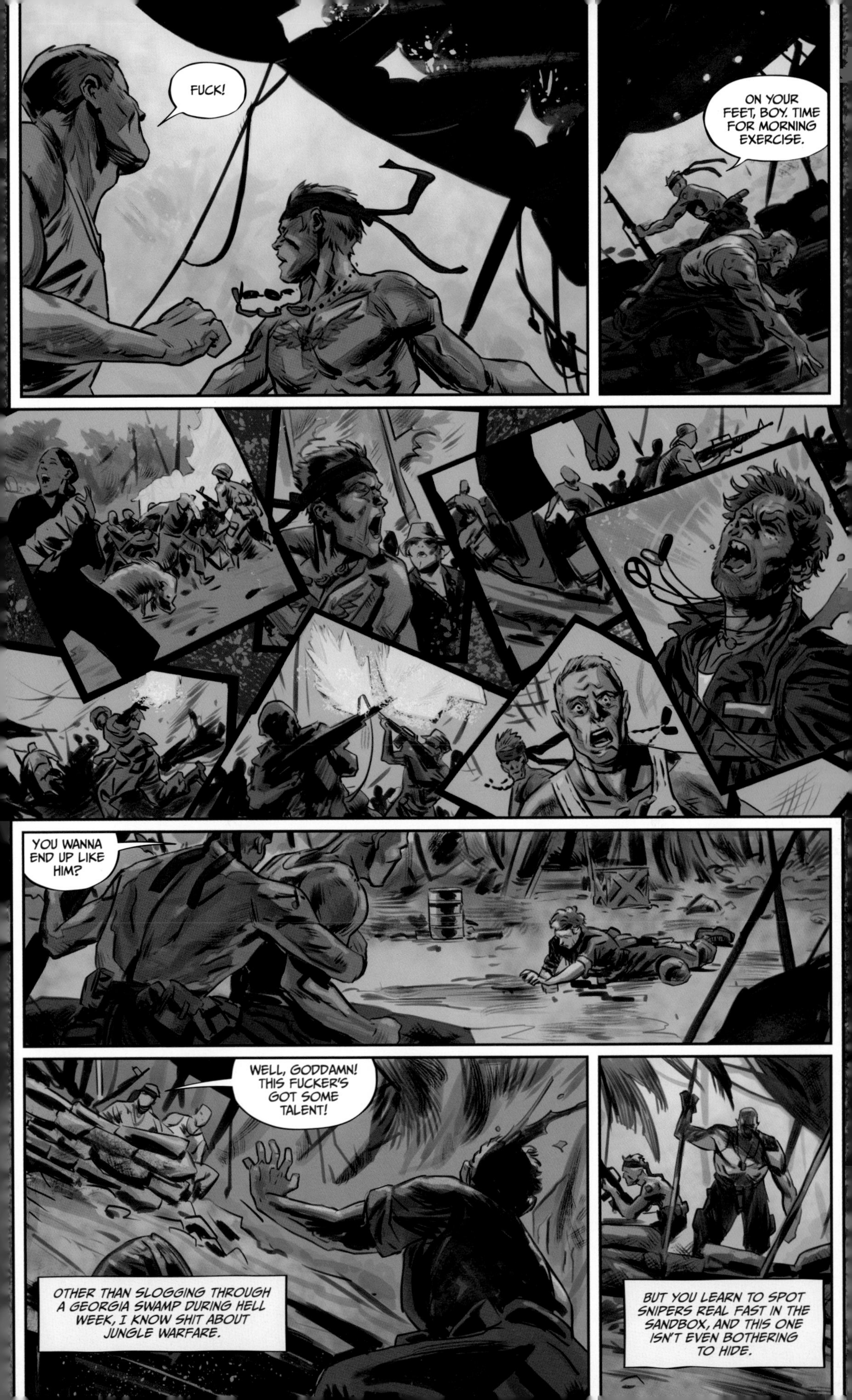
FUCK!
ON YOUR FEET, BOY. TIME FOR MORNING EXERCISE.
YOU WANNA END UP LIKE HIM?
WELL, GODDAMN! THIS FUCKER'S GOT SOME TALENT!
OTHER THAN SLOGGING THROUGH A GEORGIA SWAMP DURING HELL WEEK, I KNOW SHIT ABOUT JUNGLE WARFARE.
BUT YOU LEARN TO SPOT SNIPERS REAL FAST IN THE SANDBOX, AND THIS ONE ISN'T EVEN BOTHERING TO HIDE.

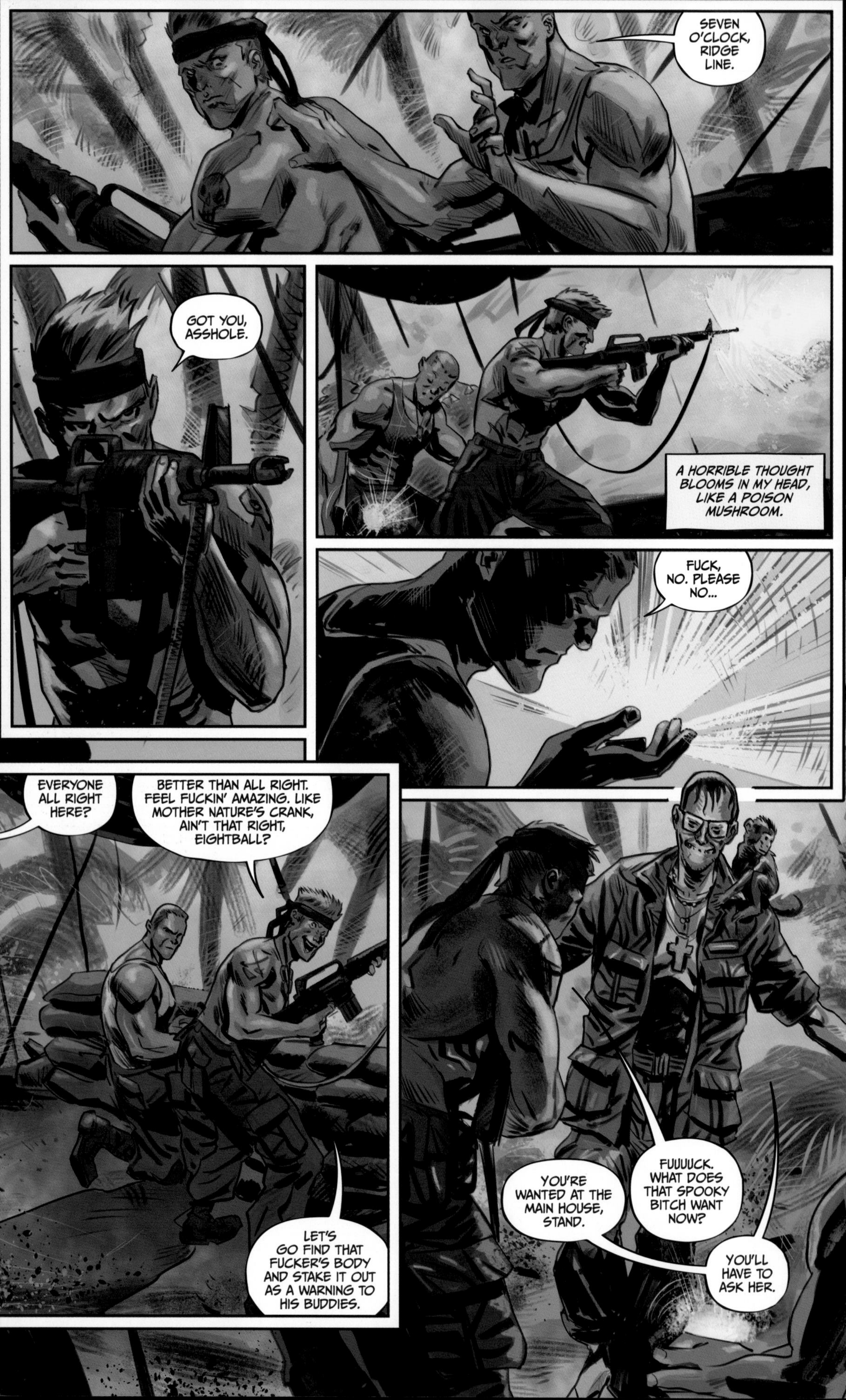
SEVEN O'CLOCK, RIDGE LINE.
GOT YOU, ASSHOLE.
A HORRIBLE THOUGHT BLOOMS IN MY HEAD, LIKE A POISON MUSHROOM.
FUCK, NO. PLEASE NO...
EVERYONE ALL RIGHT HERE?
BETTER THAN ALL RIGHT. FEEL FUCKIN' AMAZING. LIKE MOTHER NATURE'S CRANK, AIN'T THAT RIGHT, EIGHTBALL?
LET'S GO FIND THAT FUCKER'S BODY AND STAKE IT OUT AS A WARNING TO HIS BUDDIES.
YOU'RE WANTED AT THE MAIN HOUSE, STAND.
FUUUUCK. WHAT DOES THAT SPOOKY BITCH WANT NOW?
YOU'LL HAVE TO ASK HER.

ARE YOU ALL RIGHT, MY SON?

BARKING UP THE WRONG TREE, FATHER. TRUST ME.

THEN PERHAPS SOME HELP WITH THE DEAD.

YOU PEOPLE DON'T BUG OUT OF HERE, YOU'RE ALL GONNA JOIN THAT GUY. SCOUT SNIPERS MEAN THE ENEMY'S A DAY OUT.

IF YOU'RE LUCKY.

NO. THEY WON'T BE HERE FOR WEEKS.

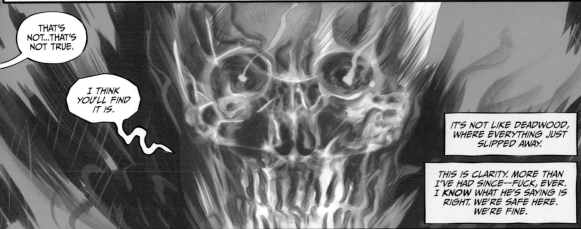

THAT'S NOT...THAT'S NOT TRUE.

I THINK YOU'LL FIND IT IS.

IT'S NOT LIKE DEADWOOD, WHERE EVERYTHING JUST SLIPPED AWAY.

THIS IS CLARITY. MORE THAN I'VE HAD SINCE--FUCK, EVER. I *KNOW* WHAT HE'S SAYING IS RIGHT. WE'RE SAFE HERE. WE'RE FINE.

THERE'S YOUR MISTAKE, JERKOFF-- NOTHING IN MY LIFE HAS EVER BEEN FINE.

NO, WAIT--

THIS IS YOUR OWN FAULT.

SHOULD HAVE JUST LET ME DO MY JOB, LUCAS.

HERO'S NOT A GOOD LOOK ON YOU.

WHATEVER ALICIA DOSED ME WITH SHARPENS MY MEMORY LIKE A KNIFE. THIS IS LIKE YESTERDAY.

THE ITCHY CARPET, THE STINK OF MY GRANDMA'S MENTHOLS, THE WORDS I'D READ SO MANY TIMES IN THE FIVE YEARS SINCE MOM HANDED THEM OVER I HAD THEM ALL MEMORIZED.

WHEN DID MOM SAY SHE'D BE BACK?

HELL IF I KNOW.

PROBABLY WHEN THAT HORSE-FACED MORON SHE'S DATING RUNS OUTTA MONEY AT THE INDIAN CASINO.

HORSE-FACE WOULD BE RON. RON WASN'T SO BAD. HE NEVER GOT DRUNK AND THREW ALL MY SHIT OUT IN THE YARD, OR BROKE TWO OF MY RIBS BECAUSE HE DIDN'T LIKE THE WAY I WAS EATING CEREAL.

WHAT WAS MY DAD LIKE?

A SHINING EXAMPLE OF HUMANITY.

COME ON. FOR REAL. WAS HE AN OKAY GUY?

WHAT'S WITH YOU ALL OF A SUDDEN? PUBERTY MAKIN' YOU EMOTIONAL?

GO GET YOURSELF A GIRLFRIEND OR A BOYFRIEND OR WHATEVER TICKLES YOUR PICKLE. DON'T WHINE ABOUT THE PAST.

GRANDMA. GROSS.

THEN PUT A CORK IN IT. I'M TRYIN' TO WATCH DYNASTY.

SHE WASN'T A MEAN WOMAN, JUST TIRED. LIKE MOST EVERYONE IN OUR SHITHOLE FACTORY TOWN.

BUT ALL I HAD TO DO WAS READ THOSE WORDS, AND IT WAS OKAY. ALL OF IT.

Dear Lucas,
I know that as you get older, you'll have questions. I won't be there to answer them, but I want you to think of me as you find your way in the world as a man.

I REPEATED THOSE FUCKING SENTENCES A HUNDRED THOUSAND TIMES.

Dear Lucas, I know that as you get older, you'll have questions. I won't be there to answer them. I want you to think of me in the world as a man.

THROUGH HIGH SCHOOL, THROUGH BASIC, THROUGH HELL WEEK, EVERY NIGHT I FELL ASLEEP NOT KNOWING IF A TALIBAN ROCKET WAS GOING TO LIGHT ME UP BEFORE MORNING.

I'M SORRY ABOUT THAT.

ARE YOU?

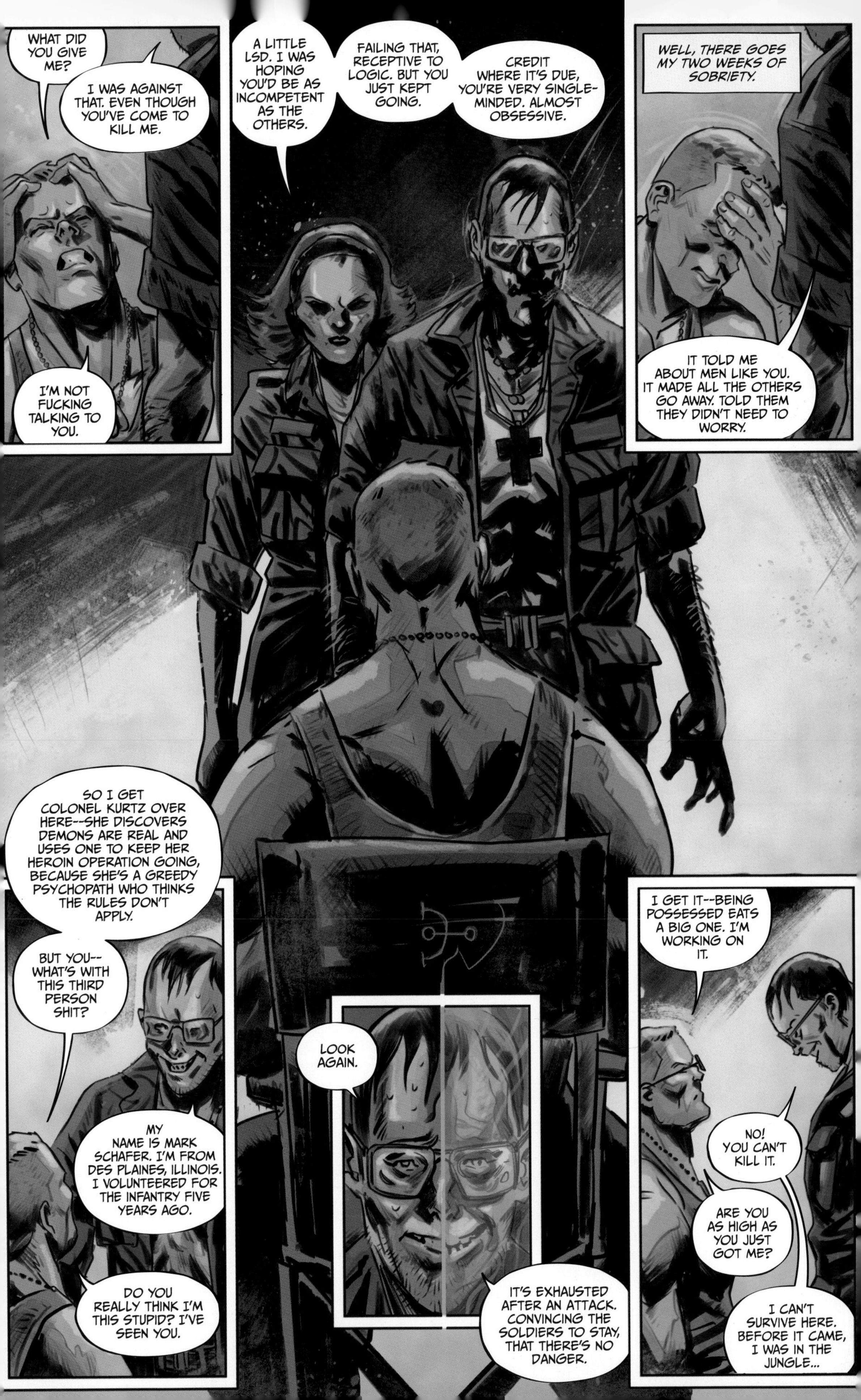
WHAT DID YOU GIVE ME?
I WAS AGAINST THAT. EVEN THOUGH YOU'VE COME TO KILL ME.
I'M NOT FUCKING TALKING TO YOU.
A LITTLE LSD. I WAS HOPING YOU'D BE AS INCOMPETENT AS THE OTHERS.
FAILING THAT, RECEPTIVE TO LOGIC. BUT YOU JUST KEPT GOING.
CREDIT WHERE IT'S DUE, YOU'RE VERY SINGLE-MINDED. ALMOST OBSESSIVE.
WELL, THERE GOES MY TWO WEEKS OF SOBRIETY.
IT TOLD ME ABOUT MEN LIKE YOU. IT MADE ALL THE OTHERS GO AWAY. TOLD THEM THEY DIDN'T NEED TO WORRY.
SO I GET COLONEL KURTZ OVER HERE--SHE DISCOVERS DEMONS ARE REAL AND USES ONE TO KEEP HER HEROIN OPERATION GOING, BECAUSE SHE'S A GREEDY PSYCHOPATH WHO THINKS THE RULES DON'T APPLY.
BUT YOU--WHAT'S WITH THIS THIRD PERSON SHIT?
MY NAME IS MARK SCHAFER. I'M FROM DES PLAINES, ILLINOIS. I VOLUNTEERED FOR THE INFANTRY FIVE YEARS AGO.
DO YOU REALLY THINK I'M THIS STUPID? I'VE SEEN YOU.
LOOK AGAIN.
IT'S EXHAUSTED AFTER AN ATTACK. CONVINCING THE SOLDIERS TO STAY, THAT THERE'S NO DANGER.
I GET IT--BEING POSSESSED EATS A BIG ONE. I'M WORKING ON IT.
NO! YOU CAN'T KILL IT.
ARE YOU AS HIGH AS YOU JUST GOT ME?
I CAN'T SURVIVE HERE. BEFORE IT CAME, I WAS IN THE JUNGLE...

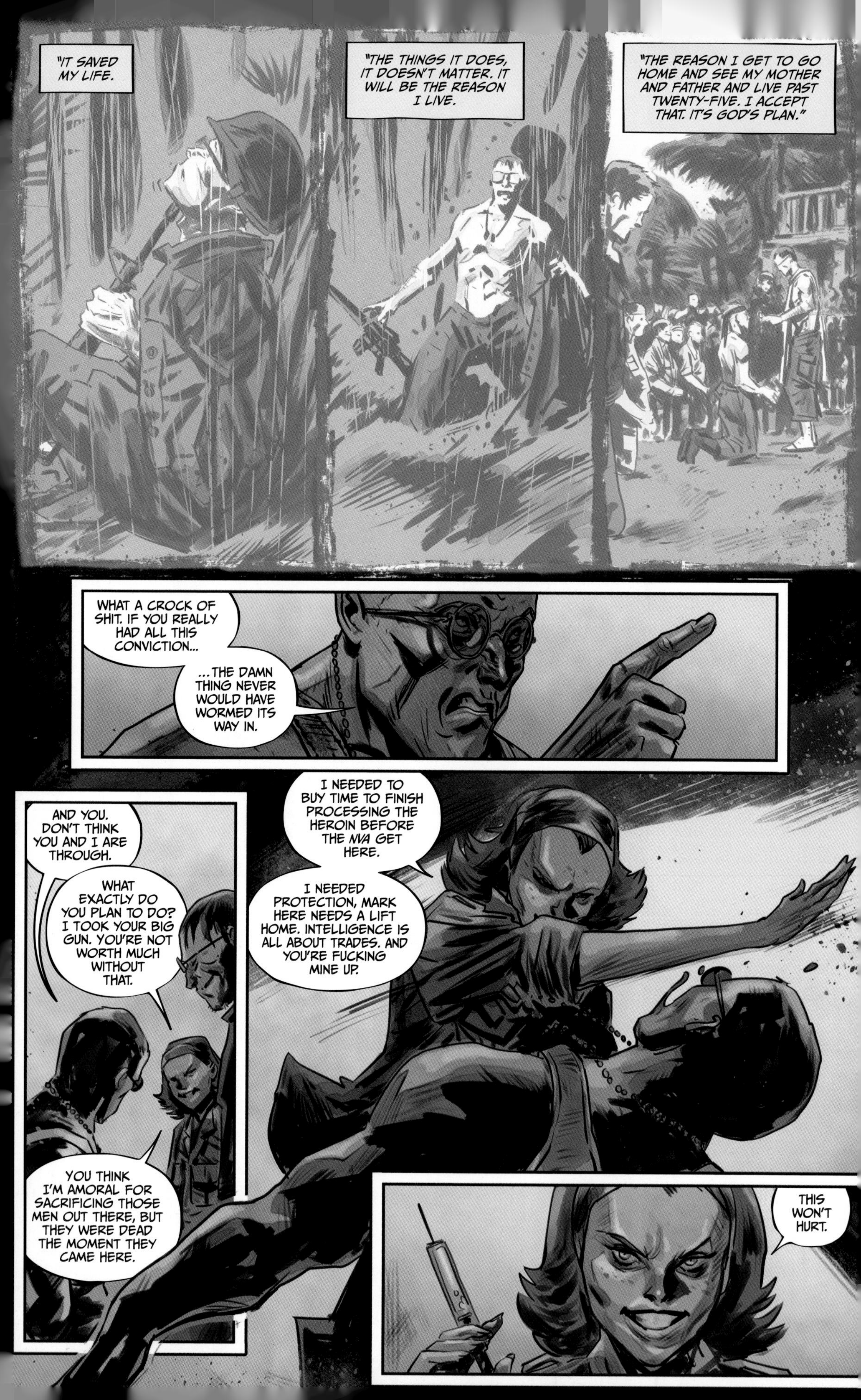
"IT SAVED MY LIFE.
"THE THINGS IT DOES, IT DOESN'T MATTER. IT WILL BE THE REASON I LIVE.
"THE REASON I GET TO GO HOME AND SEE MY MOTHER AND FATHER AND LIVE PAST TWENTY-FIVE. I ACCEPT THAT. IT'S GOD'S PLAN."
WHAT A CROCK OF SHIT. IF YOU REALLY HAD ALL THIS CONVICTION...
...THE DAMN THING NEVER WOULD HAVE WORMED ITS WAY IN.
AND YOU. DON'T THINK YOU AND I ARE THROUGH.
WHAT EXACTLY DO YOU PLAN TO DO? I TOOK YOUR BIG GUN. YOU'RE NOT WORTH MUCH WITHOUT THAT.
YOU THINK I'M AMORAL FOR SACRIFICING THOSE MEN OUT THERE, BUT THEY WERE DEAD THE MOMENT THEY CAME HERE.
I NEEDED TO BUY TIME TO FINISH PROCESSING THE HEROIN BEFORE THE *NVA* GET HERE.
I NEEDED PROTECTION, MARK HERE NEEDS A LIFT HOME. INTELLIGENCE IS ALL ABOUT TRADES. AND YOU'RE FUCKING MINE UP.
THIS WON'T HURT.

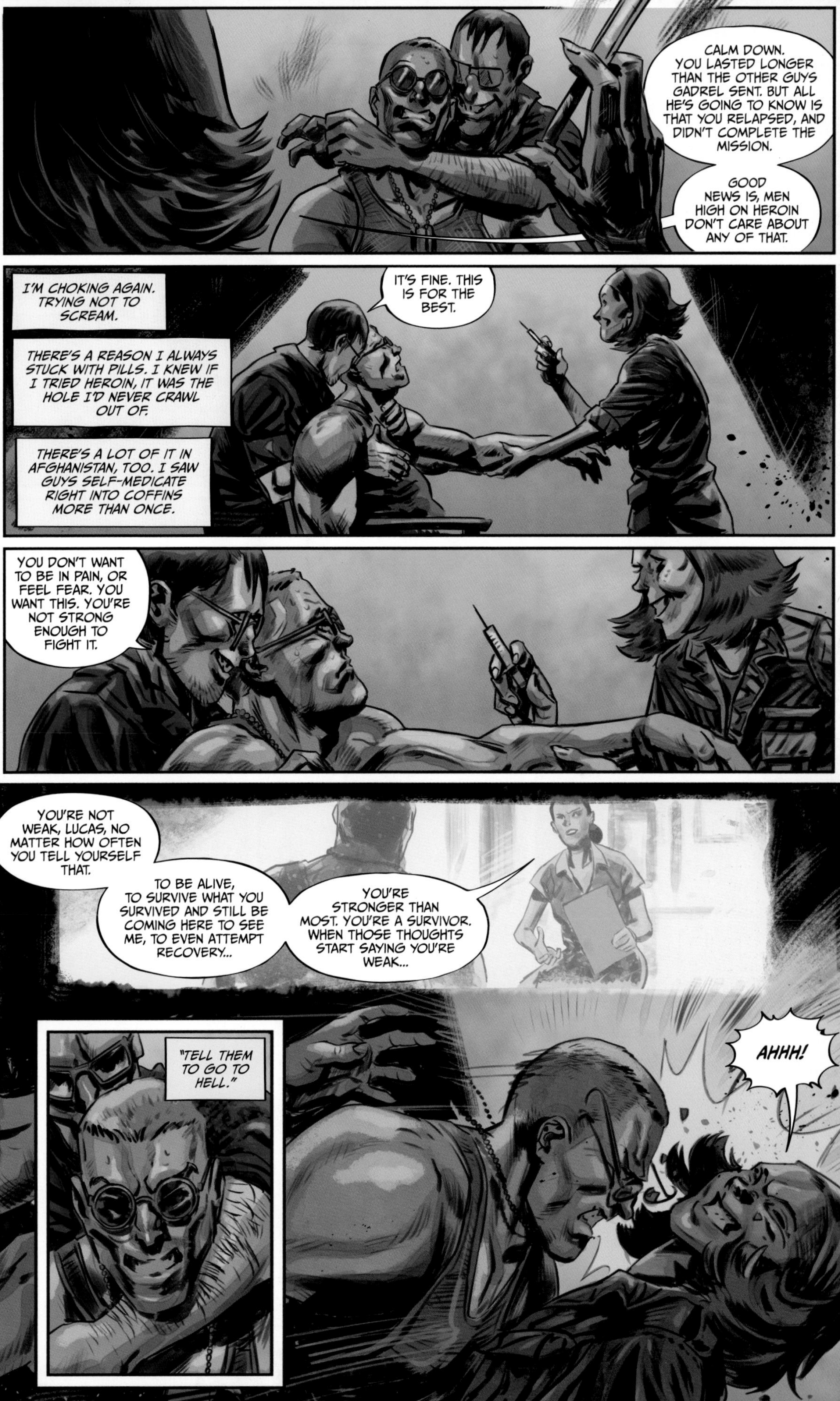
CALM DOWN. YOU LASTED LONGER THAN THE OTHER GUYS GADREL SENT. BUT ALL HE'S GOING TO KNOW IS THAT YOU RELAPSED, AND DIDN'T COMPLETE THE MISSION.
GOOD NEWS IS, MEN HIGH ON HEROIN DON'T CARE ABOUT ANY OF THAT.
I'M CHOKING AGAIN. TRYING NOT TO SCREAM.
IT'S FINE. THIS IS FOR THE BEST.
THERE'S A REASON I ALWAYS STUCK WITH PILLS. I KNEW IF I TRIED HEROIN, IT WAS THE HOLE I'D NEVER CRAWL OUT OF.
THERE'S A LOT OF IT IN AFGHANISTAN, TOO. I SAW GUYS SELF-MEDICATE RIGHT INTO COFFINS MORE THAN ONCE.
YOU DON'T WANT TO BE IN PAIN, OR FEEL FEAR. YOU WANT THIS. YOU'RE NOT STRONG ENOUGH TO FIGHT IT.
YOU'RE NOT WEAK, LUCAS, NO MATTER HOW OFTEN YOU TELL YOURSELF THAT.
TO BE ALIVE, TO SURVIVE WHAT YOU SURVIVED AND STILL BE COMING HERE TO SEE ME, TO EVEN ATTEMPT RECOVERY...
YOU'RE STRONGER THAN MOST. YOU'RE A SURVIVOR. WHEN THOSE THOUGHTS START SAYING YOU'RE WEAK...
"TELL THEM TO GO TO HELL."
AHHH!

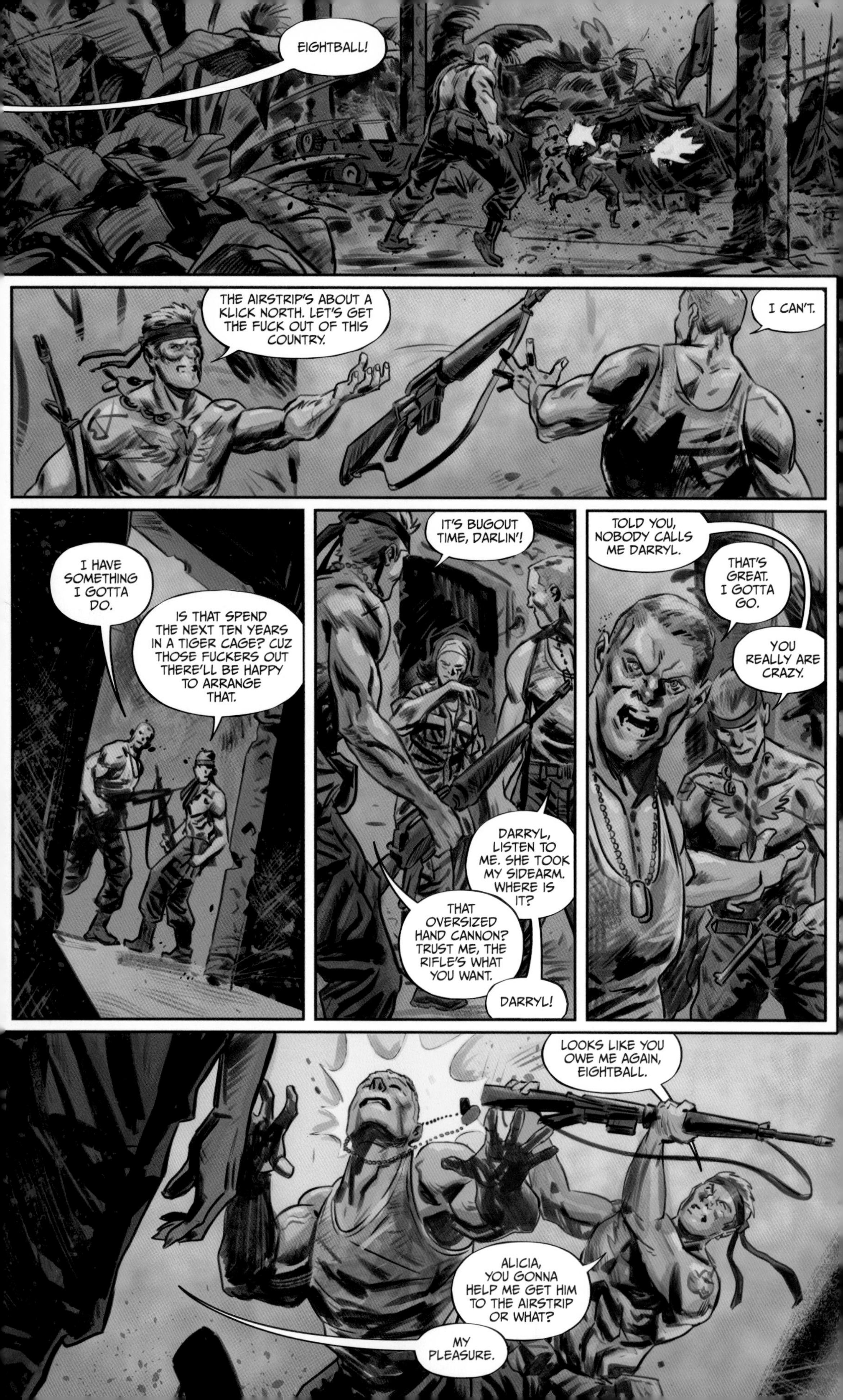
EIGHTBALL!
THE AIRSTRIP'S ABOUT A KLICK NORTH. LET'S GET THE FUCK OUT OF THIS COUNTRY.
I CAN'T.
I HAVE SOMETHING I GOTTA DO.
IS THAT SPEND THE NEXT TEN YEARS IN A TIGER CAGE? CUZ THOSE FUCKERS OUT THERE'LL BE HAPPY TO ARRANGE THAT.
IT'S BUGOUT TIME, DARLIN'!
DARRYL, LISTEN TO ME. SHE TOOK MY SIDEARM. WHERE IS IT?
THAT OVERSIZED HAND CANNON? TRUST ME, THE RIFLE'S WHAT YOU WANT.
DARRYL!
TOLD YOU, NOBODY CALLS ME DARRYL.
THAT'S GREAT. I GOTTA GO.
YOU REALLY ARE CRAZY.
LOOKS LIKE YOU OWE ME AGAIN, EIGHTBALL.
ALICIA, YOU GONNA HELP ME GET HIM TO THE AIRSTRIP OR WHAT?
MY PLEASURE.

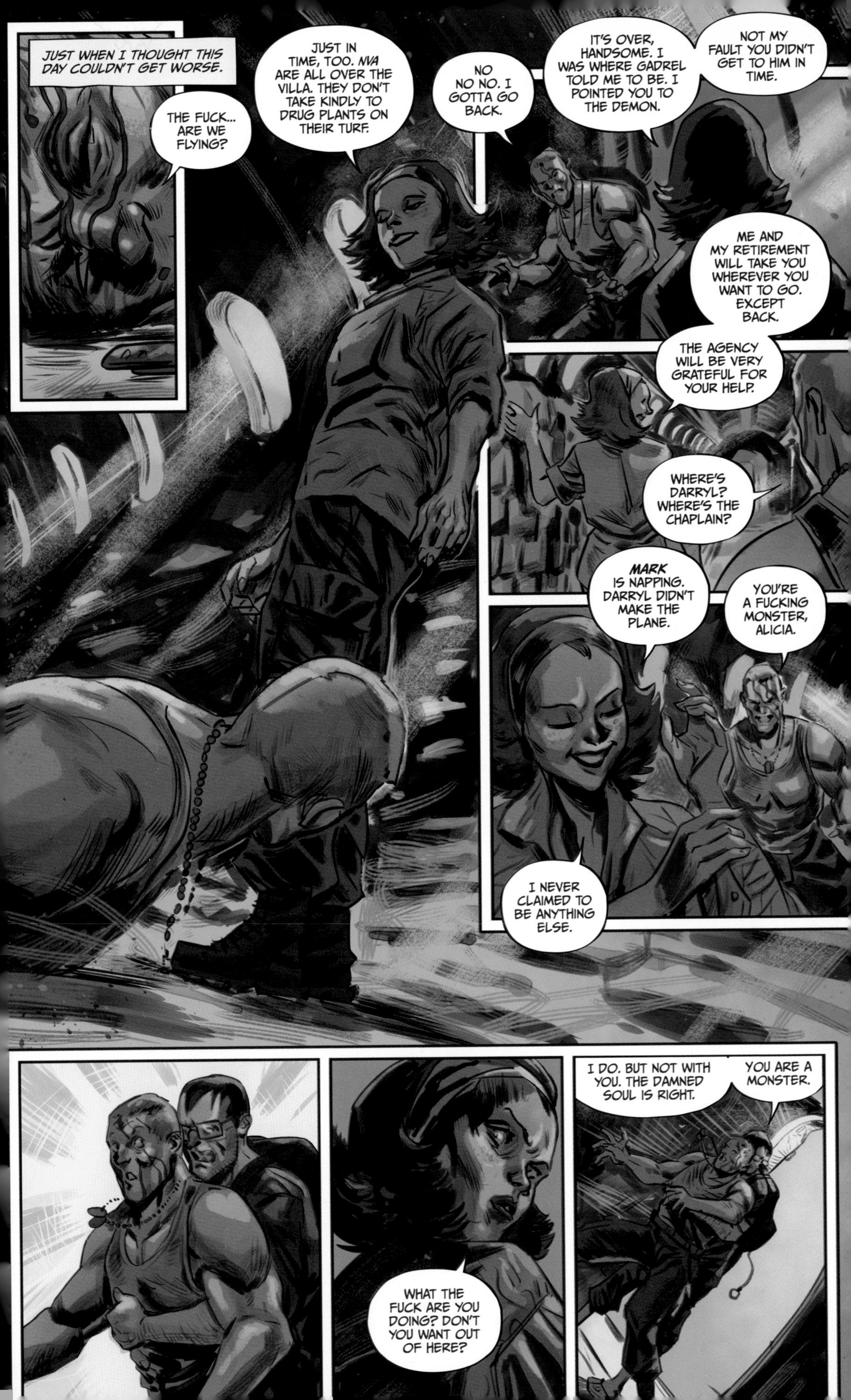
JUST WHEN I THOUGHT THIS DAY COULDN'T GET WORSE.
THE FUCK... ARE WE FLYING?
JUST IN TIME, TOO. NVA ARE ALL OVER THE VILLA. THEY DON'T TAKE KINDLY TO DRUG PLANTS ON THEIR TURF.
NO NO NO. I GOTTA GO BACK.
IT'S OVER, HANDSOME. I WAS WHERE GADREL TOLD ME TO BE. I POINTED YOU TO THE DEMON.
NOT MY FAULT YOU DIDN'T GET TO HIM IN TIME.
ME AND MY RETIREMENT WILL TAKE YOU WHEREVER YOU WANT TO GO. EXCEPT BACK.
THE AGENCY WILL BE VERY GRATEFUL FOR YOUR HELP.
WHERE'S DARRYL? WHERE'S THE CHAPLAIN?
MARK IS NAPPING. DARRYL DIDN'T MAKE THE PLANE.
YOU'RE A FUCKING MONSTER, ALICIA.
I NEVER CLAIMED TO BE ANYTHING ELSE.
WHAT THE FUCK ARE YOU DOING? DON'T YOU WANT OUT OF HERE?
I DO. BUT NOT WITH YOU. THE DAMNED SOUL IS RIGHT.
YOU ARE A MONSTER.

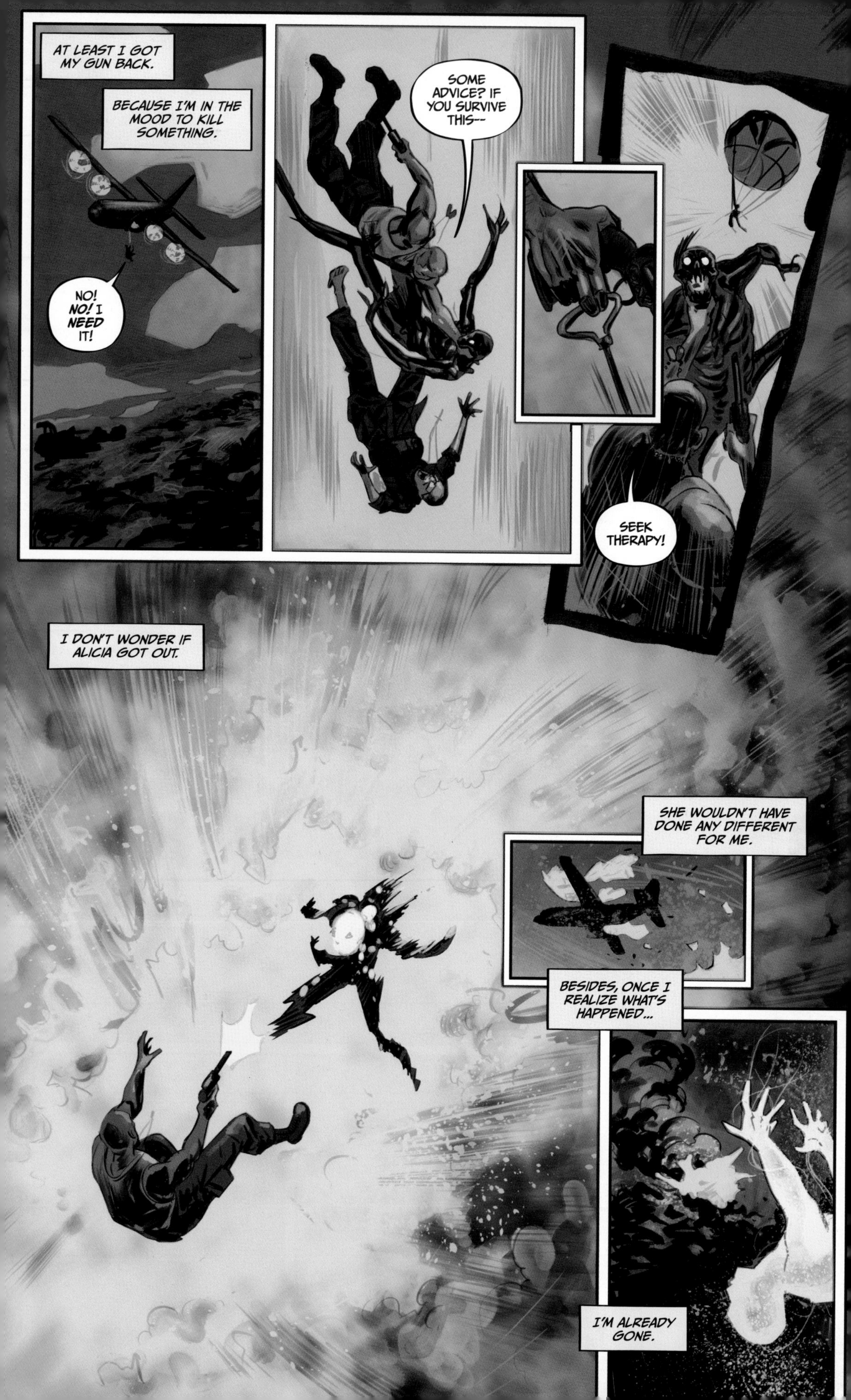

AT LEAST I GOT MY GUN BACK.
BECAUSE I'M IN THE MOOD TO KILL SOMETHING.
NO! NO! I NEED IT!
SOME ADVICE? IF YOU SURVIVE THIS--
SEEK THERAPY!
I DON'T WONDER IF ALICIA GOT OUT.
SHE WOULDN'T HAVE DONE ANY DIFFERENT FOR ME.
BESIDES, ONCE I REALIZE WHAT'S HAPPENED...
I'M ALREADY GONE.

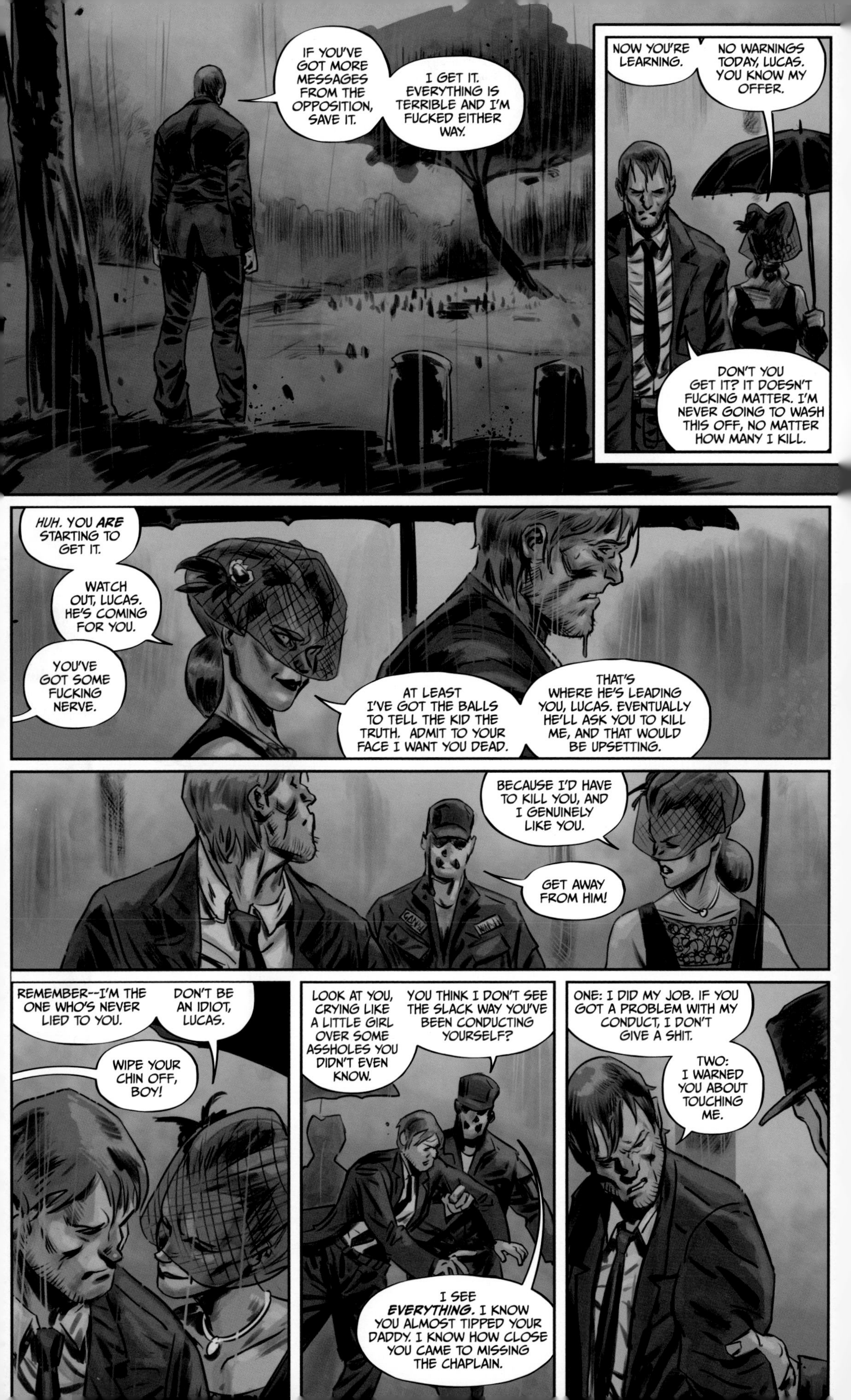
IF YOU'VE GOT MORE MESSAGES FROM THE OPPOSITION, SAVE IT.
I GET IT. EVERYTHING IS TERRIBLE AND I'M FUCKED EITHER WAY.
NOW YOU'RE LEARNING.
NO WARNINGS TODAY, LUCAS. YOU KNOW MY OFFER.
DON'T YOU GET IT? IT DOESN'T FUCKING MATTER. I'M NEVER GOING TO WASH THIS OFF, NO MATTER HOW MANY I KILL.
HUH. YOU ***ARE*** STARTING TO GET IT.
WATCH OUT, LUCAS. HE'S COMING FOR YOU.
YOU'VE GOT SOME FUCKING NERVE.
AT LEAST I'VE GOT THE BALLS TO TELL THE KID THE TRUTH. ADMIT TO YOUR FACE I WANT YOU DEAD.
THAT'S WHERE HE'S LEADING YOU, LUCAS. EVENTUALLY HE'LL ASK YOU TO KILL ME, AND THAT WOULD BE UPSETTING.
BECAUSE I'D HAVE TO KILL YOU, AND I GENUINELY LIKE YOU.
GET AWAY FROM HIM!
REMEMBER--I'M THE ONE WHO'S NEVER LIED TO YOU.
DON'T BE AN IDIOT, LUCAS.
WIPE YOUR CHIN OFF, BOY!
LOOK AT YOU, CRYING LIKE A LITTLE GIRL OVER SOME ASSHOLES YOU DIDN'T EVEN KNOW.
YOU THINK I DON'T SEE THE SLACK WAY YOU'VE BEEN CONDUCTING YOURSELF?
I SEE ***EVERYTHING.*** I KNOW YOU ALMOST TIPPED YOUR DADDY. I KNOW HOW CLOSE YOU CAME TO MISSING THE CHAPLAIN.
ONE: I DID MY JOB. IF YOU GOT A PROBLEM WITH MY CONDUCT, I DON'T GIVE A SHIT.
TWO: I WARNED YOU ABOUT TOUCHING ME.

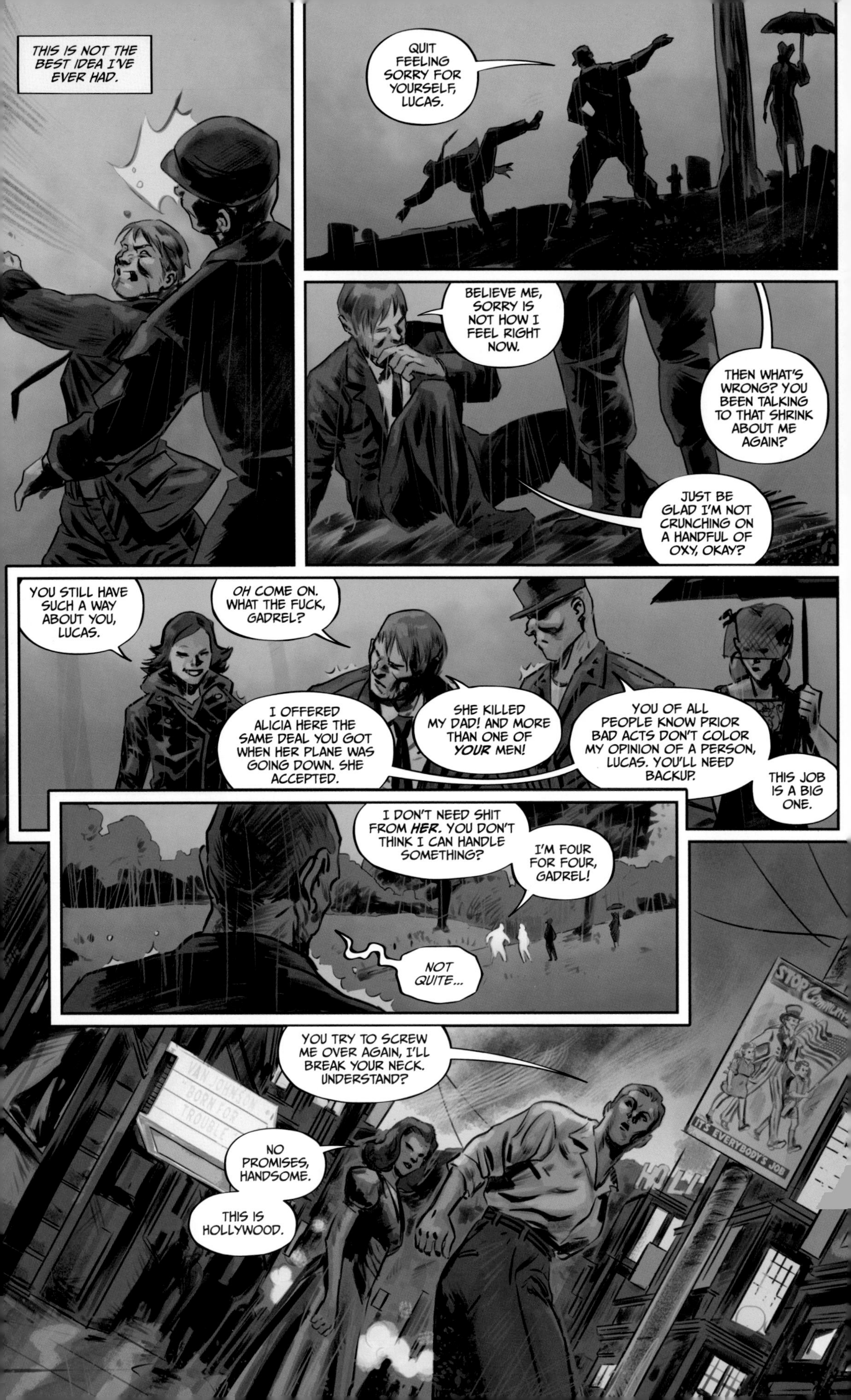
THIS IS NOT THE BEST IDEA I'VE EVER HAD.
QUIT FEELING SORRY FOR YOURSELF, LUCAS.
BELIEVE ME, SORRY IS NOT HOW I FEEL RIGHT NOW.
THEN WHAT'S WRONG? YOU BEEN TALKING TO THAT SHRINK ABOUT ME AGAIN?
JUST BE GLAD I'M NOT CRUNCHING ON A HANDFUL OF OXY, OKAY?
YOU STILL HAVE SUCH A WAY ABOUT YOU, LUCAS.
OH COME ON. WHAT THE FUCK, GADREL?
I OFFERED ALICIA HERE THE SAME DEAL YOU GOT WHEN HER PLANE WAS GOING DOWN. SHE ACCEPTED.
SHE KILLED MY DAD! AND MORE THAN ONE OF YOUR MEN!
YOU OF ALL PEOPLE KNOW PRIOR BAD ACTS DON'T COLOR MY OPINION OF A PERSON, LUCAS. YOU'LL NEED BACKUP.
THIS JOB IS A BIG ONE.
I DON'T NEED SHIT FROM HER. YOU DON'T THINK I CAN HANDLE SOMETHING?
I'M FOUR FOR FOUR, GADREL!
NOT QUITE...
YOU TRY TO SCREW ME OVER AGAIN, I'LL BREAK YOUR NECK. UNDERSTAND?
VAN JOHNSON
"BORN FOR TROUBLE"
STOP
IT'S EVERYBODY'S JOB
NO PROMISES, HANDSOME.
THIS IS HOLLYWOOD.

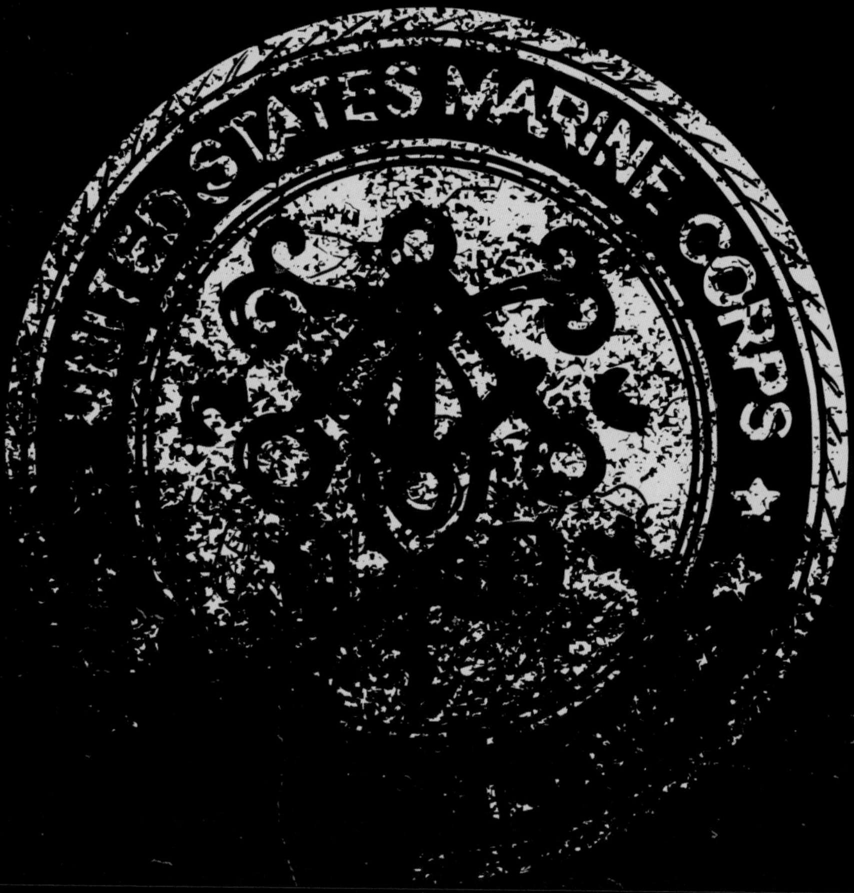
UNITED STATES MARINE CORPS

CHAPTER
FIVE

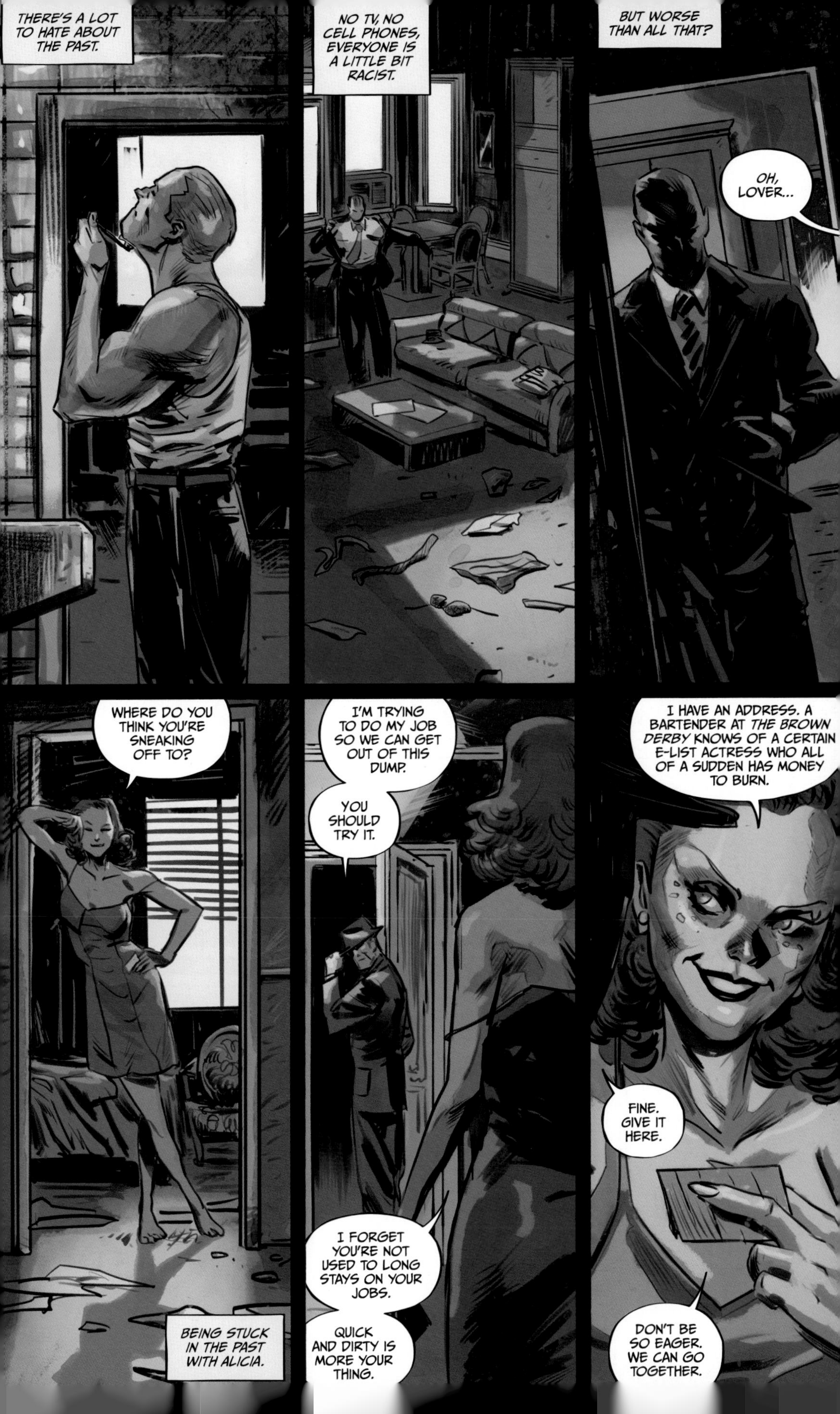
THERE'S A LOT TO HATE ABOUT THE PAST.
NO TV, NO CELL PHONES, EVERYONE IS A LITTLE BIT RACIST.
BUT WORSE THAN ALL THAT?
OH, LOVER...
WHERE DO YOU THINK YOU'RE SNEAKING OFF TO?
BEING STUCK IN THE PAST WITH ALICIA.
I'M TRYING TO DO MY JOB SO WE CAN GET OUT OF THIS DUMP.
YOU SHOULD TRY IT.
I FORGET YOU'RE NOT USED TO LONG STAYS ON YOUR JOBS.
QUICK AND DIRTY IS MORE YOUR THING.
I HAVE AN ADDRESS. A BARTENDER AT *THE BROWN DERBY* KNOWS OF A CERTAIN E-LIST ACTRESS WHO ALL OF A SUDDEN HAS MONEY TO BURN.
FINE. GIVE IT HERE.
DON'T BE SO EAGER. WE CAN GO TOGETHER.

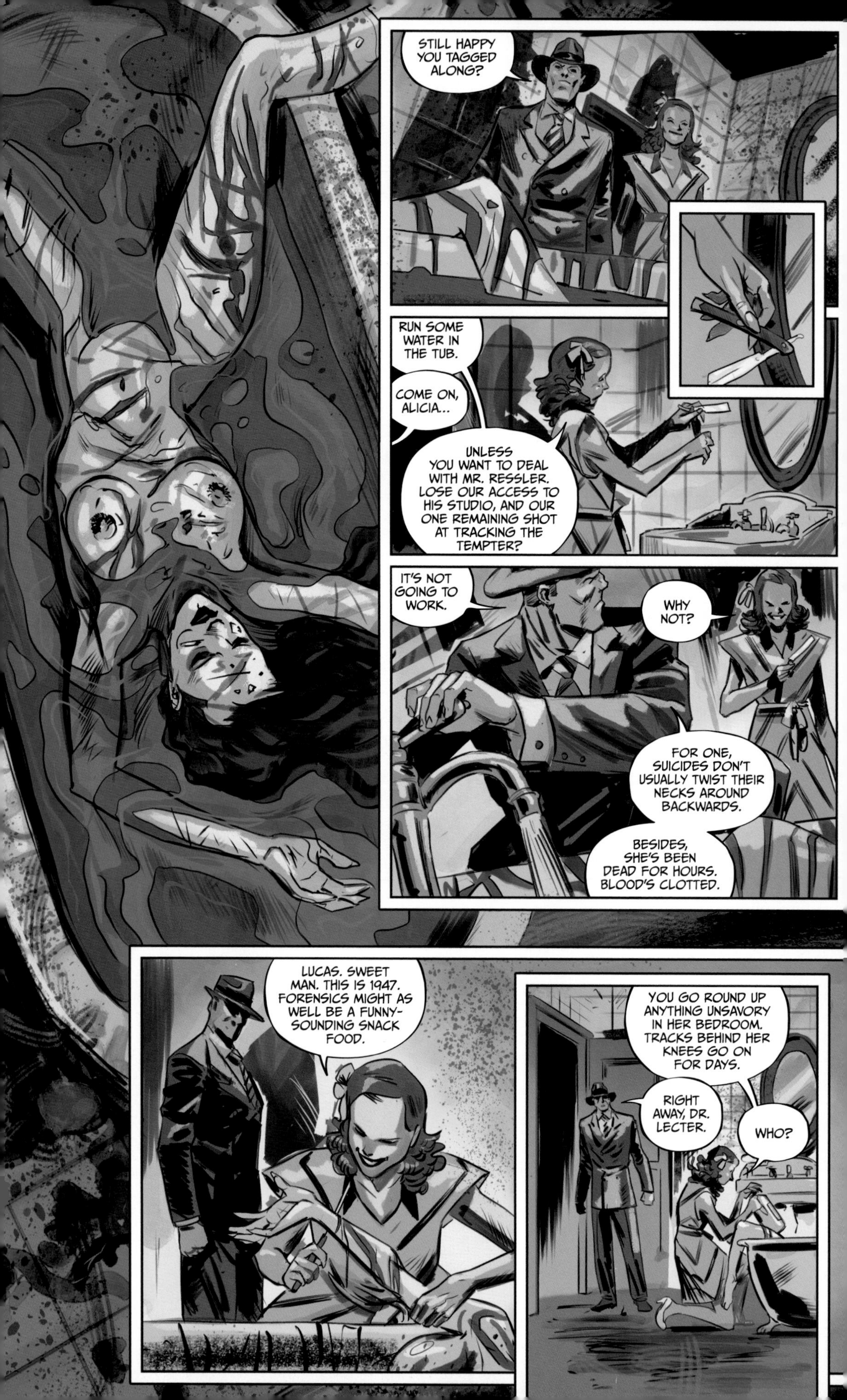
STILL HAPPY YOU TAGGED ALONG?
RUN SOME WATER IN THE TUB.
COME ON, ALICIA...
UNLESS YOU WANT TO DEAL WITH MR. RESSLER. LOSE OUR ACCESS TO HIS STUDIO, AND OUR ONE REMAINING SHOT AT TRACKING THE TEMPTER?
IT'S NOT GOING TO WORK.
WHY NOT?
FOR ONE, SUICIDES DON'T USUALLY TWIST THEIR NECKS AROUND BACKWARDS.
BESIDES, SHE'S BEEN DEAD FOR HOURS. BLOOD'S CLOTTED.
LUCAS. SWEET MAN. THIS IS 1947. FORENSICS MIGHT AS WELL BE A FUNNY-SOUNDING SNACK FOOD.
YOU GO ROUND UP ANYTHING UNSAVORY IN HER BEDROOM. TRACKS BEHIND HER KNEES GO ON FOR DAYS.
RIGHT AWAY, DR. LECTER.
WHO?

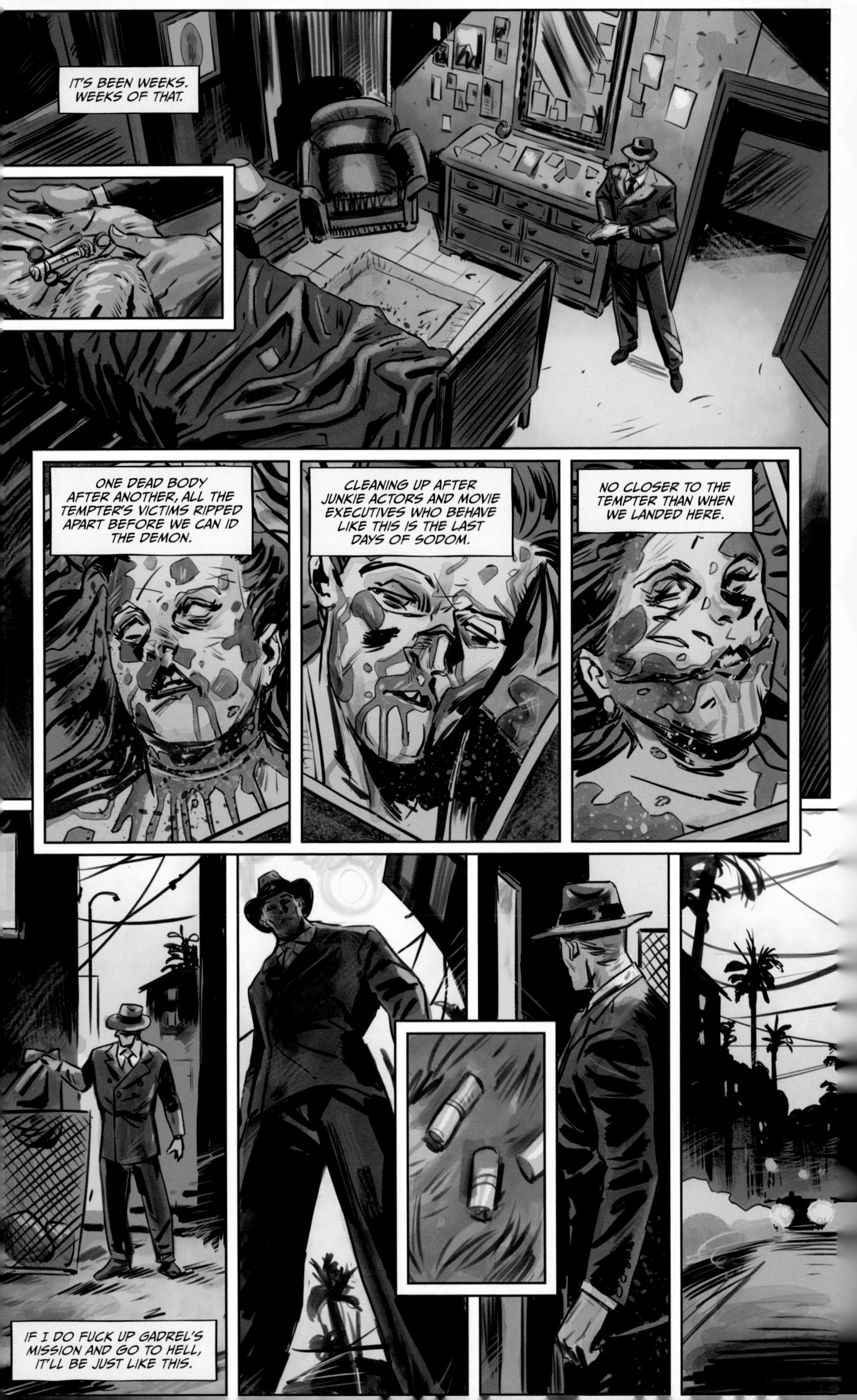
IT'S BEEN WEEKS. WEEKS OF THAT.
ONE DEAD BODY AFTER ANOTHER, ALL THE TEMPTER'S VICTIMS RIPPED APART BEFORE WE CAN ID THE DEMON.
CLEANING UP AFTER JUNKIE ACTORS AND MOVIE EXECUTIVES WHO BEHAVE LIKE THIS IS THE LAST DAYS OF SODOM.
NO CLOSER TO THE TEMPTER THAN WHEN WE LANDED HERE.
IF I DO FUCK UP GADREL'S MISSION AND GO TO HELL, IT'LL BE JUST LIKE THIS.

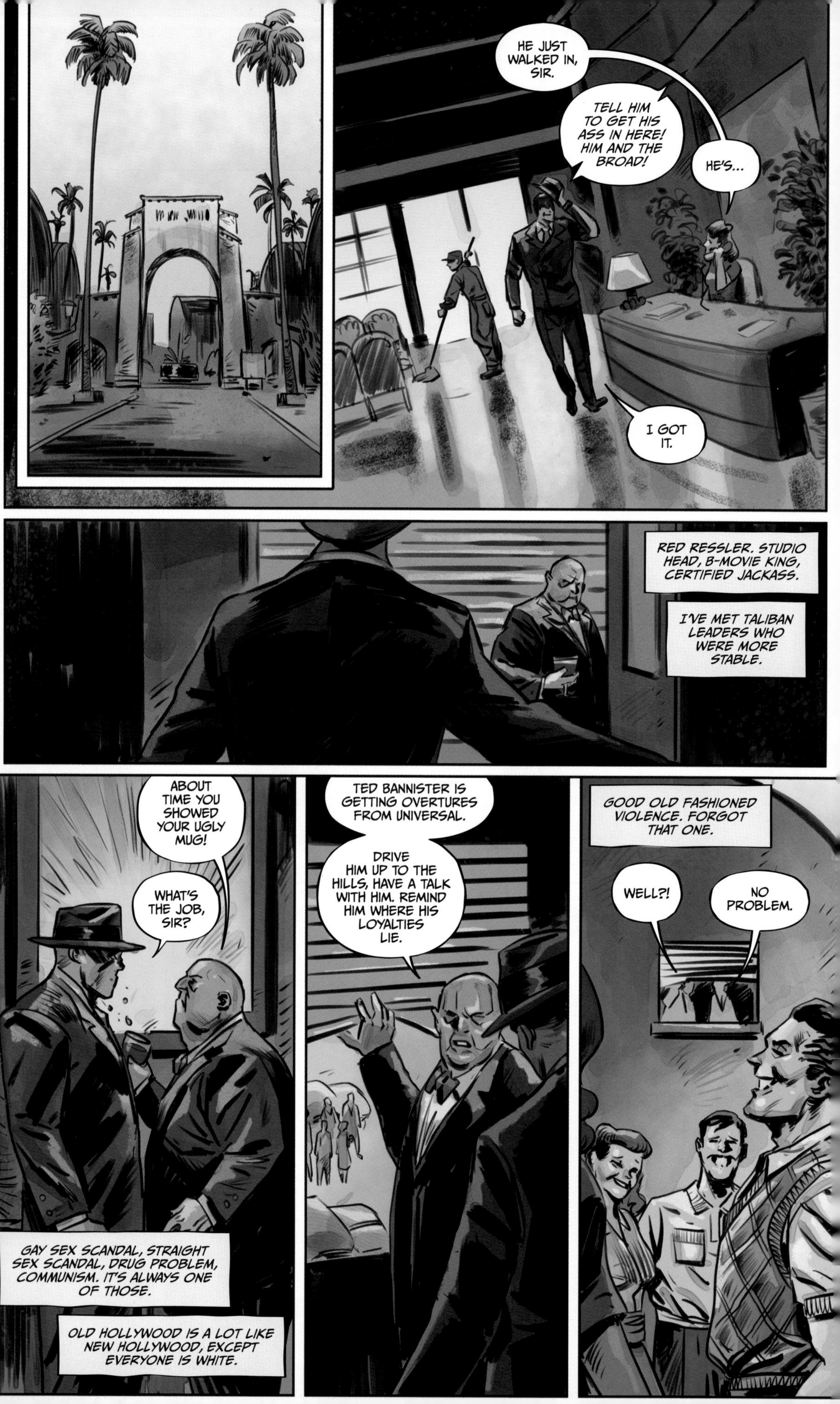
HE JUST WALKED IN, SIR.
TELL HIM TO GET HIS ASS IN HERE! HIM AND THE BROAD!
HE'S...
I GOT IT.
RED RESSLER. STUDIO HEAD, B-MOVIE KING, CERTIFIED JACKASS.
I'VE MET TALIBAN LEADERS WHO WERE MORE STABLE.
ABOUT TIME YOU SHOWED YOUR UGLY MUG!
WHAT'S THE JOB, SIR?
GAY SEX SCANDAL, STRAIGHT SEX SCANDAL, DRUG PROBLEM, COMMUNISM. IT'S ALWAYS ONE OF THOSE.
OLD HOLLYWOOD IS A LOT LIKE NEW HOLLYWOOD, EXCEPT EVERYONE IS WHITE.
TED BANNISTER IS GETTING OVERTURES FROM UNIVERSAL.
DRIVE HIM UP TO THE HILLS, HAVE A TALK WITH HIM. REMIND HIM WHERE HIS LOYALTIES LIE.
GOOD OLD FASHIONED VIOLENCE. FORGOT THAT ONE.
WELL?!
NO PROBLEM.

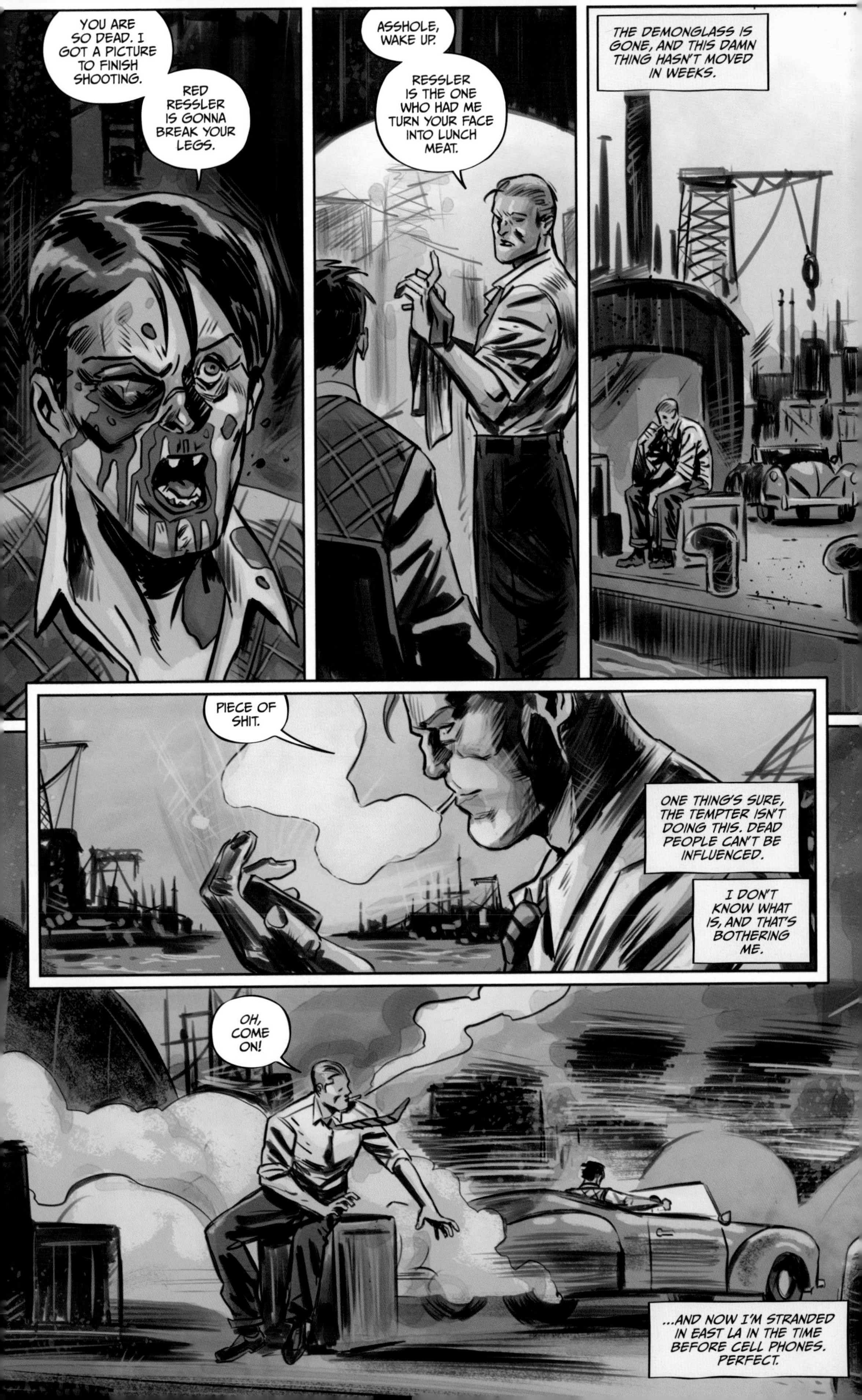

YOU ARE SO DEAD. I GOT A PICTURE TO FINISH SHOOTING.
RED RESSLER IS GONNA BREAK YOUR LEGS.
ASSHOLE, WAKE UP.
RESSLER IS THE ONE WHO HAD ME TURN YOUR FACE INTO LUNCH MEAT.
THE DEMONGLASS IS GONE, AND THIS DAMN THING HASN'T MOVED IN WEEKS.
PIECE OF SHIT.
ONE THING'S SURE, THE TEMPTER ISN'T DOING THIS. DEAD PEOPLE CAN'T BE INFLUENCED.
I DON'T KNOW WHAT IS, AND THAT'S BOTHERING ME.
OH, COME ON!
...AND NOW I'M STRANDED IN EAST LA IN THE TIME BEFORE CELL PHONES. PERFECT.

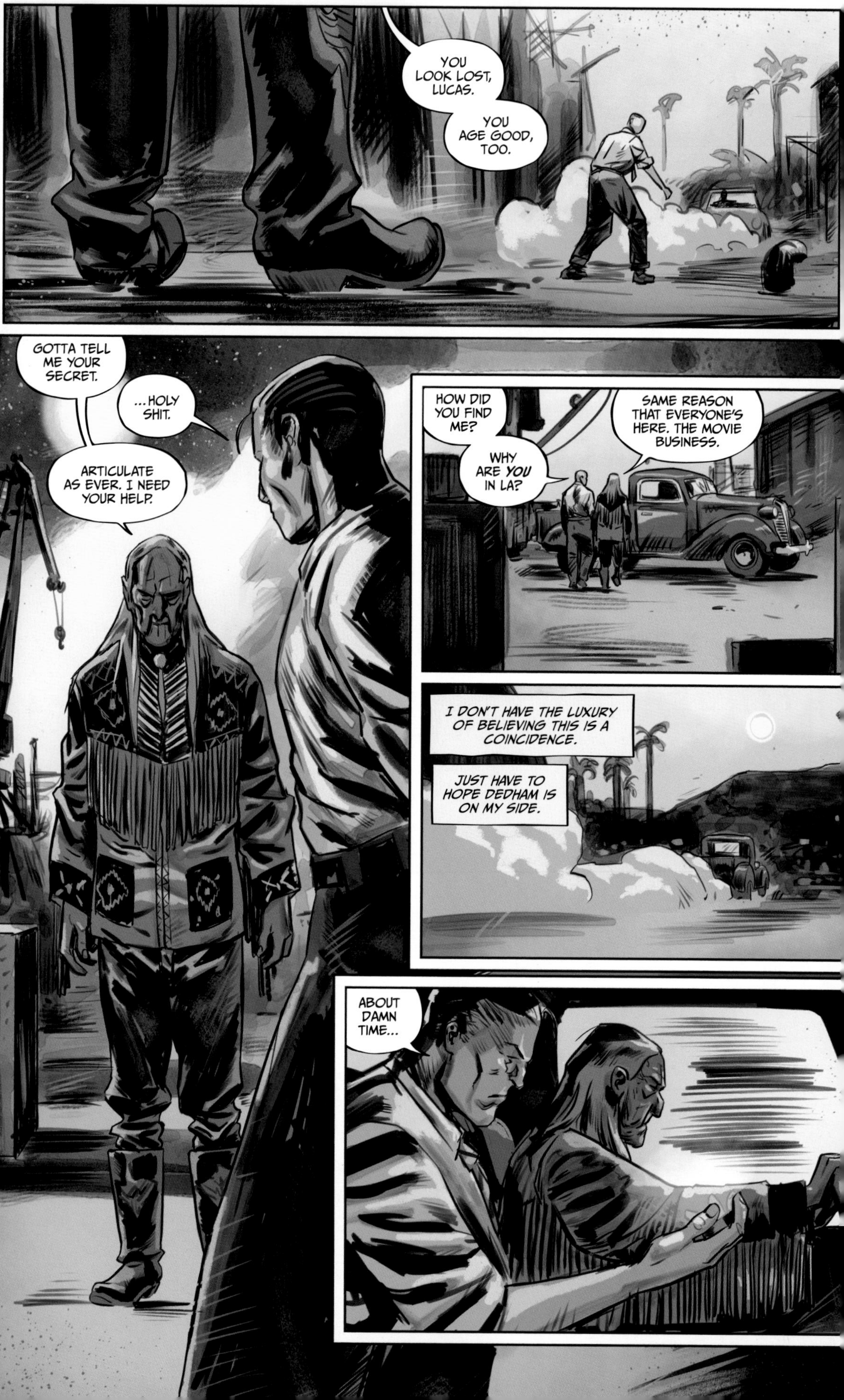
YOU LOOK LOST, LUCAS.
YOU AGE GOOD, TOO.
GOTTA TELL ME YOUR SECRET.
...HOLY SHIT.
ARTICULATE AS EVER. I NEED YOUR HELP.
HOW DID YOU FIND ME?
WHY ARE *YOU* IN LA?
SAME REASON THAT EVERYONE'S HERE. THE MOVIE BUSINESS.
I DON'T HAVE THE LUXURY OF BELIEVING THIS IS A COINCIDENCE.
JUST HAVE TO HOPE DEDHAM IS ON MY SIDE.
ABOUT DAMN TIME...

YOU STILL HAVE THAT BIG GUN?

AM I GOING TO NEED IT?

BETTER TO HAVE A GUN AND NOT NEED IT.

MY HANDS AREN'T SO STEADY THESE DAYS.

SO YOU'RE STILL HUNTING THEM.

NEVER STOPPED.

ME EITHER.

I WISH I HAD THE DEMONGLASS ABOUT NOW. FOR WHATEVER'S UP THESE STAIRS AND TO GET A GOOD LOOK AT DEDHAM.

LAST TIME I SAW HIM, IN DEADWOOD...

I DON'T KNOW WHAT I SAW. AND I LIKE UNKNOWNS LESS AND LESS THE LONGER I DO GADREL'S DIRTY WORK.

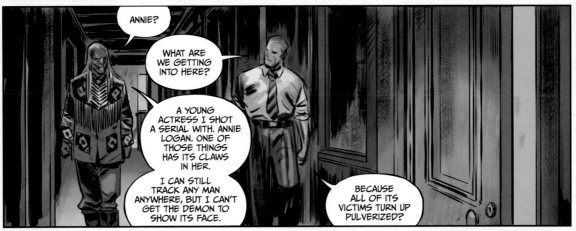

ANNIE?

WHAT ARE WE GETTING INTO HERE?

A YOUNG ACTRESS I SHOT A SERIAL WITH. ANNIE LOGAN. ONE OF THOSE THINGS HAS ITS CLAWS IN HER.

I CAN STILL TRACK ANY MAN ANYWHERE, BUT I CAN'T GET THE DEMON TO SHOW ITS FACE.

BECAUSE ALL OF ITS VICTIMS TURN UP PULVERIZED?

LET ME GO FIRST.

I'M OLD, BUT I'M NOT HELPLESS.

ARE YOU BULLETPROOF?

HMPH.

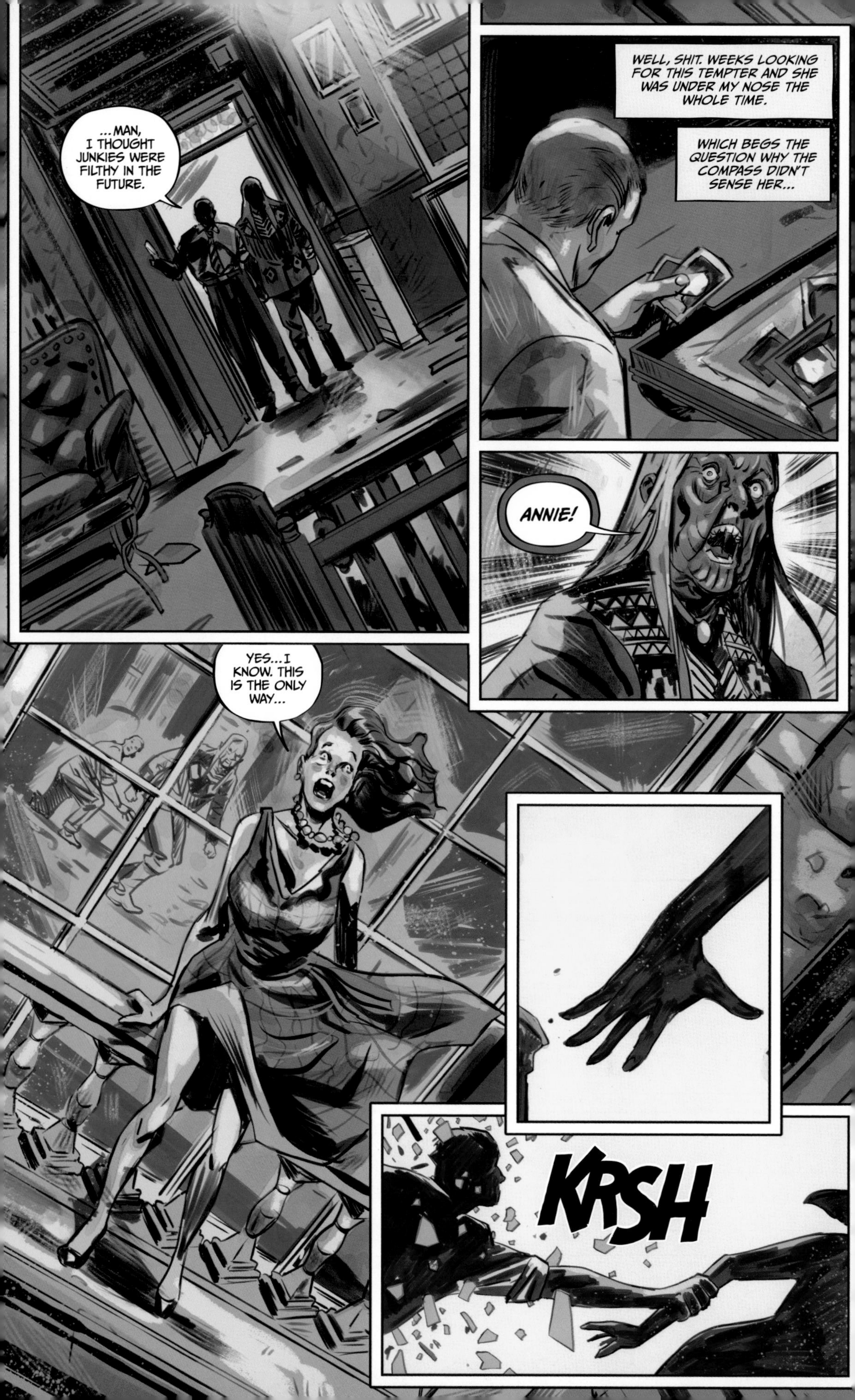
...MAN, I THOUGHT JUNKIES WERE FILTHY IN THE FUTURE.
WELL, SHIT. WEEKS LOOKING FOR THIS TEMPTER AND SHE WAS UNDER MY NOSE THE WHOLE TIME.
WHICH BEGS THE QUESTION WHY THE COMPASS DIDN'T SENSE HER...
ANNIE!
YES...I KNOW. THIS IS THE ONLY WAY...
KRSH

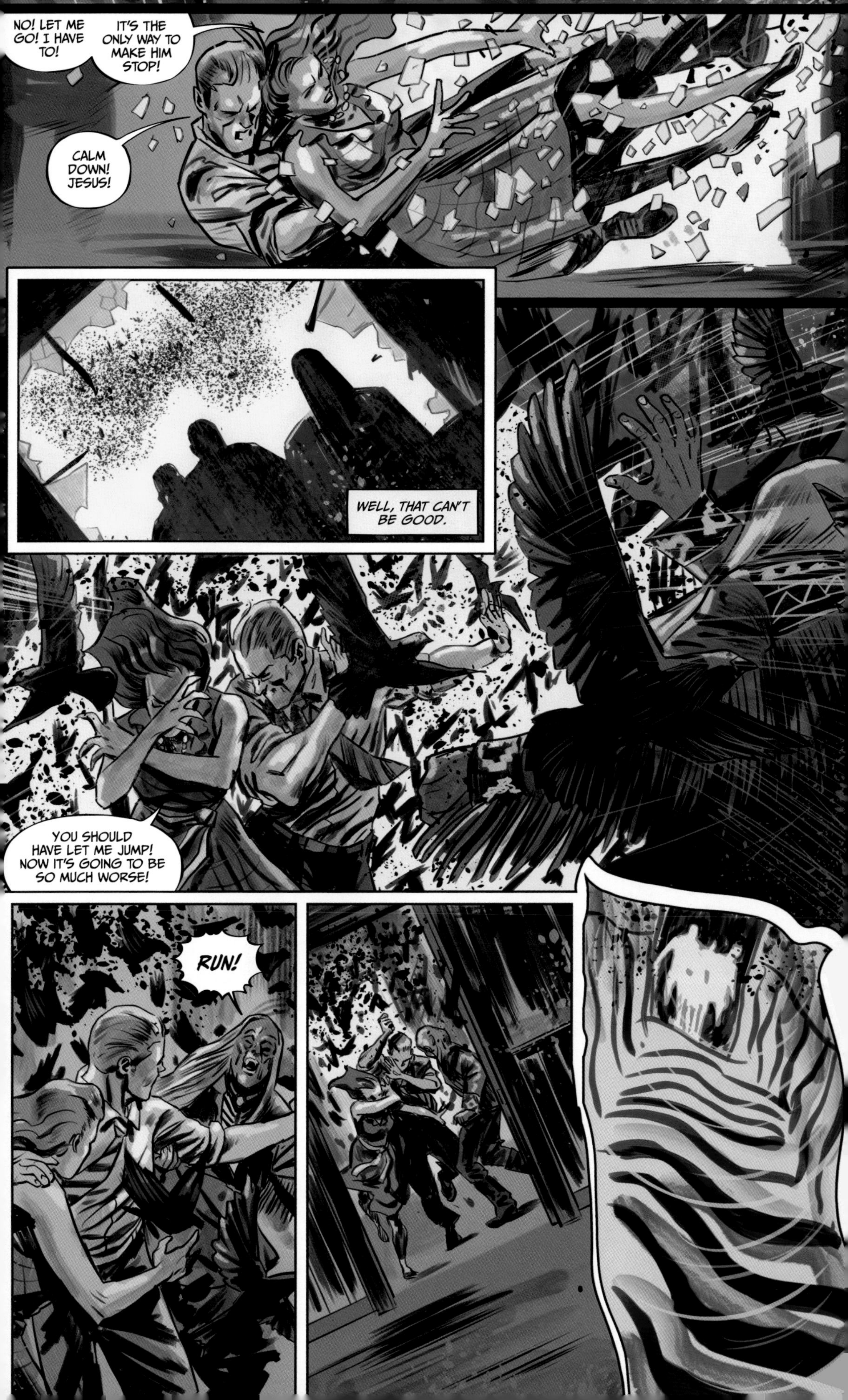

NO! LET ME GO! I HAVE TO!
IT'S THE ONLY WAY TO MAKE HIM STOP!
CALM DOWN! JESUS!
WELL, THAT CAN'T BE GOOD.
YOU SHOULD HAVE LET ME JUMP! NOW IT'S GOING TO BE SO MUCH WORSE!
RUN!

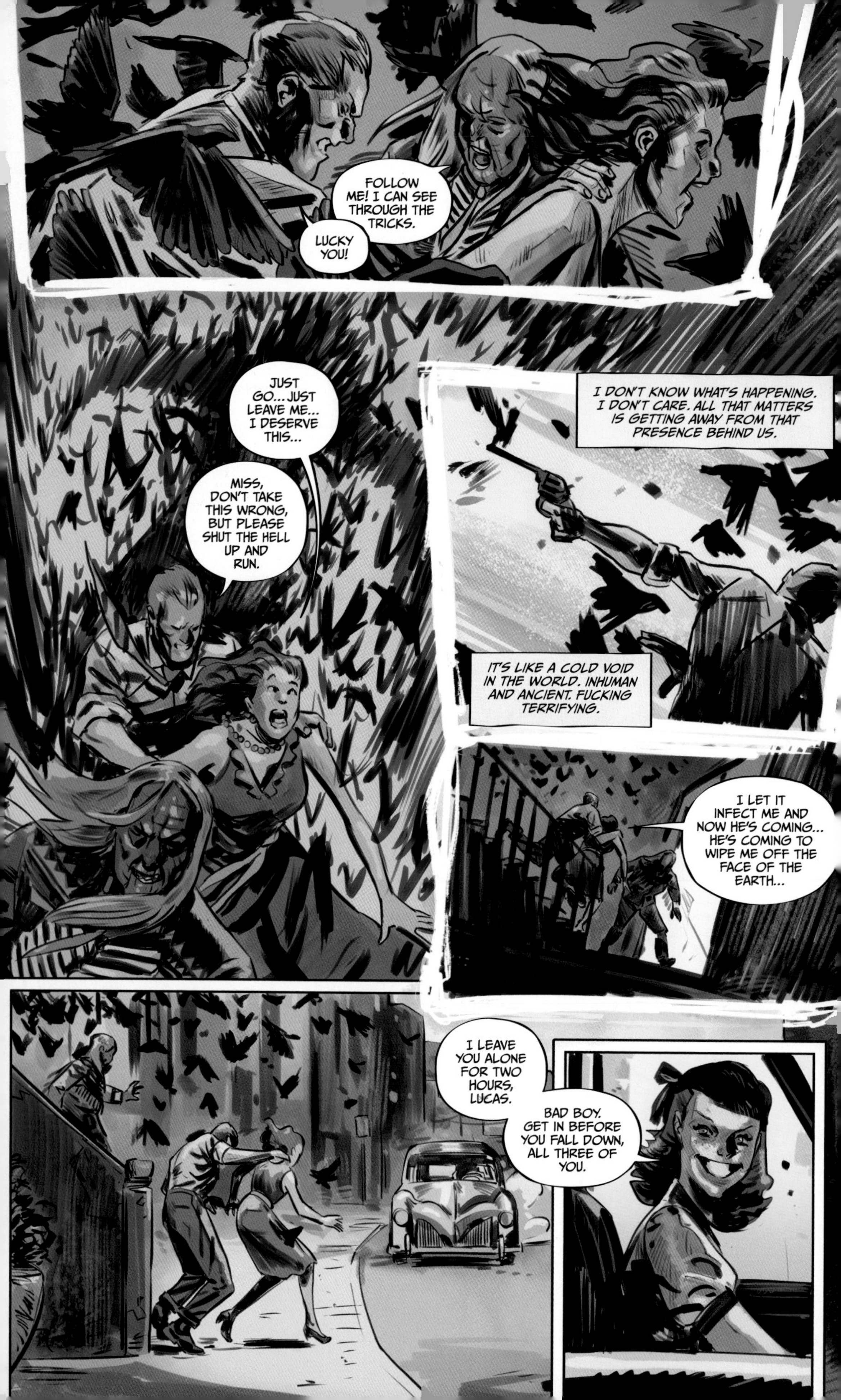
FOLLOW ME! I CAN SEE THROUGH THE TRICKS.
LUCKY YOU!
JUST GO... JUST LEAVE ME... I DESERVE THIS...
MISS, DON'T TAKE THIS WRONG, BUT PLEASE SHUT THE HELL UP AND RUN.
I DON'T KNOW WHAT'S HAPPENING. I DON'T CARE. ALL THAT MATTERS IS GETTING AWAY FROM THAT PRESENCE BEHIND US.
IT'S LIKE A COLD VOID IN THE WORLD. INHUMAN AND ANCIENT. FUCKING TERRIFYING.
I LET IT INFECT ME AND NOW HE'S COMING... HE'S COMING TO WIPE ME OFF THE FACE OF THE EARTH...
I LEAVE YOU ALONE FOR TWO HOURS, LUCAS.
BAD BOY. GET IN BEFORE YOU FALL DOWN, ALL THREE OF YOU.

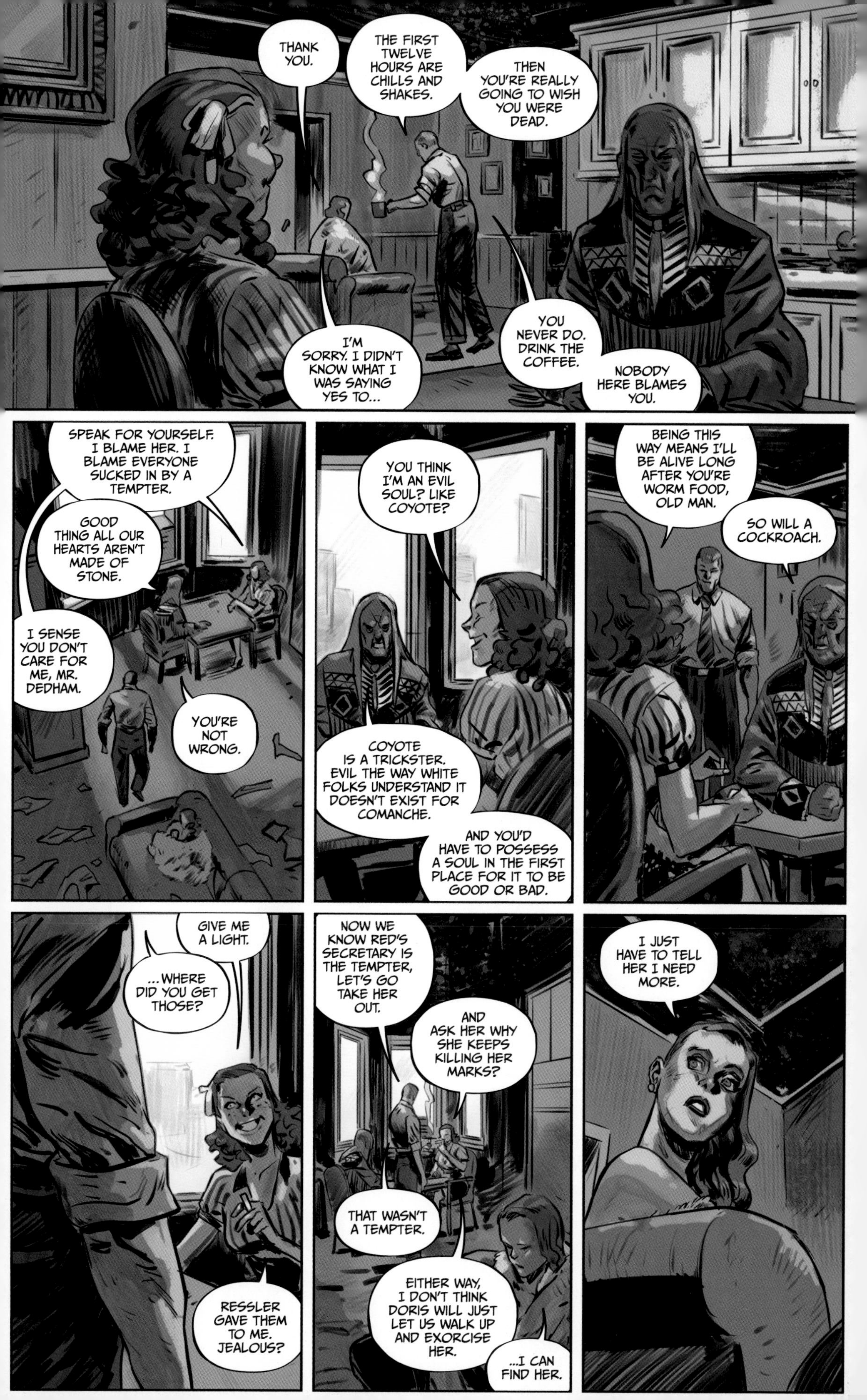
THANK YOU.
THE FIRST TWELVE HOURS ARE CHILLS AND SHAKES.
THEN YOU'RE REALLY GOING TO WISH YOU WERE DEAD.
I'M SORRY. I DIDN'T KNOW WHAT I WAS SAYING YES TO...
YOU NEVER DO. DRINK THE COFFEE.
NOBODY HERE BLAMES YOU.
SPEAK FOR YOURSELF. I BLAME HER. I BLAME EVERYONE SUCKED IN BY A TEMPTER.
GOOD THING ALL OUR HEARTS AREN'T MADE OF STONE.
I SENSE YOU DON'T CARE FOR ME, MR. DEDHAM.
YOU'RE NOT WRONG.
YOU THINK I'M AN EVIL SOUL? LIKE COYOTE?
COYOTE IS A TRICKSTER. EVIL THE WAY WHITE FOLKS UNDERSTAND IT DOESN'T EXIST FOR COMANCHE.
AND YOU'D HAVE TO POSSESS A SOUL IN THE FIRST PLACE FOR IT TO BE GOOD OR BAD.
BEING THIS WAY MEANS I'LL BE ALIVE LONG AFTER YOU'RE WORM FOOD, OLD MAN.
SO WILL A COCKROACH.
GIVE ME A LIGHT.
...WHERE DID YOU GET THOSE?
RESSLER GAVE THEM TO ME. JEALOUS?
NOW WE KNOW RED'S SECRETARY IS THE TEMPTER, LET'S GO TAKE HER OUT.
AND ASK HER WHY SHE KEEPS KILLING HER MARKS?
THAT WASN'T A TEMPTER.
EITHER WAY, I DON'T THINK DORIS WILL JUST LET US WALK UP AND EXORCISE HER.
...I CAN FIND HER.
I JUST HAVE TO TELL HER I NEED MORE.

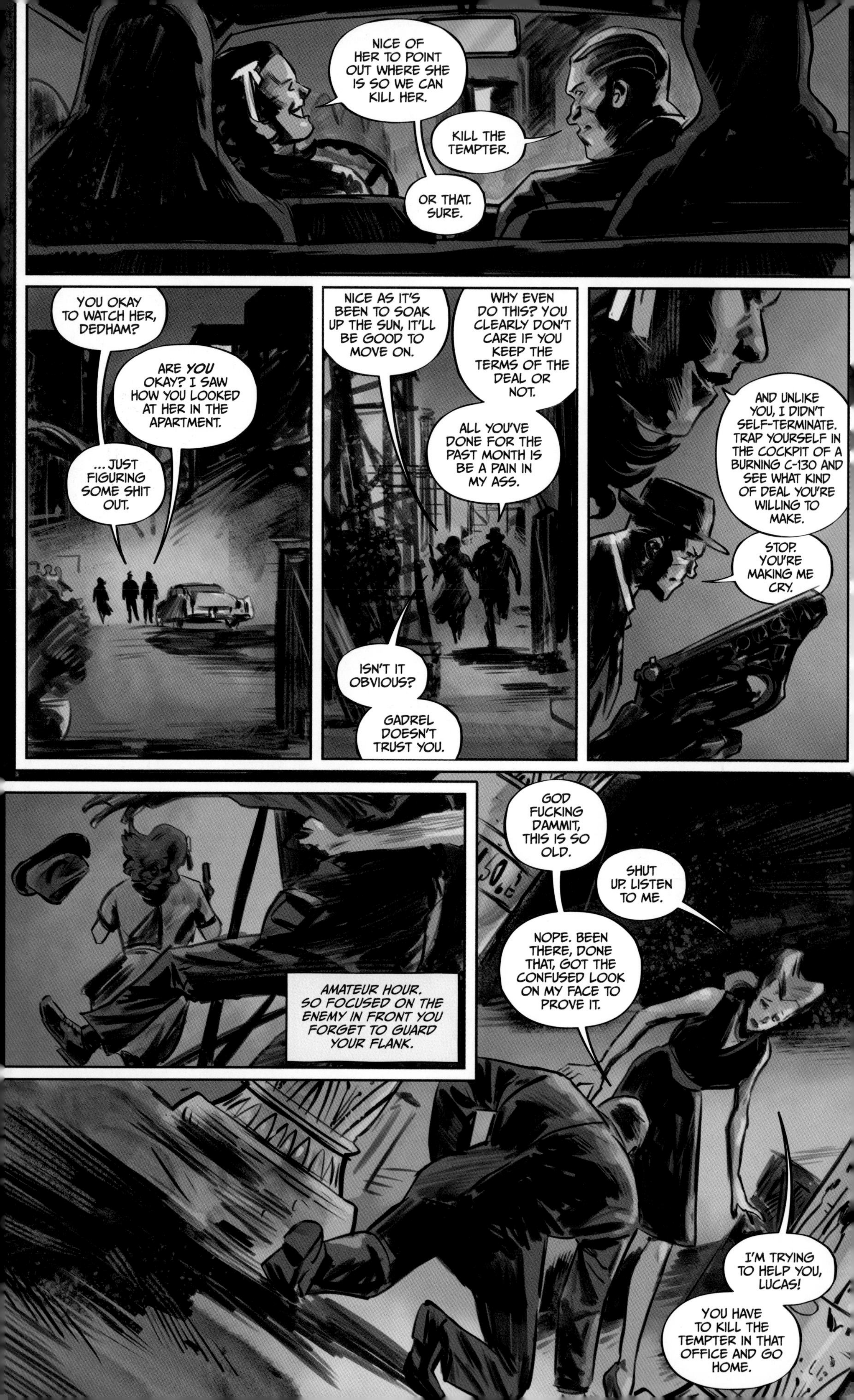
NICE OF HER TO POINT OUT WHERE SHE IS SO WE CAN KILL HER.
KILL THE TEMPTER.
OR THAT. SURE.
YOU OKAY TO WATCH HER, DEDHAM?
ARE *YOU* OKAY? I SAW HOW YOU LOOKED AT HER IN THE APARTMENT.
...JUST FIGURING SOME SHIT OUT.
NICE AS IT'S BEEN TO SOAK UP THE SUN, IT'LL BE GOOD TO MOVE ON.
WHY EVEN DO THIS? YOU CLEARLY DON'T CARE IF YOU KEEP THE TERMS OF THE DEAL OR NOT.
ALL YOU'VE DONE FOR THE PAST MONTH IS BE A PAIN IN MY ASS.
ISN'T IT OBVIOUS?
GADREL DOESN'T TRUST YOU.
AND UNLIKE YOU, I DIDN'T SELF-TERMINATE. TRAP YOURSELF IN THE COCKPIT OF A BURNING C-130 AND SEE WHAT KIND OF DEAL YOU'RE WILLING TO MAKE.
STOP. YOU'RE MAKING ME CRY.
AMATEUR HOUR. SO FOCUSED ON THE ENEMY IN FRONT YOU FORGET TO GUARD YOUR FLANK.
GOD FUCKING DAMMIT, THIS IS SO OLD.
SHUT UP. LISTEN TO ME.
NOPE. BEEN THERE, DONE THAT, GOT THE CONFUSED LOOK ON MY FACE TO PROVE IT.
I'M TRYING TO HELP YOU, LUCAS!
YOU HAVE TO KILL THE TEMPTER IN THAT OFFICE AND GO HOME.

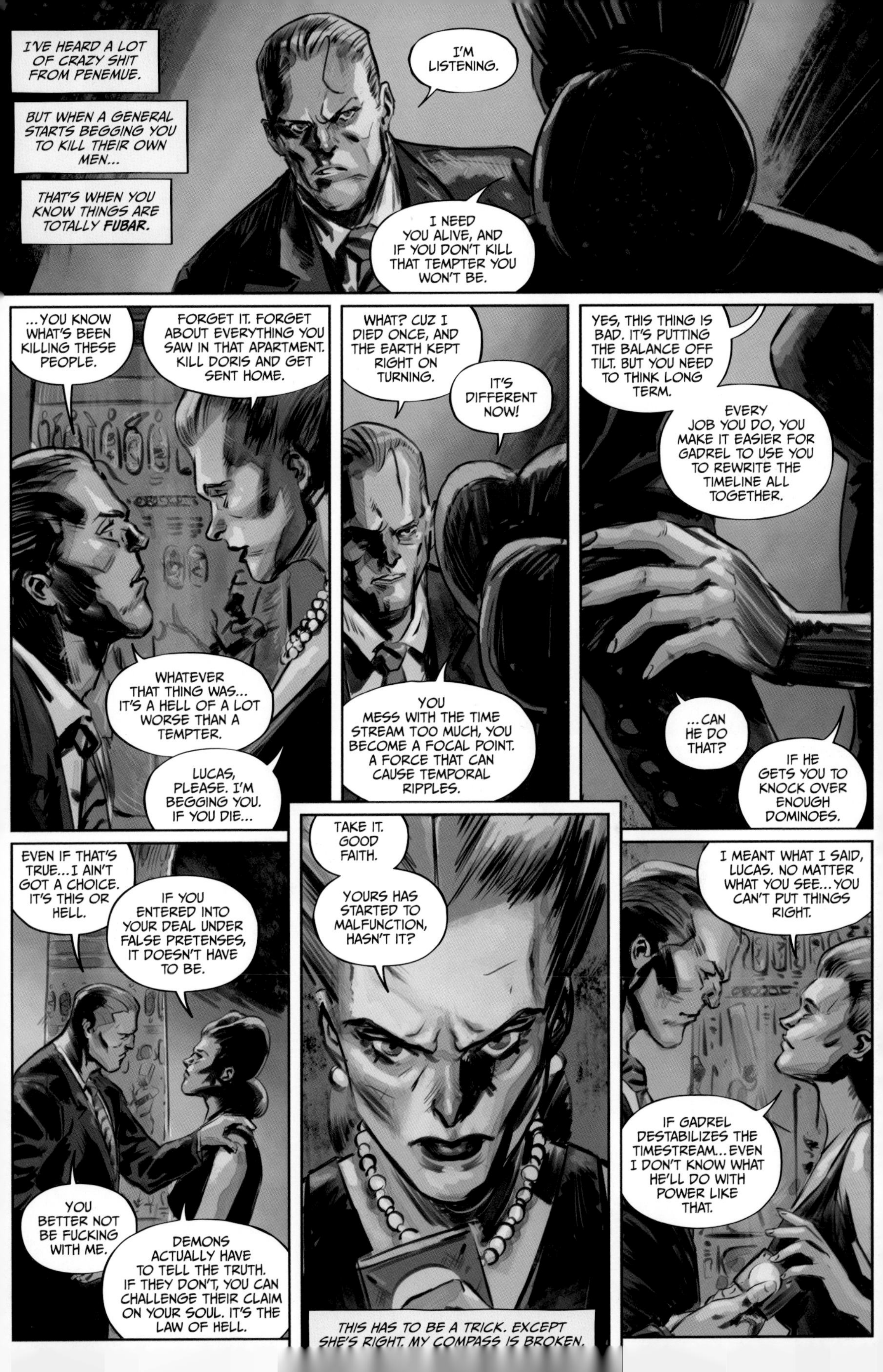
I'VE HEARD A LOT OF CRAZY SHIT FROM PENEMUE.
BUT WHEN A GENERAL STARTS BEGGING YOU TO KILL THEIR OWN MEN...
THAT'S WHEN YOU KNOW THINGS ARE TOTALLY FUBAR.
I'M LISTENING.
I NEED YOU ALIVE, AND IF YOU DON'T KILL THAT TEMPTER YOU WON'T BE.
...YOU KNOW WHAT'S BEEN KILLING THESE PEOPLE.
FORGET IT. FORGET ABOUT EVERYTHING YOU SAW IN THAT APARTMENT. KILL DORIS AND GET SENT HOME.
WHATEVER THAT THING WAS... IT'S A HELL OF A LOT WORSE THAN A TEMPTER.
LUCAS, PLEASE. I'M BEGGING YOU. IF YOU DIE...
WHAT? CUZ I DIED ONCE, AND THE EARTH KEPT RIGHT ON TURNING.
IT'S DIFFERENT NOW!
YOU MESS WITH THE TIME STREAM TOO MUCH, YOU BECOME A FOCAL POINT. A FORCE THAT CAN CAUSE TEMPORAL RIPPLES.
YES, THIS THING IS BAD. IT'S PUTTING THE BALANCE OFF TILT. BUT YOU NEED TO THINK LONG TERM.
EVERY JOB YOU DO, YOU MAKE IT EASIER FOR GADREL TO USE YOU TO REWRITE THE TIMELINE ALL TOGETHER.
...CAN HE DO THAT?
IF HE GETS YOU TO KNOCK OVER ENOUGH DOMINOES.
EVEN IF THAT'S TRUE...I AIN'T GOT A CHOICE. IT'S THIS OR HELL.
IF YOU ENTERED INTO YOUR DEAL UNDER FALSE PRETENSES, IT DOESN'T HAVE TO BE.
YOU BETTER NOT BE FUCKING WITH ME.
DEMONS ACTUALLY HAVE TO TELL THE TRUTH. IF THEY DON'T, YOU CAN CHALLENGE THEIR CLAIM ON YOUR SOUL. IT'S THE LAW OF HELL.
TAKE IT. GOOD FAITH.
YOURS HAS STARTED TO MALFUNCTION, HASN'T IT?
THIS HAS TO BE A TRICK. EXCEPT SHE'S RIGHT. MY COMPASS IS BROKEN.
I MEANT WHAT I SAID, LUCAS. NO MATTER WHAT YOU SEE...YOU CAN'T PUT THINGS RIGHT.
IF GADREL DESTABILIZES THE TIMESTREAM...EVEN I DON'T KNOW WHAT HE'LL DO WITH POWER LIKE THAT.

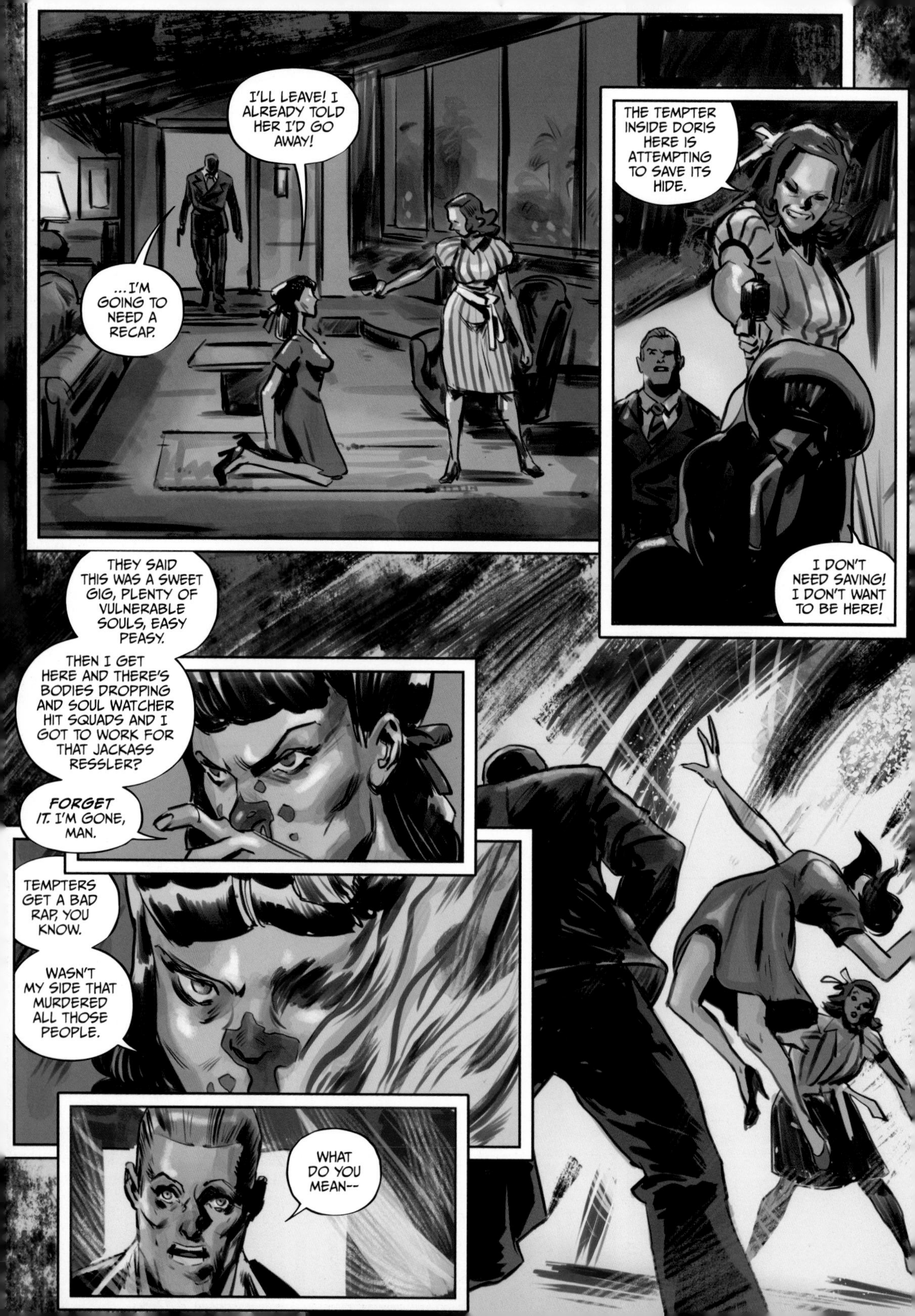
I'LL LEAVE! I ALREADY TOLD HER I'D GO AWAY!
...I'M GOING TO NEED A RECAP.
THE TEMPTER INSIDE DORIS HERE IS ATTEMPTING TO SAVE ITS HIDE.
I DON'T NEED SAVING! I DON'T WANT TO BE HERE!
THEY SAID THIS WAS A SWEET GIG, PLENTY OF VULNERABLE SOULS, EASY PEASY.
THEN I GET HERE AND THERE'S BODIES DROPPING AND SOUL WATCHER HIT SQUADS AND I GOT TO WORK FOR THAT JACKASS RESSLER?
FORGET IT. I'M GONE, MAN.
TEMPTERS GET A BAD RAP, YOU KNOW.
WASN'T MY SIDE THAT MURDERED ALL THOSE PEOPLE.
WHAT DO YOU MEAN--

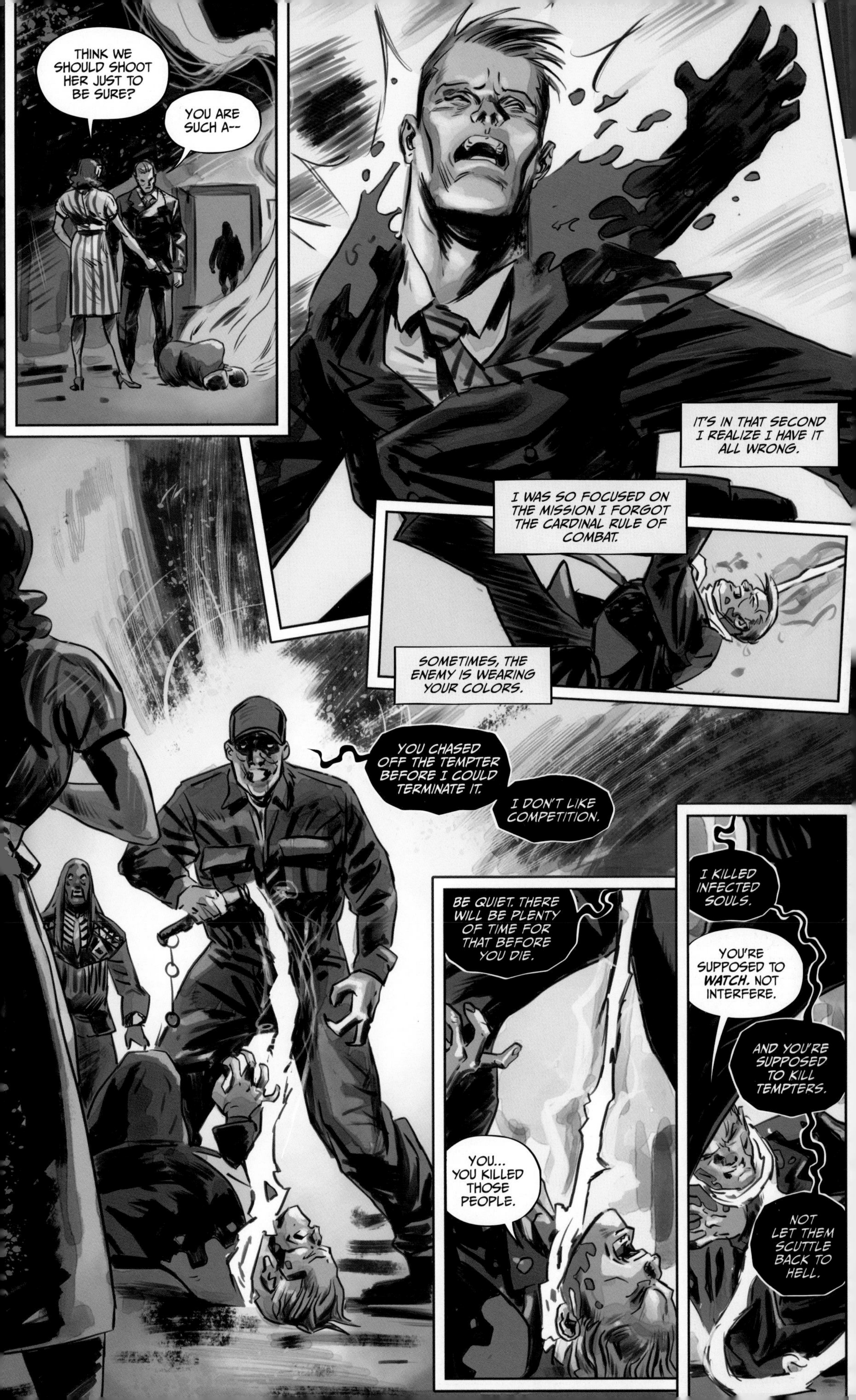
THINK WE SHOULD SHOOT HER JUST TO BE SURE?
YOU ARE SUCH A--
IT'S IN THAT SECOND I REALIZE I HAVE IT ALL WRONG.
I WAS SO FOCUSED ON THE MISSION I FORGOT THE CARDINAL RULE OF COMBAT.
SOMETIMES, THE ENEMY IS WEARING YOUR COLORS.
YOU CHASED OFF THE TEMPTER BEFORE I COULD TERMINATE IT.
I DON'T LIKE COMPETITION.
YOU... YOU KILLED THOSE PEOPLE.
BE QUIET. THERE WILL BE PLENTY OF TIME FOR THAT BEFORE YOU DIE.
I KILLED INFECTED SOULS.
YOU'RE SUPPOSED TO WATCH. NOT INTERFERE.
AND YOU'RE SUPPOSED TO KILL TEMPTERS.
NOT LET THEM SCUTTLE BACK TO HELL.

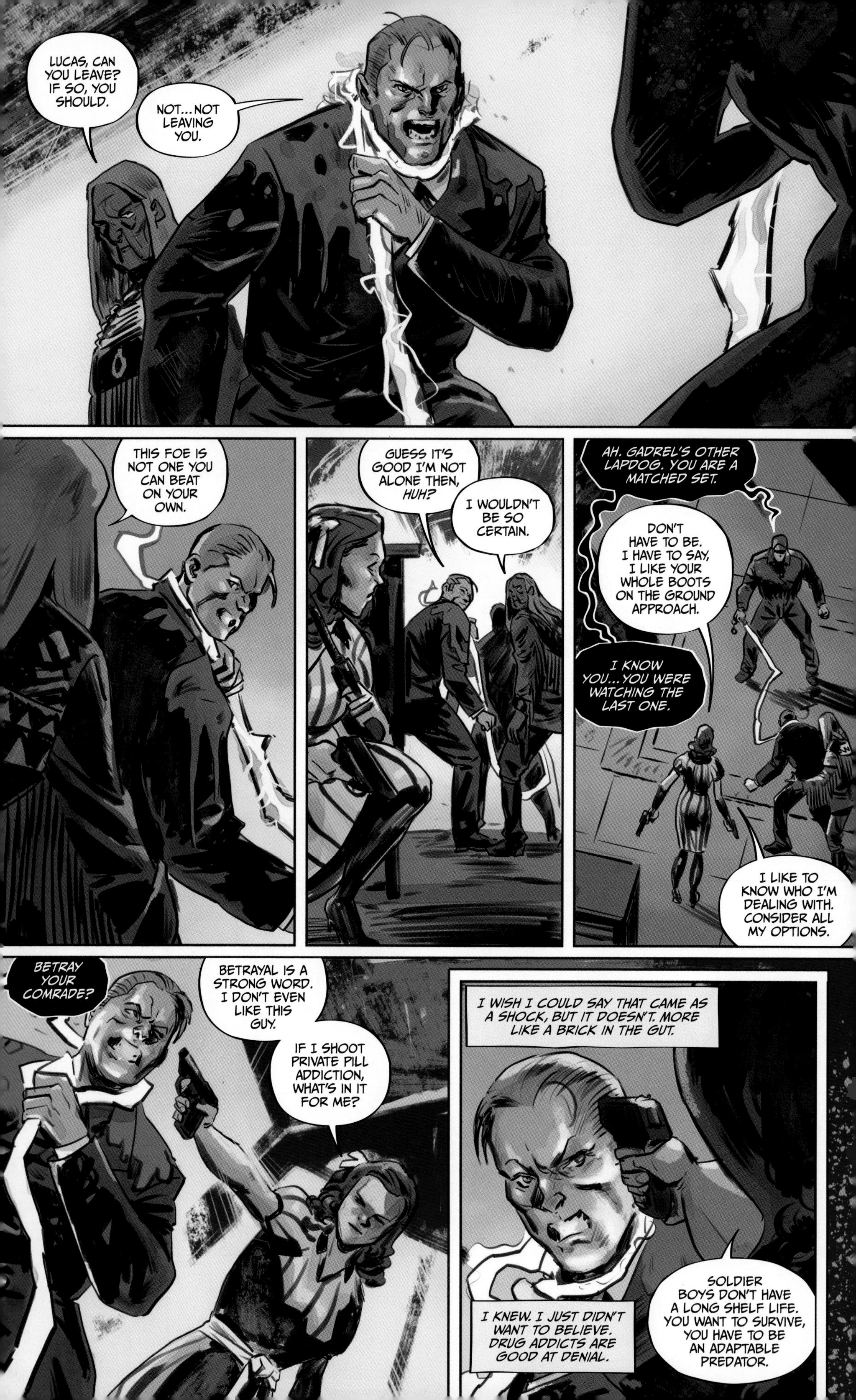
LUCAS, CAN YOU LEAVE? IF SO, YOU SHOULD.
NOT...NOT LEAVING YOU.
THIS FOE IS NOT ONE YOU CAN BEAT ON YOUR OWN.
GUESS IT'S GOOD I'M NOT ALONE THEN, HUH?
I WOULDN'T BE SO CERTAIN.
AH. GADREL'S OTHER LAPDOG. YOU ARE A MATCHED SET.
DON'T HAVE TO BE. I HAVE TO SAY, I LIKE YOUR WHOLE BOOTS ON THE GROUND APPROACH.
I KNOW YOU...YOU WERE WATCHING THE LAST ONE.
I LIKE TO KNOW WHO I'M DEALING WITH. CONSIDER ALL MY OPTIONS.
BETRAY YOUR COMRADE?
BETRAYAL IS A STRONG WORD. I DON'T EVEN LIKE THIS GUY.
IF I SHOOT PRIVATE PILL ADDICTION, WHAT'S IN IT FOR ME?
I WISH I COULD SAY THAT CAME AS A SHOCK, BUT IT DOESN'T. MORE LIKE A BRICK IN THE GUT.
I KNEW. I JUST DIDN'T WANT TO BELIEVE. DRUG ADDICTS ARE GOOD AT DENIAL.
SOLDIER BOYS DON'T HAVE A LONG SHELF LIFE. YOU WANT TO SURVIVE, YOU HAVE TO BE AN ADAPTABLE PREDATOR.

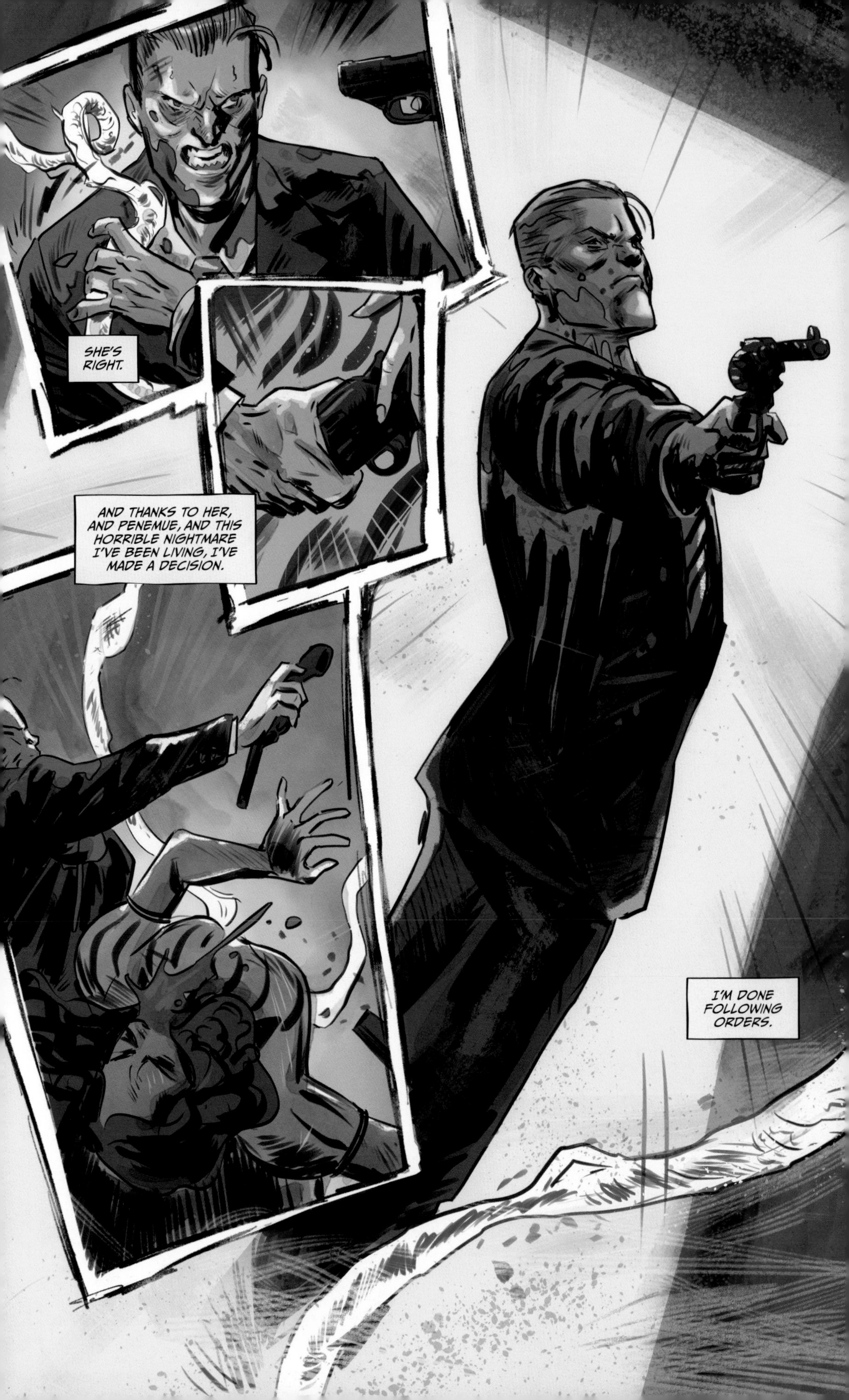
SHE'S RIGHT.
AND THANKS TO HER, AND PENEMUE, AND THIS HORRIBLE NIGHTMARE I'VE BEEN LIVING, I'VE MADE A DECISION.
I'M DONE FOLLOWING ORDERS.

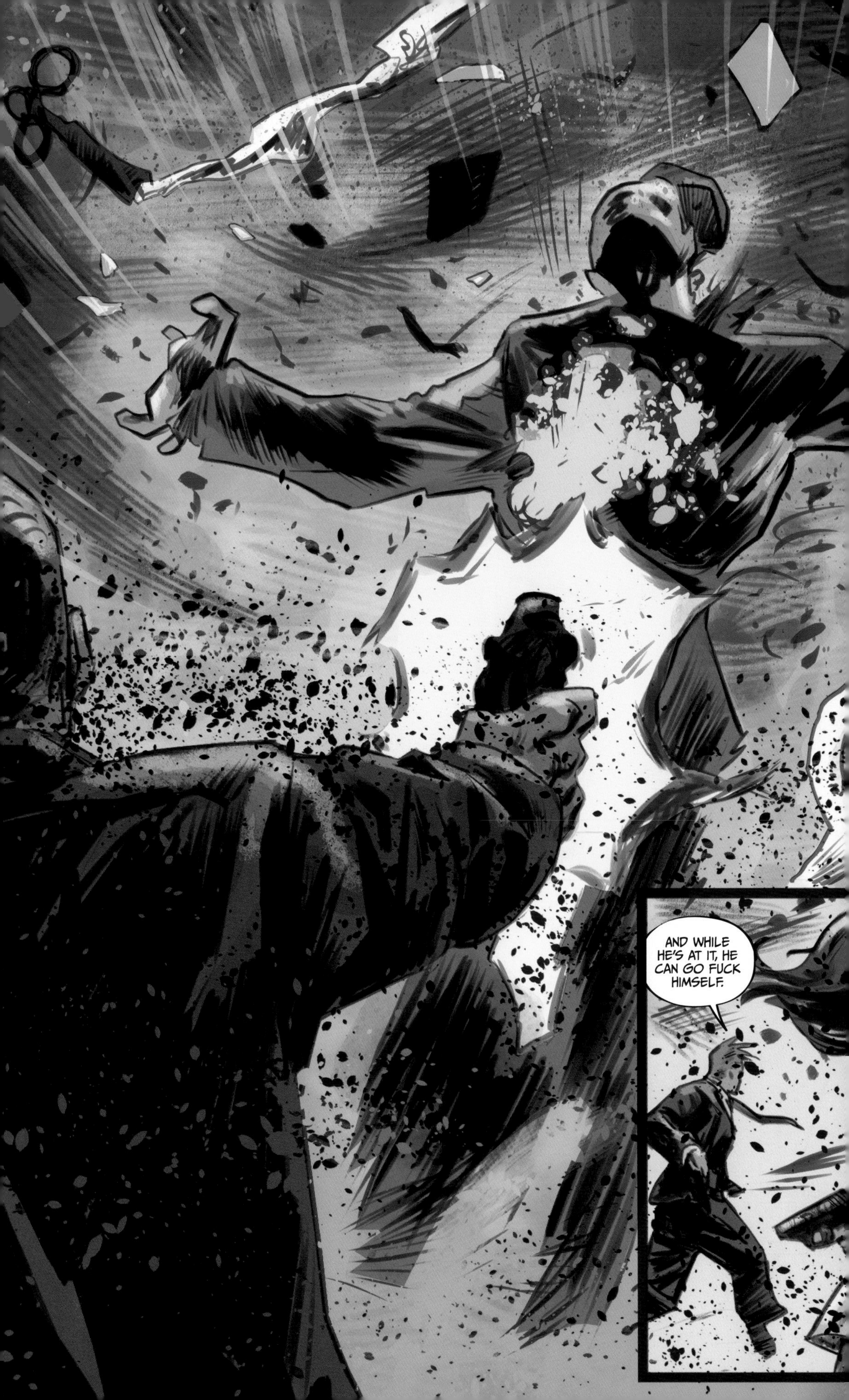
AND WHILE HE'S AT IT, HE CAN GO FUCK HIMSELF.

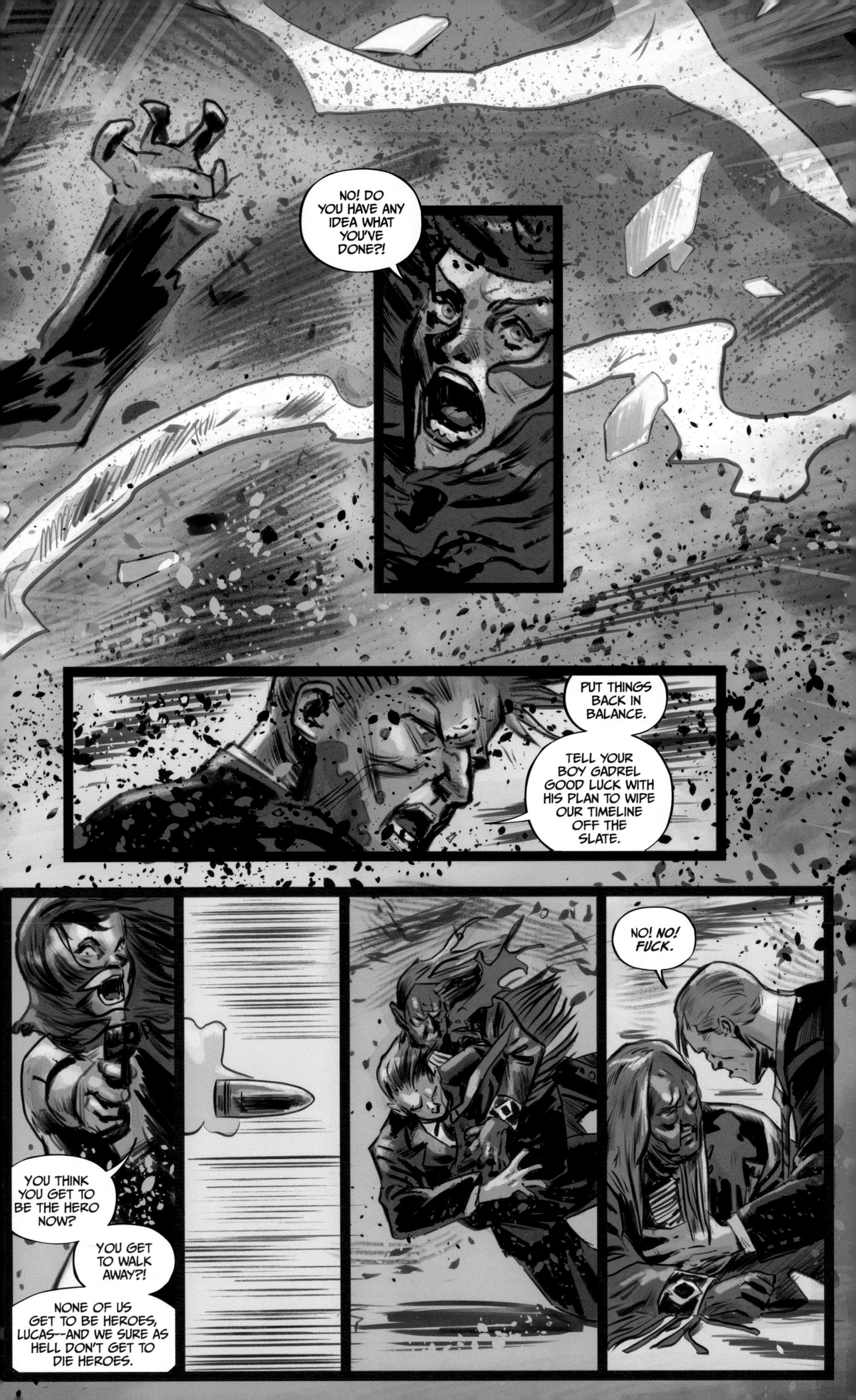
NO! DO YOU HAVE ANY IDEA WHAT YOU'VE DONE?!
PUT THINGS BACK IN BALANCE.
TELL YOUR BOY GADREL GOOD LUCK WITH HIS PLAN TO WIPE OUR TIMELINE OFF THE SLATE.
YOU THINK YOU GET TO BE THE HERO NOW?
YOU GET TO WALK AWAY?!
NONE OF US GET TO BE HEROES, LUCAS--AND WE SURE AS HELL DON'T GET TO DIE HEROES.
NO! *NO!* ***FUCK.***

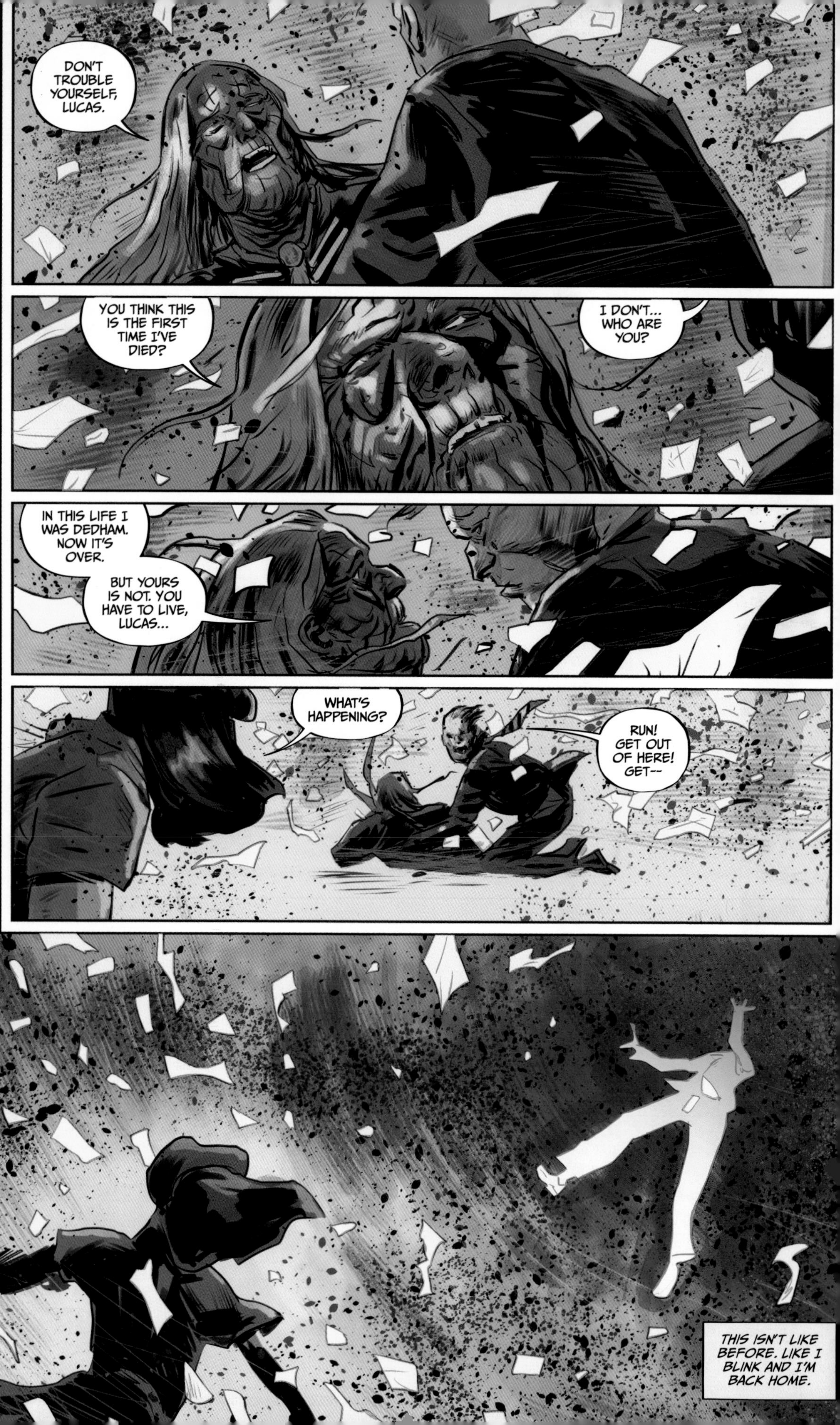
DON'T TROUBLE YOURSELF, LUCAS.
YOU THINK THIS IS THE FIRST TIME I'VE DIED?
I DON'T... WHO ARE YOU?
IN THIS LIFE I WAS DEDHAM. NOW IT'S OVER.
BUT YOURS IS NOT. YOU HAVE TO LIVE, LUCAS...
WHAT'S HAPPENING?
RUN! GET OUT OF HERE! GET--
THIS ISN'T LIKE BEFORE. LIKE I BLINK AND I'M BACK HOME.

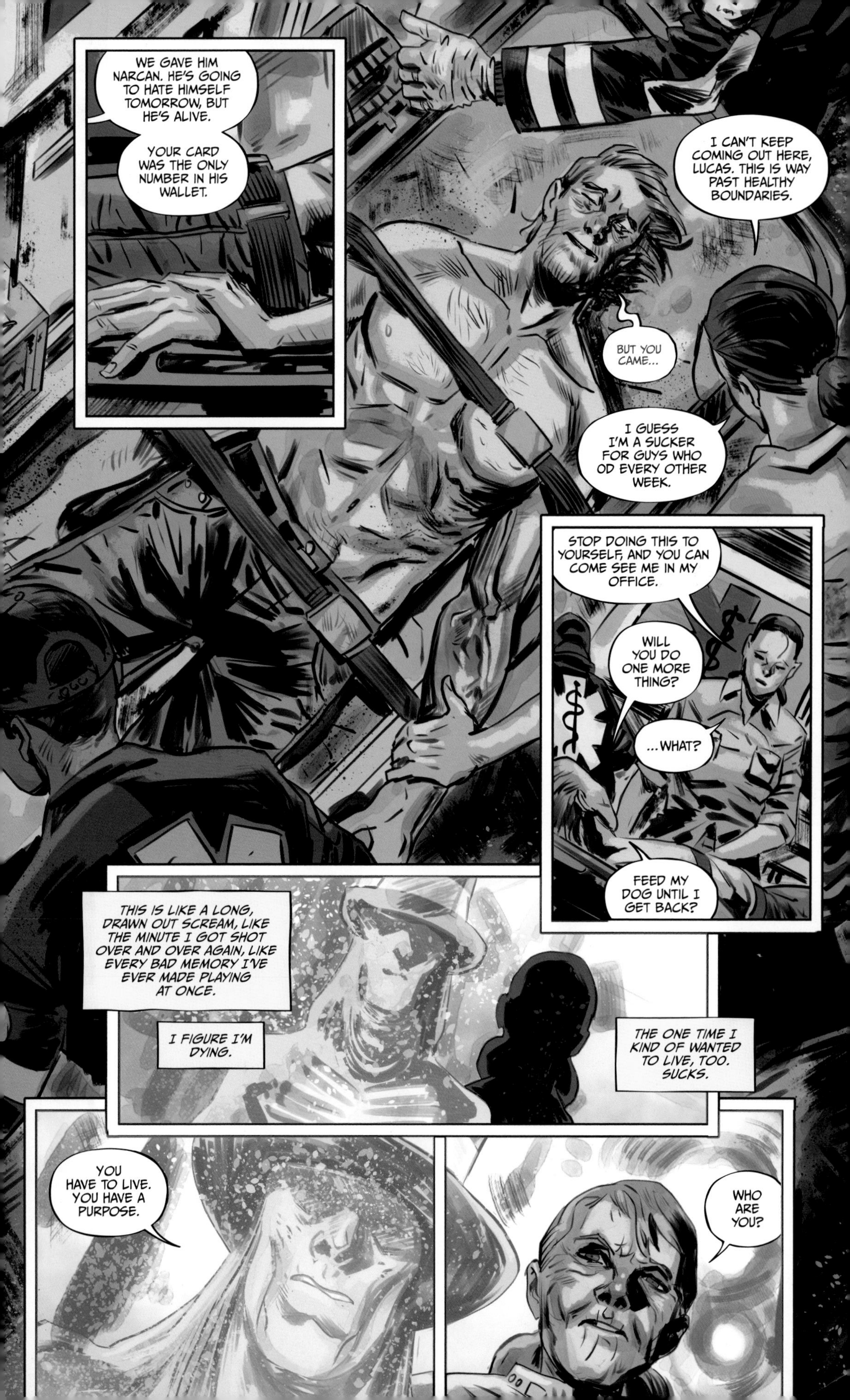
WE GAVE HIM NARCAN. HE'S GOING TO HATE HIMSELF TOMORROW, BUT HE'S ALIVE.
YOUR CARD WAS THE ONLY NUMBER IN HIS WALLET.
I CAN'T KEEP COMING OUT HERE, LUCAS. THIS IS WAY PAST HEALTHY BOUNDARIES.
BUT YOU CAME...
I GUESS I'M A SUCKER FOR GUYS WHO OD EVERY OTHER WEEK.
STOP DOING THIS TO YOURSELF, AND YOU CAN COME SEE ME IN MY OFFICE.
WILL YOU DO ONE MORE THING?
...WHAT?
FEED MY DOG UNTIL I GET BACK?
THIS IS LIKE A LONG, DRAWN OUT SCREAM, LIKE THE MINUTE I GOT SHOT OVER AND OVER AGAIN, LIKE EVERY BAD MEMORY I'VE EVER MADE PLAYING AT ONCE.
I FIGURE I'M DYING.
THE ONE TIME I KIND OF WANTED TO LIVE, TOO. SUCKS.
YOU HAVE TO LIVE. YOU HAVE A PURPOSE.
WHO ARE YOU?

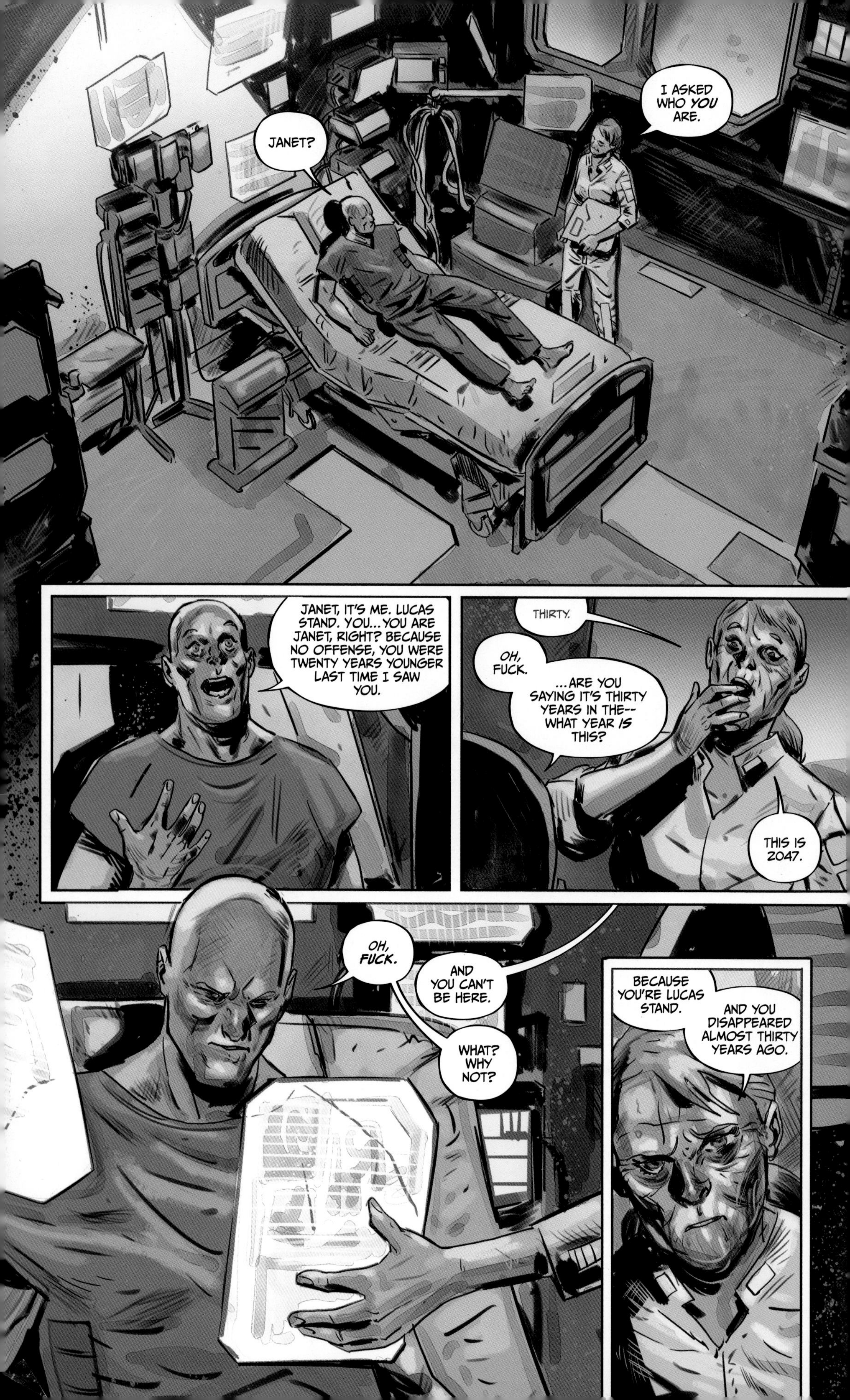
I ASKED WHO YOU ARE.
JANET?
JANET, IT'S ME. LUCAS STAND. YOU... YOU ARE JANET, RIGHT? BECAUSE NO OFFENSE, YOU WERE TWENTY YEARS YOUNGER LAST TIME I SAW YOU.
THIRTY.
OH, FUCK.
...ARE YOU SAYING IT'S THIRTY YEARS IN THE-- WHAT YEAR IS THIS?
THIS IS 2047.
OH, FUCK.
AND YOU CAN'T BE HERE.
WHAT? WHY NOT?
BECAUSE YOU'RE LUCAS STAND.
AND YOU DISAPPEARED ALMOST THIRTY YEARS AGO.

CHAPTER SIX

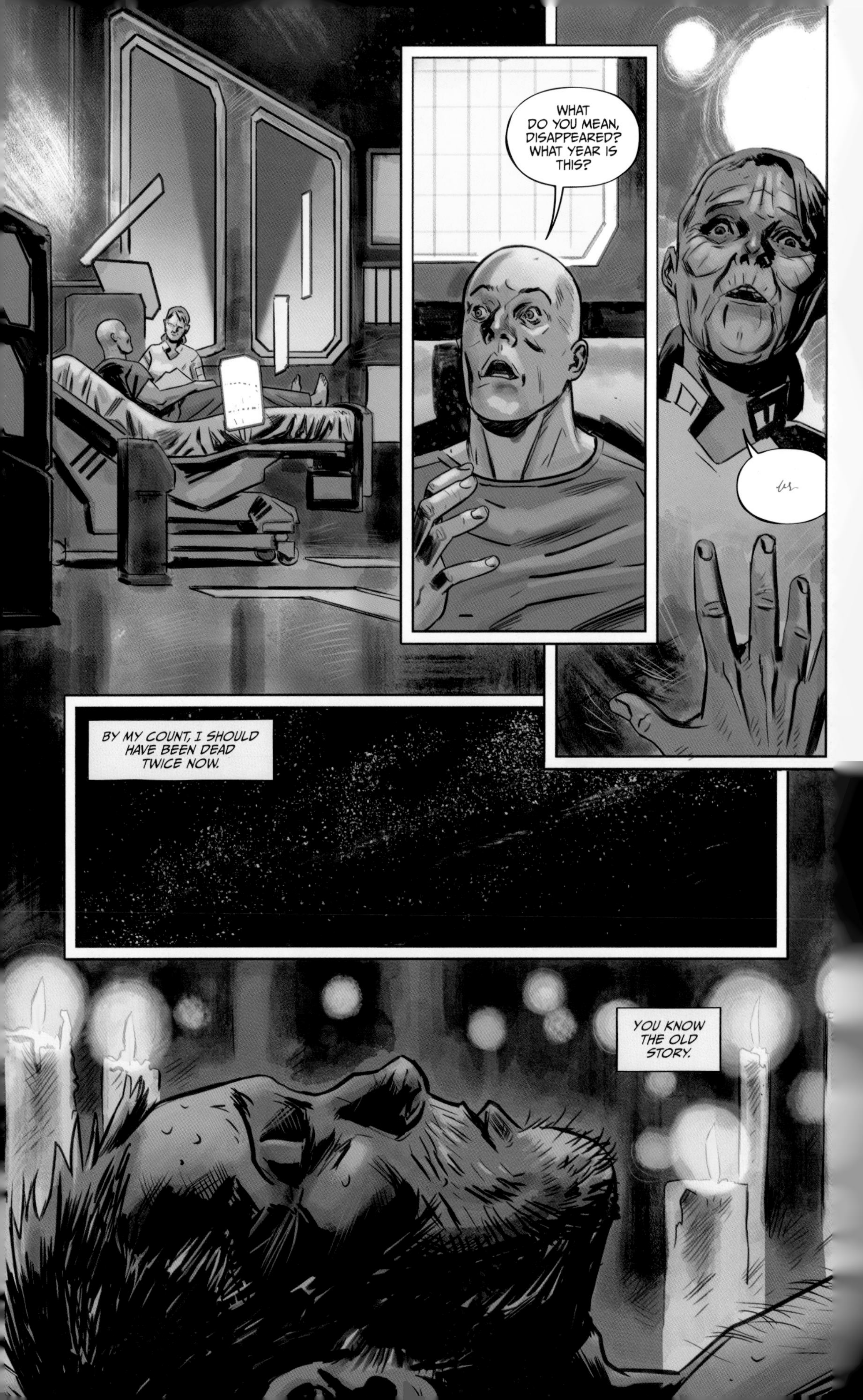
WHAT DO YOU MEAN, DISAPPEARED? WHAT YEAR IS THIS?
BY MY COUNT, I SHOULD HAVE BEEN DEAD TWICE NOW.
YOU KNOW THE OLD STORY.

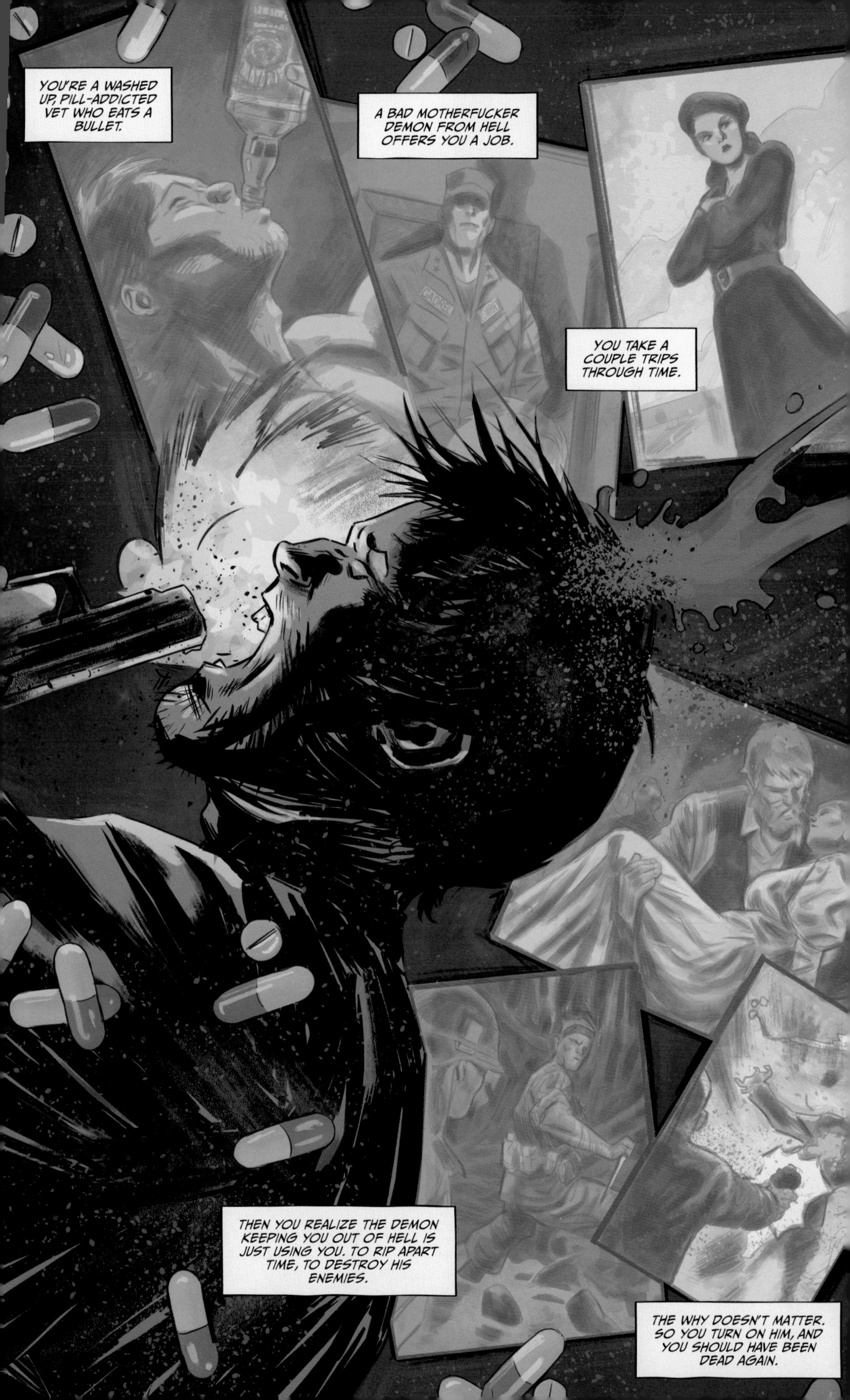
YOU'RE A WASHED UP, PILL-ADDICTED VET WHO EATS A BULLET.
A BAD MOTHERFUCKER DEMON FROM HELL OFFERS YOU A JOB.
YOU TAKE A COUPLE TRIPS THROUGH TIME.
THEN YOU REALIZE THE DEMON KEEPING YOU OUT OF HELL IS JUST USING YOU. TO RIP APART TIME, TO DESTROY HIS ENEMIES.
THE WHY DOESN'T MATTER. SO YOU TURN ON HIM, AND YOU SHOULD HAVE BEEN DEAD AGAIN.

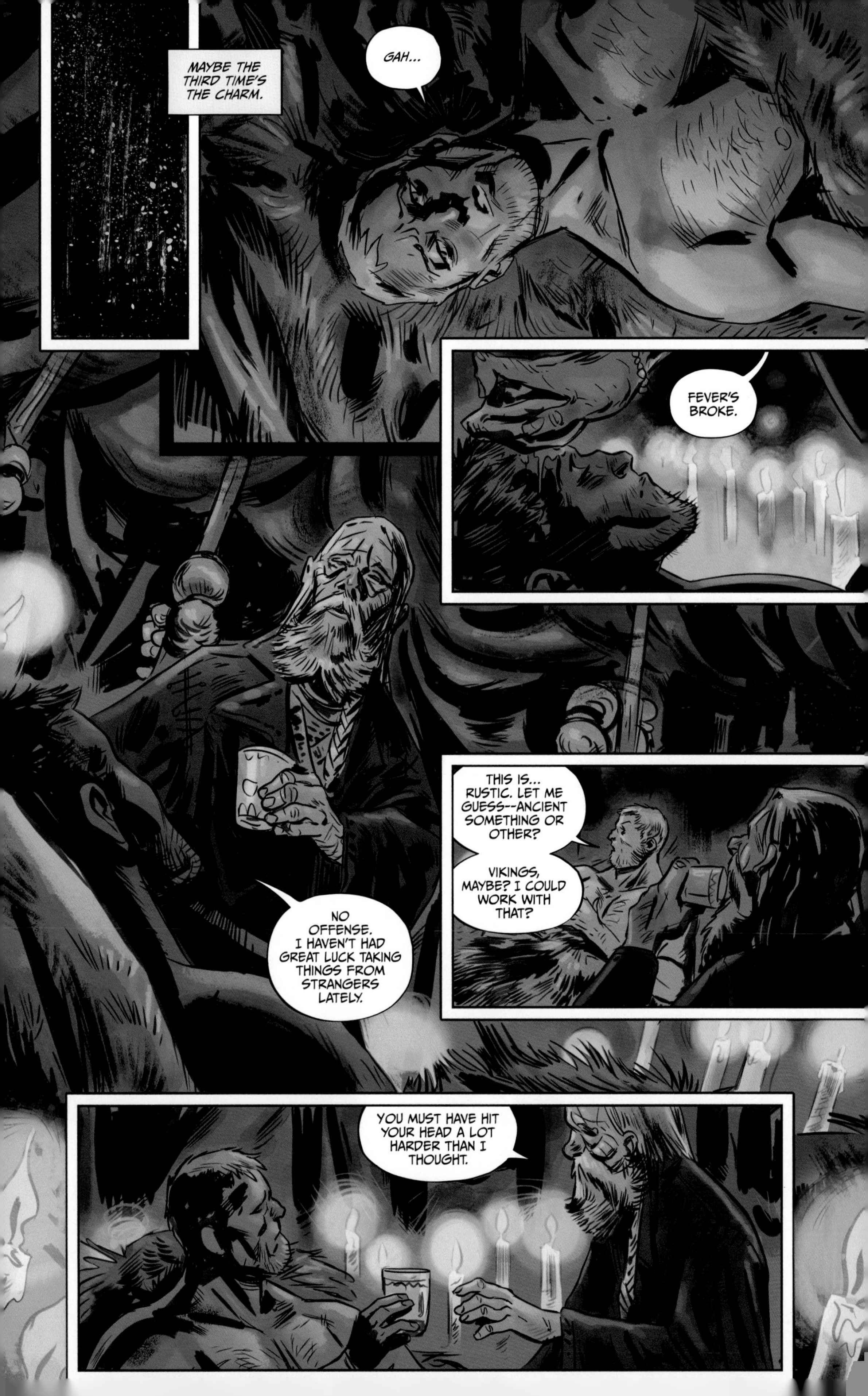
MAYBE THE THIRD TIME'S THE CHARM.
GAH...
FEVER'S BROKE.
NO OFFENSE. I HAVEN'T HAD GREAT LUCK TAKING THINGS FROM STRANGERS LATELY.
THIS IS... RUSTIC. LET ME GUESS--ANCIENT SOMETHING OR OTHER?
VIKINGS, MAYBE? I COULD WORK WITH THAT?
YOU MUST HAVE HIT YOUR HEAD A LOT HARDER THAN I THOUGHT.

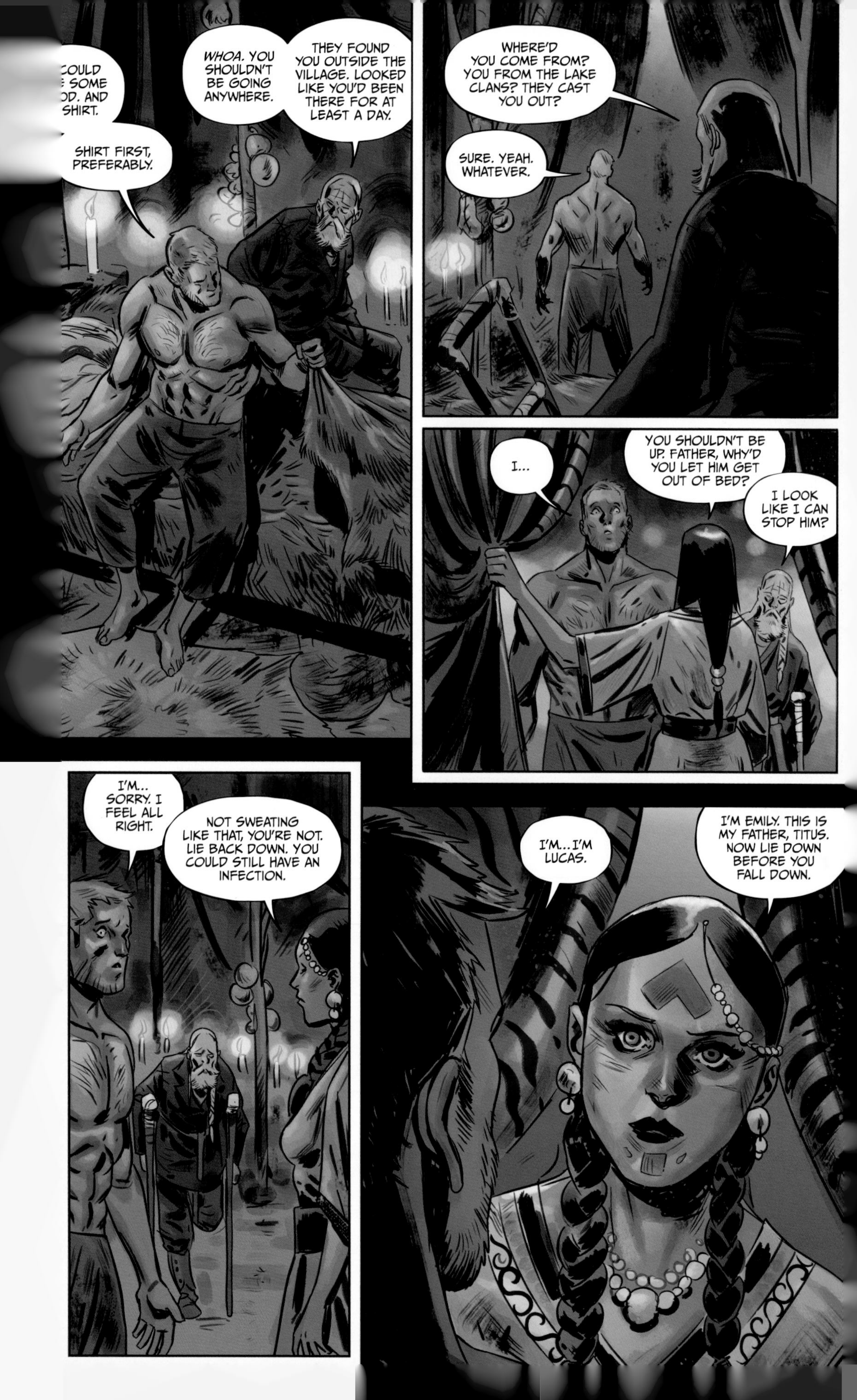
COULD
SOME
OD. AND
SHIRT.
SHIRT FIRST, PREFERABLY.
WHOA. YOU SHOULDN'T BE GOING ANYWHERE.
THEY FOUND YOU OUTSIDE THE VILLAGE. LOOKED LIKE YOU'D BEEN THERE FOR AT LEAST A DAY.
WHERE'D YOU COME FROM? YOU FROM THE LAKE CLANS? THEY CAST YOU OUT?
SURE. YEAH. WHATEVER.
I...
YOU SHOULDN'T BE UP. FATHER, WHY'D YOU LET HIM GET OUT OF BED?
I LOOK LIKE I CAN STOP HIM?
I'M... SORRY. I FEEL ALL RIGHT.
NOT SWEATING LIKE THAT, YOU'RE NOT. LIE BACK DOWN. YOU COULD STILL HAVE AN INFECTION.
I'M...I'M LUCAS.
I'M EMILY. THIS IS MY FATHER, TITUS. NOW LIE DOWN BEFORE YOU FALL DOWN.

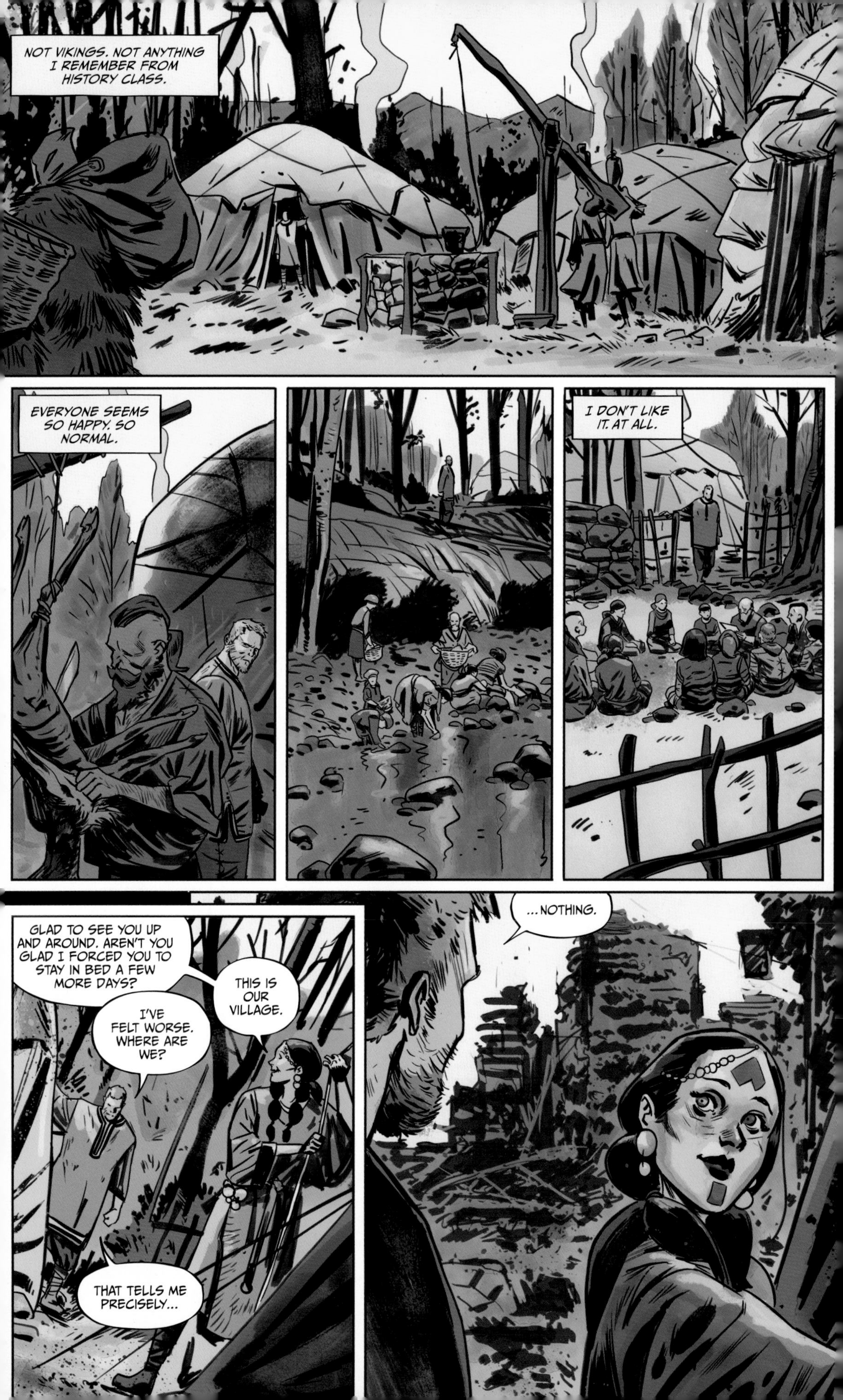
NOT VIKINGS. NOT ANYTHING I REMEMBER FROM HISTORY CLASS.
EVERYONE SEEMS SO HAPPY. SO NORMAL.
I DON'T LIKE IT. AT ALL.
GLAD TO SEE YOU UP AND AROUND. AREN'T YOU GLAD I FORCED YOU TO STAY IN BED A FEW MORE DAYS?
I'VE FELT WORSE. WHERE ARE WE?
THIS IS OUR VILLAGE.
THAT TELLS ME PRECISELY...
...NOTHING.

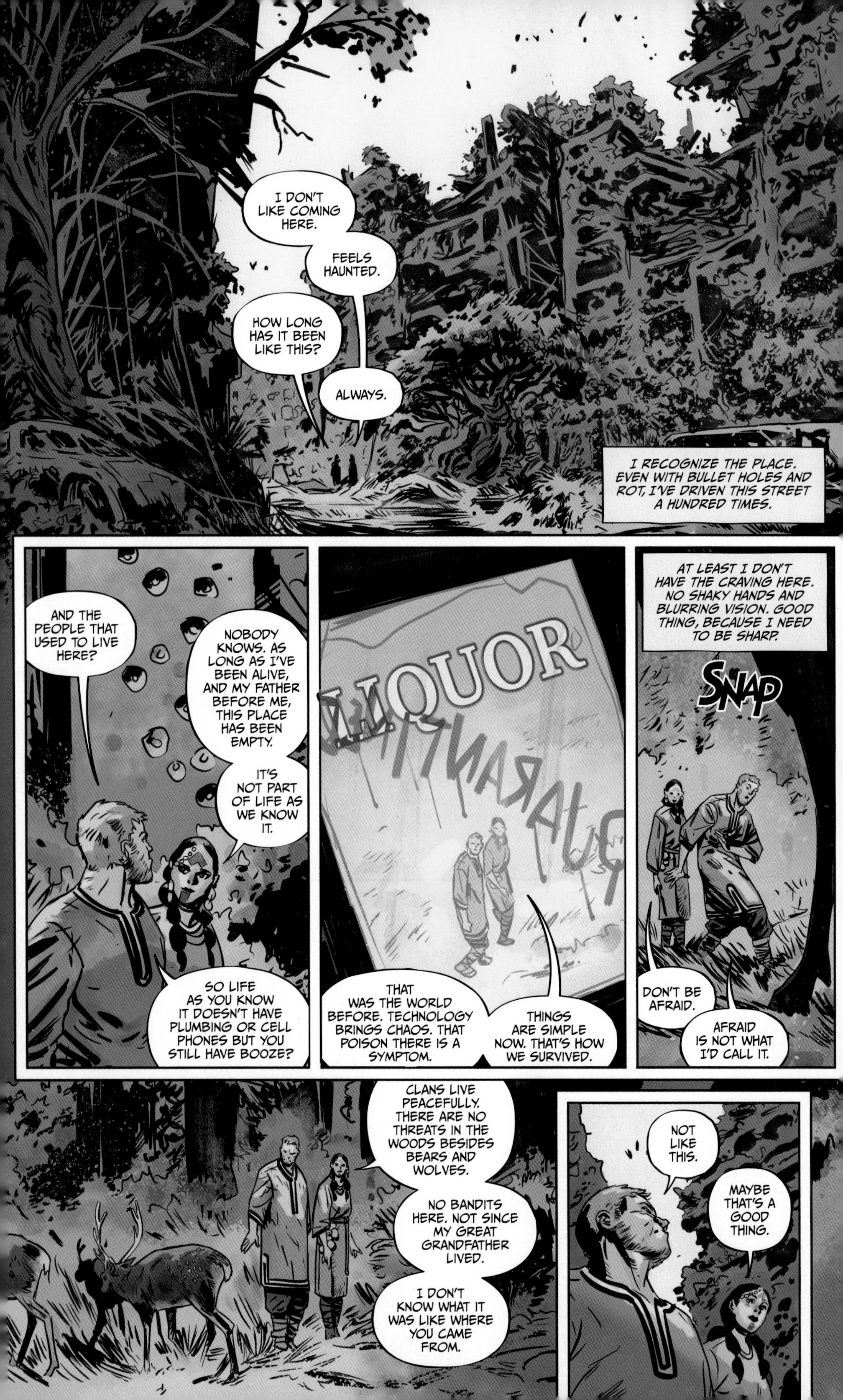
I DON'T LIKE COMING HERE.
FEELS HAUNTED.
HOW LONG HAS IT BEEN LIKE THIS?
ALWAYS.
I RECOGNIZE THE PLACE. EVEN WITH BULLET HOLES AND ROT, I'VE DRIVEN THIS STREET A HUNDRED TIMES.
AND THE PEOPLE THAT USED TO LIVE HERE?
NOBODY KNOWS. AS LONG AS I'VE BEEN ALIVE, AND MY FATHER BEFORE ME, THIS PLACE HAS BEEN EMPTY.
IT'S NOT PART OF LIFE AS WE KNOW IT.
SO LIFE AS YOU KNOW IT DOESN'T HAVE PLUMBING OR CELL PHONES BUT YOU STILL HAVE BOOZE?
LIQUOR
THAT WAS THE WORLD BEFORE. TECHNOLOGY BRINGS CHAOS. THAT POISON THERE IS A SYMPTOM.
THINGS ARE SIMPLE NOW. THAT'S HOW WE SURVIVED.
AT LEAST I DON'T HAVE THE CRAVING HERE. NO SHAKY HANDS AND BLURRING VISION. GOOD THING, BECAUSE I NEED TO BE SHARP.
SNAP
DON'T BE AFRAID.
AFRAID IS NOT WHAT I'D CALL IT.
CLANS LIVE PEACEFULLY. THERE ARE NO THREATS IN THE WOODS BESIDES BEARS AND WOLVES.
NO BANDITS HERE. NOT SINCE MY GREAT GRANDFATHER LIVED.
I DON'T KNOW WHAT IT WAS LIKE WHERE YOU CAME FROM.
NOT LIKE THIS.
MAYBE THAT'S A GOOD THING.

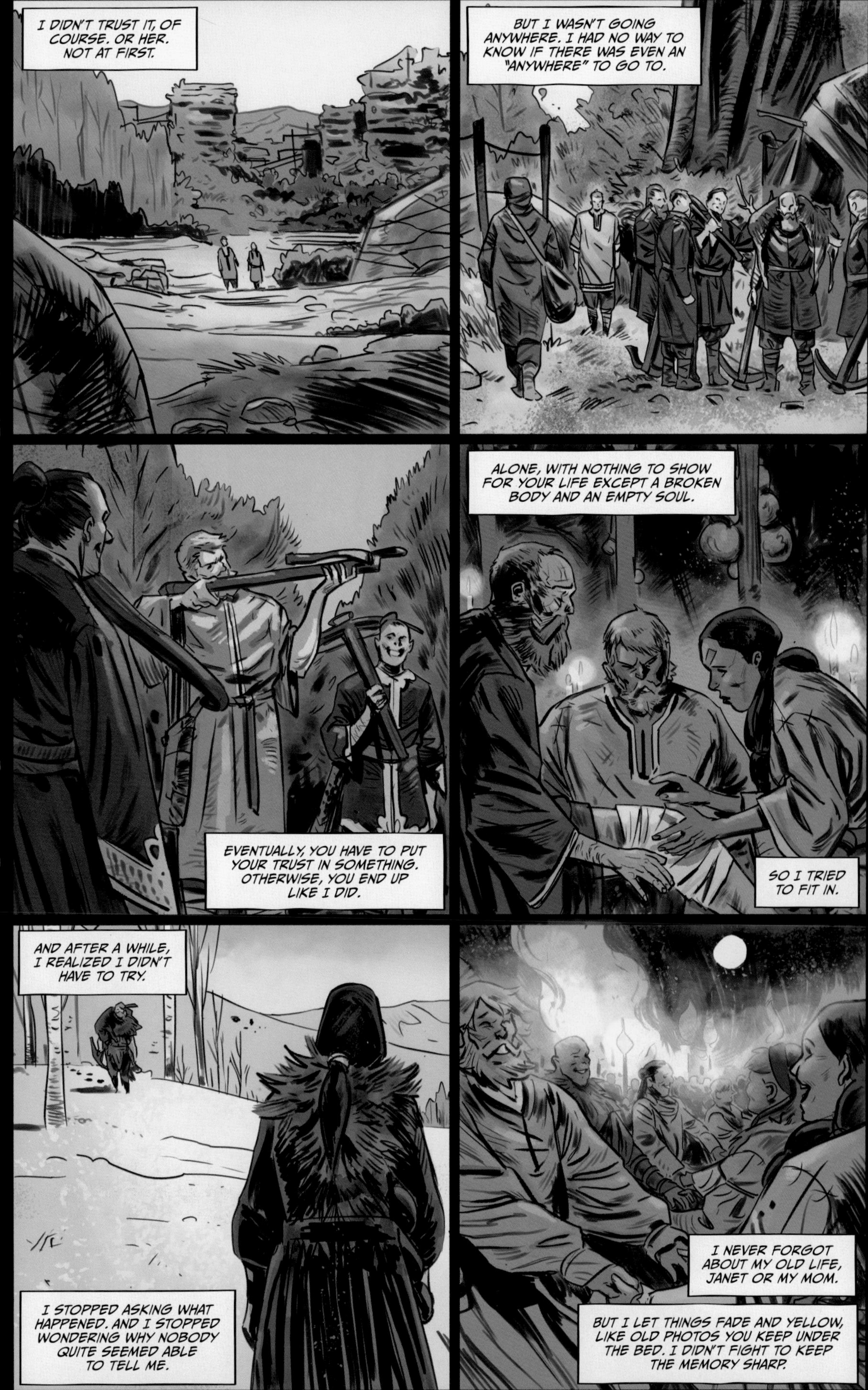
I DIDN'T TRUST IT, OF COURSE. OR HER. NOT AT FIRST.
BUT I WASN'T GOING ANYWHERE. I HAD NO WAY TO KNOW IF THERE WAS EVEN AN "ANYWHERE" TO GO TO.
EVENTUALLY, YOU HAVE TO PUT YOUR TRUST IN SOMETHING. OTHERWISE, YOU END UP LIKE I DID.
ALONE, WITH NOTHING TO SHOW FOR YOUR LIFE EXCEPT A BROKEN BODY AND AN EMPTY SOUL.
SO I TRIED TO FIT IN.
AND AFTER A WHILE, I REALIZED I DIDN'T HAVE TO TRY.
I STOPPED ASKING WHAT HAPPENED. AND I STOPPED WONDERING WHY NOBODY QUITE SEEMED ABLE TO TELL ME.
I NEVER FORGOT ABOUT MY OLD LIFE, JANET OR MY MOM.
BUT I LET THINGS FADE AND YELLOW, LIKE OLD PHOTOS YOU KEEP UNDER THE BED. I DIDN'T FIGHT TO KEEP THE MEMORY SHARP.

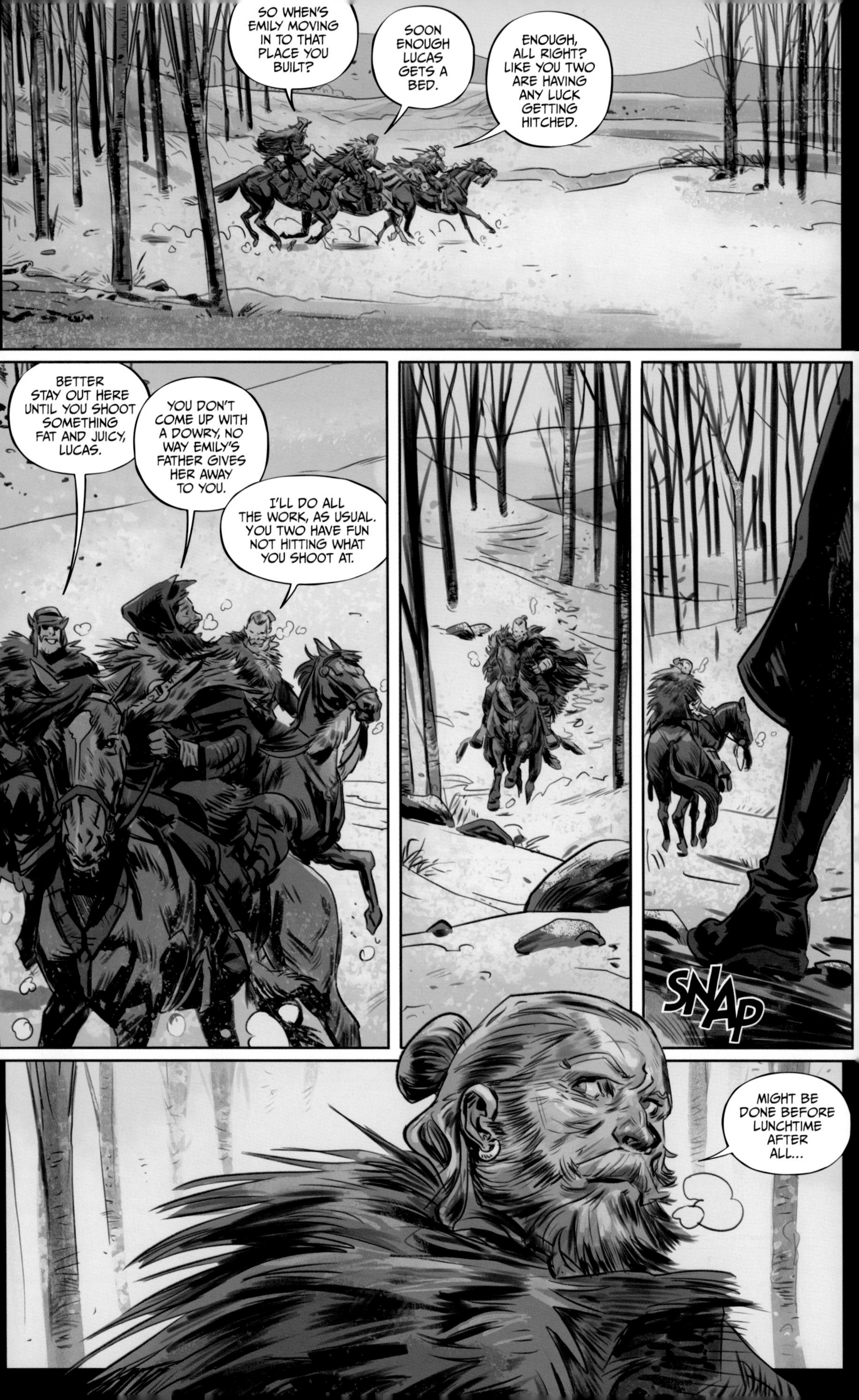
SO WHEN'S EMILY MOVING IN TO THAT PLACE YOU BUILT?
SOON ENOUGH LUCAS GETS A BED.
ENOUGH, ALL RIGHT? LIKE YOU TWO ARE HAVING ANY LUCK GETTING HITCHED.
BETTER STAY OUT HERE UNTIL YOU SHOOT SOMETHING FAT AND JUICY, LUCAS.
YOU DON'T COME UP WITH A DOWRY, NO WAY EMILY'S FATHER GIVES HER AWAY TO YOU.
I'LL DO ALL THE WORK, AS USUAL. YOU TWO HAVE FUN NOT HITTING WHAT YOU SHOOT AT.
SNAP
MIGHT BE DONE BEFORE LUNCHTIME AFTER ALL...

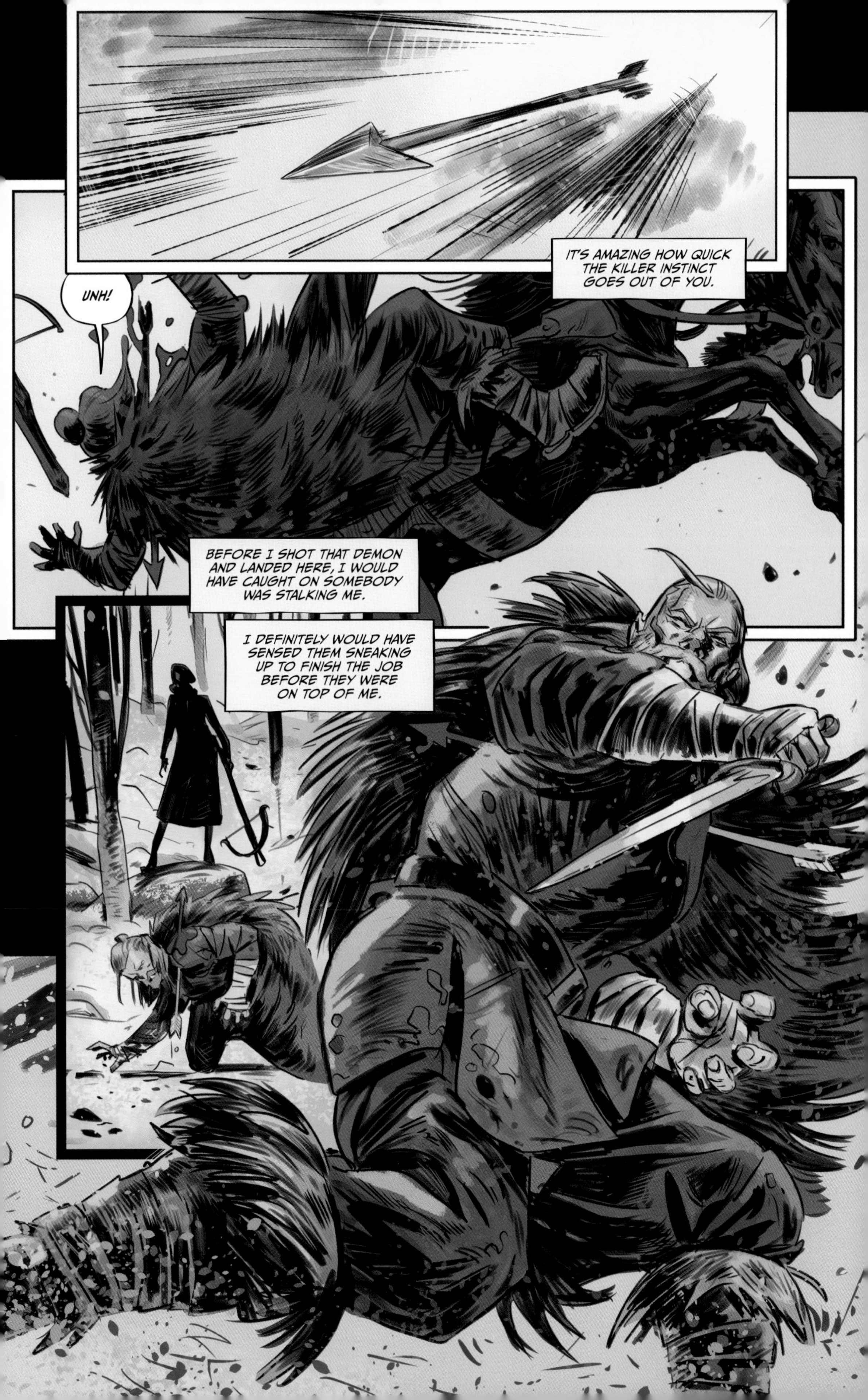
IT'S AMAZING HOW QUICK THE KILLER INSTINCT GOES OUT OF YOU.
UNH!
BEFORE I SHOT THAT DEMON AND LANDED HERE, I WOULD HAVE CAUGHT ON SOMEBODY WAS STALKING ME.
I DEFINITELY WOULD HAVE SENSED THEM SNEAKING UP TO FINISH THE JOB BEFORE THEY WERE ON TOP OF ME.

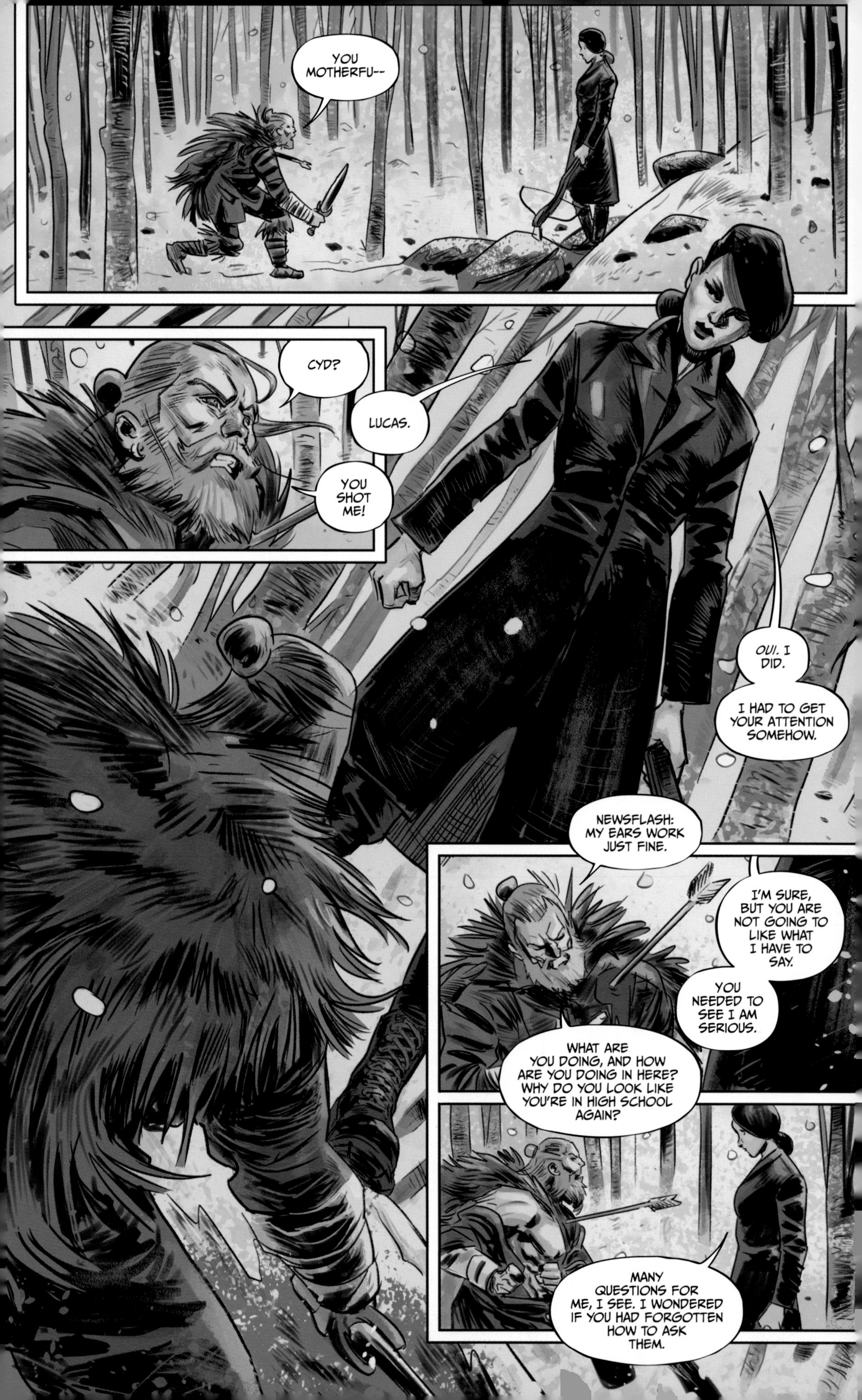
YOU MOTHERFU--
CYD?
LUCAS.
YOU SHOT ME!
OUI. I DID.
I HAD TO GET YOUR ATTENTION SOMEHOW.
NEWSFLASH: MY EARS WORK JUST FINE.
I'M SURE, BUT YOU ARE NOT GOING TO LIKE WHAT I HAVE TO SAY.
YOU NEEDED TO SEE I AM SERIOUS.
WHAT ARE YOU DOING, AND HOW ARE YOU DOING IN HERE? WHY DO YOU LOOK LIKE YOU'RE IN HIGH SCHOOL AGAIN?
MANY QUESTIONS FOR ME, I SEE. I WONDERED IF YOU HAD FORGOTTEN HOW TO ASK THEM.

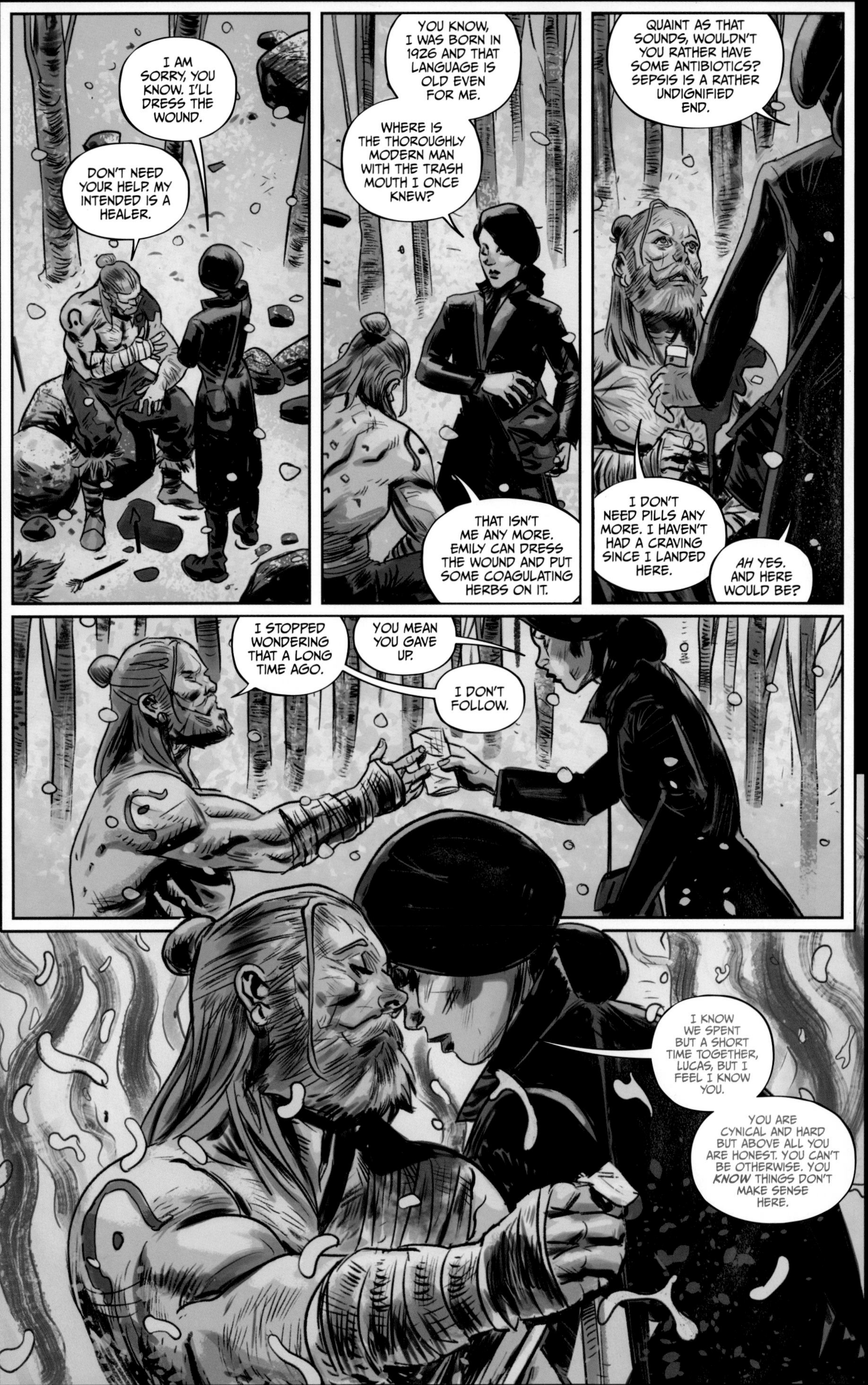
I AM SORRY, YOU KNOW. I'LL DRESS THE WOUND.
DON'T NEED YOUR HELP. MY INTENDED IS A HEALER.
YOU KNOW, I WAS BORN IN 1926 AND THAT LANGUAGE IS OLD EVEN FOR ME.
WHERE IS THE THOROUGHLY MODERN MAN WITH THE TRASH MOUTH I ONCE KNEW?
THAT ISN'T ME ANY MORE. EMILY CAN DRESS THE WOUND AND PUT SOME COAGULATING HERBS ON IT.
QUAINT AS THAT SOUNDS, WOULDN'T YOU RATHER HAVE SOME ANTIBIOTICS? SEPSIS IS A RATHER UNDIGNIFIED END.
I DON'T NEED PILLS ANY MORE. I HAVEN'T HAD A CRAVING SINCE I LANDED HERE.
AH YES. AND HERE WOULD BE?
I STOPPED WONDERING THAT A LONG TIME AGO.
YOU MEAN YOU GAVE UP.
I DON'T FOLLOW.
I KNOW WE SPENT BUT A SHORT TIME TOGETHER, LUCAS, BUT I FEEL I KNOW YOU.
YOU ARE CYNICAL AND HARD BUT ABOVE ALL YOU ARE HONEST. YOU CAN'T BE OTHERWISE. YOU KNOW THINGS DON'T MAKE SENSE HERE.

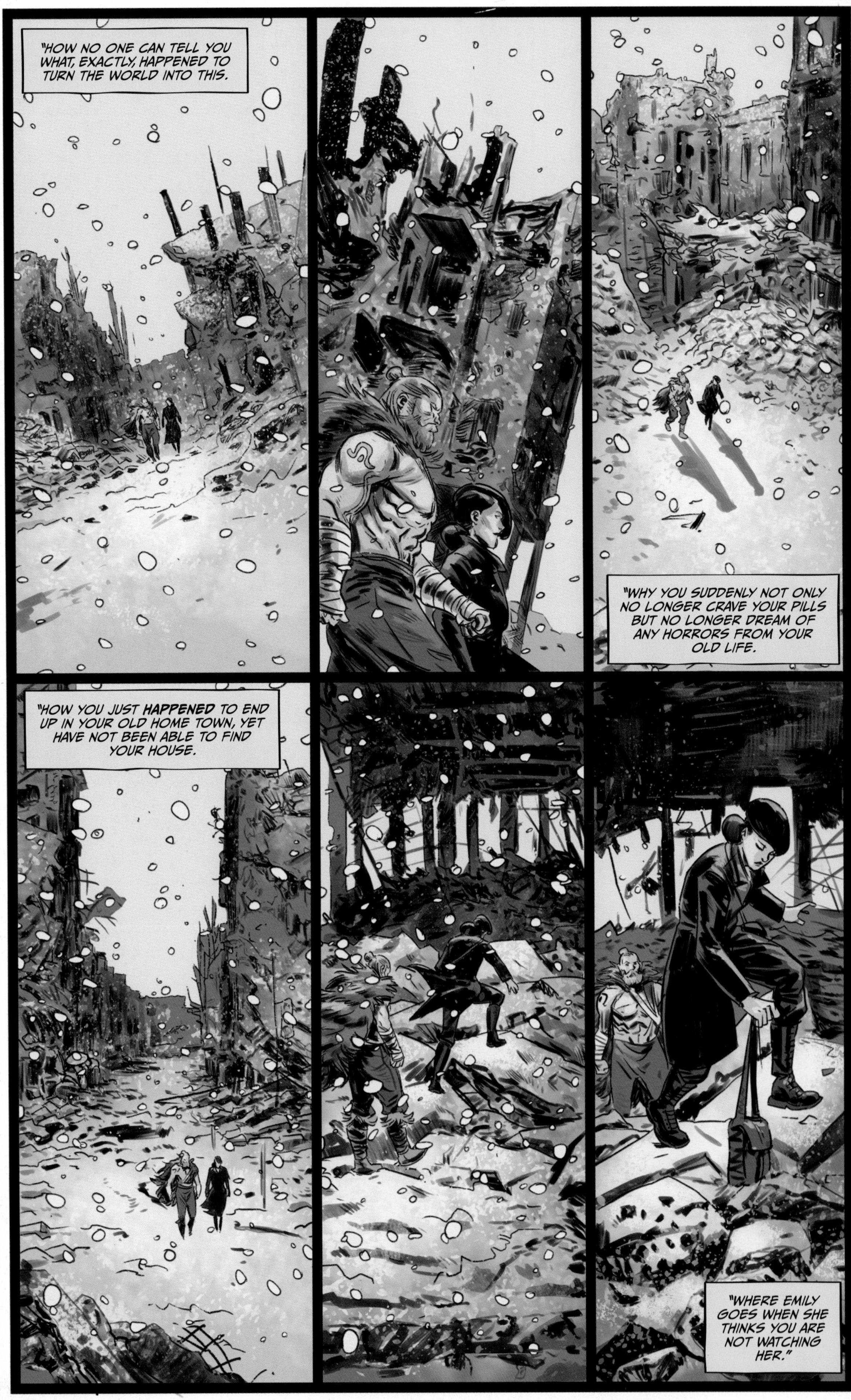
"HOW NO ONE CAN TELL YOU WHAT, EXACTLY, HAPPENED TO TURN THE WORLD INTO THIS.
"WHY YOU SUDDENLY NOT ONLY NO LONGER CRAVE YOUR PILLS BUT NO LONGER DREAM OF ANY HORRORS FROM YOUR OLD LIFE.
"HOW YOU JUST HAPPENED TO END UP IN YOUR OLD HOME TOWN, YET HAVE NOT BEEN ABLE TO FIND YOUR HOUSE.
"WHERE EMILY GOES WHEN SHE THINKS YOU ARE NOT WATCHING HER."

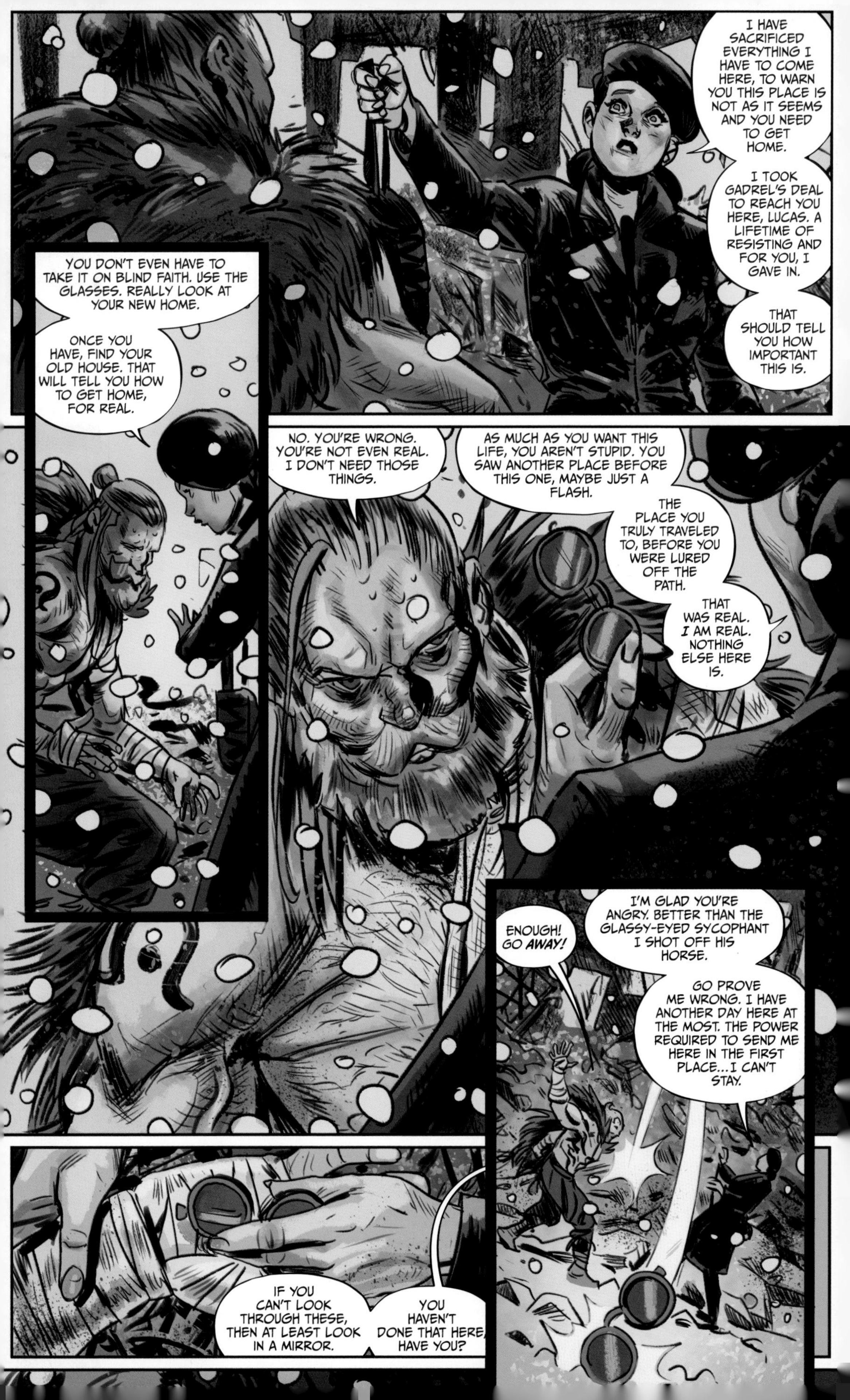
I HAVE SACRIFICED EVERYTHING I HAVE TO COME HERE, TO WARN YOU THIS PLACE IS NOT AS IT SEEMS AND YOU NEED TO GET HOME.
I TOOK GADREL'S DEAL TO REACH YOU HERE, LUCAS. A LIFETIME OF RESISTING AND FOR YOU, I GAVE IN.
THAT SHOULD TELL YOU HOW IMPORTANT THIS IS.
YOU DON'T EVEN HAVE TO TAKE IT ON BLIND FAITH. USE THE GLASSES. REALLY LOOK AT YOUR NEW HOME.
ONCE YOU HAVE, FIND YOUR OLD HOUSE. THAT WILL TELL YOU HOW TO GET HOME, FOR REAL.
NO. YOU'RE WRONG. YOU'RE NOT EVEN REAL. I DON'T NEED THOSE THINGS.
AS MUCH AS YOU WANT THIS LIFE, YOU AREN'T STUPID. YOU SAW ANOTHER PLACE BEFORE THIS ONE, MAYBE JUST A FLASH.
THE PLACE YOU TRULY TRAVELED TO, BEFORE YOU WERE LURED OFF THE PATH.
THAT WAS REAL. *I* AM REAL. NOTHING ELSE HERE IS.
IF YOU CAN'T LOOK THROUGH THESE, THEN AT LEAST LOOK IN A MIRROR.
YOU HAVEN'T DONE THAT HERE, HAVE YOU?
ENOUGH! GO ***AWAY!***
I'M GLAD YOU'RE ANGRY. BETTER THAN THE GLASSY-EYED SYCOPHANT I SHOT OFF HIS HORSE.
GO PROVE ME WRONG. I HAVE ANOTHER DAY HERE AT THE MOST. THE POWER REQUIRED TO SEND ME HERE IN THE FIRST PLACE...I CAN'T STAY.

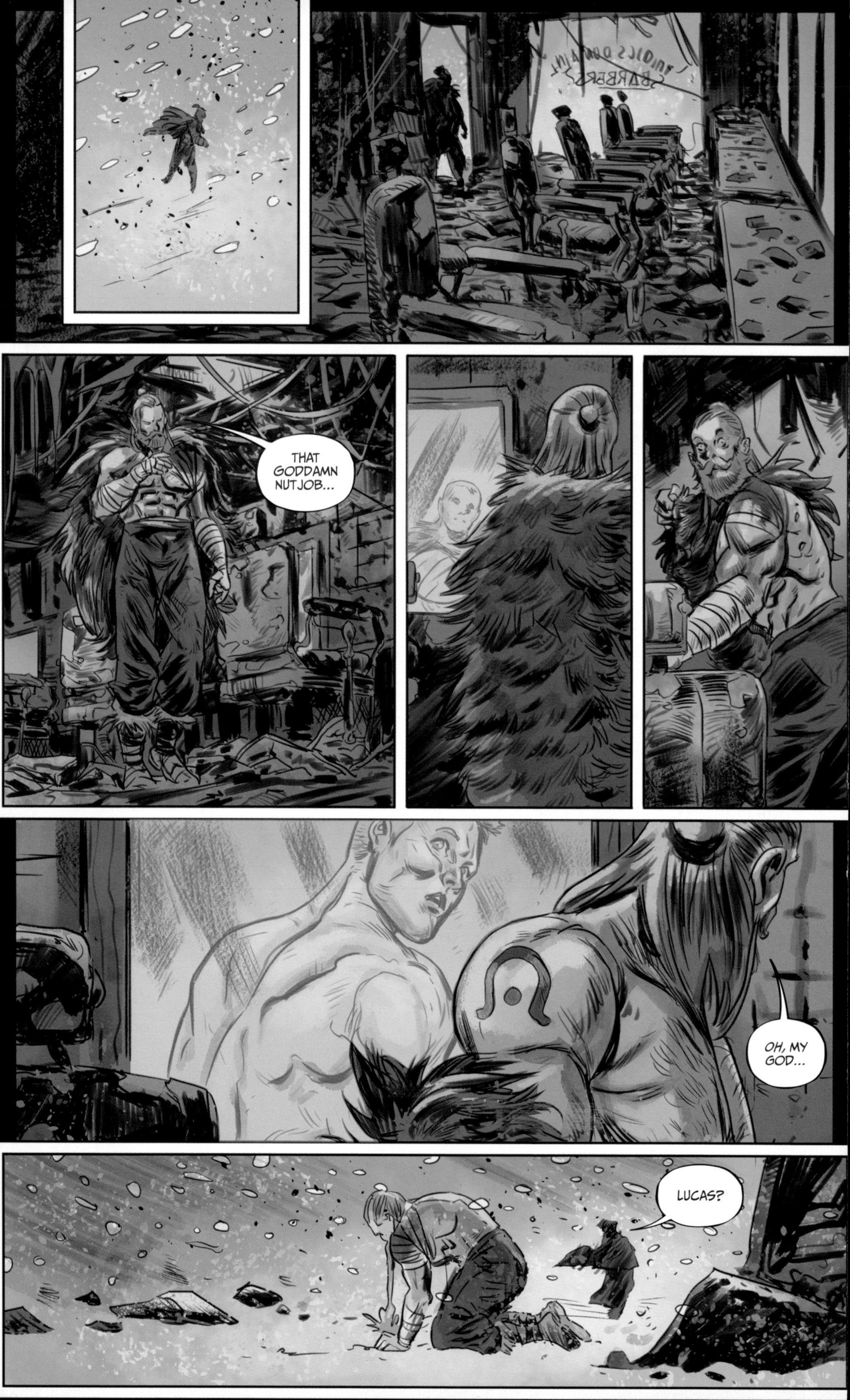
THAT GODDAMN NUTJOB...
OH, MY GOD...
LUCAS?

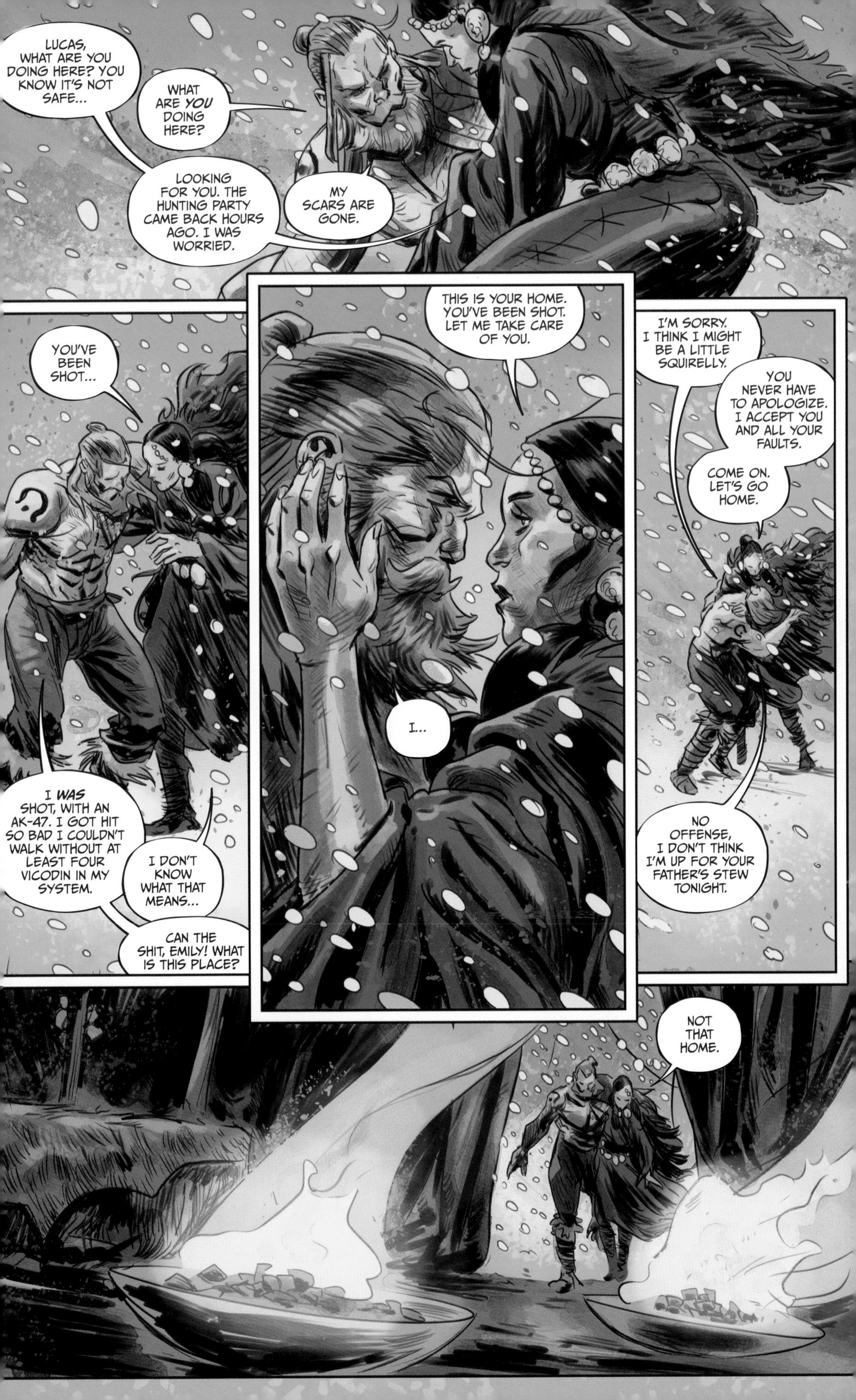
LUCAS, WHAT ARE YOU DOING HERE? YOU KNOW IT'S NOT SAFE...
WHAT ARE *YOU* DOING HERE?
LOOKING FOR YOU. THE HUNTING PARTY CAME BACK HOURS AGO. I WAS WORRIED.
MY SCARS ARE GONE.
YOU'VE BEEN SHOT...
I *WAS* SHOT, WITH AN AK-47. I GOT HIT SO BAD I COULDN'T WALK WITHOUT AT LEAST FOUR VICODIN IN MY SYSTEM.
I DON'T KNOW WHAT THAT MEANS...
CAN THE SHIT, EMILY! WHAT IS THIS PLACE?
THIS IS YOUR HOME. YOU'VE BEEN SHOT. LET ME TAKE CARE OF YOU.
I...
I'M SORRY. I THINK I MIGHT BE A LITTLE SQUIRELLY.
YOU NEVER HAVE TO APOLOGIZE. I ACCEPT YOU AND ALL YOUR FAULTS.
COME ON. LET'S GO HOME.
NO OFFENSE, I DON'T THINK I'M UP FOR YOUR FATHER'S STEW TONIGHT.
NOT THAT HOME.

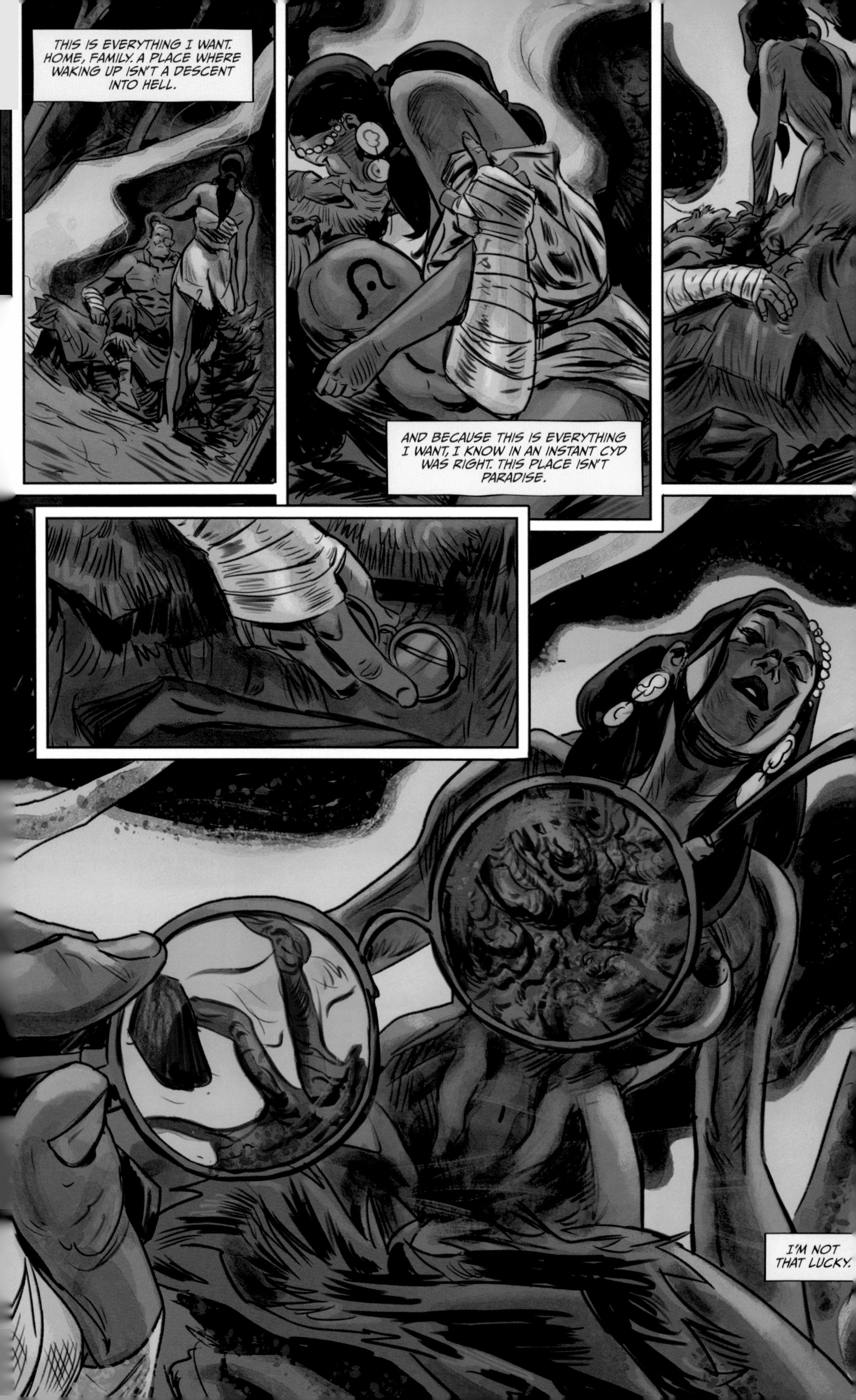
THIS IS EVERYTHING I WANT. HOME, FAMILY. A PLACE WHERE WAKING UP ISN'T A DESCENT INTO HELL.
AND BECAUSE THIS IS EVERYTHING I WANT, I KNOW IN AN INSTANT CYD WAS RIGHT. THIS PLACE ISN'T PARADISE.
I'M NOT THAT LUCKY.

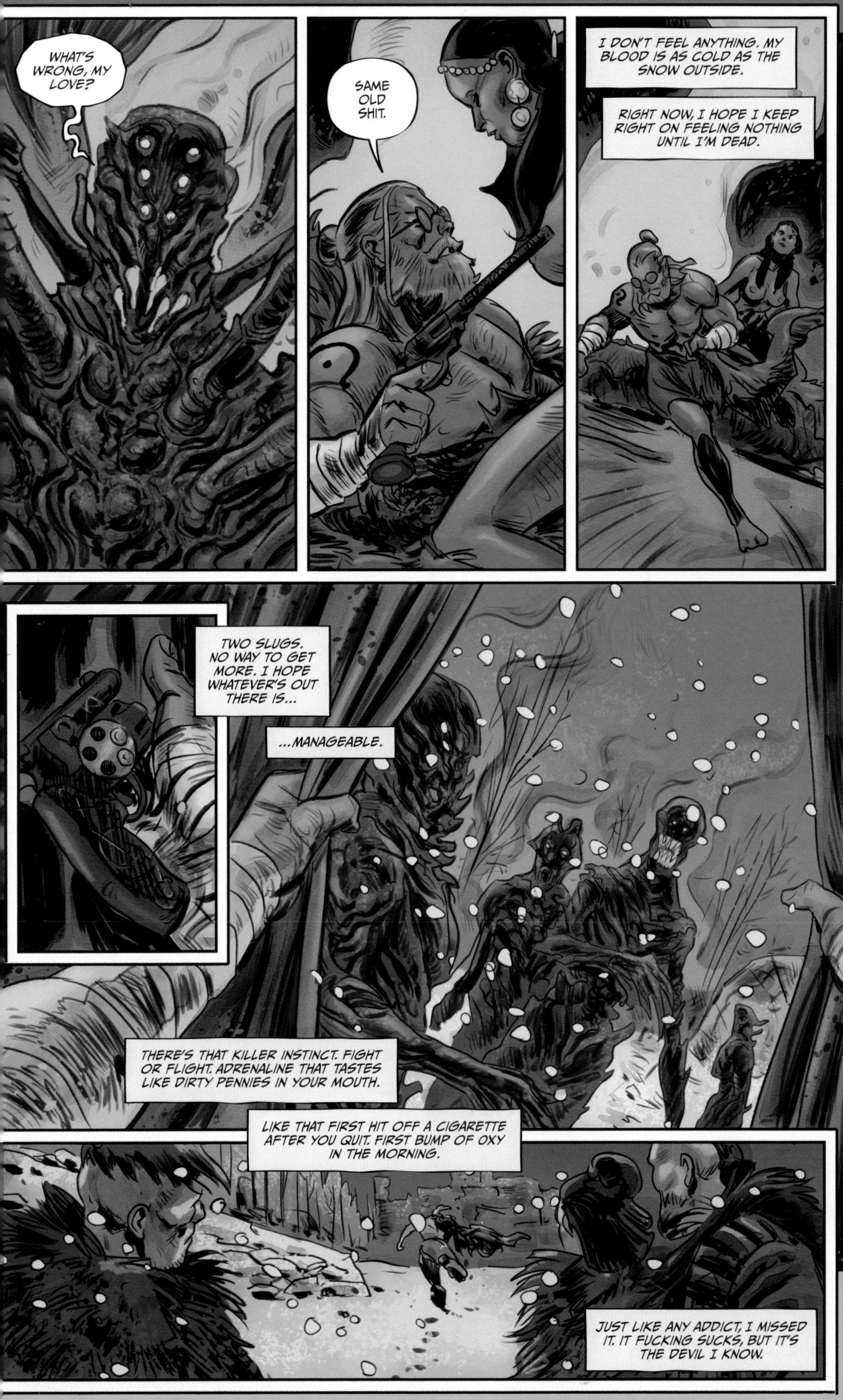
WHAT'S WRONG, MY LOVE?
SAME OLD SHIT.
I DON'T FEEL ANYTHING. MY BLOOD IS AS COLD AS THE SNOW OUTSIDE.
RIGHT NOW, I HOPE I KEEP RIGHT ON FEELING NOTHING UNTIL I'M DEAD.
TWO SLUGS. NO WAY TO GET MORE. I HOPE WHATEVER'S OUT THERE IS...
...MANAGEABLE.
THERE'S THAT KILLER INSTINCT. FIGHT OR FLIGHT. ADRENALINE THAT TASTES LIKE DIRTY PENNIES IN YOUR MOUTH.
LIKE THAT FIRST HIT OFF A CIGARETTE AFTER YOU QUIT. FIRST BUMP OF OXY IN THE MORNING.
JUST LIKE ANY ADDICT, I MISSED IT. IT FUCKING SUCKS, BUT IT'S THE DEVIL I KNOW.

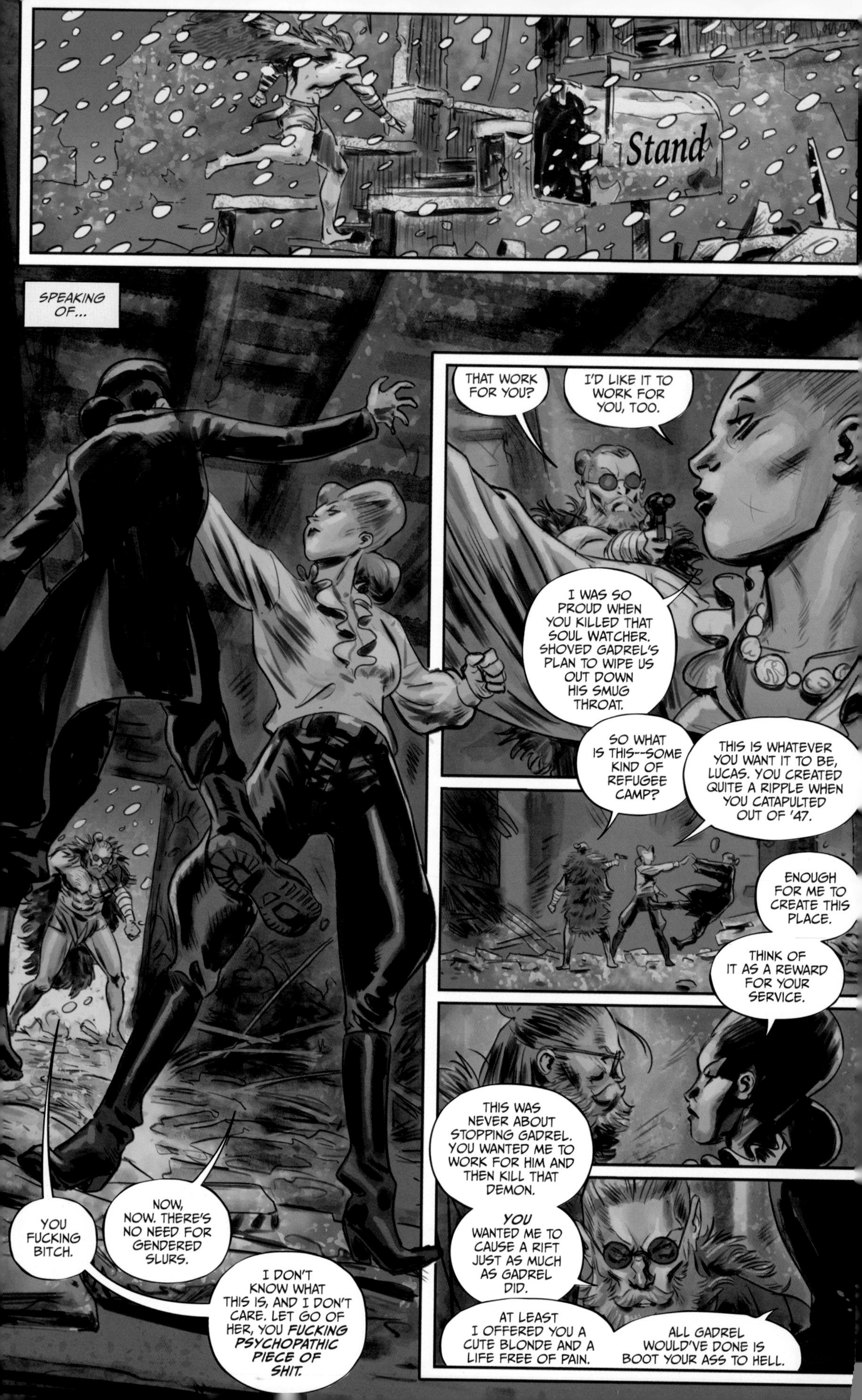
Stand
SPEAKING OF...
THAT WORK FOR YOU?
I'D LIKE IT TO WORK FOR YOU, TOO.
I WAS SO PROUD WHEN YOU KILLED THAT SOUL WATCHER. SHOVED GADREL'S PLAN TO WIPE US OUT DOWN HIS SMUG THROAT.
SO WHAT IS THIS--SOME KIND OF REFUGEE CAMP?
THIS IS WHATEVER YOU WANT IT TO BE, LUCAS. YOU CREATED QUITE A RIPPLE WHEN YOU CATAPULTED OUT OF '47.
ENOUGH FOR ME TO CREATE THIS PLACE.
THINK OF IT AS A REWARD FOR YOUR SERVICE.
THIS WAS NEVER ABOUT STOPPING GADREL. YOU WANTED ME TO WORK FOR HIM AND THEN KILL THAT DEMON.
YOU WANTED ME TO CAUSE A RIFT JUST AS MUCH AS GADREL DID.
AT LEAST I OFFERED YOU A CUTE BLONDE AND A LIFE FREE OF PAIN.
ALL GADREL WOULD'VE DONE IS BOOT YOUR ASS TO HELL.
YOU FUCKING BITCH.
NOW, NOW. THERE'S NO NEED FOR GENDERED SLURS.
I DON'T KNOW WHAT THIS IS, AND I DON'T CARE. LET GO OF HER, YOU FUCKING PSYCHOPATHIC PIECE OF SHIT.

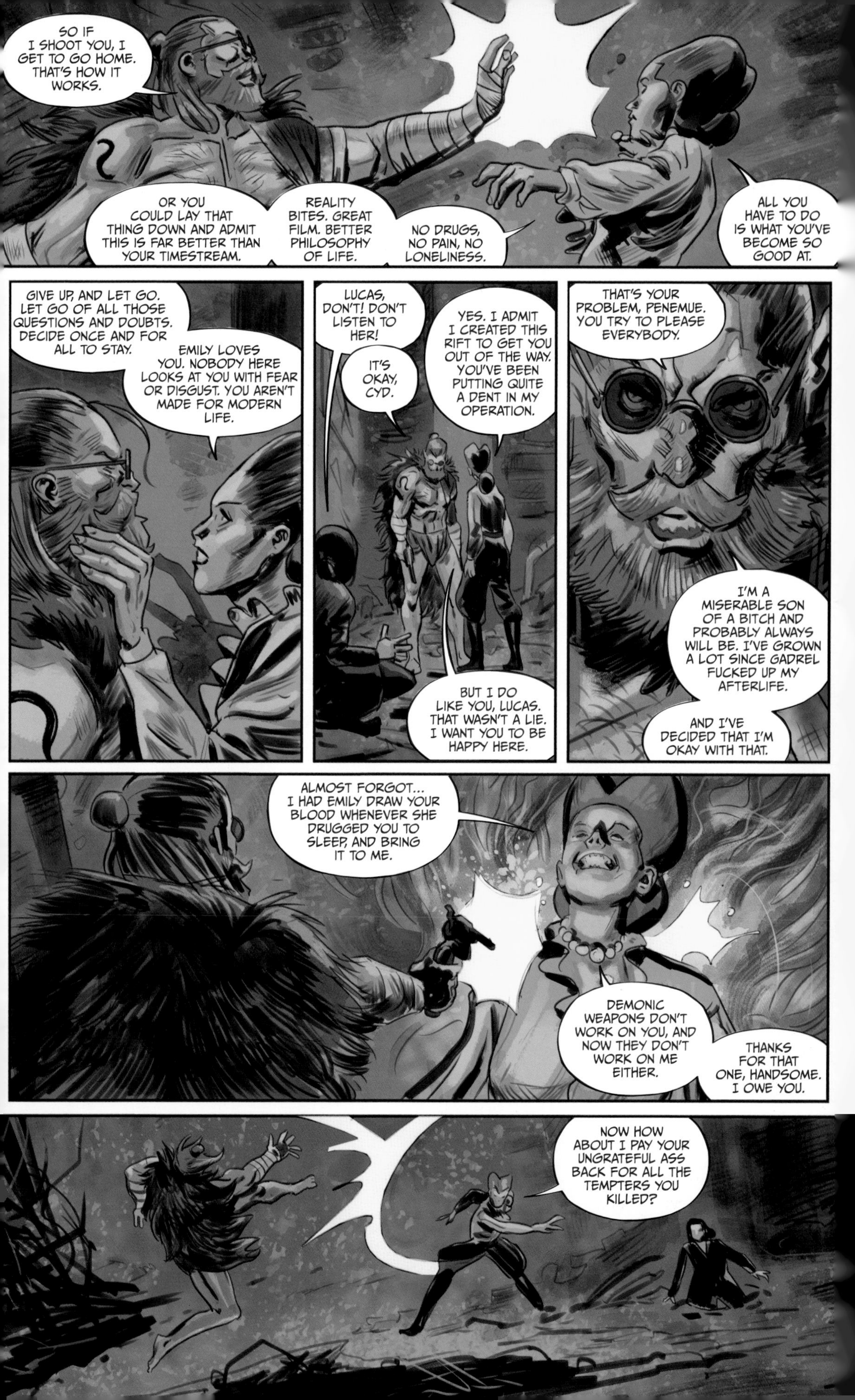

SO IF I SHOOT YOU, I GET TO GO HOME. THAT'S HOW IT WORKS.
OR YOU COULD LAY THAT THING DOWN AND ADMIT THIS IS FAR BETTER THAN YOUR TIMESTREAM.
REALITY BITES. GREAT FILM. BETTER PHILOSOPHY OF LIFE.
NO DRUGS, NO PAIN, NO LONELINESS.
ALL YOU HAVE TO DO IS WHAT YOU'VE BECOME SO GOOD AT.
GIVE UP, AND LET GO. LET GO OF ALL THOSE QUESTIONS AND DOUBTS. DECIDE ONCE AND FOR ALL TO STAY.
EMILY LOVES YOU. NOBODY HERE LOOKS AT YOU WITH FEAR OR DISGUST. YOU AREN'T MADE FOR MODERN LIFE.
LUCAS, DON'T! DON'T LISTEN TO HER!
IT'S OKAY, CYD.
YES. I ADMIT I CREATED THIS RIFT TO GET YOU OUT OF THE WAY. YOU'VE BEEN PUTTING QUITE A DENT IN MY OPERATION.
BUT I DO LIKE YOU, LUCAS. THAT WASN'T A LIE. I WANT YOU TO BE HAPPY HERE.
THAT'S YOUR PROBLEM, PENEMUE. YOU TRY TO PLEASE EVERYBODY.
I'M A MISERABLE SON OF A BITCH AND PROBABLY ALWAYS WILL BE. I'VE GROWN A LOT SINCE GADREL FUCKED UP MY AFTERLIFE.
AND I'VE DECIDED THAT I'M OKAY WITH THAT.
ALMOST FORGOT... I HAD EMILY DRAW YOUR BLOOD WHENEVER SHE DRUGGED YOU TO SLEEP, AND BRING IT TO ME.
DEMONIC WEAPONS DON'T WORK ON YOU, AND NOW THEY DON'T WORK ON ME EITHER.
THANKS FOR THAT ONE, HANDSOME. I OWE YOU.
NOW HOW ABOUT I PAY YOUR UNGRATEFUL ASS BACK FOR ALL THE TEMPTERS YOU KILLED?

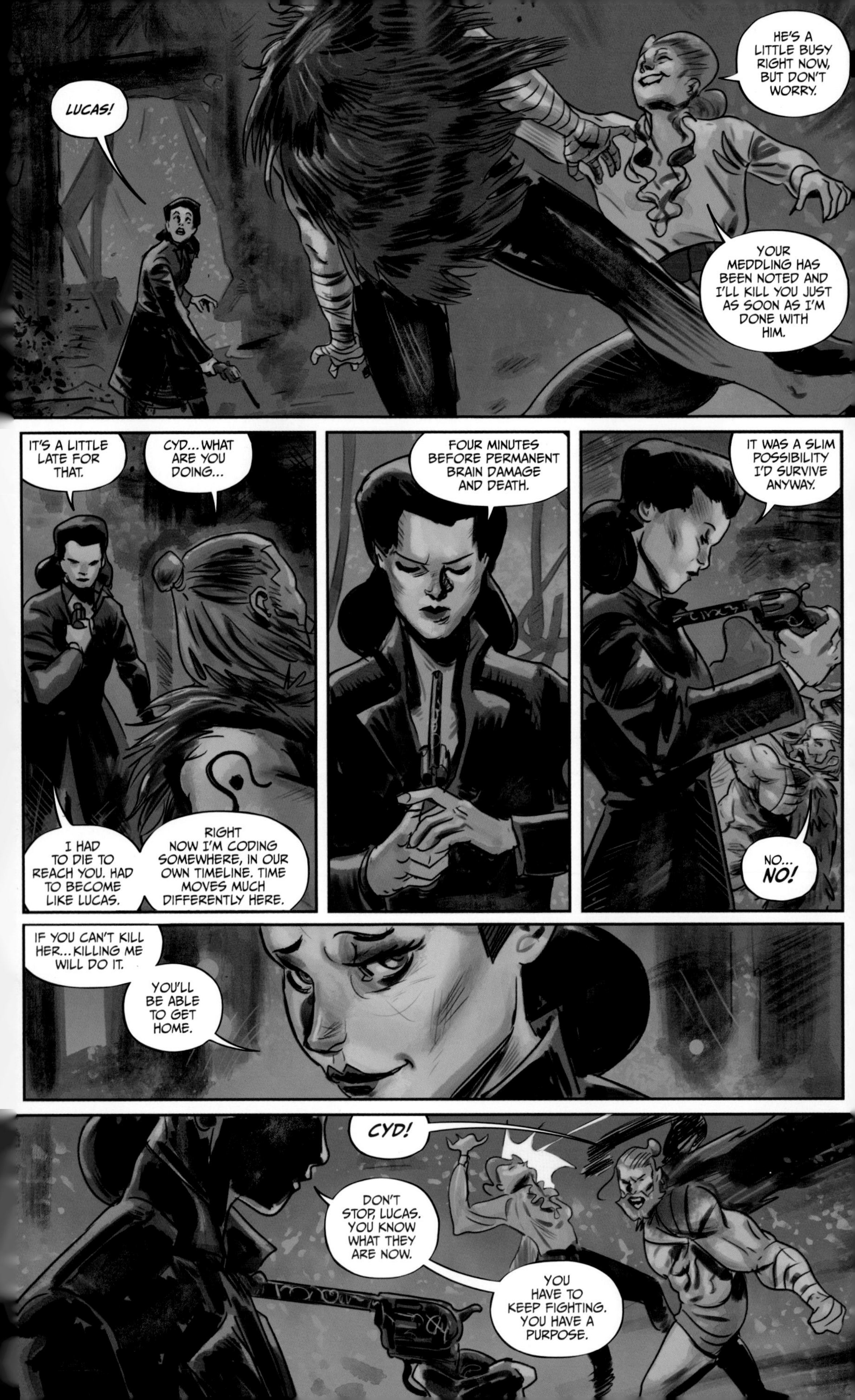
LUCAS!
HE'S A LITTLE BUSY RIGHT NOW, BUT DON'T WORRY.
YOUR MEDDLING HAS BEEN NOTED AND I'LL KILL YOU JUST AS SOON AS I'M DONE WITH HIM.
IT'S A LITTLE LATE FOR THAT.
CYD... WHAT ARE YOU DOING...
I HAD TO DIE TO REACH YOU. HAD TO BECOME LIKE LUCAS.
RIGHT NOW I'M CODING SOMEWHERE, IN OUR OWN TIMELINE. TIME MOVES MUCH DIFFERENTLY HERE.
FOUR MINUTES BEFORE PERMANENT BRAIN DAMAGE AND DEATH.
IT WAS A SLIM POSSIBILITY I'D SURVIVE ANYWAY.
NO... NO!
IF YOU CAN'T KILL HER... KILLING ME WILL DO IT.
YOU'LL BE ABLE TO GET HOME.
CYD!
DON'T STOP, LUCAS. YOU KNOW WHAT THEY ARE NOW.
YOU HAVE TO KEEP FIGHTING. YOU HAVE A PURPOSE.

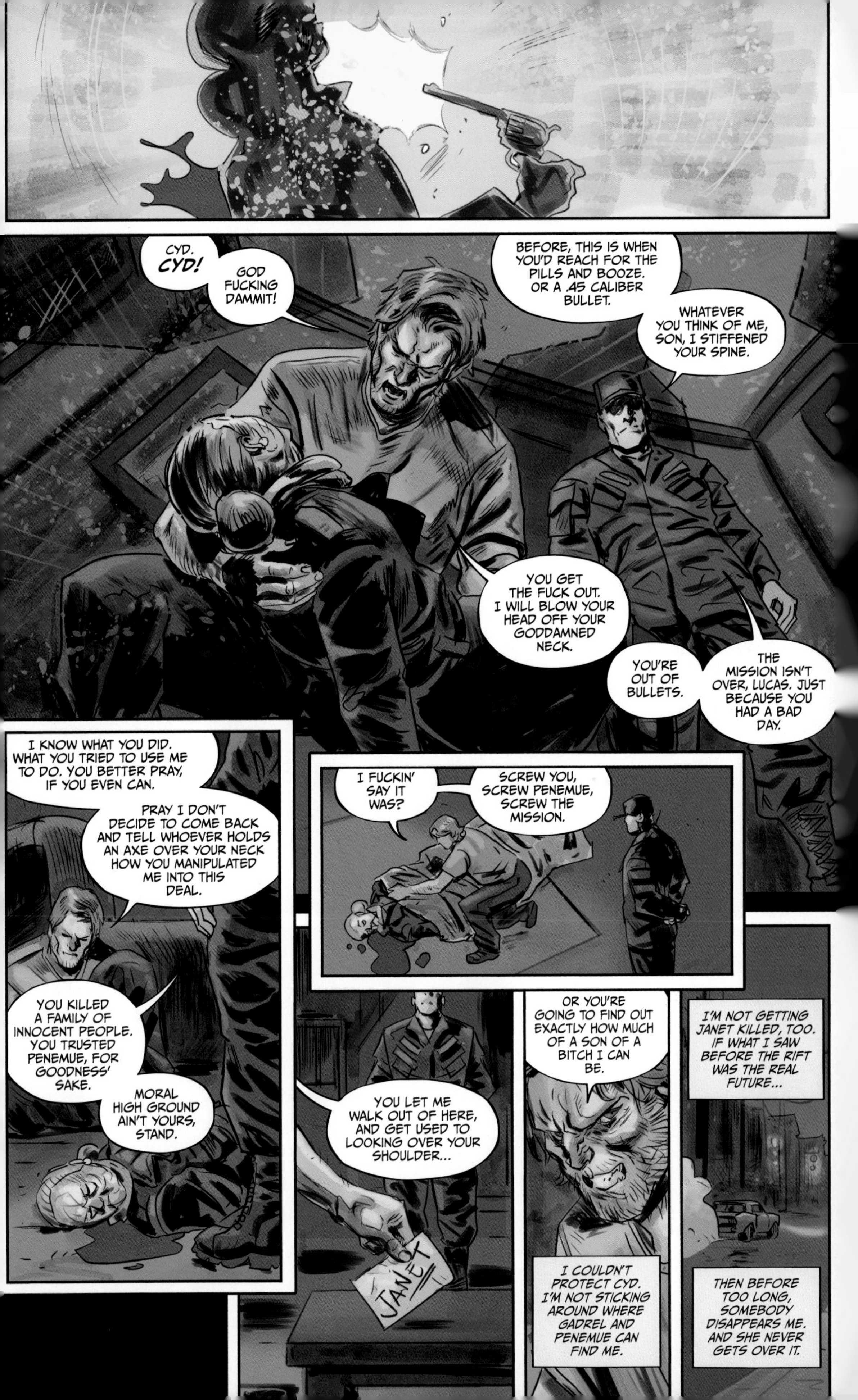
CYD. CYD!
GOD FUCKING DAMMIT!
BEFORE, THIS IS WHEN YOU'D REACH FOR THE PILLS AND BOOZE. OR A .45 CALIBER BULLET.
WHATEVER YOU THINK OF ME, SON, I STIFFENED YOUR SPINE.
YOU GET THE FUCK OUT. I WILL BLOW YOUR HEAD OFF YOUR GODDAMNED NECK.
YOU'RE OUT OF BULLETS.
THE MISSION ISN'T OVER, LUCAS. JUST BECAUSE YOU HAD A BAD DAY.
I KNOW WHAT YOU DID. WHAT YOU TRIED TO USE ME TO DO. YOU BETTER PRAY, IF YOU EVEN CAN.
PRAY I DON'T DECIDE TO COME BACK AND TELL WHOEVER HOLDS AN AXE OVER YOUR NECK HOW YOU MANIPULATED ME INTO THIS DEAL.
YOU KILLED A FAMILY OF INNOCENT PEOPLE. YOU TRUSTED PENEMUE, FOR GOODNESS' SAKE.
MORAL HIGH GROUND AIN'T YOURS, STAND.
I FUCKIN' SAY IT WAS?
SCREW YOU, SCREW PENEMUE, SCREW THE MISSION.
YOU LET ME WALK OUT OF HERE, AND GET USED TO LOOKING OVER YOUR SHOULDER...
JANET
OR YOU'RE GOING TO FIND OUT EXACTLY HOW MUCH OF A SON OF A BITCH I CAN BE.
I COULDN'T PROTECT CYD. I'M NOT STICKING AROUND WHERE GADREL AND PENEMUE CAN FIND ME.
I'M NOT GETTING JANET KILLED, TOO. IF WHAT I SAW BEFORE THE RIFT WAS THE REAL FUTURE...
THEN BEFORE TOO LONG, SOMEBODY DISAPPEARS ME. AND SHE NEVER GETS OVER IT.

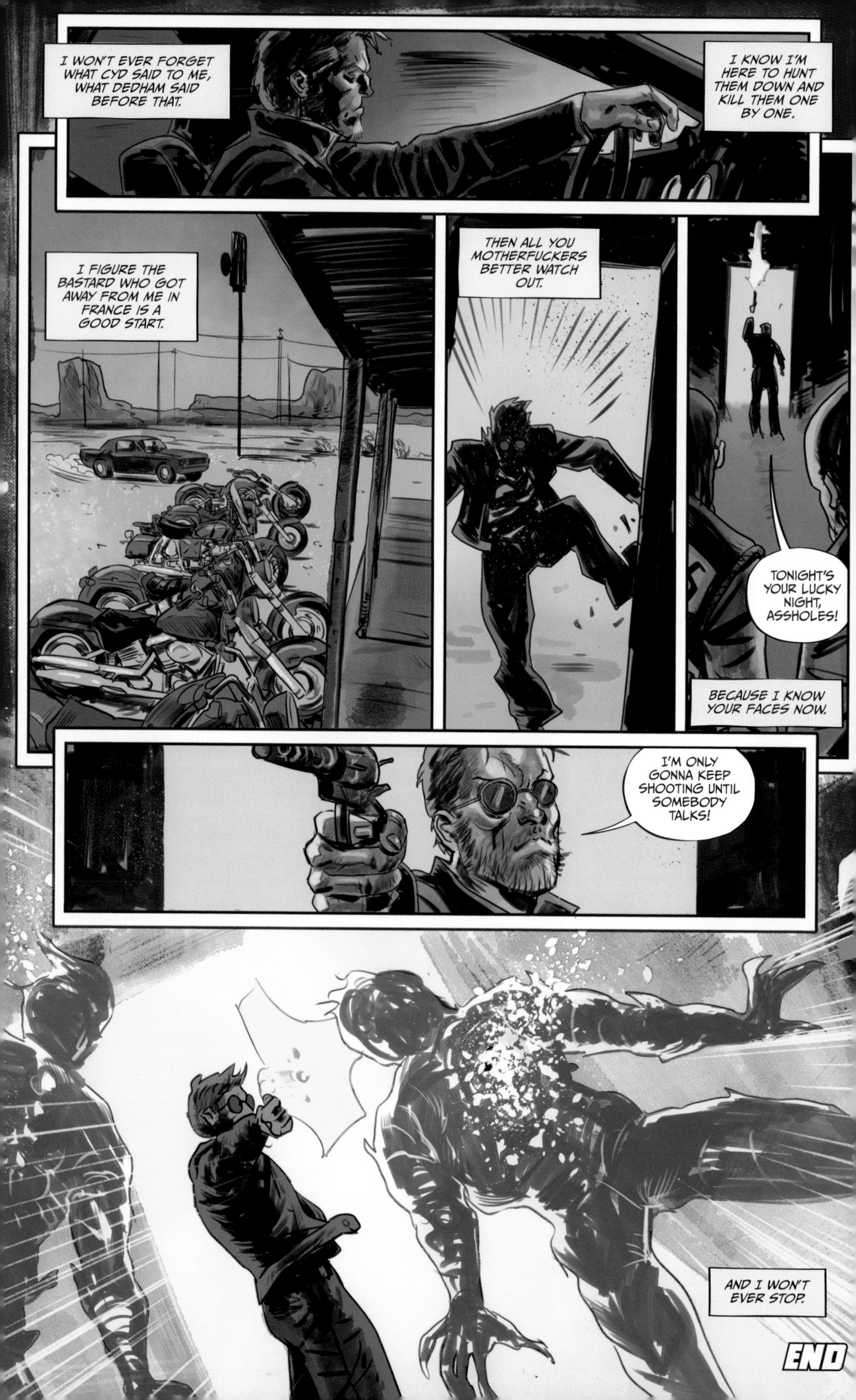
I WON'T EVER FORGET WHAT CYD SAID TO ME, WHAT DEDHAM SAID BEFORE THAT.
I KNOW I'M HERE TO HUNT THEM DOWN AND KILL THEM ONE BY ONE.
I FIGURE THE BASTARD WHO GOT AWAY FROM ME IN FRANCE IS A GOOD START.
THEN ALL YOU MOTHERFUCKERS BETTER WATCH OUT.
TONIGHT'S YOUR LUCKY NIGHT, ASSHOLES!
BECAUSE I KNOW YOUR FACES NOW.
I'M ONLY GONNA KEEP SHOOTING UNTIL SOMEBODY TALKS!
AND I WON'T EVER STOP.
END

COVER
GALLERY

ISSUE ONE MAIN COVER

LEE BERMEJO

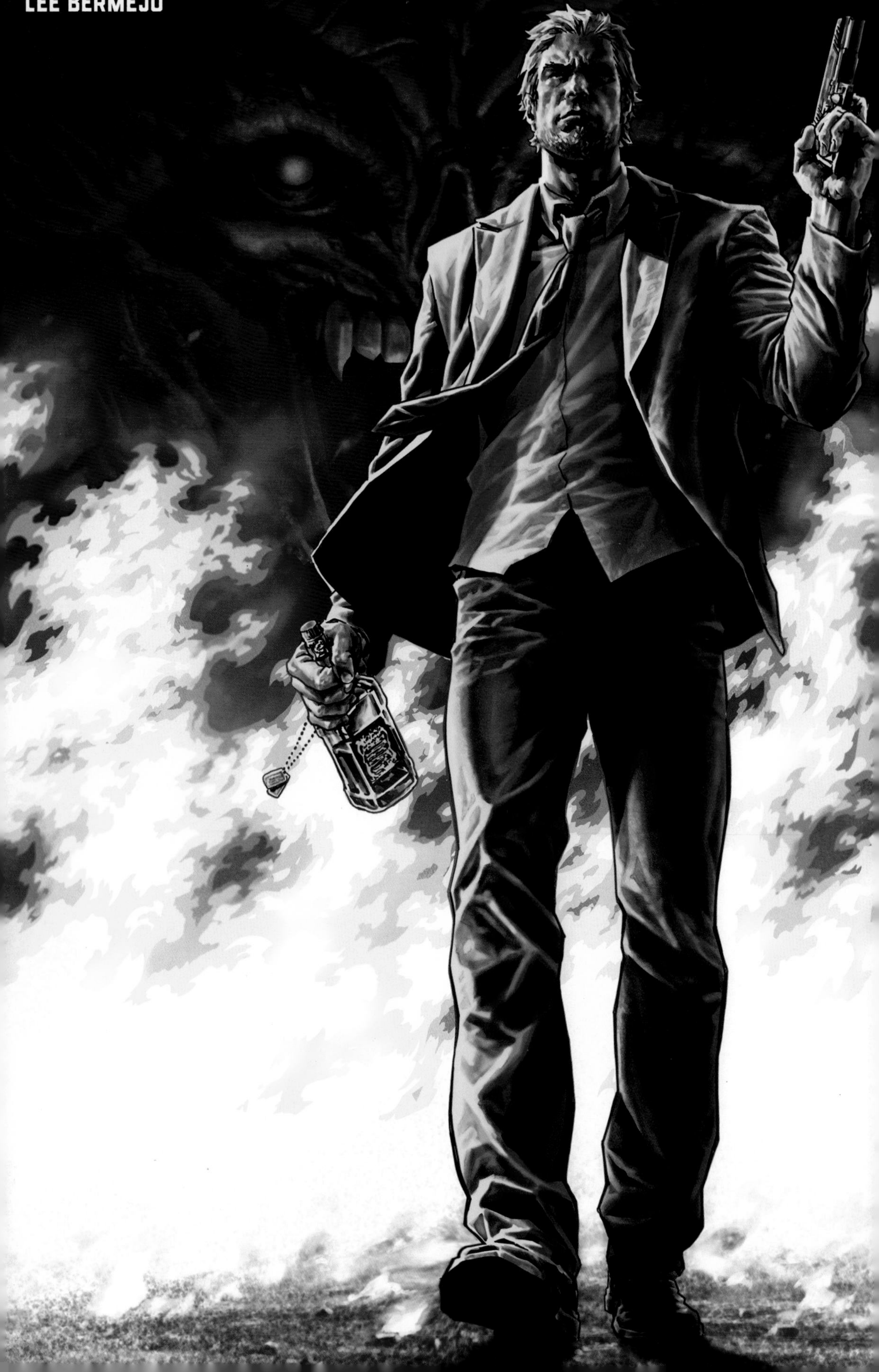

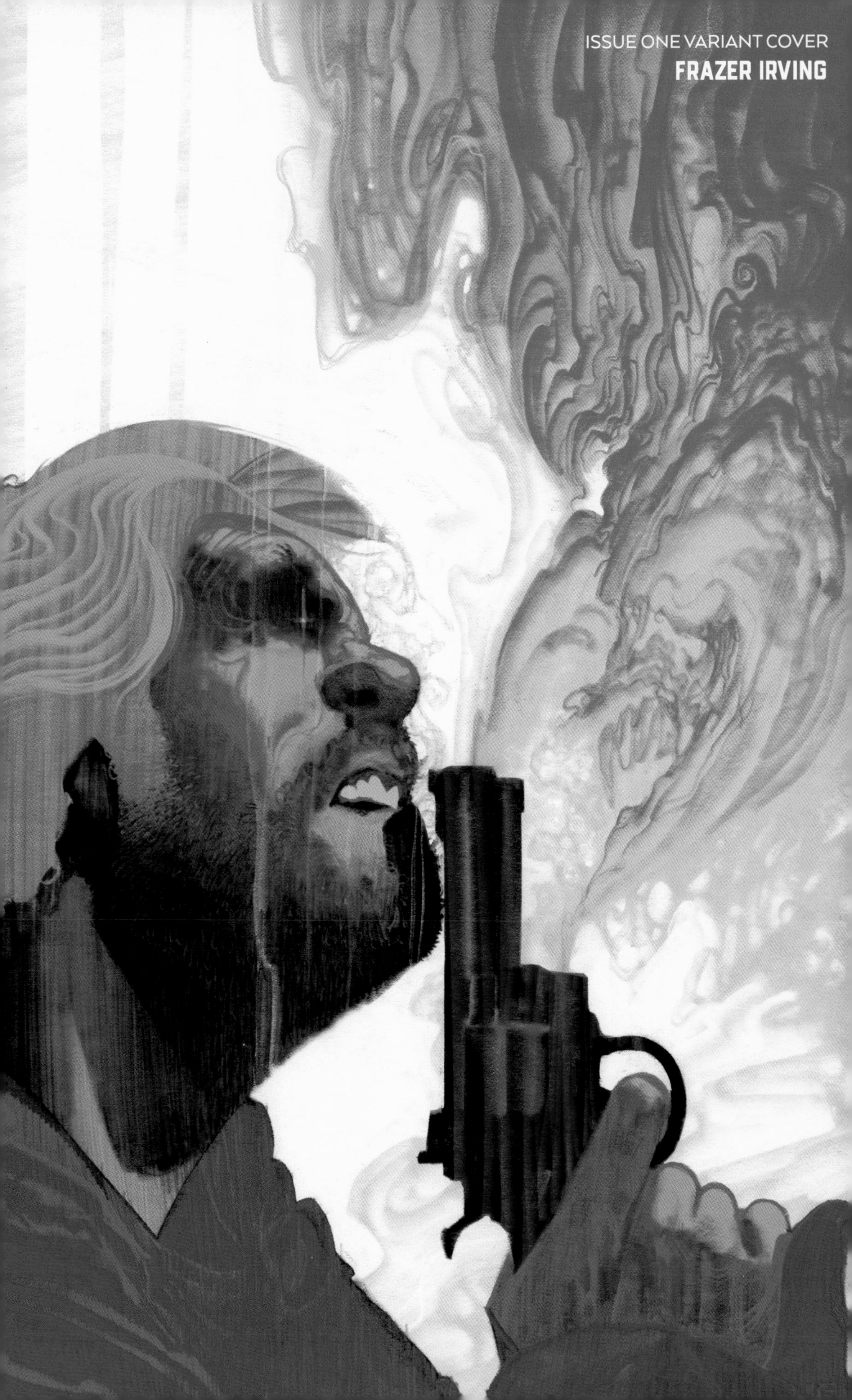

ISSUE ONE VARIANT COVER
FRAZER IRVING

ISSUE ONE VARIANT COVER

RILEY ROSSMO

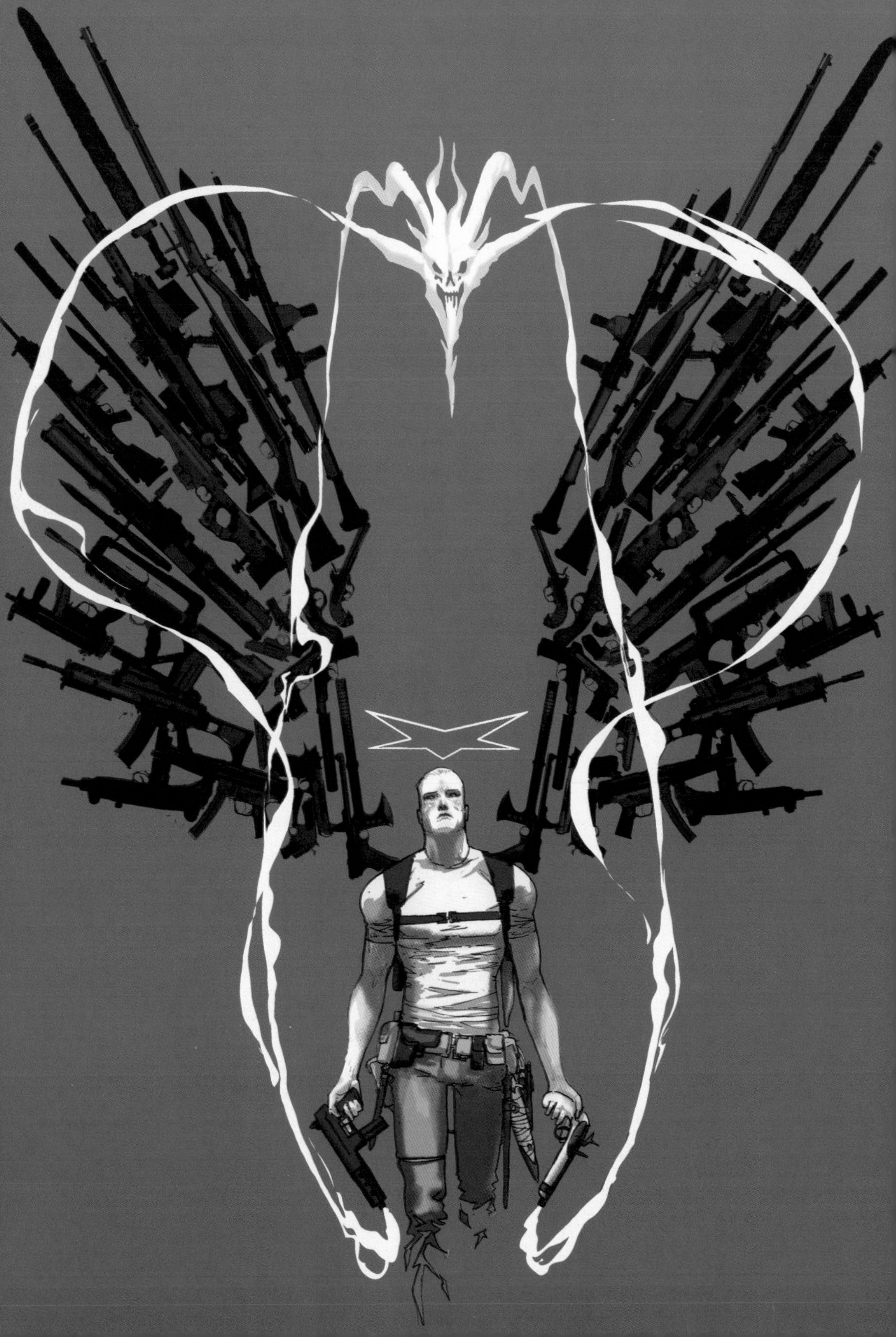

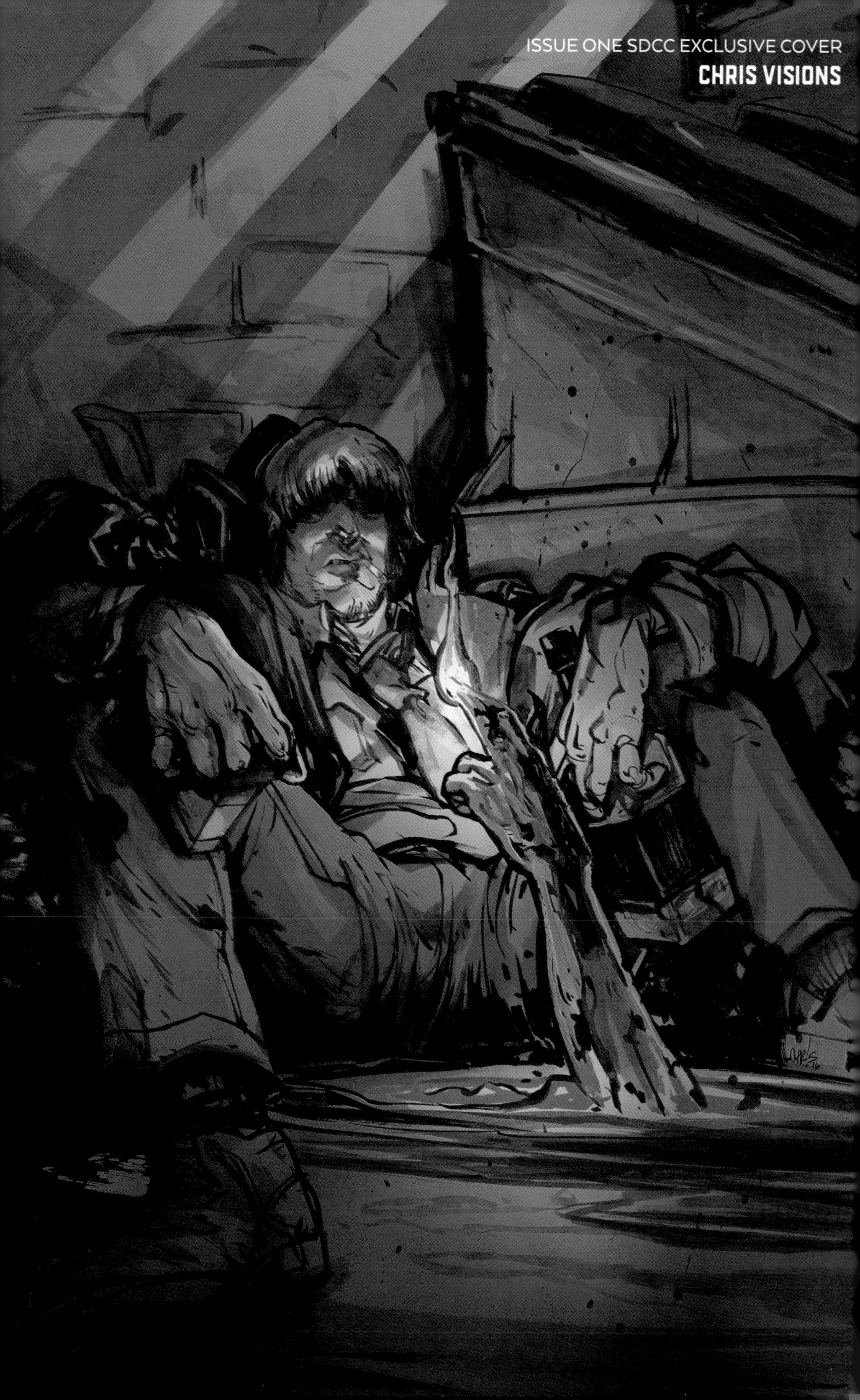

ISSUE ONE SDCC EXCLUSIVE COVER
CHRIS VISIONS

ISSUE ONE CHALLENGE COIN SIGNED VARIANT COVER

JESÚS HERVÁS WITH **KELSEY DIETERICH**

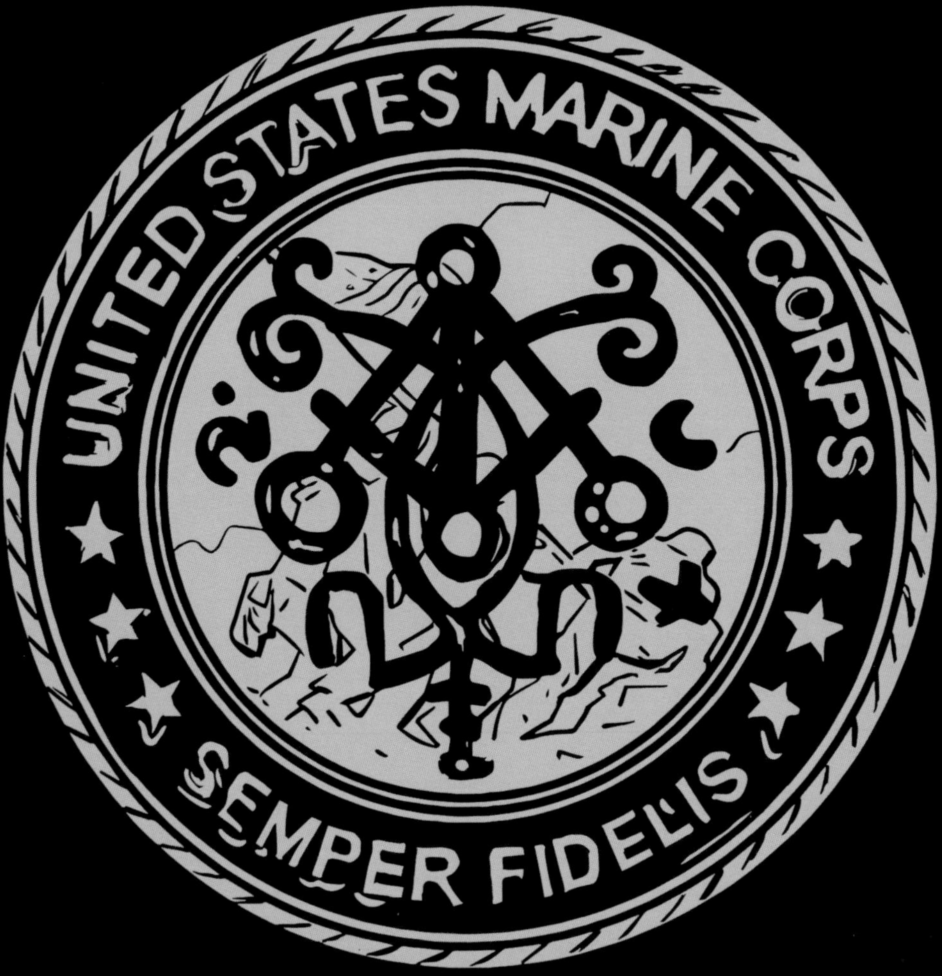
UNITED STATES MARINE CORPS
SEMPER FIDELIS

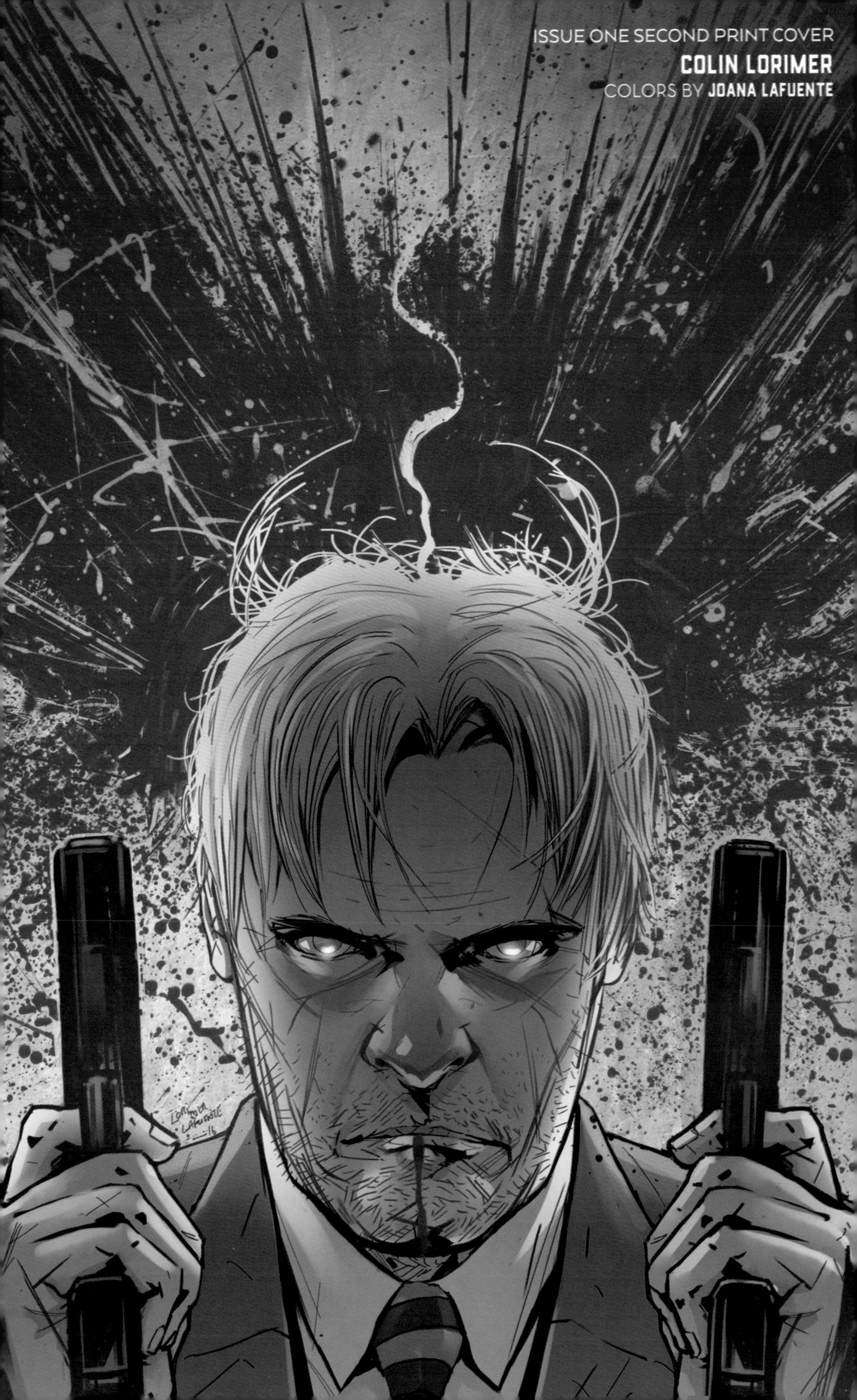

ISSUE ONE SECOND PRINT COVER
COLIN LORIMER
COLORS BY **JOANA LAFUENTE**

ISSUE TWO MAIN COVER

RILEY ROSSMO

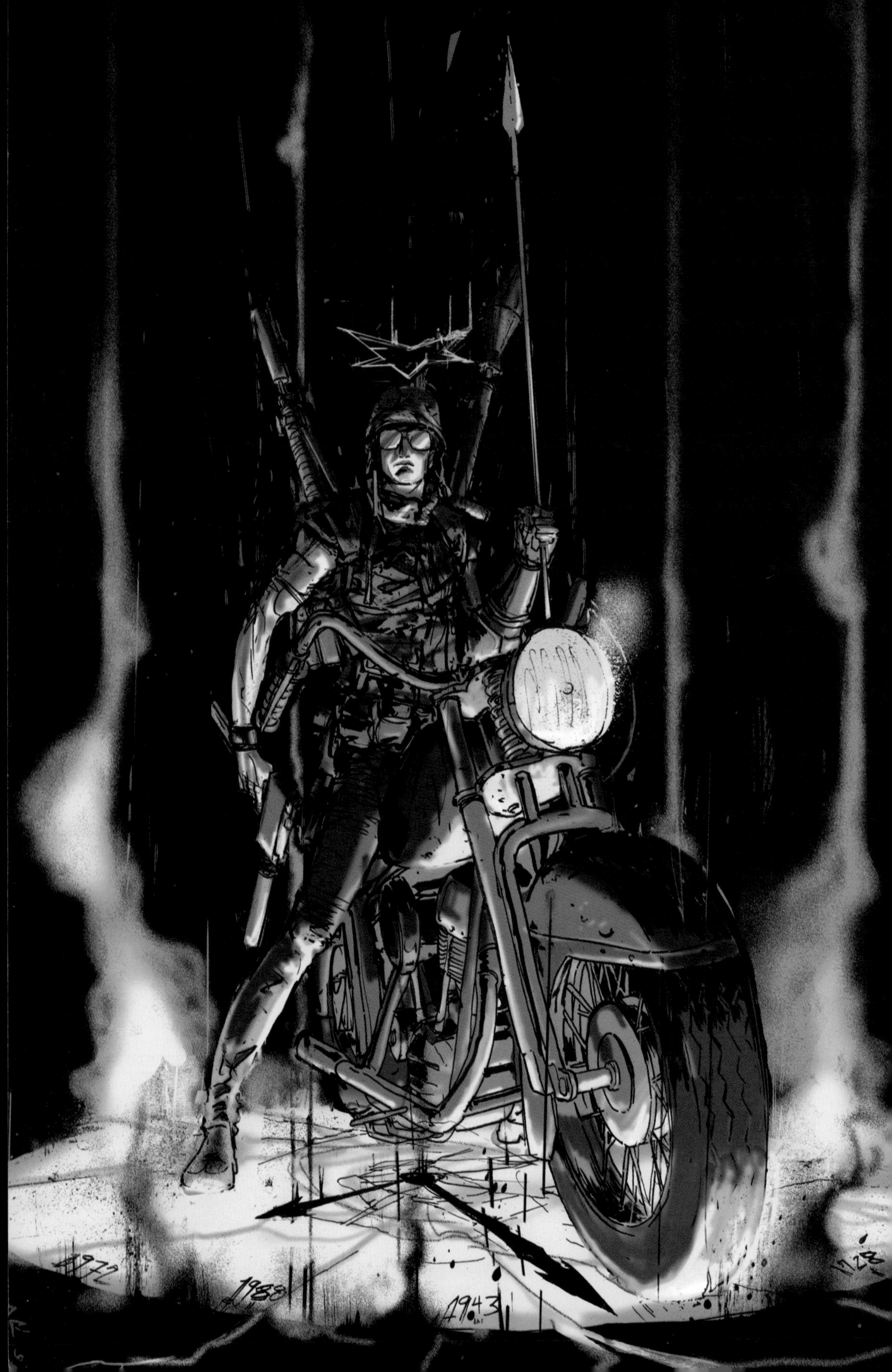
1988
1943

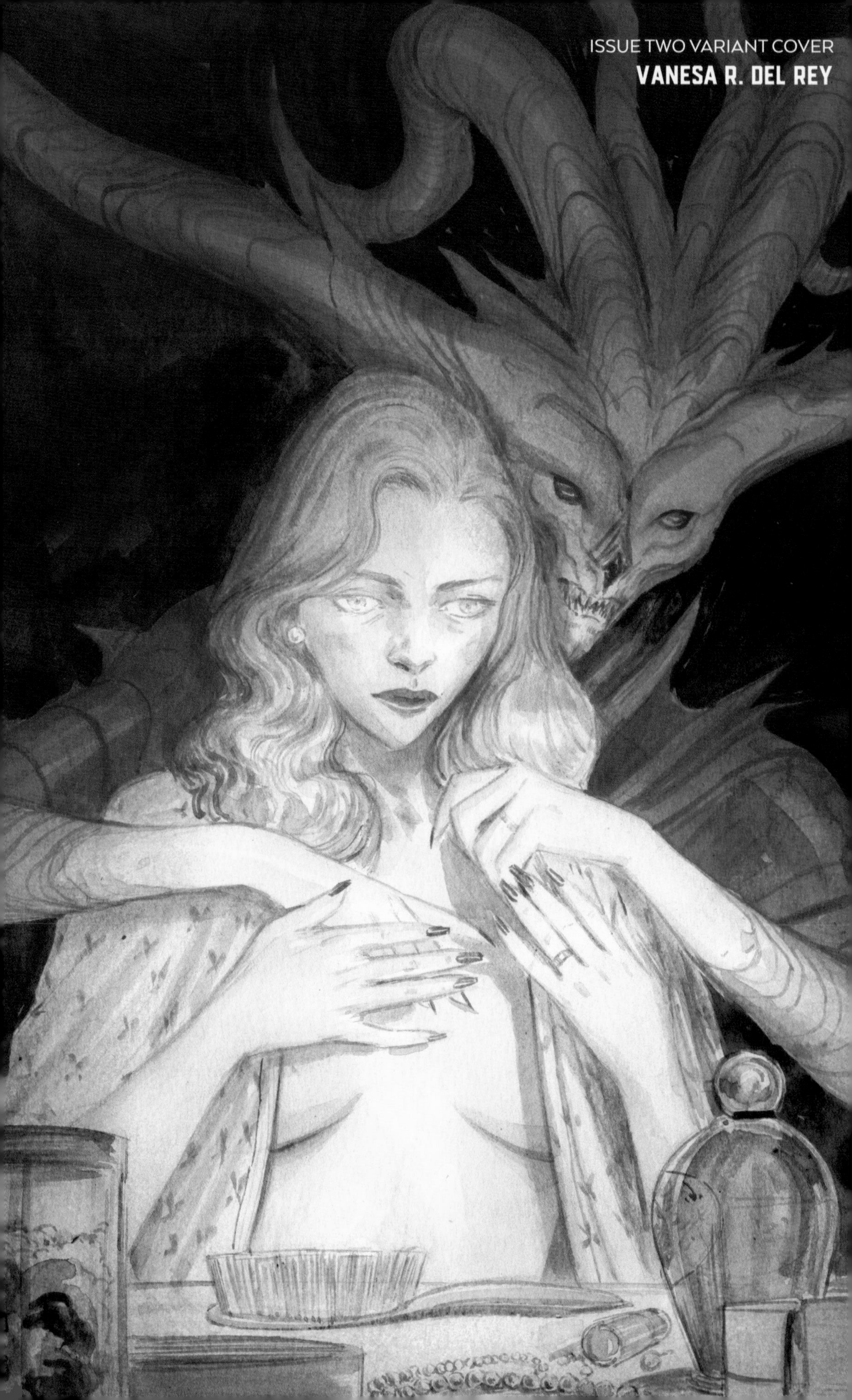

ISSUE TWO VARIANT COVER
VANESA R. DEL REY

ISSUE THREE COVER

RILEY ROSSMO

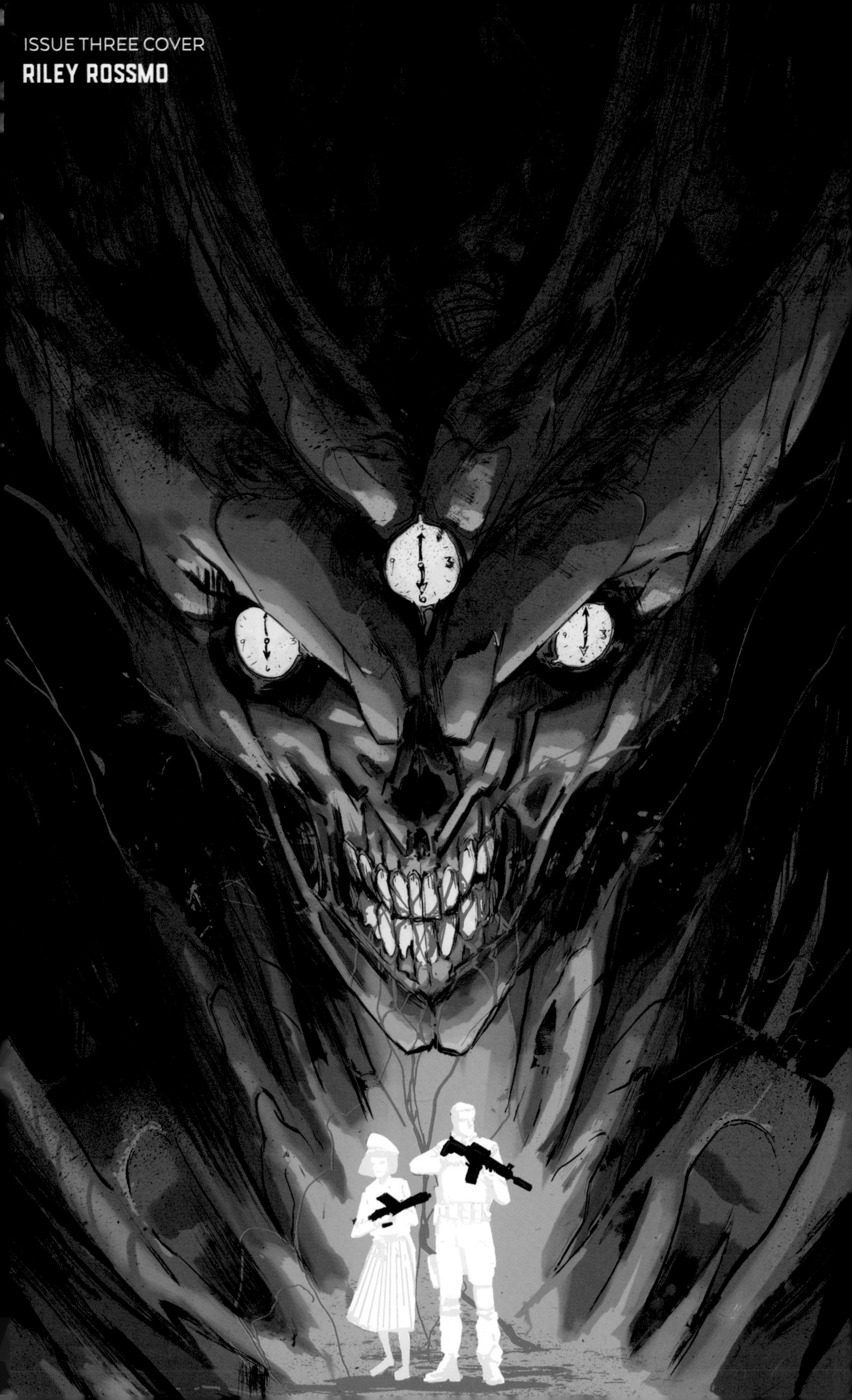

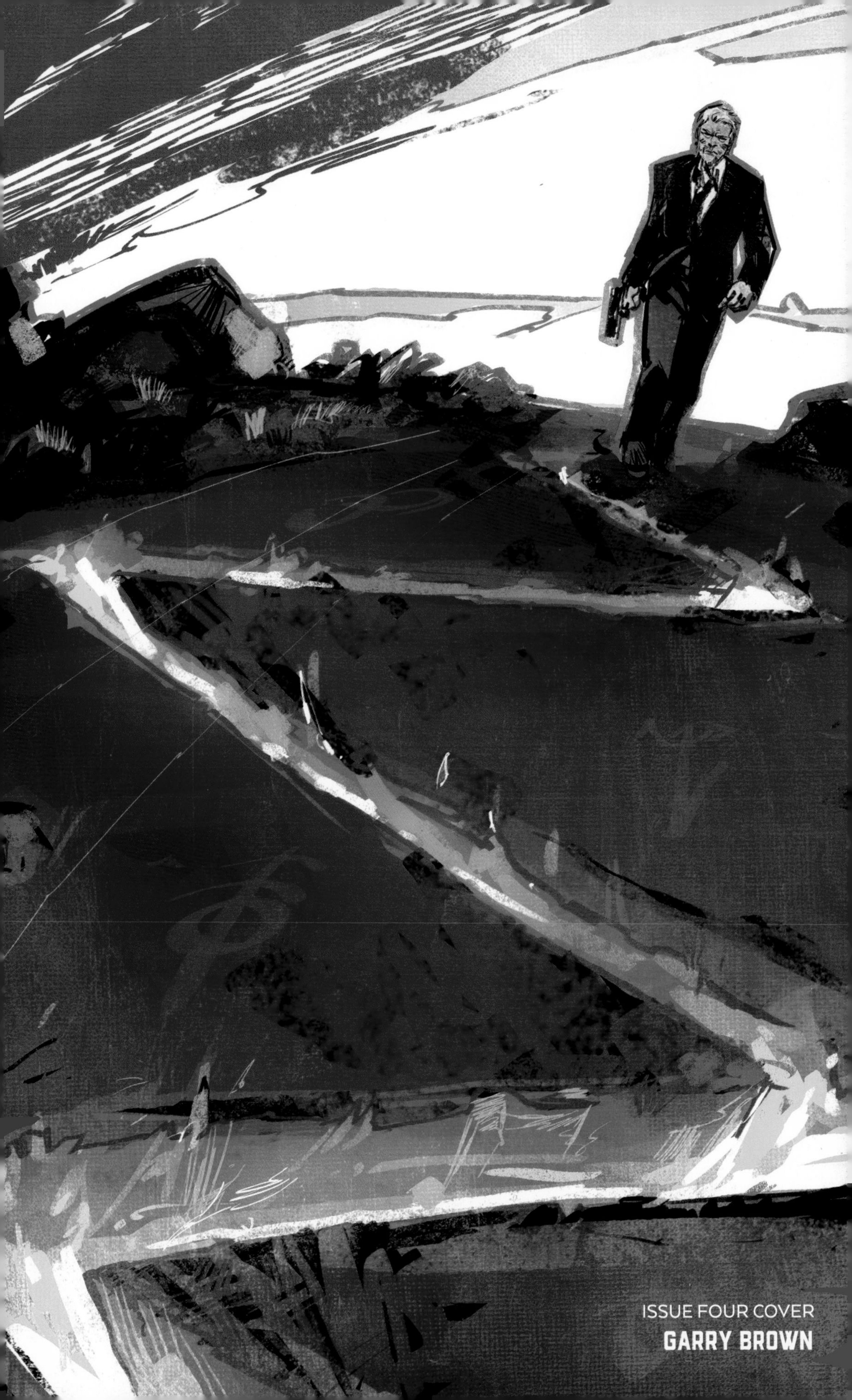

ISSUE FOUR COVER

GARRY BROWN

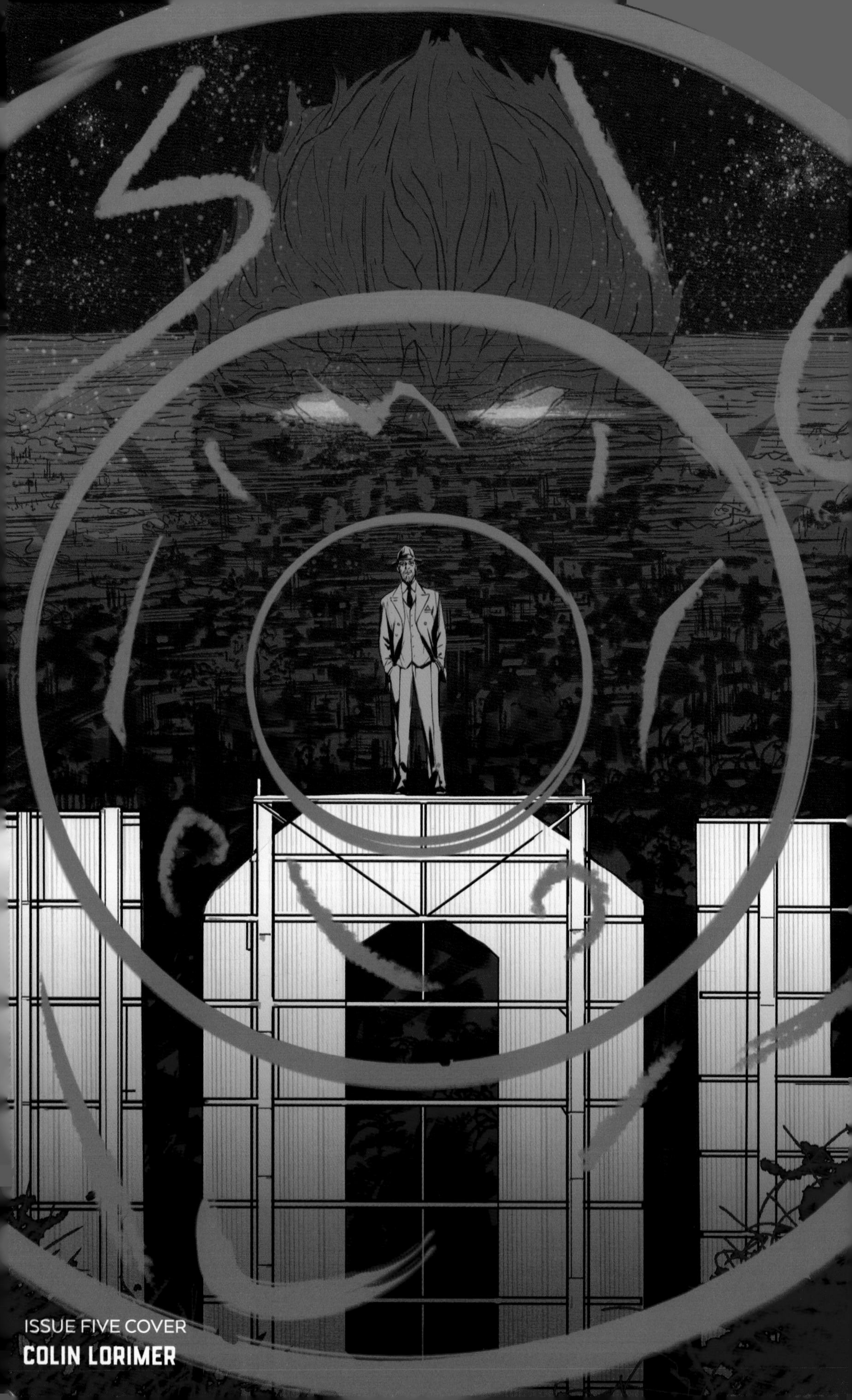

ISSUE FIVE COVER
COLIN LORIMER

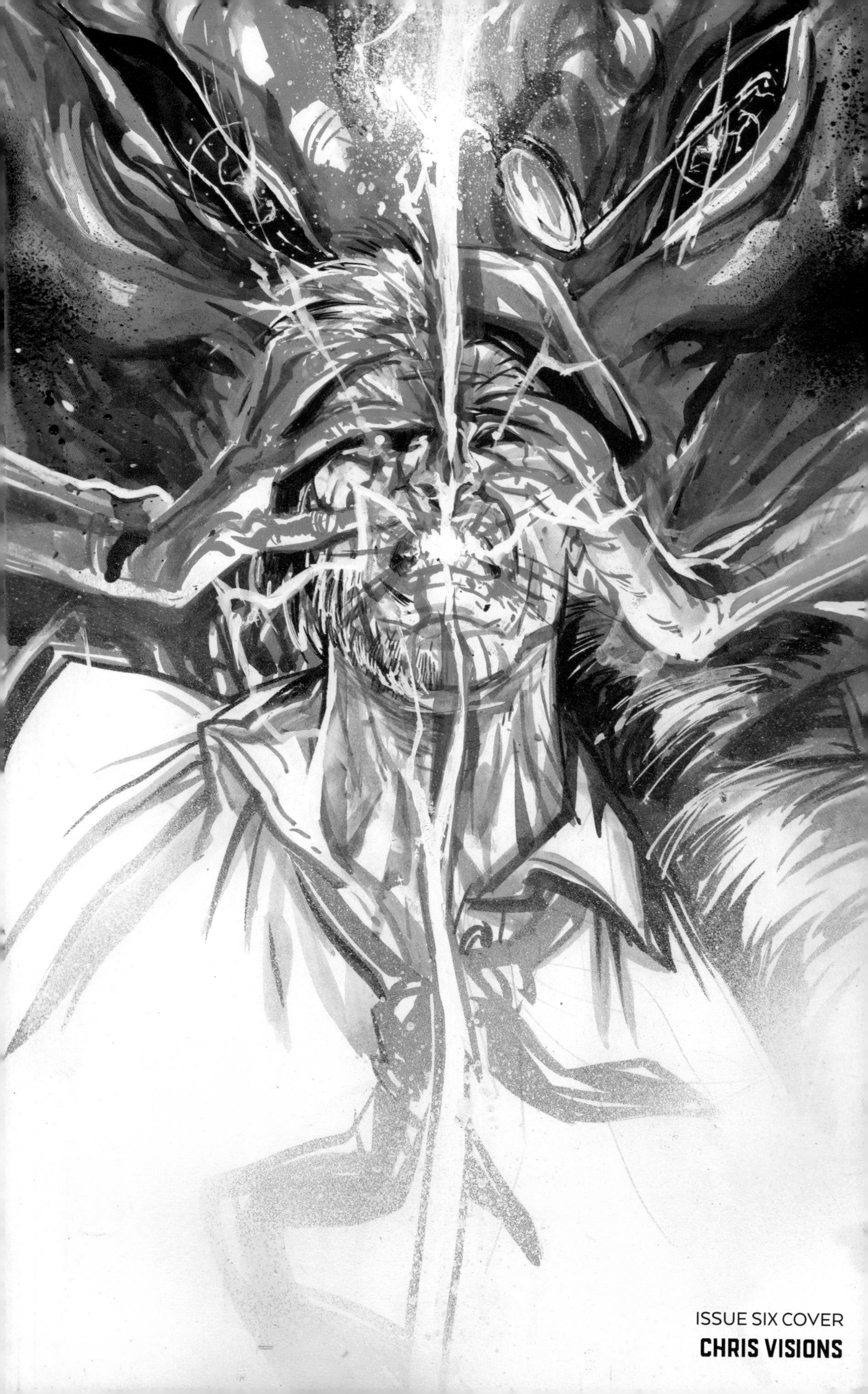

ISSUE SIX COVER
CHRIS VISIONS